CHALLENGING PROFESSIONS

Historical and Contemporary Perspectives on Women's Professional Work
Edited by Elizabeth Smyth, Sandra Acker, Paula Bourne, and Alison Prentice

Challenging Professions is an innovative, interdisciplinary collection of thirteen thematically linked yet methodologically diverse essays that explore Canadian women's engagement with professional education and employment in the twentieth century. Guided by a co-authored introduction, *Challenging Professions* critically examines how women's entry into and continued participation in the professions not only contested but also challenged a concept of professionalism that was and remains profoundly gendered. This book is the product of a three-year collaboration among sixteen researchers from a variety of fields, who joined together in an interdisciplinary network funded by the Social Sciences and Humanities Research Council of Canada to explore collectively their individual research on women and professional education.

The collection as a whole examines change over time and the differences between professions peopled mostly by men and those whose members are chiefly women. The difficulties of combining family and professional commitment and the impact of professional on personal life are further integrating themes. *Challenging Professions* raises questions not only about women's relationships to the professions but about the professions themselves, adding to the literature that demonstrates that the meaning of professionalism is historically and culturally contingent. This collection offers readers the opportunity to examine critically both the challenges of professional work for women and the ways in which women have challenged professions.

ELIZABETH SMYTH is Associate Professor, Northwest Centre, Ontario Institute for Studies in Education / University of Toronto.

SANDRA ACKER is Professor, Department of Sociology and Equity Studies in Education, Ontario Institute for Studies in Education / University of Toronto.

PAULA BOURNE is Coordinator, Centre for Women's Studies in Education, Ontario Institute for Studies in Education / University of Toronto.

ALISON PRENTICE is Professor Emeritus, Ontario Institute for Studies in Education / University of Toronto, and Adjunct Professor, University of Victoria.

Challenging Professions:

Historical and Contemporary Perspectives on Women's Professional Work

Edited by
Elizabeth Smyth, Sandra Acker,
Paula Bourne, and Alison Prentice

UNIVERSITY OF TORONTO PRESS
Toronto Buffalo London

© University of Toronto Press Incorporated 1999
Toronto Buffalo London
Printed in Canada

ISBN 0-8020-4319-4 (cloth)
ISBN 0-8020-8143-6 (paper)

∞

Printed on acid-free paper

Canadian Cataloguing in Publication Data

Main entry under title:

Challenging professions : historical and contemporary perspectives on women's professional work

Includes index.
ISBN 0-8020-4319-4 (bound)   ISBN 0-8020-8143-6 (pbk.)

1. Women in the professions – Canada – History.   I. Smyth, Elizabeth M. (Elizabeth Marian), 1954–   .

HD6054.2.C3C42 1999   331.4′81′000971   C99-930099-7

University of Toronto Press acknowledges the financial assistance to its publishing program of the Canada Council for the Arts and the Ontario Arts Council.

This book has been published with the help of a grant from the Humanities and Social Sciences Federation of Canada, using funds provided by the Social Sciences and Humanities Research Council of Canada.

Contents

ACKNOWLEDGMENTS   vii

Introduction   3

Part I   Individual Odysseys

Pentecostalism and Professionalism: The Experience and Legacy of
Aimee Semple McPherson
JANICE DICKIN   25

Professor Elizabeth Govan: An Outsider in Her Own Community
CAROL BAINES   44

Beyond 'Women's Work for Women': Dr Florence Murray and
the Practice and Teaching of Western Medicine in Korea,
1921–1942
RUTH COMPTON BROUWER   65

Music and Marginality: Jean Coulthard and the University of British
Columbia, 1947–1973
WILLIAM BRUNEAU   96

Part II   Multiple Reflections

Three Women in Physics
ALISON PRENTICE   119

From the Science of Housekeeping to the Science of Nutrition:
Pioneers in Canadian Nutrition and Dietetics at the University of
Toronto's Faculty of Household Science, 1900–1950
RUBY HEAP   141

War and Peace: Professional Identities and Nurses' Training,
1914–1930
MERYN STUART   171

The Feminine Face of Forestry in Canada
PEGGY TRIPP-KNOWLES   194

Part III   Collective Case Studies

'Medettes': Thriving or Just Surviving? Women Students in the
Faculty of Medicine, University of Toronto, 1910–1951
W.P.J. MILLAR and R.D. GIDNEY   215

Professionalization among the Professed: The Case of Roman
Catholic Women Religious
ELIZABETH SMYTH   234

Who's Accounting? Women Chartered Accountants in Nova Scotia
CYNDY ALLEN with MARGARET CONRAD   255

Caring as Work for Women Educators
SANDRA ACKER   277

Pawns between Patriarchies: Women in Canadian Pharmacy
LINDA MUZZIN with PATRICIA SINNOTT and CLAUDIA LAI   296

CONTRIBUTORS   315

ILLUSTRATION CREDITS   319

INDEX   321

Acknowledgments

The editors wish to thank the Social Sciences and Humanities Research Council of Canada, Women and Change Strategic Grant initiative, for supporting our collaborative network 'Women and Professional Education.'

In addition to all the contributors to the collection, the researchers who supported them, and the archivists who so generously gave their time and expertise, there are a few people who deserve particular mention. We thank our editor, Gerry Hallowell, the staff of the University of Toronto Press who assisted in the technical production of the book, and Beth McAuley, who created our index.

We could not have undertaken either the project or the production of this manuscript without the ongoing assistance of the administration and staff of the Ontario Institute for Studies in Education of the University of Toronto (OISE/UT). We owe particular thanks to the Centre for Women's Studies in Education of OISE/UT, staffed by Paula Bourne and Caralee Price, for administering our grant, expediting communication, and arranging our network meetings. A further debt of gratitude is owed to Michael Fullan, Angela Hildyard, Mary Stager, Moira Cascone, Jane King, Alyson King, Wayne Seller, and Margaret Gerry.

Finally, to our friends, colleagues, families, and students, who were patient, kind, and understanding, we give both our love and our thanks.

CHALLENGING PROFESSIONS

Introduction

In the early 1960s, as a centennial project, the Canadian Federation of University Women commissioned Mary Quayle Innis to edit a collection of biographical essays on Canadian women. The result of her efforts, entitled *The Clear Spirit: Twenty Canadian Women and Their Times*, was published in 1966. It contained a number of studies of professional women. In her introduction, Innis outlined the considerations that had guided the CFUW editorial committee in its selection of subjects. Musicians and actresses had been ruled out, as most had typically carried on their careers outside Canada. Women who were still living were also considered unacceptable candidates for the collection. Finally, the committee had decided not to include 'members of the traditional women's professions – the teachers, nurses, and librarians.' The problem in their case was that their numbers were myriad; most had lived their lives, moreover, on the regional, rather than the national, stage.[1]

In the interval between the CFUW's book and our own, feminist scholars have been among those who have challenged the dominance of national events and themes in Canadian studies. They have argued that, for the vast majority of women, whose lives are lived in local communities, what goes on in Canada's towns and cities, provinces and territories, *is* important. Similarly, focusing on the stars in politics, the arts, or the professions has been challenged, and much written about ordinary women and men in everyday walks of life.[2] At the same time, boundaries between the disciplines where one might study ordinary women and men have begun to crumble, as interdisciplinary work in women's studies illustrates. Historians and sociologists, in particular, are increasingly discovering topics of mutual interest. One such topic is the study of the professions.

Studying Professions

Long a subject mainly for sociologists, understanding the professions has also become a goal for historians, who have often found sociological paradigms helpful as they strive to make sense of the histories of individual professional groupings. When Mary Quayle Innis was composing the introduction to her book in the 1960s, however, few Canadian historians were thinking along these lines. Not surprisingly, then, the concept of 'professional women' was not really analysed in *The Clear Spirit*. There is a hint that Innis and the members of her committee, when they used the term 'profession,' meant simply the common-sense definition: an occupation providing the possibility of earning one's living. By the 1960s, Innis noted in her introduction, artists 'could be professional'; she cited as an example – rather ironically, given her extreme financial difficulties at certain points in her career – the British Columbia artist Emily Carr,[3] to whom a chapter of the Innis volume was devoted.

The editors of the present volume can only confess that, three decades later, it is not necessarily easier to come up with satisfactory definitions. What is a profession and what is not, who is in a given profession and who is outside it, in any time and place, have been and remain matters for debate, political manoeuvring, and rule-making, as members, non-members, would-be members, and legislators have struggled over issues of place and power in the workforce. As Mary Kinnear has shown in her ground-breaking Canadian study of professional women prior to 1970, even census takers could change their minds about which occupations to include under the category 'professional' over the years.[4] In most fields investigators interested in the subject now agree that the professions, and what is commonly referred to as 'professionalization' in any given occupation, are historically and culturally contingent.[5]

If we go back to the early nineteenth century, we find that members of the most powerful professions characterized themselves as 'learned' and 'gentlemen.' But where there were shortages of such gentlemen, as R.D. Gidney and W.J.P. Millar have pointed out, physicians, lawyers, and clergymen in fact shared the professional stage with many who were not, strictly speaking, either well educated or members of the 'gentle' classes. The question of what constituted a profession became a serious issue as the nineteenth century progressed. The professions became crowded, and interlopers increasingly demanded access to the work that professional gentlemen had formerly monopolized.[6]

Among the most anomalous of those demanding entry to the professions were women. Indeed, it may well have been women knocking at the door which led to the obsession with the idea of professionalism – and eventually produced what amounted to a twentieth-century scholarly industry. Professionals, the new sociologists of professionalism opined, had special bodies of knowledge, acquired through extensive study, which defined them as highly educated experts; they accepted fees for particular work, rather than hourly or weekly wages; many had been 'called' to their profession and believed that their work constituted service to clients whom they agreed to serve, rather than customers whom they had not chosen; all had concerns about the ethical conduct of their occupations. Professionals had organizations to define pertinent bodies of knowledge and appropriately ethical practices. Through these organizations they attempted to control recruitment to their professional groups.[7]

To speak about recruitment to a profession is, however, almost oxymoronic. Since the late nineteenth century in the industrialized West, members of professional bodies have worried far less about recruitment and far more about creating boundaries to keep the 'right people' in and the persons and groups whom they saw as unworthy or undesirable out. Boundary-making and the education of future professionals came together as, increasingly, professional training moved out of the workplace and into universities – institutions to which, of course, women initially had no access. Yet even when women were admitted to faculties of arts or sciences, they were often denied admission to particular professional schools, such as those dedicated to theology. Although the subject is only beginning to come under scrutiny in Canada, it is clear that some professional schools instituted formal or informal quotas in order to limit the numbers of women, as they did with regard to Jews and other minorities.[8] Or in the case of lawyers and doctors, if access were granted to the law or medical school, women could be turned away from law firms or hospitals and thus denied the articling or interning experience that they needed to be licensed. Women physicians responded to this difficulty in early-twentieth-century Ontario by founding their own hospital.[9] And if Manitoba and Ontario were typical, more often than not, budding women lawyers in this period – and later – obtained articles chiefly through family influence. Jewish women experienced double discrimination; even if they managed to get articling positions in Jewish law firms, they joined their non-Jewish sisters in finding these apprenticeships difficult and sometimes very unpleasant because of their gender. For women lawyers, a further exclusion consisted in their typical inability to penetrate practising lawyers' informal networks – networks that greatly eased the professional paths of the men who belonged to them.[10] In other professional fields, access to funding has been difficult for women. A Swedish study of funding practices in biomedical research has demonstrated that, in a 1995 competition, women had to be two and half times as good as men in order to get a research grant.[11] Given these different forms of exclusion, it is not surprising to find one analyst describing the professions as 'historically specific closure projects.'[12] As much as any labour union – perhaps more so – they have been closed shops, albeit shops that have changed over time.

It was with the intention of exploring these themes, primarily in the Canadian context, that the present collection came into existence. Our authors have been members of an interdisciplinary network on women and professional education, and *Challenging Professions* is the culmination of the ongoing discussions of this group. The purpose of our network has been to allow persons with related research areas to meet each other, discuss joint interests, and eventually pursue further research and scholarship collaboratively. The idea of the network arose initially from discussions in 1995 among Alison Prentice, Elizabeth Smyth, Sandra Acker, and Paula Bourne, all working at the Ontario Institute for Studies in Education of the University of Toronto (OISE/UT).[13] We sought to bring together scholars from across Canada who were studying historical and contemporary topics related to women and professional education. A grant from the Social Sciences and Humanities Research Council of Canada[14] allowed us to administer the project through the Centre for Women's Studies in Education at OISE/UT, set up a communication network over electronic mail, and hold two workshops in Toronto. The grant also supported bibliographical research[15] and the development of this volume.[16] Finally, it permitted us to invite a number of other scholars interested in the topic to join us in a third workshop in order to explore the topic further and to think about future directions for this kind of work.[17]

We came to our network discussions and our research with considerable scepticism regarding the professions: their claims to exclusive expertise, the power of one profession over another, the relegation of some groups to categories such as the 'semi-professions,'[18] even the use of terms such as 'non-professional' or 'unprofessional.' In our scepticism we echoed recent sociological analyses that have seen professionalism as something between a mystique and a conspiracy, rather than as a series of admirable traits.[19] Most of us have been involved in or profoundly influenced by feminist scholarship – scholarship that not only supports critical investigation but also calls attention to the way in which gender organizes everyday life. In this volume we hope to pare away some of the mystique of professionalism, by putting particular professional groupings under scrutiny and examining their gendering and its consequences, in various places and over time.

With this idea at the core, we aimed for as much diversity as we could muster. Yet we ourselves were less diverse, as authors, than we might have wished. Although there is one young woman among us, we are otherwise a group of white, middle-class, middle-aged women and (two) white, middle-class, middle-aged men. There is some variation in ethnic and religious background among us, but not as much as would be desirable to represent Canada's multicultural society. We attempted to achieve regional representation, but were only partly successful in that respect and ended up with a majority of Ontario members – in part reflecting the concentration of universities in Canada's most heavily populated province.[20] Not surprisingly, the focus in much of our work was on English-Canadian, white women.

This bias can be further explained by the historical nature of many of our explorations: we were often looking at pioneers in fields initially inhospitable to women or at women who pioneered by pushing at the boundaries of traditional work. Although some of those who were pioneering professionals came from modest origins, many in such roles were from privileged backgrounds and lived in a nation that at the time was not as diverse ethnoculturally as it has since become. Moreover, by restricting coverage to 'the professions,' however broadly defined, we have not by and large discussed poor and working-class women, although a full examination of 'ordinary women' would certainly call for such a study. There is clearly much work still remaining: to identify and investigate the women (and men) from all groups who contribute to contemporary Canadian professions and to understand gender and other social divisions and relations within these occupations. Scholars such as Himani Bannerji, Agnes Calliste, Linda Carty, Adriane Dorrington, Annette Henry, Patricia Monture, and Helen Ralston have already begun this task.[21]

There is the further limitation that we could not 'cover' all the professions in which women are or have been involved. There are no essays on artists, dentists, lawyers, journalists, or women in the military, among the many occupations that might have been considered. Somewhat to our surprise, despite the fact that several of us have been interested in and written extensively about teachers,[22] we seem to have followed, at least in this respect, in the footsteps of Mary Quayle Innis: we have included no study that focuses exclusively upon elementary or secondary teachers, although one essay compares schoolteachers and academics. Higher education, health care, social service, and religion are important in the collection, in essays analysing women in nursing, dietetics, social work, medicine, missionary and academic work, and religious communities. However, women's work as accountants, composers, pharmacists, physicists, and foresters also comes under scrutiny.

Approaches/Methodologies/Questions

Most of the huge corpus of literature on 'professions' can only be described as by men, for men, about men; advances in feminist scholarship have, however, called a halt to business (even professional business) as usual. In Canada a growing periodical literature has now been enriched by the pioneering monographs of R.D. Gidney and W.P.J. Millar and Mary Kinnear. Our reading of this Canadian work and the international literature suggested to us that a focus solely on women in the established professions would exclude most of the jobs that women do.[23] Once again it seemed that we could not simply 'add women and stir.'

Indeed, the concentration on women – and more so, the concentration on gender relations – brings greater depth and different details to the study of professions. Definitions of professions and professionalism begin to expand. And as Mary Kinnear's work has implied, Canadian women's experience of the professions may have been somewhat different from that of women in other countries, with further variations arising from religious or ethnic identity.[24] Although her statistical evidence suggests that the picture might be similar across Canada,[25] we would argue that future researchers should reopen the question of regional differences.

The essays gathered here not only draw on research from several provinces but also illustrate a variety of methodologies and academic styles that can be used to explore our topic. The authors have chosen the tools of analysis that in their view worked best, given the sources available and the focus they wished to develop. Several studies are quantitative and show how relatively large numbers of women were inducted into or have experienced their professional careers. Thus we have essays on medical students at the University of Toronto and on accountants in Nova Scotia which try to give the broad picture in particular times and places. Many of the authors, in contrast, have turned to biography in the gendering of the professions. We are well aware of the cautions that have been expressed about focusing on 'women worthies' in historical or contemporary studies; indeed, in the past many of us have studiously avoided biography because of these concerns. Yet recently there has been a return to explorations of individual women's lives.[26] Often it is only detailed studies of single individuals that allow us to see how and why things happened, or how and why certain choices were made; these insights, in turn, can be explanatory of larger trends in history. For example, Allie Vibert Douglas's analysis of her departure from a career in atomic physics is the study of one woman's feelings only, but it suggests why other women may have found this field less than sympathetic. The careers of Elizabeth Govan, Elizabeth Laird, and the women religious reveal other factors and circumstances that limited women's options. Moreover, when the subjects were still alive (as was the case for Elizabeth Allin, Jean Coulthard, and the foresters), it was sometimes possible to gain special insight into motivation and emotional response, since the authors were able to interview or observe the individuals involved. In some cases the persons studied must remain anonymous, but thoughts and feelings are nevertheless conveyed to us, as the words of interviewees rise vividly from the page.

Increasingly, and in line with much feminist writing, we recognize that our own personal and occupational concerns are integral to our scholarly work. Most of us are employed as professors in universities. Coming from other perspectives are one author who, at the time she was conducting the research, was a graduate student and another who has worked largely as an independent scholar. Most of us are women, although we cannot thereby claim universal insight into the situation of women, given the vast diversity among persons in this category. At the same time, being female (or, in two cases, being male) has inevitably shaped the experiences that we have had as citizens and as scholars, and those experiences find some resonance in our work. At times some of us have encountered difficulties in the gendered academy: lack of encouragement as graduate students or of support and recognition later on; difficulty getting academic jobs or slow promotion once we were employed. Other facets of our identities – ethnicity, national origin, sexual orientation, marital status, age – have sometimes worked against us in traditional universities. Yet we have also experienced much success. We are all too aware of how difficult it is currently even to enter academic life in a tenure-track position, let alone to survive in the present regime of cutbacks and downsizing. Will the generation following the one to which most of us belong be able to overcome gender prejudice in such strained circumstances? Many of us are concerned for the future of women's work in universities.

Some of the connections that we have to our work are less obvious. Alison Prentice, for example, is married to a retired member of a university physics department; she thus observed physics and physicists from the perspective of a faculty wife. Bill Bruneau's interest in music extends beyond the academic, for he performs the works of the composer he writes about. Although we might elaborate further on the personal ties that bind the authors to their work, it is sufficient perhaps to pose the questions that arise when we consider such ties. As insiders, or scholars near to insiders, do we see more of the flaws than others would? Or, on the contrary, are we less inclined to be critical? Do our contemporary subjects trust us more because we understand their world? Or do they hesitate to reveal secrets that might be passed on to others in the work community? Do we gain greater understanding because we know what people in the field are talking about? Or do we lose information because informants assume that, because we know things already, there is no need to elaborate? Do some of us project our own feelings and experiences, as professional women and men, onto the subjects of our essays? It is not always clear how our various positions affect our understandings. Some of the authors try to come to grips with these questions, while others do not attempt that exercise in this context. We leave such questions to our readers, who, we hope and believe, will have their own insights and experiences to bring to the subjects explored here.

Previous work on gender and the professions has been invaluable in helping us to ask questions and develop ideas. Anne Witz and David Coburn, writing in British and Canadian contexts respectively, have called attention to the complexity of the interactions among various professions and the importance of looking at *systems* of employment and how they change over time. Coburn's interest is in how the work of certain groups becomes deskilled or proletarianized as other, related groups professionalize – or, indeed, how professionalization and proletarianization of an occupation can take place simultaneously. The main focus for Witz is the gendering of different professions as more-powerful ones engage in strategies of exclusion, segregation, or demarcation in order to contain women's professional ambitions.[27] We see echoes of their arguments in the essays that follow.

Witz joins the American scholars Penina Glazer and Miriam Slater in insisting that we explore women's own motives and tactics – or 'female professional projects'[28] – in the world of professionalization. The latter have argued that turn-of-the-century women pioneering entry into the professions employed four main strategies: superperformance, innovation, segregation, and subordination.[29] Mary Kinnear, examining the lives of women teachers, university professors, doctors, lawyers, and nurses in Manitoba prior to the 1970s, found that willingness to accept a subordinate role was the most typical strategy for her subjects. They were loath or unable to take on the workload of the superperformer and had little opportunity to innovate or to pursue their goals in segregated environments.[30] The essays in our book suggest that, for many women in many fields, accepting subordinate roles has indeed been the dominant strategy. And yet we also see public-health nurses managing to create segregated universes where they could enjoy greater autonomy than some of their sisters in the nursing field. The dietitians and Roman Catholic sisters described in this volume also operated much of the time in segregated worlds. Innovators and superperformers, it has to be said, are also represented here.

Other explorations raise further questions for comparative study. In her analysis of the lives of African-American professional women whom she interviewed, Gwendolyn Etter-Lewis notes how differently the fathers and mothers of her subjects were portrayed. Fathers spoke directly, encouraging their daughters to attend university or seek independence through professional careers; mothers were depicted as community-oriented role models. In her attention to the language of her informants and to the intricacies of their interactions with herself, the interviewer, Etter-Lewis makes a case for narrative: the telling of women's stories, often using their own words, to illuminate the history of their encounters with the professions.[31] Many of the essays in this anthology similarly argue for the usefulness of narrative, for historical as well as living women, although none of our authors takes the argument for oral history 'as autobiography'[32] as far as Etter-Lewis does for her African-American subjects.

Broken Patterns: Professional Women and the Quest for a New Feminine Identity, an American study by Anita Harris, explores the fragmented lives often reported by contemporary women in the professions and the ways in which one generation of women has resisted following the patterns of the previous generation.[33] Have generations of Canadian women been similarly motivated? Have women of each era fought to escape from one kind of patriarchy, only to find themselves enmeshed in another? Harris's study reminds us that earlier women often eschewed marriage in order to adopt professional lives parallel to men's. Many contemporary women, in contrast, have rejected this pattern and tried to combine family and professional work. Both choices entail costs. Has the struggle – encapsulated by the Australian scholar Alison Mackinnon as 'love' versus 'freedom' – been worth it?[34] Mackinnon has explored the connections between fertility decline in modern Western nations and contemporary women's engagement with higher education and the professions. Clearly, many women have chosen to remain single in their quest for personal and economic autonomy. But their lives were not necessarily loveless. Mackinnon called her book *Love* and *Freedom*. As her study shows, and as some of the essays in our volume also demonstrate, women have often sought and found love outside marriage and child rearing. In addition, married women have limited their fertility. Indeed, Mackinnon provides persuasive evidence that women's higher education and professional involvement, as well as more-egalitarian marriages, are implicated in this trend. The choice to have no or fewer children was often a conscious and negotiated choice for women professionals.[35] Do we see reflections of Mackinnon's arguments in the lives explored in the pages that follow?

Despite its importance, the difficulty of combining commitments to family, friends, or partners with the heavy demands of professional work is not the only, or even necessarily the most important, issue as we contemplate women's professional careers in the past and present. The British sociologists Anne Spencer and David Podmore, for example, find that child-rearing responsibilities are only one among many factors that contribute to the marginalization of women in male-dominated professions.[36] On the same theme, participants in a 1997 Stockholm workshop on women and higher education were reminded more than once that focusing on women's family responsibilities makes women the 'problem,' when the real issue is the structuring of institutions and careers to conform to a man's (idealized) life pattern: that of the full-time breadwinner supported by a wife who takes care of all domestic and family responsibilities. The myth of the male breadwinner and full-time wife, we all know, no longer matches the reality of most married couples in the post-industrial age. But there is another way of looking at this conundrum. The Swedish scholar Inga Elgqvist-Saltzman argues that the caring responsibilities undertaken by women should be regarded less as impediment and more as enrichment in professional lives that increasingly demand flexibility and the ability to communicate. Her vivid picture contrasting men's and women's careers over time suggests that we reverse our priorities. If we do, we see that the vision, experience, and career patterns typical of men may have been constricted, compared to the broader, more flexible, and more socially oriented experience of comparable women.[37]

The American anthropologist, English teacher, and former college administrator Mary Catherine Bateson has made a case for the positive challenges and even the satisfactions of women professionals' fragmented lives. Drawing on the biographies of four friends and on her own life story, Bateson talks about women composing their lives as works of art. As one reviewer put it, she shows us that 'marginality can be celebrated for its space and creativity.' Although it is hard to see Bateson and her friends as truly marginal in the grand scheme of things, they felt themselves to be so in some respects and at various times in their lives; improvisation and adaptation were important strategies in their encounters with even temporary marginality. The vision is similar to Elgqvist-Saltzman's: that 'winding tracks' may be more interesting and educational than straight ones.[38] Readers may wish to ponder these arguments as they peruse the essays gathered here.

Network discussions have raised further questions. One certainly is the role of political context. What, for example, has been the impact of war on the gendering of the professions? The First World War, it is clear, gave some Canadian women the opportunity both to extend the boundaries of certain professions and to create new ones. The Second World War has been less examined, but it appears to have had a more ambiguous effect, at least in some professional arenas. We know that, following the war, married women were less discriminated against in the hiring process in many professions and that the war itself created more jobs for women in fields such as nursing. Mary Kinnear has noted that the Second World War provided opportunities for women in university teaching both during the war and afterwards as, first, male professors left their posts for war-related jobs and, later, teachers were needed for the veterans who flooded university campuses after 1945. But these same veterans and the returning professors also competed for jobs, and the percentages of faculty members who were female dropped off quickly after the 1940s. It also seems to have been during the Second World War that quotas were put in place to prevent large numbers of women (and other non-favoured groups) from entering medical schools in Manitoba and Ontario.[39] Were patterns in other provinces similar? And what other events have marked women's entry into or affected their engagement with the professions?

Second, we have found ourselves confronted with the impact that the professionalization of women's work had on the professions. Their presence has redefined the professions, just as their experiences in the professions have redefined women's lives as persons, mothers, and wives. Has the entry of women, in fact, contributed to divided professions, as knowledge (and work) separate into two streams: the theoretical and the practical? Has women's entry in fact resulted in the creation of underclasses within the professions?

Third, we are increasingly intrigued with professional-knowledge claims. Who decides which knowledge particular professions may (or must) lay claim to and who controls access to that knowledge? By what mechanisms do prescribed bodies of knowledge change over time? These complex issues find varying degrees of space in our essays. Several deal with the University of Toronto, and one looks at the Faculty of Music at the University of British Columbia; in both these universities decisions about what subjects ought to be studied to become a doctor, a dietitian, a physicist, or a musician mattered to women. Some authors take up this question more explicitly than others.

A fourth issue, barely touched upon in these essays but certainly an issue for women, is that of professional cultures. We need to know more about the external accoutrements of professional life and culture – the language, dress, and ritual – which give many professionals their power and that women have often found hard to accept, let alone reproduce or imitate.[40] What other aspects of professional culture have women's absence or presence in the professions shaped or reshaped?

Also little examined here is a fifth question: the gendered nature of political leverage when it comes to the professions. This is an especially important angle to consider, since governments determine which professionals may legally practise and which may not, and the remuneration, status, and power of particular professional groups.[41] As Mary Kinnear has noted, this factor is especially important in Canada, since the universities and schools that now train most professionals are almost entirely funded by government. In the absence, also, of large numbers of private hospitals, Canadian governments have enormous power over the health-care professions.[42] Whether or not, and in what manner, midwives may legally practise and Toronto's Women's College Hospital can survive government-driven restructuring are obvious examples of issues that deeply concern women not only as professionals but also as clients of professionals. A related question is the interplay between women's professional work and the shifting boundaries between voluntary and state intervention in the health and well-being of Canadian citizens. Women's work in previously private and philanthropic spheres has over time become both institutionalized and state controlled. What will happen to women's professional work when governments dismantle the welfare state, as they appear to be doing in Canada and elsewhere?

In sum, when we engage in analyses of women's work in the professions, we enter into debates about power. And there are many factors that contribute to or take away from women's power in the world of work, in the professions as elsewhere. In a study of anti-Semitism in Ontario, Stephen Speisman has noted that Jews entering the professions tended to prefer those in which they could be self-employed, such as law and medicine. Professions such as accountancy, architecture, and engineering, he suggests, offered less opportunity for such autonomy.[43] One wonders if women have had to make similar choices. The findings of Barbara Lawrence are relevant here. Exploring contemporary trends for women general practitioners in the United Kingdom, she observes that they are moving away from group practice. Questioned about the trend, her respondents reported that they had experienced both financial and personal exploitation in group practice; many preferred to work longer hours for less pay in order to have greater control over their working lives. They wanted the power to practise the kind of medicine they believed in and to do things their own way.[44]

Putting It All Together

The authors of the essays in this collection have not been able to tackle all the questions we have raised here. Nor, as we have seen, have they explored the issues that they have tackled from identical angles. Indeed, we hope that the essays in our volume will illustrate not only the many issues and problems raised by the gendering of the professions and professional education but also the diverses approaches that are available to students of the subject.

Although a chronological organization for this book initially suggested itself, and other organizational schemes might also have been useful, in the end we have chosen to group the essays according to these approaches. We begin with biographical studies. Their subjects include an evangelist who made her career chiefly in the United States, a University of Toronto professor of social work, a missionary doctor whose career unfolded in Korea, and a west-coast composer. Their stories suggest the opportunities that professional life has provided for some Canadian women. Aimee Semple McPherson, the daughter of working farmers, Elizabeth Govan and Florence Murray, raised in urban middle-class homes, and Jean Coulthard, from an urban upper-middle-class background, all grappled with the possibilities and made unique and unforgettable uses of them. Readers might ponder the different problems that these women faced, the impact that class or the regional (and even national) location of their work had on their careers, and the varying ways in which they dealt with – or did not deal with – the issues raised by gender in their professional and personal lives.

The essays in the second section might best be characterized as studies in group biography; here the authors have made comparisons, often over time, as they explore different women's responses and approaches to the opportunities encountered – or denied, redefined, and grasped – in their chosen fields. In public-health nursing, physics, dietetics, and forestry, women have found a variety of niches, and the authors of the essays dealing with these areas have chosen to focus on more than one woman partly in order to illustrate this variety. Have women's opportunities been different, depending on whether the field developed largely as women's work (nursing and dietetics) or men's (physics and forestry)? How have these fields changed for women over time?

Finally, a third section explores larger collectivities of women engaged with the professions. Here we include studies dealing with women's access to the Faculty of Medicine at the University of Toronto during the first half of the twentieth century; the professional concerns of Canadian women religious over time; the changing status of women in Nova Scotia accountancy up to 1970; and the conditions under which teachers, academics, and pharmacists currently work, and how they respond to these conditions. Here again, differences emerge both with respect to the authors' approaches to their subjects and among the subjects themselves. How and why are the problems faced by women accountants different from those faced by women pharmacists, medical students, academics, or religious? Here, perhaps more than in the other sections, is displayed the power of the corporate bodies to which many professionals must relate. As pharmaceutical companies, universities, or religious organizations grow in size, what happens to the women whose professional work is largely under their control? Does size matter? And once again we are faced with the differences between 'men's professions' and 'women's.' How have these differences been played out as the organizations employing women professionals have developed and become more complex over time?

The essays in this collection represent a sampling of current work being done in Canada on women and the professions. They indicate that the issues related to the role of gender in the professions engage researchers employed in a variety of fields. The essays also point clearly to the fact that this is an area of research that cries out for ongoing exploration, employing a variety of approaches, to examine the past, reflect on the present, and think about the future. We have attempted to be scholarly, provocative, and accessible, while at the same time resisting the urge to draw sweeping conclusions from the cases presented here. It is too early within the scholarly process to undertake such a synthesis.

We hope that our readers will enjoy the products of our collective efforts as much as we enjoyed both working on our different subjects and exploring them together. There continue to be, needless to say, differences of opinion among us; spaces between and across disciplines; gaps in our understanding. There certainly remains, as we have learned, much more to do. It is our hope that the ideas presented here will expand our knowledge not only of how the professions have challenged women but of how women's engagement with the professions has both challenged and changed them.

NOTES

1 Mary Quayle Innis, ed., *The Clear Spirit: Twenty Canadian Women and Their Times* (Toronto: University of Toronto Press, 1966), ix–xii. Soon after the publication of *The Clear Spirit*, Innis did put together a collection of essays dealing with Canadian nursing: Innis, ed., *Nursing Education in a Changing Society* (Toronto: University of Toronto Press, 1970).

2 For a sampling of Canadian monographs and collections of essays dealing with 'ordinary' women, see Janice Acton, Penny Goldsmith, and Bonnie Shepard, eds., *Women at Work: Ontario 1850–1930* (Toronto: Canadian Women's Educational Press, 1974); Francine Barry, *Le travail de la femme au Québec: L'évolution de 1940 à 1970* (Montréal: Université de Québec, 1977); Hugh and Pat Armstrong, *The Double Ghetto: Canadian Women and Their Segregated Work* (Toronto: McClelland and Stewart, 1978; 2nd ed., 1984; 3rd ed., 1994); Sara Diamond, *Chambermaids and Whistlepunks: An Oral History of Women in B.C. Labour, 1930–1955* (Vancouver: Press Gang, 1983); Marie Lavigne and Yolande Pinard, eds., *Travailleuses et féministes: Les femmes dans la société québécoise* (Montréal: Boréal Express, 1983); Paula Bourne, ed., *Women's Paid and Unpaid Work: Historical and Contemporary Perspectives* (Toronto: New Hogtown Press, 1985); Joy Parr, *The Gender of Breadwinners: Women, Men, and Change in Two Industrial Towns 1880–1950* (Toronto: University of Toronto Press, 1990); Annalee Golz, David Millar, and Barbara Roberts, *A Decent Living: Women in the Winnipeg Garment Industry* (Toronto: New Hogtown Press, 1991); Ruth A. Frager, *Sweatshop Strife:*

Class, Ethnicity, and Gender in the Jewish Labour Movement of Toronto, 1900–1939 (Toronto: University of Toronto Press, 1992); Joan Sangster, *Earning Respect: The Lives of Working Women in Small-Town Ontario, 1920–1960* (Toronto: University of Toronto Press, 1995). A more complete listing of historical works may be found in Diana Pedersen, *Changing Women, Changing Society: A Bibliography of the History of Women in Canada* (Ottawa: Carleton University Press, 1996).

3 Innis, *The Clear Spirit*, xi.

4 Mary Kinnear, *In Subordination: Professional Women, 1870–1970* (Montreal and Kingston: McGill-Queen's University Press, 1995), 7.

5 We add 'culturally' to the phrase 'historically contingent,' which we have borrowed from R.D. Gidney and W.J.P. Millar, to suggest how professions will differ from one cultural or national community to another. See Gidney and Millar, *Professional Gentlemen: The Professions in Nineteenth-Century Ontario* (Toronto: University of Toronto Press, 1994), xii.

6 Gidney and Millar, *Professional Gentlemen*, especially part 2, 'Reconstructing Profession,' and chapter 15, 'Who Was Then a Gentleman?'

7 This list of characteristics draws on a number of studies, including Burton J. Bledstein, *The Culture of Professionals: The Middle Class and the Development of Higher Education in America* (New York: W.W. Norton, 1976); Dee Garrison, *Apostles of Culture: The Public Librarian and American Society, 1876–1920* (New York: The Free Press, 1979); Penina Migdal Glazer and Miriam Slater, *Unequal Colleagues: The Entrance of Women into the Professions* (New Brunswick, NJ: Rutgers University Press, 1987); Kinnear, *In Subordination*; Gidney and Millar, *Professional Gentlemen*.

8 For an discussion of this practice at the University of Manitoba's Faculty of Medicine in the 1940s, see Kinnear, *In Subordination*, 63–6. While Gidney and Millar find no evidence for quotas in the University of Toronto's Faculty of Medicine in the years following the admission of women up to the 1940s, they suggest that Toronto employed them beginning in that decade. See their essay '"Medettes": Thriving or Just Surviving? Women Students in the Faculty of Medicine, University of Toronto, 1910–1951,' in this volume.

9 See Lykke de la Cour and Rose Sheinin, 'The Ontario Medical College for Women, 1883 to 1906: Lessons from Gender Separation in Medical Education,' *Canadian Woman Studies/Les cahiers de la femme* 7, 3 (fall 1986); reprinted in Marianne Gosztonyi Ainley, ed., *Despite the Odds: Essays on Canadian Women in Science* (Montreal: Véhicule Press, 1990), 112–20.

10 Kinnear, *In Subordination*, chapter 4; Constance Backhouse, '"To Open the Way for Others of My Sex": Clara Brett Martin's Career as Canada's First Woman Lawyer,' *Canadian Journal of Women and the Law* 1, 1 (1985): 1–41; Gidney and Millar, *Professional Gentlemen*, 322–5 and 328–32; Cecilia Morgan, '"An

Embarrassing and Severely Masculine Atmosphere'": Women, Gender and the Legal Profession at Osgoode Hall, 1920s–1960s,' *Canadian Journal of Law and Society* 11, 2 (fall 1996): 32–4.

11 Christine Wenneras and Agnes Wold, 'Nepotism and Sexism in Peer Review,' *Nature* 387 (22 May 1997). As the title suggests, knowledge of and connections to candidates were also sources of bias.

12 Anne Witz, *Professions and Patriarchy* (London: Routledge, 1992), 37.

13 In 1996 the former OISE was officially renamed the Ontario Institute for Studies in Education of the University of Toronto.

14 The SSHRC grant was offered under the strategic theme 'Women and Change.'

15 Alyson King, *Women and the Professions: A Bibliography* (Toronto: OISE/UT, 1999).

16 The papers collected here were first vetted and then presented at two workshops, as well as circulated among members. Taking into account feedback from the group, authors refined their papers further and eventually sent them to the editors, who provided further feedback. All the papers went through at least one revision at that point. Finally, the editors met in twos and threes to make decisions about the book's organization and to write the introduction.

17 The SSHRC grant covered a third workshop, held in April 1998, which included additional participants. As a result of that meeting, participants initiated plans for further dissemination of research on women in the professions through special issues of journals and agreed to explore possibilities for the expansion and continuation of the research network.

18 See, for example, Amitai Etzioni, *The Semi-Professions and Their Organization* (New York: Free Press, 1969).

19 See, for example, Margali Sarfatti Larson, *The Rise of Professionalism* (Berkeley: University of California Press, 1977); Mike Saks, 'Removing the Blinkers? A Critique of Recent Contributions to the Sociology of the Professions,' *Sociological Review* 31, 1 (1983): 1–21.

20 In addition, this weakness illustrates the difficulty that Canadian scholars still have in finding, communicating with, and getting to know their counterparts in other regions of the country, especially when attempting interdisciplinary work. It also reflects the nature of our funding and institutional arrangements; money for bringing in scholars who lived at a distance from Toronto was limited.

21 Himani Bannerji, 'But Who Speaks for Us? Experience and Agency in Conventional Feminist Paradigms,' and Linda Carty, 'Black Women in Academia: A Statement from the Periphery,' in Bannerji et al., eds., *Unsettling Relations: The*

University as a Site of Feminist Struggle (Toronto: Women's Press, 1991), 67–107; Agnes Calliste, 'Antiracism, Organizing and Resistance in Nursing: African Canadian Women,' *Canadian Review of Sociology and Anthropology* 33, 3 (August 1996): 361–90; Adriane Dorrington, 'Nova Scotia Black Female Educators: Lessons from the Past,' (EdD thesis, University of Toronto, 1995); Annette Henry, 'African Canadian Women Teachers' Activism: Recreating Communities of Caring and Resistance,' *Journal of Negro Education* 61, 3 (1992): 392–404; Patricia A. Monture, 'Ka-Nin-Geh-Heh-Gah-E-Sa-Nonh-Yah-Gah,' in The Chilly Collective, eds., *Breaking Anonymity: The Chilly Climate for Women Faculty* (Waterloo: Wilfrid Laurier University Press, 1995), 265–78; Helen Ralston, 'Race, Class, Gender and Work Experience of South Asian Women in Atlantic Canada,' in Wendy Mitchinson et al., eds., *Canadian Women: A Reader* (Toronto: Harcourt Brace Canada, 1996), 405–15.

22 For example, Sandra Acker, ed., *Teachers, Gender and Careers* (London: Falmer Press, 1989); Acker, *Gendered Education: Sociological Reflections on Women, Teaching and Feminism* (Buckingham: Open University Press, 1994), and 'Gender and Teachers' Work,' in Michael Apple, ed., *Review of Research in Education*, vol. 21 (Washington, DC: American Educational Research Association, 1995–6), 99–162; Alison Prentice and Marjorie Theobald, eds., *Women Who Taught: Perspectives on the History of Women and Teaching* (Toronto: University of Toronto Press, 1991); Elizabeth Smyth, '"Much Exertion of Voice and Great Application of the Mind": Teacher Education within the Congregation of the Sisters of St Joseph of Toronto 1851–1920,' *Historical Studies in Education* 6, 3 (1994): 97–113, and 'Christian Perfection and Service of Neighbour,' in E. Muir and M. Whiteley, eds., *Changing Roles of Women within the Christian Church in Canada* (Toronto: University of Toronto Press, 1995), 38–54.

23 Gidney and Millar, *Professional Gentlemen*; Kinnear, *In Subordination*; Witz, *Professions and Patriarchy*; Margaret W. Rossiter, *Women Scientists in America: Struggles and Strategies to 1940* (Baltimore and London: Johns Hopkins University Press, 1982), and *Women Scientists in America: Before Affirmative Action* (Baltimore and London: Johns Hopkins University Press, 1995); Glazer and Slater, *Unequal Colleagues*; Gwendolyn Etter-Lewis, *My Soul Is My Own: Oral Narratives of African American Women in the Professions* (New York and London: Routledge, 1993).

24 Kinnear, *In Subordination*; see especially chapter 7, 'In Retrospect: "Delighted to Be Accepted,"' 163–5, and her references to the experiences of Jewish women professionals in Manitoba.

25 Ibid., appendix 1, 171–86.

26 Indeed, Natalie Zemon Davis, who gave us the expression 'women worthies,' has herself recently turned to biography in a fascinating study of three

women whose lives exemplify choices that were available to some relatively prosperous and prominent Roman Catholic, Jewish, and Protestant women in early modern Europe. Zemon Davis, *Women on the Margins: Three Seventeenth-Century Lives* (Cambridge, Mass.: Harvard University Press, 1995). See also the discussion of the biographical approach to exploring women's roles and status in the sciences in Alison Prentice, 'Three Women in Physics,' in this volume.

27 David Coburn, 'Professionalization and Proletarianization: Medicine, Nursing, and Chiropractic in Historical Perspective,' *Labour/Le travail* 34 (fall 1994): 139–62; Witz, *Professions and Patriarchy*, especially 30–8. For an earlier discussion of how the structure of professions changed with the entry of women, see Michael J. Carter and Susan Boslego Carter, 'Women's Recent Progress in the Professions; or, Women Get a Ticket to Ride after the Gravy Train Has Left the Station,' *Feminist Studies* 7, 3 (fall 1981): 477–504.

28 Witz, *Professions and Patriarchy*, 39.

29 Glazer and Slater, *Unequal Colleagues*, especially chapter 1, 'The Context of Professionalization.'

30 Kinnear, *In Subordination*, 163–7.

31 Etter-Lewis, *My Soul Is My Own*, especially 82–91 and following.

32 Ibid., chapter 4, 'African American Women's Oral Narratives as Autobiography: The Care and Feeding of "Mongrel Offspring."'

33 Anita M. Harris, *Broken Patterns: Professional Women and the Quest for a New Feminine Identity* (Detroit: Wayne State University Press, 1995).

34 Alison Mackinnon, *Love and Freedom: Professional Women and the Reshaping of Personal Life* (Cambridge: Cambridge University Press, 1997).

35 Ibid., especially chapters 4 and 5.

36 Anne Spencer and David Podmore, eds., *In a Man's World: Essays on Women in Male-Dominated Professions* (London: Tavistock, 1987). They list ten factors: stereotypes about women; stereotypes about the nature of the professions and professionals; the sponsorship system; the lack of models and peers; informal relationships; the concept of professional commitment; the unplanned nature of many women's careers; 'women's work'; clients' expectations; and fear of competition.

37 'The Promised Land ... The Gendered Character of Higher Education,' a conference sponsored by the Council for Studies of Higher Education, Stockholm, Sweden, 14–17 August 1997; Inga Elgqvist-Saltzman, 'Straight Roads and Winding Tracks: Swedish Educational Policy from a Gender Perspective,' *Gender and Education* 4, 1–2 (1992): 41–56; 'Gravel in the Machinery or the Hub of the Wheel?' in Maud L. Eduards et al., *Rethinking Change: Current Swedish Feminist Research* (Uppsala: Humanistisk-samhallsvetenskapliga

forskiningsradet, 1992), especially the discussion of the graphs on 79–80. See also Gunilla Bjerén and Inga Elgqvist-Saltzman, eds., *Gender and Education in a Life Perspective* (Aldershot: Avebury, 1994).

38 Mary Catherine Bateson, *Composing a Life* (New York: Plume, 1990); review from *7 Days*, reprinted inside front cover of *Composing a Life*; Elgqvist-Saltzman, 'Straight Roads and Winding Tracks,' 41; see also Zemon Davis, *Women on the Margins*.

39 Kinnear, *In Subordination*, 18, 35, 63–5, 111, and 134; Millar and Gidney, '"Medettes": Thriving or Just Surviving?' in this volume.

40 See Kim Thomas, *Gender and Subject in Higher Education* (Buckingham: Open University Press, 1990); Jennifer Coates, 'The Language of the Professions: Discourse and Career,' in Julia Evetts, ed., *Women and Career: Continuity between Private and Professional Identity* (London and New York: Longman, 1994); Alyson M. Worrall, 'Suit-able for Promotion: A Game of Educational Snakes and Ladders,' in Diane M. Dunlap and Patricia A. Schmuck, eds., *Women Leading in Education* (Albany: State University of New York Press, 1995).

41 This is a major theme in Gidney and Millar, *Professional Gentlemen*.

42 Kinnear, *In Subordination*, 13. For a discussion of the power of the federal government over its own civil service employees, see Annis May Timpson, 'The Politics of Employment Inequality in Canada: Gender and the Public Sector,' in Evetts, ed., *Women and Career*.

43 Stephen Speisman, 'Antisemitism in Ontario: The Twentieth Century,' in Alan Davis, ed., *Antisemitism in Canada: History and Interpretation* (Waterloo: Wilfrid Laurier Press, 1992), 121.

44 Barbara Lawrence, 'The Fifth Dimension – Gender and General Practice,' in Spencer and Podmore, *In a Man's World*.

PART I:

INDIVIDUAL ODYSSEYS

Pentecostalism and Professionalism: The Experience and Legacy of Aimee Semple McPherson

JANICE DICKIN

Pentecostal evangelist Aimee Semple McPherson was an enigma. Material on her life frequently offers conflicting versions of what even biographers are prone to call 'facts.'[1] For example, Aimee was at one and the same time everybody's 'Sister' and nobody's 'sister.' The first description alludes to both her familiar style with congregations and the honorific for women commonly used by some Protestant sects. This double entendre has been used as the subtitle for the most recent biography of her.[2] In the very first line of that book she is described as 'an American phenomenon' (ix). In fact, she was an Ontario farm girl with three older half-siblings whom she never mentioned publicly.

Aimee's professional life is equally enigmatic. The survivor of three marriages but widowed only once, she founded a sect that did not condone divorce. Publicly opposed to both dancing and movies, she drew texts for sermons from popular tunes and Hollywood films, as well as from the Bible. Part of a movement that shunned worldliness, she took the basically itinerant form of the revival and built for it a theatre that rivalled Radio City Music Hall in size and facilities. Her Saviour preached poverty; she dressed in expensive clothes, drove in expensive cars, and travelled first class. Her job as a revivalist was to support old, not create new, denominations. In fact, she established a church that claims to be the fourth largest Pentecostal organization in the world. And as a guiding light in a movement which believes fundamentally that the only knowledge worth having is granted, not learned, she established a bible college aimed at turning out professionally trained Pentecostal evangelists.

The juxtaposition of Pentecostalism and professionalism moves us out of the realm of enigma and into that of contradiction. The traditional

Pentecostal doctrine is one of justification by faith alone and embraces the belief in a priesthood of all believers. Only one credential gains entry as both a believer and a preacher: a cataclysmic emotional experience described variously as being born again, being baptized by fire, and being filled with the Holy Spirit. Preferably, the experience is made manifest by a form of spontaneous utterance called 'speaking in tongues,' or glossolalia.

The biblical authority classically used for this phenomenon is Acts 2:1–4. Christ's disciples were waiting, on a traditional Jewish holy day seven weeks after His crucifixion, for a promised sign: 'And when the day of Pentecost was fully come, they were all with one accord in one place. And suddenly there came a sound from heaven as of a rushing mighty wind, and it filled all the house where they were sitting. And there appeared unto them cloven tongues like as of fire, and it sat upon each of them. And they were all filled with the Holy Ghost, and began to speak with other tongues, as the Spirit gave them utterance.' From here and because of this experience, the disciples set forth on their careers of spreading the Gospel.

Spreading the Gospel, or evangelizing (from a Greek word to do with reward for bringing good news), can be a part of any Christian sect, but Pentecostalism is set off by its insistence on being born again – that is, baptism by fire in addition to baptism by water. In the latter act, if one is old enough, one makes a pledge and is accepted into the sect. In the case of infants the pledge is made by – literally – godparents. Most sects prescribe reaffirmation and repetition of this pledge through confirmation and/or rebaptism as an adult. Theoretically at least, this process can be accomplished with a modicum of intense feeling. But baptism by fire requires, as an essential, a very high degree of emotional expression as well as feeling. This is, in one way, a very onerous task. Perhaps we can take as a sign of the difficulty with which most people perceive the achievement of this state the fact that many consider it possible or at least likely only through fakery.

In addition to the reward of feeling at one with God, the experience of baptism by fire gives one, as mentioned above, automatic entry into what other sects call the ministry. Christ said, 'Except a man be born again, he cannot see the kingdom of God' (John 3:3). From this passage of Scripture was drawn the justification for the concept of an almost 'instant ministry' of the type possible within the Pentecostal movement at the turn of the century. Though one can trace Pentecostalism back through the evangelistic arms of Methodism and Anglicanism, these denominations prescribe (in common with Catholicism) a priesthoood serially passed on from Christ (Acts 19:6) through His disciples in one long, continuous historical chain by the laying on of hands. In breaking away from this tradition and insisting instead on anointment directly by the Holy Spirit, Pentecostals short-circuited and made redundant two millennia of entrenched, hard-fought-for, and carefully assembled church hierarchy. When more-staid Christians dismissed baptism by fire as evidence of being out of control, they could not have been more right. While Pentecostalism insisted that one seek and find one's Saviour personally, it also freed one to do so.

And who better to help an individual in this endeavour than one already so baptized, a person who had already seen, in one possible reading of John 3:3, the kingdom of God? Pentecostals, in short, found another gate into Heaven, a gate manned only by St Peter, not by his earthly ecclesiastical descendants. In doing so, they not only made it possible for individuals to find God without bowing to the doctrinal and social demands of the established Christian sects, but they also opened the gate of priesthood to persons who were called rather than trained, individuals barred by other sects for reasons which have to do with gender and class, not belief. Pentecostal religious stewards were expected to help people to find Christ through their emotions, not through theology. If this is not precisely an anti-intellectual concept, it is certainly an 'extra-intellectual' one.

The power invested by believers in this emotional, charismatic approach to religion is no better demonstrated than in their belief in the gift of tongues. This gift not only was resistant to training, could not be accomplished by training, and short-circuited the need for training; it was believed to grant in one coup the benefits of training. It was thought to provide direct access to the word of God and instant knowledge of any language needed for its propagation. No wonder that Pentecostalism was often dismissed as appealing mainly to the lower classes. For obvious reasons, it did.

Tongues-speaking as a spiritual experience pre-dates Christianity. In ancient Greece gods sometimes used mortals to pass on messages. Interpretation was key to revealing the true meaning of these messages, even when they were couched in the vernacular. Christian sects previous to and other than Pentecostalism which have practised tongues-speaking value the experience not only for the message being passed on (still requiring interpretation) but also as evidence of being spirit-filled. Come the twentieth century, glossolalia bore the distinction of not only being disapproved of by less charismatic Christians; it also fell prey to the new science of psychology. Glossolalics were dismissed as 'illiterate, uncontrolled, neurotic, ruled by mob emotion, subject to auto-suggestion and self-hypnosis, suffering from disease or derangement of the nervous system, and classified with hysterics, cataleptics, and schizophrenics.'[3]

By the mid-1920s Aimee herself would relegate tongues-speaking, along with faith healing (another ability granted solely by gift from God), to an inner room of her temple. If she never precisely stated a loss of trust in the power of faith alone, she had begun to act in a manner that indicated a belief in training. She had opened a bible school, thereby professionalizing a role that for her had been a calling. No matter how practical and worthy her intentions were in passing along the benefits of her experience, by formalizing education for a Pentecostal ministry, she became a gatekeeper. By providing a mechanism for professionalism, she helped to undermine the meaning of Pentecostalism, barring rather than laying the way for others like herself.

Personally, Aimee gloried in the knowledge that she had been directly chosen by God to do His work. For a short period she did carry credentials from the Assemblies of God, but by and large she spent most of her ministry unrecognized by anyone other than herself and her followers. And God. She went to great trouble in various versions of her story of her life to establish not only that God had personally chosen her to preach but that indeed He had almost killed her when she resisted. Married to a husband at the time unenthusiastic about her re-entry into 'the work,' Aimee argued with God that she must remain a dutiful wife and care for her two young children. She became both physically and mentally ill. Finally, as she lay dying on an operating table, the voice of God asked her, 'NOW – WILL – YOU – GO?' As she told the story year after year, usually on her birthday, she knew that she would 'go' one way or the other and chose to answer the call to preach. In this one act she resolved the conundrum of giving herself to her children (by staying alive) while giving herself to God (by bartering her soul). The marriage was sacrificed.

Emotionally, Aimee claimed her credentials from suffering: 'Oh, don't you ever tell me that a woman cannot be called to preach the Gospel! If any man ever went through one-hundreadth [sic] part of the hell on earth that I lived in, those months when out of God's will and work, they would never say that again.'[4] Scripturally, she claimed her credentials from Acts 2:16–18: 'But this is that which was spoken by the prophet Joel; And it shall come to pass in the last days, saith God, I will pour out my Spirit upon all flesh: and your sons and your daughters shall prophesy, and your young men shall see visions, and your old men shall dream dreams: And on my servants and on my handmaidens I will pour out in these days of my Spirit; and they shall prophesy.'

Aimee took 'this is that' as the title of her first book. In her frequent quoting of these few obscure verses, she remedied the gender imbalance of God's word by editing out the 'young men having visions and old men dreaming dreams' part. So far as she was concerned, the daughters and handmaidens were equal to the sons and the servants. She never made a particularly big issue out of this matter. As far as she was concerned, just as God made her preach, this was simply the way that things were ordained to be, and that was that. She offered re-gendered interpretations of the Bible time and again, casting Mary as the main character in the Christmas story and telling the Easter narrative from the point of view of the women seeking Christ's body in the garden.

In later years, after she had broken bitterly with her mother and business partner, Minnie Kennedy, Aimee took to describing her first husband, Robert Semple, as 'my only Bible College.' This was, in fact, a misrepresentation. It was to her mother that she owed her early religious education, her faith in the strength of women, and her respect for practicality. Robert encouraged aspects of herself that her mother could never have understood – in particular, a personal recklessness – but Minnie Kennedy, through the Salvation Army, provided Aimee with the training base for her professional evangelistic career.

The story is that at the age of either three weeks or six weeks Aimee was plopped into an open pram by Minnie and pushed the five miles to Ingersoll in order to be dedicated to God and the Salvation Army.[5] Since Aimee was born on 9 October 1890, the date of this occurrence was either late October or mid-November. Whichever age is correct, Minnie was making clear her determination to have her daughter follow her own religion as well as her husband's. James Kennedy sang in the choir of the Salford Methodist Church just up the road. Presumably Aimee had already been presented there. Also presumably James was not keen to have the Salvation Army link cemented in any way. He could easily have hitched up the team for Minnie to drive to town, thereby alleviating his own sister's fears that the baby would die of pneumonia in the cold autumn weather. Since he figures in none of the tellings of this story, we can assume that either he disapproved and would not help Minnie get to town or that she was making good her escape in his absence. Later Minnie would tell her granddaughter Roberta that the most important modern invention was the self-starter on the motor car. It meant that no woman need wait for a man to hitch up a team or crank a motor.[6] As it was, even as a teenaged mother, Minnie was not going to let her husband or his sister, both in their fifties, stand in the way of her plans for her daughter.

Orphaned at twelve and handed over to be raised in the itinerant life of the early Salvation Army, Minnie Clark had met James Kennedy when, at the suggestion of the Army, she took a job nursing his dying first wife. For reasons that are unclear, she stayed on in the house with James (and perhaps his mentally handicapped son) after Mrs Kennedy's death. James proposed and she accepted. It is easy to see his appeal to her. James was prosperous, he was handsome, and he was old enough to be the father she had barely known. Still, she seems to have regretted her decision almost immediately. Her daughter later described Minnie's feelings at that time as having been 'caught in the devil's net,' 'helpless as far as active service was concerned,' forced to 'grind in the prison house.' Her only hope was to pray for pregnancy. She asked God for a female child to 'preach the word I should have preached, fill the place I should have filled, and live the life I should have lived.'[7]

Such specific parental expectations would have been a heavy load for any child to carry, and indeed, the separation of mother and daughter into two personalities would only be accomplished years later and in circumstances bitterly painful to them both. Aimee was born with all the strengths of both her strong parents. Minnie was tough-minded and ambitious; James was successful and creative. Minnie got her preacher daughter, as it turned out, but one who could not be contained by the Salvation Army. With a mother who thought of her life as the wife of a prosperous farmer to be grinding in a prison house, Aimee was unlikely to be content to stay in Salford. In addition, she had an overwhelming need to be popular, the centre of attention. A number of factors in her life can explain this trait. One was her early and constant exposure to the Salvation Army, an organization that depended on its 'Hallelujah Lasses' for much of its work.[8] Not only was she taught and encouraged to speak up within the Army, but she was forced to defend herself from harassment by those who disapproved of it. She revelled in the retelling of a story in which she persuaded scoffing classmates to form an impromptu rhythm band and march around the school yard. It was a technique right out of the Army book: Don't flinch in public and offer the crowd something fun – and preferably musical – to do.

Aimee no doubt was also made to suffer for the scandal surrounding her parents' marriage. With more than thirty-five years separating their ages, James and Minnie felt sufficiently sheepish to lie on their marriage licence. It is clear that Aimee's surviving half-sister never accepted Minnie or her daughter. Aimee's description of her childhood is one of a lonely, isolated youngster, albeit a defiantly cheerful one. She preached sermons to farm animals, hung around the hired hands, set herself off from her contemporaries by early establishing a reputation as an elocutionist, set her cap at winning (flauntingly, by entering the contest at the last minute) what was called a 'popularity contest' but was really a test of salesmanship sponsored by a local newspaper, read novels, and played ragtime on the piano. She wrote letters to the education page of the Montreal *Star* on evolution and was, at a very young age, the leading witness (complete with newspaper coverage) at the trial of a neighbour accused of poisoning her husband.

This was all a little more than Minnie thought she had prayed for, and Aimee refers to herself as a rebellious teenager. One has to be careful in taking this sort of admission at face value. In order to be saved – a necessity for the Pentecostal – one has to be lost in the first place. It would have been pretty hard for a girl as spoiled and as fiercely protected as Aimee to get too lost in a town such as Ingersoll just after the turn of the century. She was a regular student at the collegiate there (far surpassing both her parents in terms of education) and was well known to both the Methodist and the Salvation Army congregations, as well as the Woman's Christian Temperance Union, in whose elocution competitions she shone. She went to dances, seemingly against her parents' wishes, but had her first dance with a young Presbyterian minister. Her soul may have been at risk, as she later claimed, but not much else.

One wonders what type of life she saw opening for herself. Later, critics as well as admirers said that she had the talent to have been a great actress. Certainly, with her educational and cultural advantages, she was being raised above the rank and file of the Salvation Army. If she ever considered working her way up in that organization, she never admitted to such ambitions in anything she wrote, and they seem out of character. More probable would have been marriage slightly higher on the social scale. James was well respected in the community, and Aimee had certainly been supplied with sufficient education and social graces to perform well as a middle-class wife. Her daughter, Roberta, claims that Aimee had a serious teenage boyfriend in James Clark, who later became speaker of the Ontario legislature.

But Aimee was the child of a discontented farm wife and had been raised with adventurous stories of the mission field, of the Bible, of *Fox's Book of Martyrs*, and of Grace Darling, the Victorian lighthouse heroine of the Faeroe Islands. She must have been dying to get out of Salford, out of Ingersoll, out from under the thumb of her doting parents, out into the world. Her chance came in the form of a romantic, itinerant evangelist whose religion had plenty of room for emotionalism and (unintentionally) eroticism, surely attractions for a nubile girl of sixteen.

Robert Semple was not only Aimee's ticket out of Ingersoll; he was also her route to the imagined adventures of China. The unconscious sexuality apparent in her every retelling of their meeting is almost painful. In a recording made more than twenty years after his death, her voice quivers as she describes first laying eyes on him: 'I had such a longing for the WORD!'[9] Clearly, she also had a longing for this

tall young man, six feet two inches in height [who] rose to his feet on the platform and taking his Bible in his hand opened it and began to read. His was a frank, kindly face, with Irish blue eyes that had the light of heaven in them, chestnut brown hair, with one rebellious brown curl which would insist in falling down close to his eye no matter how often he brushed it back ...

Suddenly, in the midst of his sermon, the Evangelist closed his eyes and with radiant face began to speak in a language that was not his own – but the words of the Holy Spirit. To me it was the voice of God thundering into my soul awful words of conviction and condemnation, and though the message was spoken in tongues it seemed as though God had said to me – 'YOU are a poor, lost miserable, hell-deserving sinner!' I want to say right here that I *knew* this was God speaking by His Spirit through the lips of clay.[10]

There is much that is revealing in this passage. One aspect is the fact that Aimee considered Robert beautiful, an assessment that is borne out by their wedding photo. But while they were certainly a match in terms of physical attractiveness, Robert was her inferior in every other measurable sense of the term. He was a penniless foundry worker. His prospects in his home town of Magherafelt, in northern Ireland, had been insufficiently attractive to keep him there. After nearly a decade in the United States, he does not seem even to have established a home base. Not only was Robert Aimee's inferior in terms of social class and money, but his education was minimal. Nor is there any indication that he had either her drive or her intelligence. In his late twenties he was preaching part-time in other people's missions; in her own late twenties, widowed and separated from a second husband, with two small children, Aimee would have her own tent, her own newsletter, and invitations to preach at U.S. national camp meetings.

Although Aimee was not the first woman to try to turn an unsuitable match into a suitable one, typically she found an unusual way. Speaking in tongues in terms of prophecy always required an interpreter. The ability to interpret was another of the gifts bestowed as a manifestation of the Holy Spirit (I Cor. 12:10). Note that this was the form of Aimee's manifestation. She *knew* that God was speaking to her through Robert and that she was a poor miserable sinner. It is in fact very handy to be a poor miserable sinner if one wants to gain the attention of the evangelist. In turn, it is helpful to be sexually attractive if one wants to gain the attention of poor miserable sinners. Robert Semple, unequal to Aimee in class terms as a prospective mate, could in fact offer her several things: sexual attractiveness on her own level, a public physical presence that matched her own, a position of prominence as a minister's wife, and the chance to travel.

Robert also held out to Aimee a role of considerable importance within the Pentecostal belief system. He was the one who spoke in tongues; she would be the interpreter. This convenient arrangement actually made a virtue out of the fact that she was the more highly educated and intelligent. When the spirit moved him, the emotional Robert could segue into his talent for tongues, something he was clearly very effective at. Aimee could then take over, in effect, to complete his sermon by interpreting the words of God that came from his mouth.

In order to do so, she immediately set about learning the underlying doctrines of Pentecostalism. Although the gift of interpretation was given by God, not all interpretations were accepted as having been so sent. There were false interpreters – for example, those whose interpretations did not find favour with the leaders of Pentecostalism – and true ones. The fact that Aimee was regarded as a true interpreter and gained a reputation for this gift within a year of her marriage indicates that she was a quick study and that she worked hard.

Aimee received her early training in Pentecostal theology and practice at two important missions. The first was the Hebden Mission in Toronto,[11] where Robert had 'tarried' (a term used by Pentecostals to encompass the concept of waiting for God to make his will known) immediately before starting his storefront mission in Ingersoll and to which he and Aimee hurried directly after their wedding on 12 August 1908. Established four years earlier by Ellen Hebden and her husband, James, the mission had contact with the Azusa Apostolic Faith Street Mission, a small black congregation in Los Angeles which had become a sort of mecca for Pentecostals after a widely publicized mass conversion experience there in 1906.[12] Shortly after the fire fell on Azusa Street, Mrs Hebden became the first Canadian to be similarly baptized, on 17 November 1906. Within five months, between seventy and eighty individuals who had undergone the same experience at the Hebden Mission and had spoken in tongues went out to spread the word throughout Ontario. As news of the work circulated, others flocked to the mission, among them Robert Semple, who had been in the United States since 1898, most recently in Chicago, where he had embraced Pentecostalism only a few months earlier.

After tarrying in Toronto, Robert and Aimee also went out to spread the word, notably in Stratford; they then settled for a few months at W.H. Durham's North Avenue Mission in Chicago. Durham was an early Pentecostal leader who had personally visited Azusa Street and was possibly the person whom Robert had first turned to at his conversion. During their time in Chicago, Aimee and Robert received both donations and encouragement for their hopes to minister in China. They moved on to places such as London, Ontario, and Findley, Ohio, collecting further financial and moral support.

Early in 1910, married less than two years, Aimee and Robert took the train from Toronto to Saint John, New Brunswick. There they caught a boat for Liverpool on the first leg of their long journey to China, bent on fulfilling their Pentecostal destiny of bringing Christ's word to unbelievers. Their last few days at the Hebden Mission were a triumph. According to the biographer most closely associated with the Pentecostal movement, the 'faithful believed Robert Semple to be particularly "led by the Spirit," and they hung on his words, while they thrilled to "Sister Semple's gift of interpretation." Her powerful gift defied ordinary decription: she spoke "the very words in given tongues that ... made the presence of God very manifest to all."'[13]

Their mission to China was a disaster. Within months, Aimee would be a widow and a mother, in that order. The couple were greeted at the harbour in Hong Kong on 1 June 1910 by a small group of Pentecostals who had already been working hard for three years to establish a mission home. Dissatisfied with Hong Kong as a mission field because he felt that the worldly lifestyle of the foreigners there turned the Chinese from God, Robert longed to move farther inland. He and Aimee spent their days seeking guidance through prayer and study. Denied the gift of any Chinese tongue, Robert began to hope for that of healing. Instead, six weeks after their arrival, he contracted dysentery; by the time of their second wedding anniversary on 12 August both were confined to the Matilda Hospital in Hong Kong with malaria. Robert died a week later, but Aimee lived – to give birth to their daughter, Roberta, on 17 September and to mourn her romantic young husband for the rest of her days.

As soon as she could gather herself and some money together, she sailed to San Francisco. She completed her round-the-world trip by train, joining her mother, who had left James, at least temporarily, to take up active work in New York City for the Salvation Army. Aimee collaborated with Minnie for a while in Army work, but mostly she drifted in and out of depression, back and forth between Chicago and New York. On 5 February 1912 she married Harold McPherson, a committed Christian but primarily a man interested in settling down and having a family. Just over a year later, on 23 March 1913, their son, Rolf, was born. This event marked the beginning of the two years of bad health which Aimee described as 'those months when out of God's will and work.' In late June 1915 she secretly loaded herself and her children into a taxi and onto a train, and went back to the farm in Salford, where Minnie was once again installed with the elderly James.

In the seven years since she had left Salford as a bride, Aimee had learned several things. One was that she felt called to the itinerant evangelistic life to which Robert had introduced her. It is possible that, like other widows, she took up her husband's profession in order to keep him 'alive.' However, it is more likely that, having experienced some success before her trip to China, she wanted to recapture that sense of joy in accomplishment. She also knew that happiness and fulfilment were not to be found through trying to re-establish herself at the Chicago mission or others like it. She had tried that approach. She had lost the partner who had spoken so eloquently in tongues. Instead, she undertook to function without this middleman, continuing her work of 'interpreting' God's word to rural people who, like herself, longed for it.

Although she would never return to The Salvation Army, now too regimented in its growing respectability for her free spirit, she would not forget the lessons she had learned from it. As her tent ministry grew – at first with an uncomfortable Harold and then alone – she asked her practical, Salvation Army–trained mother to join her to take over its administration. In short order the two women abandoned the seasonal toing and froing along the American Atlantic coast and headed for Los Angeles, ostensibly in order to settle down someplace for the good of the children but, at least subconsciously, also to go to the source, to the volatile social and religious climate of the city where the fire had fallen on Azusa Street just over twelve years before their arrival in late December 1918. Aimee also had contacts in Los Angeles within the large Canadian community, and one of these organized her first mission there – a successful venture that soon had to to move to a hall seating 3,500 and lasted from Christmas to Valentine's Day.

Her car trip across the United States, with her mother and her children and a secretary to whom Aimee dictated *This Is That* as she drove, marked a watershed in her career. Once her family was established in Los Angeles, she headed back onto the road, criss-crossing the continent and holding revivals in Canadian and American cities eager to give thanks for the end of the Great War and the passing of the devastating influenza epidemic that came near its close. Riding on the coat-tails of these events and of a fear of Godless communism sparked by the Russian Revolution, her organizational details handled by Minnie, Aimee took off as an evangelist.

On 1 January 1923 she opened the 5,000-seat Angelus Temple in Los Angeles, entirely paid for with money that she had raised in just four years of transcontinental preaching. At the peak of her glory, she was also on the point of exhaustion, and it is not surprising that her thoughts turned, as they had before while she trekked up and down the east coast, to a desire for assistants – or, in other words, disciples. As the historian of the International Church of the Foursquare Gospel portrays her situation: 'In earlier times, after one of her great city-wide campaigns, Mrs. McPherson would retire to her quarters, slump exhausted into a chair or prop herself up in bed. There she would visualize what might happen if such a revival could be followed up with a group of trained workers going with the resounding message to all parts of the city. But alas, such workers were not available!'[14]

Aimee had buried herself in work since setting out on her own as an evangelist. She needed helpers, but even more she needed more of herself. It was her charismatic style, her sexual attraction, that won many of the converts, just as she had been drawn to Robert. In later years she would try to handle the fact that there was simply not enough of her to go around with bizarre schemes which gave people an illusion of having her personal attention. One was a vacation camp at which she was to maintain a house: 'Vacation with Aimee.' Another was a cemetery where plots were sold surrounding what was to be her grave: 'Go up with Aimee.' More successful were her use of the radio (KFSG, Kalling Foursquare Gospel), recordings, and, through L.I.F.E. Bible College, the cloning of enthusiastic versions of herself.

In the early days of Angelus Temple, Aimee preached at least six sermons a week when she was in residence. She followed an even more gruelling schedule on revival tours. There were also calls to set up new congregations throughout North America, most notably along the west coast up to Vancouver, British Columbia. And of course there was the mission field. She must have felt a special kinship with these workers in particular; she knew at first hand the disaster that could come from insufficient preparation and inadequate organization. To provide that organization, there was no point looking to the charismatic Pentecostalism that Robert and Aimee had followed as a couple. Trusting their fate to God, its wandering preachers often had no idea where they would spend the night. By acquiring her own tent and her own car before picking up again after Robert's death, she had in effect given notice that she was not going to allow herself ever again to be at the mercy of others for a place to sleep and a way to get home. In starting her college, she sought to ensure that any Foursquare Gospel missionaries whom she sent out had practical training on how to get their jobs done and how to look after themselves.

Aimee could make use of earlier training schools for revivalists when preparing plans for her own,[15] but she also drew heavily on the Salvation Army. She, in fact, called her training institute the L.I.F.E. Bible College, the initials standing for 'Lighthouse of International Foursquare Evangelism.' She even set up a Salvation Navy (complete with uniforms and automobiles decked out as L.I.F.E. boats) to go along with it, until the U.S. Navy complained and she had to relent. Started only three months after the temple opened, the bible college moved into a new five-storey building three years later. By this point, enrolment had grown from 50 to 650, and by 1929 there were 1,000 students from Australia, the British Isles, South America, and Germany, as well as from across North America. Aimee gathered around her a faculty headed by Harriet Jordan, a former teacher who claimed to have been healed of intestinal agony by Aimee.

Classes were meant to produce what has been referred to as 'after-care' workers, charged with taking on what were essentially ministerial, rather than evangelical, duties. In short, they were being trained to shepherd, not to lead.[16] In this training, L.I.F.E. Bible College offered bible and practical evangelism; practical ministry; the Gospels, Epistles, and life of Christ; divine healing and church history; major prophets and the pentateuch; and the doctrine and philosophy of the cross. Organization of the bible school was put in the hands of the Reverend John Quincy Adams, a former Texas state educational director for the Baptist Church.[17]

Aimee recruited an impressive array of talent and experience to teach under Jordan, Adams, and herself, but it was a long, long way from her

L.I.F.E. students cheering Aimee Semple McPherson, possibly chanting 'We are McPherson's boys and girls.'

own apprenticeship in Toronto, where in 1909 Mrs Hebden had 'rejected totally any form of structure for the new Movement ... She ridiculed, for example, the use of the designation "Reverend" for gospel workers ... [and] also feared the negative impact that any form of organization might have on the level of spirituality among the early Pentecostals.'[18] In fact, Mrs Hebden's reaction to the fact that hers was becoming the focal point for a growing organization had been to 'state most emphatically' that she refused to allow this development to occur. Inevitably, the Hebden Mission withered away. Aimee chose another fate and was more than willing to have her mission become a centre of organization, despite wanting to keep its revival traditions. Inevitably, Angelus Temple would become the focus of a new denomination.

L.I.F.E. Bible College still kept to the basic tenet of Pentecostalism in that it did not require any particular level of education for enrolment. In that way anyone touched by God could still be a preacher. The crucial difference was that, if they wanted to feed into the impressive and growing Foursquare organization, students had to acquire credentials in a way that Aimee had not. She 'convocated' her inaugural class with these words of Christ from the Gospel according to Mark (16:15–18): 'Go ye into all the world, and preach the gospel to every creature. He that believeth and is baptized shall be saved; but he that believeth not shall be damned. And these signs shall follow them that believe; In my name shall they cast out devils; they shall speak with new tongues; They shall take up serpents; and if they drink any deadly thing, it shall not hurt them; they shall lay hands on the sick, and they shall recover.'[19] By moving from non-affiliated mission to fully organized denomination, Aimee gave her graduates a better chance at fulfilling the ambitions of Pentecostalism than she and the hapless Robert had ever had.

This is, of course, the contradiction. While Aimee could produce more-efficient missionaries, people who fared better than she had done at her first chosen profession, she could not produce another of herself. In fact, the two women most obviously her successors ran into terrible struggles with her, ending in legal suits. Her daughter, Roberta Star Semple, originally raised to succeed Aimee in the pulpit, made a final break in the 1930s, instead having a successful career behind the scenes in the New York radio world. Rheba Crawford, the 'angel of Broadway' upon whom the Hallelujah Lass in the musical *Guys and Dolls* is based, lasted only a couple of years as Aimee's associate before shifting her full attention to the California state welfare department. Simply put, there was no room in the temple of a flamboyant woman evangelist for another flamboyant woman evangelist. Angelus Temple, with its services and its offshoots, its bible schools and its social programs, can be compared to an anthill of activity, and anthills have only one queen. What was needed was workers to support the exhausting work of that queen, and that is what L.I.F.E. Bible College was set up to do.

Aimee's successor would instead be her stolid son, Rolf, offspring of the taciturn Harold. When she started the temple, much of her support came from women – from her daughter, from her mother, from many members of her board and congregation. Women were highly visible, and in the photo of the first class of the bible college, they outnumber men two to one. This presence began to erode in the 1930s. As in so many other areas of society, economic depression moved women back into the home and into unpaid service work. In the case of Angelus Temple, they were gradually uprooted from their leadership roles. Aimee even took a third husband, extolling his manliness and her need to be looked after. But when the large and oppressive David Hutton – promoted overnight from his baritone role as Pharoah in her religious opera, *The Iron Furnace* – tried to make good on this prospect and take over running the temple, Aimee first went on a round-the-world cruise, leaving him to be savaged by her worker ants, and then, when she returned, had him turned out of the nest.

Rolf was the better person to take over. He had in fact been largely kept out of Angelus Temple politics, the son deprived of his father and sent off to be raised on a ranch by members of the congregation so as to benefit from male contact. Rolf was a dull speaker, a hard worker, and a doting son. It is to him that the denomination owes its longevity. Building on the structures that his practical grandmother Minnie had put in place before she too fell afoul of Aimee, he set up a new type of church board, overwhelmingly male. Rolf McPherson – Dr McPherson, by right of the honorary degree bestowed on him by L.I.F.E. – would put the International Church of the Foursquare Gospel on a firm business footing, backed up with solid training in the Scriptures. Although there is still talk at the temple of these being 'the latter days' before Christ's second coming, the organization is in the meantime digging in for the long term.

Fascinatingly – and chillingly – Rolf married his charisma. His wife, Lorna De McPherson, had been a student in his mother's bible college. Like so many of these young women, she dressed like Aimee, bleached and coiffed her hair like Aimee, and copied the trade-mark smile. Before her death in the early 1990s, Lorna De carried Aimee's torch in terms of personality and by providing the feeling that you were the only person in the world when she smiled at you. But Rolf held the power.

Aimee had set up L.I.F.E. Bible College to train 'evangelists, pastors and missionaries.'[20] Somewhere along the line, the organization also began to train an entity that was not embraced in early Pentecostalism – the 'pastor's wife.'[21] In its beginnings Pentecostalism, with its equality of even 'the least of all saints,' had opened the world for women, just as had the early Salvation Army. Aimee took advantage of this opportunity, using the education that she had acquired as a privileged child in small-town Ontario. Then she wrapped up all she knew – her social graces, her understanding of tight-knit communities, her elocution lessons, her grounding in the Bible, her knowledge of the new 'scientific' curriculum introduced into the schools at the turn of the century, her mother's and the Salvation Army's grounding in practicality – slung them over her shoulder like a beggar's sack, and set out on the road. It was the freedom of Pentecostalism that created her as an evangelist, and without it, no matter how much training one might receive in a newly enlightened, gender-equal type of bible college, one would not have the freedom to create as she had.

The lesson is probably that you cannot train a phenomenon, Canadian *or* American. What you *can* prepare are acolytes who can try to carry on the work, spreading the word of the phenomenon. However, once you get into systems, other systems start to impinge. It is no accident that, once it became hierarchical, Aimee's world started to be taken over by men. Other religions are, after all, also controlled by men, and to achieve respectability the Foursquare Gospel followed suit. Aimee's ministry, as a direct result of its own success, has been captured by the very forces that early Pentecostalism – Mrs Hebden with her refusal to be the head of *anything* – sought to escape. It tried to make a place in spirituality for those outside the power structure, and the powerless – women such as Aimee, the uneducated such as Robert – flowed in. Mrs Hebden was right: any attempt at structure would inevitably squeeze those people out again. You cannot have both Pentecostalism and professionalism, though you can have a movement that calls itself Pentecostal which purports to turn out professionals. Pentecostalism is about emotion and spirituality. At base, it is extra to the intellect and to training. It is about opening doors to feeling, not about learning how to think in a particular way.

The irony here is that the true disciples of Aimee may in fact be the New Agers rather than the Pentecostals. It is of note that Rolf's only surviving child has chosen to follow this path. Would Aimee be able to recognize herself in her granddaughter? Would she be able to find a biblical passage – no matter how obscure – for support? Could she say, as she fundamentally said of herself, 'It doesn't matter how things have always been done. God made her do it?'

NOTES

1 For an earlier discussion of the problems of working with such sources, see Janice Dickin McGinnis, 'Aimee Semple McPherson: Fantasizing the Fantasizer? Telling the Tale of a Tale-Teller,' in R.B. Fleming, ed., *Boswell's Children: The Art of the Biographer* (Toronto and Oxford: Dundurn Press, 1992), 45–56.
2 Edith Blumhofer, *Aimee Semple McPherson, Everybody's Sister* (Grand Rapids, Mich.: William B. Eerdsman Publishing Company, 1993). Another recent biography is Daniel Epstein, *Sister Aimee: The Life of Aimee Semple McPherson* (New

York: Harcourt Brace Jovanovich, 1993). The best so far is still Lately Thomas, *Storming Heaven: The Lives and Turmoils of Minnie Kennedy and Aimee Semple McPherson* (New York: William Morrow and Company, 1970).

3 David Christie-Murray, *Voices from the Gods: Speaking with Tongues* (London and Henley: Routledge & Kegan Paul, 1978), 199. This is a sympathetic review of tongues-speaking from pre-Christian times to the present.

4 Aimee Semple McPherson, *This Is That: Personal Experiences, Sermons and Writings*, (2nd ed., Los Angeles: Echo Park Evangelistic Association, 1923), 78.

5 There are several 'autobiographies' of Aimee Semple McPherson, as well as other materials of an autobiographical nature. The age of six weeks is given in McPherson, *This Is That*. It is whittled down to three weeks in *Aimee: Life Story of Aimee Semple McPherson* (Los Angeles: Foursquare Publications, 1979), 9. This latter work is a reprint of *The Story of My Life* (Waco, Tex.: Word Books, 1973), not to be confused with *The Story of My Life* (Los Angeles: Echo Park Evangelistic Association, 1951). Both *Story*s were actually ghost-written after her death by church officials who claimed as their sources sermons and other documents that Aimee left behind.

6 Interview, Roberta Salter, New York, 17–18 June 1988.

7 McPherson, *This Is That*, 15–16.

8 For a discussion of the experience of women like Minnie Kennedy, see Lynne Marks, 'The "Hallelujah Lasses": Working-Class Women in the Salvation Army in English Canada, 1882–92,' in Franca Iacovetta and Mariana Valverde, eds., *Gender Conflicts: New Essays in Women's History* (Toronto: University of Toronto Press, 1992).

9 Aimee Semple McPherson, 'Milkpail to Pulpit' (sermon recorded in 193?; tape, Foursquare Publications, n.d.).

10 McPherson, *This Is That*, 35, 37.

11 See Thomas William Miller, 'The Canadian "Azusa": The Hebden Mission in Toronto,' *PNEUMA: The Journal of the Society for Pentecostal Studies*, spring 1986, 5–29.

12 For an account of the importance of Azusa Street to Canadian Pentecostalism, see Gloria Kulbeck, *What God Hath Wrought: A History of the Pentecostal Assemblies of Canada* (Toronto: The Pentecostal Assemblies of Canada, 1958), 25–8. 'Azusa' stands for 'A to Z in the USA.'

13 Blumhofer, *Aimee Semple McPherson*, 86. The sources of her quotations are unclear.

14 Nathaniel M. Van Cleave, *The Vine and the Branches: A History of the International Church of the Foursquare Gospel* (Los Angeles: International Church of the Foursquare Gospel, 1992), 12.

15 Famous revivalist forebear Dwight L. Moody was not the first to set up such an

institution when he founded his Moody Bible Institute in 1886. See William G. McLoughlin Jr, *Modern Revivalism: Charles Grandison Finney to Billy Graham* (New York: The Ronald Press, 1959), 272–3.

16 Bryan R. Wilson, 'The Pentecostalist Minister: Role Conflicts and Status Contradictions,' *American Journal of Sociology* 64 (March 1959): 495–504. While this is a very informative article, it is hostile to Pentecostalism as a belief system.

17 Van Cleave, *The Vine and the Branches*, 49.

18 Miller, 'The Canadian "Azusa,"' 21.

19 International Church of the Foursquare Gospel Papers, Billy Graham Archives, Wheaton College, Wheaton, Ill., box 10, folder 22, L.I.F.E., Commencement Address, 1925–6.

20 *Carry On: 1927 Year Book of the International Institute of Foursquare Evangelism*, 15; quoted in Van Cleave, *The Vine and the Branches*, 47.

21 Van Cleave, *The Vine and the Branches*, 14.

Professor Elizabeth Govan:
An Outsider in Her Own Community

CAROL BAINES

I will not be squelched.[1]

These were the words of Elizabeth Govan, a young Toronto woman who was studying at Somerville College at Oxford in 1930. She was full of optimism about the possibilities that were before her. Considering herself privileged to be in such an idyllic and stimulating environment, Govan, at the age of twenty-three, decided that she wanted an academic career and approached her education in a deliberate and determined manner. Her career path was somewhat circuitous, but it culminated in her appointment as a full professor in the Faculty of Social Work at the University of Toronto in 1956.

This is an essay about Elizabeth Govan, and it illustrates the contradictory demands that women face – the restrictions that impeded Govan's career and made it difficult for her to flourish as an academic in the mid-twentieth century. There is a literature that idealizes and celebrates the lives of the women who forged professional careers for themselves in early women's colleges and in social organizations such as Hull House in Chicago.[2] Many of these women happily shared their lives with other women. Their personal and professional paths were well integrated, privileged, and for the most part not stigmatized. Lillian Faderman has described these relationships as 'Boston marriages' – bonds between women who shared their lives but usually without sexual relationships.[3] Other historians have portrayed a more pessimistic view and identified the strategies that women utilized to compensate for their marginal positions.[4] A second generation of professional women (1920–60) faced different issues. Same-sex relationships that had been publicly accepted and viewed as asexual were by the 1920s defined as lesbian and stigmatized. Aware of the public scrutiny they faced and the stress of concealing their relationships, women began to separate their public and private lives.

Elizabeth Govan (or Betty, as she was known) did not live in a long-term partnership with another woman. That she did, however, have close and loving relationships with other women during her career is evident from letters in her personal papers, donated to the University of Toronto Archives by her sister, Margaret Govan. While there is much that we do not know about Govan's personal affairs, we do know that she kept her professional and private lives separate. I was a student of hers in 1966 and remember her as a very energetic woman, strongly committed to research and the academic study of social work; she was among those who stimulated my interest in the history of the profession.

The Toronto program for social work education had its roots in the Department of Political Economy and was predicated on the belief that social service should be a masculine activity.[5] Indeed, Sara Burke has argued that the Department of Social Services at the University of Toronto was actually initiated to challenge the growing involvement of women in social work. However, despite its mission, Toronto did not succeed in attracting large numbers of men to the field. From 1914 to 1938 the university graduated 53 men compared with 478 women.[6] What it did succeed in doing was to create a climate where the leadership and administration of the profession would remain in the hands of male graduates, a division of labour that has continued to characterize the field. The marriage between university scholarship and applied social service work at the University of Toronto was thus fraught with gender issues from the outset. For many women in the early and mid-twentieth century, movement into a faculty position was circumstantial rather than planned. Applied professions such as social work often recruited women who were highly regarded as practitioners into academic positions to provide students with the knowledge and skills essential for practice; as such, these women were not expected to engage in research but were regarded as the gatekeepers for their professions. However, not all women conformed to this pattern, and rigid dichotomies like this do not help us to understand some of the variations. Some men have been very committed to social work practice, and some women, such as Govan, were viewed as academics. Although she was strongly committed and loyal to the social work profession, her background and areas of interest were history and social policy.

There is a paucity of research on the history of women in social work in Canada, particularly for those who provided leadership in social work education. In her study of professional women in Manitoba, Mary Kinnear has argued that informal barriers, hiring and promotion criteria, and a consensus by men and women as to what was appropriate behaviour for women served to keep the proportion of women in the academy low and that this pattern applied to faculty in social work as in other fields.[7] Kinnear has also pointed to the tensions that existed between women who had children and those who did not. Single women often resented married women who were employed, and this resentment limited solidarity between them. This issue was dramatically highlighted by one woman at the University of Manitoba who 'based her insight on the singular experience of having a woman mentor, a professor who encouraged and fussed over her – until the intolerable occurred: she [the student] became pregnant and was therefore no longer "professional."'[8] Prejudice of this sort largely barred married women from the academy; not surprisingly, most of the first and second generation of women were single. Although many of these women had responsibilities caring for partners and/or aging parents, like women's care-giving in general, such responsibilities were largely invisible.

In their contemporary study of women in the academy, Nadya Aisenberg and Mona Harrington have pointed out how women continue to struggle with 'family claims' – claims that are centred on care-giving responsibilities. Implicit in this view is the assumption that women are different – are more emotional and subjective and thus more suited to do what is considered women's work. According to Aisenberg and Harrington, it was the 'marriage plot' that defined women's roles whether they were married or not – 'it defines what women should want, the way they should behave and the choices they should make under the old norms.'[9] Women who are married with children need to find ways to blend their work and family lives. In addition, male colleagues prepare for their role through study and experience, but women need to take a further step. They need to move 'from a passive to an active persona ... a person prepared for autonomy.'[10] Confined by social norms that define what is appropriate and possible, women are not prepared for the 'rules of the game.'

In many ways, Govan was an exception who was prepared for the 'rules of the game.' She was the first woman with a PhD to teach at the School of Social Work at the University of Toronto, and her area of study, social policy, was viewed as a man's domain. She was regarded as fiercely rational, academic, and ambitious. She had purposely embarked on an academic career.

The Dawn of Govan's Career

There is considerable research that points to the significance of women's colleges in providing both mentors and a cultural environment that supported the careers of women as academics.[11] Experiencing such an environment was a crucial factor in setting the stage for Govan's career. After achieving a BA in history at the University of Toronto in 1930, she spent two further years completing a degree in political economy at Somerville College, a woman's institution at Oxford. Govan viewed her education there as superior to her experience at Toronto, and she was clearly more comfortable with the female environment of Somerville. There was a large network of women students from abroad at the college who formed special bonds and whose social and cultural events filled her letters home. Not a typical undergraduate student, Govan was a little older than some of her contemporaries and was aware that she was different. 'I am not fond enough of either dancing or men to go on a blind ticket,' she wrote to her parents.[12] That she would struggle with her own identity may well have dawned on her during her Oxford days as she reflected about the 'pashes' that unfolded between some female students.[13] She herself was very fond of and attached to her female tutor and had been extremely pleased that the tutor had asked her to go walking with her.

Her consciousness of the discrimination that women faced and her determination to do what Aisenberg and Harrington call 'breaking the mould' were apparent to her early in her studies. In a coeducational class in which Govan was enrolled at Somerville, she was enraged when a male professor, whom she referred to as a 'woman-hater,' addressed only the men in the class and on one occasion did not deliver his lecture since no men were present. Describing another tutor as having a reputation of trying to squelch women, she demonstrated her determination: 'I will not be squelched.' She concluded that the professor liked to argue and she was willing to take him on. Strongly competitive, she was resentful that 'what gets a man a first gets a woman a fourth,' but she set as her goal a first-class degree. A chilly climate would not dampen her spirit or hamper the education she was receiving.'I am living at the top of the world' was her way of expressing her enthusiasm and her love of this time at Oxford.[14] On another occasion, referring to the hypocrisy of men, she wrote: 'I hate these conceited reformers who are out for the cause of the weak females purely from a social point of view evidently – we poor weak females do not want sympathy and condescension, we want appreciation and recognition of equality.'[15] Unlike some women students who came to Oxford for the glamour, she came for the intellectual life and to study.[16]

For Govan, this was a holistic experience – she was in rapture about residence life, the culture that the college afforded, the athletics, and the outdoors. During vacation periods she cycled 583 miles alone through the north of England and also travelled extensively in Europe. That she felt guilty about her position of privilege during the Depression was not surprising as her study of political economy had drawn her closer to the field of social service. Her interest in this area was also fuelled by some of the excursions that she took while at Somerville, such as a trip to Wales and a study of the mines there, a lecture in London by William Beveridge on unemployment, and visits to Toynbee Hall. Her idealism was evident in her desire 'to make the world a better place.'[17]

She was also determined to pursue an academic career, and while at Oxford she wrote to E.J. Urwick, then director of the Department of Social Services at the University of Toronto, enquiring about teaching possibilities. However, it would be several years before she received an academic position. On her return to Canada in 1932, she was employed as a caseworker in the Toronto Department of Public Welfare before she returned to complete a MA in political science and a diploma in social work at the University of Toronto.

A Supportive and Integrated Career and Life in Australia

The opportunity to enter social work education came her way in 1938 when, on the recommendation of Agnes MacGregor, assistant director of the social services department at the University of Toronto, she was asked to apply for a position as casework tutor in Sydney, Australia. The Sydney school had been founded by the Board of Social Studies and was a voluntary program affiliated with, but independent of, the University or Sydney.[18] Govan's recruitment to Australia followed a troubled beginning for the Sydney program. Like its counterparts in Melbourne and Adelaide, it had struggled with the issue of combining academic study at the university with applied training in community agencies. For the school to become a department of the University of Sydney, the board needed to recruit a person with high academic standing who was prepared to undertake research and who had professional social work experience and ability.[19] Govan was appointed in 1939 and went on to become the assistant and then the director of social studies at the University of Sydney the following year.

She quickly plunged herself into the social welfare community in Australia. Still only thirty-two years of age, she carried a heavy load, including administration, development and supervision of the field practicum program, lecturing, research, and publishing, as well as commitment to the professional social work associations. Her research was focused on a study of social conditions in selected towns in New South Wales. She was the president of the New South Wales branch of the social workers' association and a member of the executive of the Council of Social Agencies of New South Wales, both positions indicating her efforts to link the university to the social work community.

The Department of Social Studies at Sydney during Govan's tenure seemed to replicate the intimacy of her experiences at Somerville. It was a small program, and the faculty members in the professional part of the program were all women. Many Australian social workers had studied in the United States or the United Kingdom, and they shared in the excitement and energy of a fledgling program. From 1941 to 1945 Govan lived with Norma Parker, the assistant director of the program. Their relationship reflected shared personal, social, and professional interests. Govan's authority and prestige has been recognized by John Lawrence in his study of Australian social work: 'Her administrative talent, complete reliability and exceptional industry placed social work training on a firm footing in the university and helped the acceptance of professional social work in the community.'[20] She seemed incredibly happy both with her work and with her personal life. She loved teaching and received excellent reports and accolades from students, administrators, and the social work community.

Govan's efforts to integrate social policy and social work practice were evident in her approach to the development of a social work program in Australia. Her background in political economy and history placed her on the academic side of the pendulum, but her women colleagues and friends were involved in practice and the delivery of services. At a time when psychiatry and casework were beginning to dominate social work education, Govan's perceptions of social work were more consistent with what has more recently been identified as a unitary or generalist model. She advanced 'a curriculum that included economics, social history, public administration and social philosophy ... [The student] also must study the individual: his behaviour, his social needs: hence the importance of biology, social hygiene, psychology and social psychiatry. These theoretical courses are not separate: it is essential to the student's thinking that he should think of the individual in his social setting, and of social organization as it affects the individual.'[21] As a generalist, Govan took an approach to social work education different from those who advocated specialization. Her colleague Norma Parker gradually adopted casework and embraced psychiatry, and this difference seems to have caused some tension in their relationship, especially when Parker urged Govan to take her PhD in casework.[22] Govan's writings suggest that, in contrast, she tried to integrate knowledge of the individual with awareness of the social environment and political structure. Influenced by her British education, she, like the idealist E.J. Urwick, was cautious about the application of the scientific method to social work and focused instead on its practical and humanistic nature.[23] On the affirmative side of a debate titled, 'Resolved that social work is a waste of time and money,' Govan won easily but was dismayed by the inability of her opponents to defend social work's mission.[24]

Despite some ambivalence about leaving Australia, in 1945 she moved back to her family home and assumed a position as assistant professor of casework and fieldwork at the University of Toronto. Her motives were both personal and professional. The war had limited her contact with her family, and she had decided to begin her PhD.

Social Policy and Social Work at the University of Toronto

By the 1940s two different approaches to social work education had emerged in the United States. The University of Chicago, under the leadership of women such as Edith Abbott, stressed a strong academic and social science foundation and a commitment to social reform and activism. The women faculty members at the University of Chicago collaborated with the practical social workers and sociologists who worked out of Hull House. This powerful group of women continued to influence the program at Chicago well into the 1950s. A contrasting approach to education developed at the New York School of Philanthropy and Smith College. Both these latter programs adopted casework as the cornerstone of the profession and had as their mission the development of practitioners.[25]

Despite the differences in their missions, both approaches to social work education adhered to the belief that science provided the answer for the advancement of social work as a profession. Efforts to emulate the male-dominated professions such as medicine and law would prove to be an ongoing thorny issue for social work. Gender was not a factor in this debate. Lillian Wald, Florence Kelley, the Abbott sisters, and Julia Lathrop, trailblazers for U.S. social work, were all advocates of scientific research. However, their success and influence were grounded in their area of expertise – child welfare – a field that was women's traditional domain. While these child welfare reformers believed that equality would prevail, they underestimated the role that the bureaucratic state would have in the evolution of social welfare – a state that would be more conducive to the career of the male social welfare expert.[26]

The development of a welfare state with graduates from the University of Toronto providing leadership was part of the agenda established by Harry Cassidy when he was appointed director of the School of Social Work in 1945. One of a new breed of social welfare experts in Canada, he has been described by Allan Irving as a Fabian socialist.[27] As an economist who had headed the Berkeley school of social welfare in San Francisco, Cassidy supported state intervention and the development of a welfare bureaucracy in which graduates in social policy from the University of Toronto would provide the expertise.

This was the setting in which Elizabeth Govan found herself on her appointment as assistant professor to teach casework and provide leadership in fieldwork at Toronto. Her rank appears to have been based not on her academic background and achievement but rather on her gender. A year later, in 1946, Charles Hendry, a man with limited academic background but with extensive experience with the YMCA, fund-raising, and community research, was appointed a full professor with tenure. 'Always more of a doer than a thinker, more a promoter than a thinker,' he never completed his doctorate but went on to be the director of the Toronto school from 1951 until his retirement in 1969.[28] Govan was clearly an ambitious woman, and returning to Canada in a junior position must have been difficult for her. As well, in a profession that was becoming increasingly divided, she was not perceived as a 'practice person.' This reputation may well have impeded the development of collegial relationships with the women practice teachers; at the same time she was not readily accepted by the male faculty members who taught social policy and research. Professor Winifred Herington, who was a student of Govan's during this period, remembers her as a 'good teacher with a commanding presence.' Interestingly, Govan invited all her students to Sunday tea, a practice that had been common in Somerville and in Australia but one that none of her colleagues at Toronto practised.[29]

Her dissatisfaction with Toronto and with Cassidy's leadership was acknowledged in a letter from Parker in January 1946, although the details were not spelled out.[30] It seems likely that, as in the past, both personal and career objectives led to her resignation from the university in June 1948. Govan had embarked on her PhD at the University of Chicago on a part-time basis in 1946, and she began full-time study there two years later when she received the Edith Abbott Fellowship. Her dissertation, 'Public and Private Responsibility in Child Welfare in New South Wales, 1788–1887,' traced the history of the care of dependent children in that state.

An Escape to Practice

On the completion of her doctorate, Govan accepted the advice of Bessie Touzel, a well-known and respected colleague, to take a break from academic life and work in the social welfare community. From 1950 to 1956 she lived in Ottawa and was employed on special projects with the Canadian Welfare Council (CWC). Why Govan heeded this advice is difficult to know. She had been asked to apply for a position at the University of Chicago and was encouraged to do so also at the University of British Columbia. What seems most likely is that the pull of her family brought her back to Ontario.

The tension between family ties and personal freedom seems to have pervaded Govan's life. Like other women who have sought to remove themselves from both institutional barriers and family obligations, she accepted temporary overseas assignments and thrived in this environment, where she could work relatively autonomously. One of these projects included her acting as a social welfare expert for the Technical Assistance Administration (TAA) of the United Nations to train women as social workers in Iraq between September 1952 and July 1953.[31] Committed to a generalist and broad-based view of social work, she advocated a role for social workers as generalists in community development and opposed the establishment of specialized services for problem groups. Govan demonstrated her ability to work in a very diverse situation and was sensitive to the cultural and social characteristics of Iraq. She was, however, troubled by the behaviour of the TAA officials, who she believed did not recognize her expertise and planned training groups without proper consultation with her.[32]

On her return to Canada Govan continued her work with the CWC, but she struggled with her interpersonal relationships and was constrained by what was viewed as appropriate behaviour for women and the ways in which they should interact with others. This dilemma is evident in notes that she made for a self-evaluation while at the CWC:

Elizabeth Govan, 1949.

People respect but only like [me] after long acquaintance because I do not let people get to know me. I am shy and seek escape from social relationships in being an intellectual. Staff are frightened (terrified) of me. I am provocative, possessive, defensive. I seem hard because I do not show people that I am really soft and feminine. I am neurotic in that I escape social relationships by working too hard – every night. I would not be able to organize people – manipulate them to get them to do things. Because I am shy I am awkward in my relationships. I create tensions when I work with staff. I am not at ease so I do not place people at ease. All the senior staff were consulted and were unanimous in saying they prefer PB [probably Phyllis Burns] as supervisor to me. [33]

That Govan saw herself as different seems apparent in her self-evaluation, but it also reflects the limited ways in which even women are able to understand and accept differing patterns of femininity. As well, it is a telling example of how social workers applied and utilized pathology to explain their own behaviour as well as that of their clients. To what extent this self-evaluation represented the perceptions of others is not clear, but we do know that Govan developed few close friendships with her colleagues at the CWC or at the University of Toronto after she returned there in 1956 to accept a full professorship and assume responsibility for curriculum coordination and development.

By that year Govan's transformation into an academic was complete. She was given opportunities for research and became heavily involved in the doctoral program. Her academic credentials, her experience, and her sense of her own authority matched those of her male colleagues. She was actively involved in research; as well she carried extensive community responsibilities, such as serving as president of the Canadian Association of Social Workers. She was the only female faculty member with publications who was listed in the report to the president of the University of Toronto in 1959–60. Professor Donald Bellamy remembers her as an extremely bright woman who asked the questions that needed to be asked but who often rocked the boat.[34]

Unlike other women in the academy, who were silent about issues of salary, throughout her career Govan enquired about the salaries of men in similar positions and insisted that she be remunerated on an equal basis.[35] These demands and her pugnacious style may well not have endeared her to her new director, Charles Hendry, or to her colleagues. She seemed to be in a unique position. Most of her women colleagues were involved in the teaching of casework, lacked a PhD, and were relegated to a subordinate status – both personally and with respect to the practice component of the curriculum. Govan was interested in the practice of social work at the community level, but her women colleagues did not perceive her as knowledgeable about practice, but saw her rather as 'one of the boys.'[36]

Her leadership and achievements in social work education were recognized by her participation in international work. She served on the board of the U.S. Council of Social Work Education and the American Public Welfare Association, as well as in major community projects in Canada. But personally and among her colleagues at Toronto, she remained an outsider – a loner – and at the end of her career seemed bitter and isolated. While individual factors and personal responsibilities may have contributed to her unhappiness, one must also conclude that she was thwarted by the personal and professional barriers that she encountered as a woman who was not prepared to accept a subordinate position. What is clear is that she embarked on and conducted her academic and professional career in a determined – even obsessive – way. Hendry expressed concern about her heavy work schedule of teaching, research, and community and family commitments. This overwork, she admitted, derailed a Social Sciences and Humanities Research Council of Canada research project that she was directing from 1964 to 1969.[37] The sadness apparent in her career is accentuated as one attempts to draw a picture of her personal life. This image presents a side of Govan that few people appreciated. It also pinpoints the difficulties that women encounter when they attempt to keep their professional and personal lives separate, and the latter closeted.

Family and Personal Claims

What we know about Govan's personal life is largely revealed through the weekly letters that she wrote to her family while at Oxford and in Australia and Iraq and the letters that she received from close women friends. Govan came from a tight-knit family who encouraged her education and fostered her independence. The letters to her parents are detailed accounts of her social and professional experiences, and they reflect the love of the outdoors, sports, and culture that she shared with her family, her warmth, sense of humour, and kindness, and the concern that she felt for her family. Interestingly, there are few letters from either her parents or her sister in her personal papers, but Govan's weekly letters from abroad were all retained by her family. As the eldest child and following a pattern typical of other academic women, she appears to have played a dominant role and frequently provided advice and support to her mother and father.[38] For example, on the prospective marriage of her brother to a Roman Catholic, she had this to say: 'The Roman Catholic issue does not worry me as I insist that everyone has to approach God in His own way, & that the way is far more often chosen by family training than by actual choice – I should love to have nieces & nephews even if I am destined not to have children! Our family has a too pronounced clannishness & it is high time it was broken – What darlings you all are & how this must have flabbergasted you but you simply must trust Bill's ideal of family life – built upon what he has seen of family such as ours can be – to be guiding his decision. I hope you have opened your hearts to her and fallen in love with her too! How I love you all.'[39]

How Govan reconciled the demands and ties that drew her to her family is not entirely clear. Letters from friends and colleagues suggest that she was, not surprisingly, torn between her career aspirations and her wish to be close and supportive to her family. During the period in Australia, she experienced a degree of freedom that was evident in her work and personal life. Yet she seemed plagued with guilt. Letters to her family were attempts both to appease them and to justify her wishes to remain in Australia. She wanted to make her parents proud of her as compensation for her absence, and she hoped that they would share her belief that she 'was putting Australian social work on the map.'[40]

Norma Parker had urged Govan to remain in Australia and cautioned her on how hard it would be for her to readjust to life in Toronto and the loss of the freedom she had gained.[41] Parker based this advice on her own visit to the Govan family home in late 1944 and on her impressions of the Toronto school, which she criticized for its emphasis on social policy. Her letters to her 'Lady Mine,' her pet name for Govan, are loving and affectionate. They highlight the women's shared personal and professional interests and describe the network of women social work educators from the United States with whom Parker was studying in 1944–5. On Govan's departure from Australia, Parker captured the supportive relationship that they had shared: 'I have loved living with you and hope we have yet another short period together.'[42]

Mary Jo Deegan has highlighted a range of relationships that existed between women who shared their lives with other women. In analysing the letters and the relationship between Sophonisba Breckinridge and Marion Talbot at the University of Chicago, Deegan refers to them as 'loving letters' and identifies the passion. She nevertheless assumes that many of these women were celibate.[43] Regardless of how one interprets the excerpts that follow, they provide a picture of the intimacy that Govan experienced with a professional colleague. Unfortunately, her own letters to her friend have not been found, so we have to infer a great deal about their relationship. Their friendship had begun in 1928, but it was rekindled in 1945 on Govan's return from Australia and was recounted in this way:

Something has lasted all these years better than we ever dreamed it would ... What is it, darling? ... What do you think? I think and know that one of the things is my joy in the way your steady old head works ... you talk well because of it ... and that is such a change from the ordinary run of things. – Another thing is the springs from which your vitality and enthusiasm and joy in living fathoms forth. Very sweet clear water ... – You really aren't any more impervious to feelings than I am ... and we're old and wise enough now to assess things like that more accurately, aren't we? It has moved out of the pathological pitfall it fell into just at first because of my need then ... and now? ... such a very tender affection my Betty ... so very dear and to be cherished, now more than ever. – Bless you ... I don't know when I have been so happy ... Yours, B[44]

The excerpts from the letters that follow highlight the empathy shown to Govan as she wrestled with family tensions.

I cannot bear the thought of anyone, much less you, being tossed about by family feelings. Probably by now Mrs. B. is back on the job and you're back on an evener keel, but I wish in some way that you could get yourself into quieter waters where you can still practice family loyalty without being periodically wrecked on shoals and rocks – I'm no person to talk as you well know ... and my conscience if I have any is quite unfettered. Unless families are the sort the sociology books talk about as ideal – and there aren't many of those, people in them should free themselves gently but firmly. I don't need to tell you this, my gosh. But there's that Scottish trait of yours that makes demands upon you ... out of all reason maybe. Anyway I don't want you to lose the notion of Vancouver ... and I do want you to do something about it before long ... just to cement the deal.[45]

I suppose I knew more than I ever really brought into words about your early conflicts ... I knew or sensed, even back in the night paths at Ocean Park, the fact of your rebellion to the family pattern ... knew and sympathized and loved you because of it. My family experience was so traumatic that it was possible for me to recover quite quickly ... yours was the sort that hangs heavy on sensitive souls like yours and distorts the world that you, expecially you were meant to *enjoy*, my darling ... not to conquer, you donkey. It still isn't easy for you at home ... I want to know all about it ... all the little things that rise to haunt you even with your well earned freedom that I rejoice with you in having ... s [sic] funny ... primitive things about people ...

I suppose we can't evade the usual implications of the conservative school ... the biddies who frown upon close attachments between women. Well, there are many kinds of those ... those that harm and those that heal. We'll have the latter kind, because we both have many friends and abiding loyalties to them, and because we haven't room for debilitating jealousies.[46]

Dear Betty-boy, I'm pausing for a cigarette and a word with you ... I can see this little routine developing into a perpetual pattern to lighten the days and make them shine. – While you were here I reacted like your heat-resisting Australian leaves ... (I remember everything you said, because you say things beautifully) ... I only wanted to listen, and look at you, and feel your presence ... You always go away from me ... that is the pattern for us apparently ... but I still feel you, my dearly beloved child, right to my fingertips. It is a miracle sort of thing that has ... in the words of King James ... been vouchsafed ... It has a religious quality ... perhaps I mean transcendent quality ... And it makes me love the world even more dearly than before ... and feel safer and freer, and surer. I'm saying all this again because it still overwhelms me ... – Thank God for our emotional health, my Betty, and for the mental capacity we both have to recognize a miracle when it happens – We have followed almost identical lines in that process, old girl ... vocationally, we're akin, and speak understandingly to each other ... but more than that, we've unfettered ourselves from old established strings ... the things you talked of. It has been easier for me than you, because my fetters were never too tight ... I grieved for the state of your being when you go back to the old setting but you are free and that will see you through. – I know that life is satisfying ... I've confidence in my own evaluation of things as they are ... and when old affinities are proven, as mine to you have been this week, I am ready to burn candles ... Instead I take deep breaths of salty Vancouver air, and long to be with you, or have you near ...[47]

These intimate and caring letters identify a shared professional and personal standpoint that must have been nurturing to Govan. Both she and her friend were deeply concerned about the state of social work in Canada and believed that its mission must be directed towards social justice, as is evident in a letter to Govan in 1945:

but Betty-boy there aren't many thinking social workers around. They just aren't interested much, except in the protective aspects of CASW. – There's a fearful timidity about social workers. They cannot bring themselves to stand up for their convictions ... if they have them, indeed, to be the influence they ought to be in fashioning social conditions.

what is wrong with social workers that they cannot be leaders? And why do so many government officials ... your Brantford story is typical ... loathe and despise the professional person[?]. Is it because social workers are not yet of sufficiently high intellectual calibre[?]. – Or is it that they are supervised to death and cramped by agency policies and hush hush? Or is it, now think hard, my Bet, because they are indoctrinated out of all reason in their professional education! Or is it that casework has been made the profession to the exclusion of all other kinds of thinking? – But what's wrong Betty? Why this dearth? I think it is a combination of all the things I've asked you ... beginning with a timidity born of intellectual self-conscious embarrassment. When asked for an opinion, the reply is usually accompanied by a smirk or a giggle or an apology ... We need a generation of people with enough courage to *state* their convictions loudly. We should be in the labour movement – We should be on the councils, Boards, commissions of government. We should let no new thing be born, affecting social conditions without expressing our ideas about it ... I simply glow with all the things we have in common – Betty my darling.[48]

Although it is not known what happened to this relationship, Govan was urged to consider an academic position in western Canada so the friendship could continue to flourish.

You have all the things that would, and did hoist you almost beyond reach of my earthly eyes ... social poise, academic honours that are staggering in comparison to mine, achievement and prestige in the top drawer of social work ... teaching. Even those dizzy heights couldn't deter me, or send me richocheting away from you as they might easily have ... Instead we reached out to each other from the ... to be analytical about this ... From the libidinal level ... The warm all together satisfying pleasure of our emotional reaction to each other. And in all our contacts, that essential element has to show ... To some degee or other ... I've been successful in my little whirlpool of teaching, as you have been in your wider reaches, because we've given of ourselves from that human enjoyable level ... Carry on with it ... Don't let the alabaster coating around Toronto deter you. If it can't be cracked, come to us ... we're sort of plain people.[49]

For whatever reason, Govan did not free herself from the 'alabaster coating,' and we know little about her later friendships. There is a real sense of loss in these loving and supportive letters. Faderman has identified two important issues about the definition of same-sex relationships as lesbian that may well help us understand some of the ambivalence that Govan experienced. The term 'lesbian,' as it emerged in the 1920s, had begun to separate women who loved women from the rest of the female community by mid-century and had forced them to accept a classification that was regarded as abnormal. A further, even more drastic effect on women who could not accept the stigma was to limit their involvement with other women.[50] Given the lack of definitive evidence, one can only speculate; but Govan's apparent uncertainty and her own recognition in 1954 that she avoided personal relationships suggest that these were difficult issues for her.

There were other women in Govan's life, but most of her correspondence was sporadic, and although personal, it gives only a partial picture of her private life in her mid and later career.[51] What we know is that her intimate relationships were with women at a distance from her family home. While there may have been significant friendships in Toronto, her later life seems to have been filled by academic responsibilities – she was actively involved in professional social work organizations and was part of a network of women who provided leadership to social work in both Canada and the United States – and the personal responsibilities of sharing in the care of her mother with her sister, Margaret. The freedom and excitement that she had experienced in her youth were not sustained in her later years.

Conclusion

Elizabeth Govan's career must be viewed in the context of the post-Second World War period, which was characterized by the expansion of the welfare state and the thrust to professionalize and defeminize social work as an occupation. Women played a commanding role in social work in its pre-professional or charity period, but the welfare state and professionalism were increasingly patriarchal. Interestingly, the first three social work programs in Australia were initiated by private, voluntary social service organizations and headed by women. But when they became university programs, efforts were made to recruit male academics. Govan's replacement at Sydney was a Scottish psychologist who had little experience in social work and was unable to provide the leadership essential to the school. Norma Parker, Govan's friend and colleague, who had been turned down for the director's position, became acting director in 1949.[52]

Govan was an atypical woman in a traditional woman's occupation who believed that meritocracy would prevail. Although she was attuned to the 'rules of the game,' she was unprepared for the barriers that she would encounter in establishing her career. A woman whose academic credentials and behaviour were more in keeping with her male colleagues, Govan found herself alienated from both her female colleagues and her male counterparts in social policy, despite her commitment to building a bridge between policy and practice. While some of her difficulties may be related to personal characteristics, it seems more likely that women who tried to do what was considered 'men's work' found themselves marginalized. That women continue to play only a minor role in social policy, the academic aspect of social work education, speaks to the powerful barriers that remain.

At one level, Govan confronted the barriers in the university. But her resulting position as a full professor at a prestigious university separated her from her women colleagues. She was not prepared to accept remuneration that was lower than that of a man occupying a similar position. She entered the academy with a defined sense of her own autonomy and exercised it throughout her career. In this way, she was different from the women identified by Aisenberg and Harrington. She did not just happen to enter an academic career; she embraced the life of an intellectual early in her education. Unlike her women colleagues, she was responsible for significant research activities and tried to play the 'rules of the game' – a game created by men for men. However, she did not achieve the same heights as two male colleagues appointed by Cassidy in the post-war period, Charles Hendry and Albert Rose, both of whom served as director and dean of the Toronto school. Govan was an ambitious woman. She exercised comparable leadership in Australia, and her work in Iraq was well recognized. Whether she had other aspirations in her academic career is difficult to know, but it is clear that she wanted authority and offered her opinions to her colleagues as well as to the president of the university.[53]

Although Govan was a strong advocate of professionalization, she had few mentors and limited collegial backing in the twilight of her career. Lacking the support that she had experienced as a student at Somerville and as a young academic in Australia, she mirrored the behaviour of successful male academics. One of the attributes that has been identified as essential for women to succeed in authority is the need to be tough. But this toughness usually provokes criticism, as Govan discovered. She was tough, but she was considered troublesome by faculty members who did not like to be challenged.[54]

On a personal level, Govan's life was evidently not a happy one. There is clearly much that is hidden from us. It is hard to know how to interpret the personal letters that she received from her friends. The private letters and the relationships that they depict must have enriched her life, and they reveal a side of her that was not visible to her colleagues. Yet these letters also speak to the difficulty that women had and still have in blending their private and public lives. Intimacy in personal relationships takes a variety of forms, and its denial evokes a heavy price. What Govan identified as her 'soft feminine side' remained largely invisible, and in a world that has a narrow definition of 'feminine caring behaviour,' her caring in both her personal and professional lives went unnoticed. As a single, unmarried woman, she was a 'dutiful daughter' caring for her mother, and she was also caring to her women friends.[55] As a social work educator, she was concerned about social justice and social work's commitment to social reform, and she relayed this concern to her students. Govan's life reminds us of the importance of recognizing diversity and of acknowledging the struggles as well as the triumphs in women's lives.

NOTES

I would like to thank Chen Xiao Bei for her research assistance and Jane Aronson and Karol Steinhouse for their helpful and thoughtful suggestions for an earlier version of this essay.

1 University of Toronto Archives (UTA), Elizabeth Govan, B79-0027/002, Letter to her family, 10 May 1931.
2 See, for example, Patricia M. Palmieri, *In Adamless Eden: The Community of Women Faculty at Wellesley* (New Haven: Yale University Press, 1995).
3 For a discussion of relationships between women, see Lillian Faderman, *Odd Girls and Twilight Lovers: A History of Lesbian Life in Twentieth Century America* (New York: Columbia University Press, 1990), and 'Nineteenth-Century Boston Marriage as a Possible Lesson for Today,' in *Boston Marriages,* eds. Esther D. Rothblum and Kathleen A. Brehony (Amherst, Mass.: University of Massachusetts Press, 1993).
4 See, for example, Mary Kinnear, *In Subordination: Professional Women, 1870– 1970* (Montreal and Kingston: McGill-Queen's University Press, 1995); Alison Prentice, 'Elizabeth Allin: Physicist,' in *Great Dames,* eds. Elspeth Cameron and Janice Dickin (Toronto: University of Toronto Press, 1997). And see also Penima Mignal Glazer and Miriam Slater, *Unequal Colleagues: The Entrance of Women into the Professions, 1890–1940* (New Brunswick, NJ, and London: Rutgers University Press, 1987).

5 Sara Z. Burke, *Seeking the Highest Good: Social Service and Gender at the University of Toronto, 1888–1937* (Toronto: University of Toronto Press, 1996), 93.

6 Ibid.

7 The proportion of women in university teaching changed very little from the 1920s to the 1970s. See Kinnear, *In Subordination*, 30.

8 Ibid.

9 Nadya Aisenberg and Mona Harrington, *Women of Academe: Outsiders in the Sacred Grove,* (Amherst, Mass.: University of Massachusetts Press, 1988), 6.

10 Ibid., 20.

11 See Glazer and Slater, *Unequal Colleagues,* and Palmieri, *In Adamless Eden.*

12 UTA, B79-0027/002, Undated letter (1930).

13 Ibid., Letter to her family, 9 November 1931.

14 Ibid., Letter to her father, 30 November 1930.

15 Ibid., Letter to her family, 5 May 1931.

16 Ibid., Letter to her family, 26 April 1931.

17 Ibid., Letter to her family 10 May 1931.

18 UTA, B79-0027/003, Letter from Aileen Fitzpatrick to Govan, 14 March 1939.

19 R.J. Lawrence, *Professional Social Work in Australia* (Canberra: The Australian National University Press, 1965), 115.

20 Ibid., 128.

21 UTA, B79-0027/015, Govan, 'The Social Worker in Public Administration,' *Journal of Australian Regional Groups of the Institute of Public Administration,* March 1942, 38.

22 UTA, B79-0027/003, Letter from Parker to Govan, 24 October 1944.

23 UTA, B79-0027/015, Govan, 'A Scientific Approach to Social Service,' *Journal of Australian Regional Groups of the Institute of Public Administration,* September 1943, 311–23.

24 UTA, B79-0027/003, Letter to her family, 29 October 1940.

25 See John Ehrenreich, *The Altruistic Imagination* (Ithaca: Cornell University Press, 1985).

26 Molly Ladd-Taylor, *Mother-Work: Women, Child Welfare and the State, 1890–1930* (Urbana and Chicago: University of Illinois Press, 1994), 75.

27 Allan Irving, 'A Canadian Fabian: The Life and Work of Harry Cassidy' (PhD thesis, Faculty of Social Work, University of Toronto, 1982).

28 John R. Graham, 'Charles Eric Hendry (1903–1979): The Pre-war Formational Origins of a Leader of Post–World War II Canadian Social Work Education,' *Canadian Social Work Review* 11, no. 2 (summer 1994).

29 Personal interview, Professor Winifred Herington, 25 October 1996.

30 UTA, B79-0027/003, Letter from Parker to Govan, 3 January 1946.

31 See Govan, 'Social Work and Culture,' *The Social Worker* 22, no. 3 (March 1954): 11–20.

32 UTA, B79-0027/016, 'Monthly Report' (June 1953), 4–5.

33 UTA, B79-0027/020, CWC file, Personal evaluation dated 8 September 1954.

34 Personal interview, Professor Don Bellamy, 27 June 1996.

35 UTA, B79-0079/020. See, for example, the letter to R. Davis in 1953, in which Govan agreed to accept a position with the CWC with the qualifier that she would be paid the same salary as a male in the position, and letter from President Sydney Smith, 20 June 1946, regarding salaries of faculty members.

36 Govan's identification with the male social policy stream was clearly articulated during personal interviews I had with Professors Bellamy and Herington.

37 UTA, B79-0027/017, Letter to Charles Hendry, 3 March 1969.

38 For a discussion of the influence of family on women in academic careers, see Palmieri, *In Adamless Eden.*

39 UTA, B79-0027/003, Letter to her family, 25 October 1939.

40 Ibid., Letters to her family, 19 March 1941 and 30 March 1941.

41 Ibid., Letter from Parker to Govan, 8 January 1945.

42 Ibid., Letter from Parker to Govan, undated, from Templeton, 1944.

43 Mary Jo Deegan, '"Dear Love, Dear Love": Feminist Pragmatism and the Chicago Female World of Love and Ritual,' *Gender and Society* 10, no. 5 (October 1996): 590–606.

44 UTA, B79-0027/003 Letter to Govan, undated (probably 1945). In the letters quoted here the writer frequently uses ellipses (dots) between sentences or phrases. Omissions in the quotations have therefore been indicated by dashes.

45 Ibid.

46 Ibid., Letter to Govan, Tuesday, 7:00 p.m., 1945.

47 Ibid., Letter to Govan, undated, Saturday morning, from Vancouver, 1945.

48 Ibid., Letter to Govan, 8 November 1945.

49 Ibid., Letter to Govan, undated, Saturday morning, from Vancouver, 1945.

50 Faderman, 'Nineteenth-Century Boston Marriages,' 30–5.

51 There is no personal correspondence from women friends after 1950 in the collection at UTA.

52 Lawrence, *Professional Social Work in Australia,* 12.

53 UTA, B79-0027/004, Letter from Govan to president, 3 December 1968.

54 Aisenberg and Harrington, *Women of Academe,* 142. In my personal interview with Professor Don Bellamy, he referred to Govan as 'tough.'

55 See Jane Aronson, 'Dutiful Daughters and Undemanding Mothers: Constraining Images of Giving and Receiving Care in Middle and Later Life,' in *Women's Caring: Feminist Perspectives on Social Welfare,* eds. Carol Baines, Patricia Evans, and Sheila Neysmith (2nd ed., Toronto: Oxford University Press, 1998).

Beyond 'Women's Work for Women': Dr Florence Murray and the Practice and Teaching of Western Medicine in Korea, 1921–1942

RUTH COMPTON BROUWER

'Women's work for women,' the rationale for single women's entry into foreign missionary service in nineteenth-century Asia, grew out of the assumption that seclusion was the norm for women in Asian societies and that male missionaries could thus not work for their conversion. Though a separate-spheres approach to missionary work developed with the Hindu and Muslim societies of South Asia particularly in mind, it also shaped women's missionary work in other parts of the non-Christian world.

The need for women, rather than men, to do medical work among Asian women was seen to be especially compelling. As a belief in the utility of Western medicine in winning a hearing for the gospel among non-Christian women gained hold among mission supporters in main-line Protestant denominations in the late nineteenth century, increasing numbers of female medical missionaries were sent abroad. By the early twentieth century enthusiasm for such work had led to the establishment of two ecumenical facilities in India for training Indian Christian medical women as assistants so that they too could use medicine as a way of demonstrating practical Christianity and winning converts.[1]

The work of female medical missionaries has so far been studied mainly within this context, that is, as one aspect of the history of Western women missionaries seeking opportunities and finding fulfilment by doing 'women's work for women.'[2] A recent non-Canadian essay collection, attempting to apply Gramsci's concept of hegemony to colonial India and Africa, does touch on the work of missionary health-care workers, male and female, in an investigation of the use of medicine as a strategy for 'the manufacture of consent' in pursuit of colonial control.[3]

Missionary medicine has also received some attention from scholars interested in discourse analysis.[4] Canadian scholar Karen Minden's *Bamboo Stone* examines the emergence of a Chinese medical elite from roots in Canadian missionary medicine as an illustration of 'the process of technology transfer over time and between cultures,' but women doctors do not figure largely in her account.[5] Overall, remarkably little attention has been paid to missionary medicine as an aspect of the social history of Western medicine, or to the ways that the practice and teaching of medicine by Western women might have altered in mission contexts in the first half of the twentieth century as a result of their own grounding in the new ideals and technologies of scientific medicine. U.S. historian Sara W. Tucker's 'A Mission for Change in China: The Hackett Women's Medical Center of Canton, China, 1900–1930' is one of the few studies to touch on this topic.[6] In the present essay I take up the subject from a Canadian perspective by focusing on aspects of the career of Florence Jessie Murray (1894–1975), a Maritime doctor who served in Korea from 1921 to 1969 save for interruptions created by the Second World War and the Korean War. The essay deals with the first phase of Murray's career, the years in northern Korea.

Dr Murray's practice was not confined to women and children. Nor were the Koreans whom she tutored in Western medicine mainly female. This essay suggests that her approach to the practice and teaching of medicine reflected changes taking place within North American society as well as her perception of what was most serviceable in the Korea of her day. It argues that Murray's commitment to the model of Western medical professionalism that gained ascendancy in early-twentieth-century North America,[7] reinforced by a variant of what Nancy Cott has called 'modern' feminism,[8] led her to regard strict sexual segregation in the practice and teaching of Western medicine in Korea as neither necessary nor desirable. The essay will begin by describing Dr Murray's origins and medical training before going on to examine episodes in her Korean career prior to 1942 that illustrate her commitment to the contemporary Western model of medical professionalism and her lack of attachment to the earlier, separate-spheres paradigm in missionary medicine. In regard to the teaching aspect of her work, it is perhaps unnecessary to state that Murray's adoption of a new approach would not have been possible had there not been 'modernizing' Korean men willing to move beyond their own society's traditional gender patterns by accepting Murray as a mentor and colleague.

I

In the late twentieth century, as Grant Wacker notes, the foreign mission enterprise has become 'almost exclusively a conservative preserve.'[9] While the beginning of this trend was already in evidence in some mission settings by the 1920s,[10] for main-line Protestant churches in Britain and North America the inter-war era was characterized not so much by a sudden and sharp drop in the number of moderate and liberal missionaries going abroad as by two broad and related changes: first, participation in an international and non-denominational missions bureaucracy with many specialized work committees and national councils headed by permanent salaried officials and linked under the umbrella of the liberal and ecumenical International Missionary Council (IMC); and second, an increased emphasis on improving the quality of missionary social services while at the same time reducing the ties between such services and overt proselytization. This second development, in turn, reflected the growth of secular tendencies at home, a new tentativeness among moderate and liberal missionaries about the appropriateness of undermining ancient faiths, and practical realities created by the rise of nationalist and anti-colonialist sentiments in host societies, where an increasing amount of proselytization was, in any case, being carried out by indigenous rather than Western Christians.[11] It was within this changing missionary climate that Florence Murray's career unfolded, though her upbringing in Maritime Canada had nourished her vocation in an earlier missionary tradition, the significance of which would be evident in her ongoing strong support for the religious as well as the practical work of Christian missions.

The eldest of the six children of a Presbyterian minister and a former schoolteacher, Murray was raised in rural communities in Nova Scotia and Prince Edward Island. In her published memoir she maintained that she had chosen medicine as a career only after learning that she could not enter the ministry herself and that she had decided on overseas missionary work as a belated substitute for her father, who had aspired to be part of the small group of ordained Maritimers chosen to establish the Presbyterian Church in Canada's mission to Korea in 1898.[12] Having decided on missionary medicine, she prepared rigorously.

Even before her five years of training (1914–19) at the Dalhousie University Faculty of Medicine had been completed, Murray had acquired a rich fund of practical experience as a result of unique opportunities for female medical students created by the First World War and her own initiative in seeking out chances for professional development outside the classroom. The most dramatic such opening came in the immediate aftermath of the Halifax explosion of 1917, when she was called on to be the official anaesthetist at the YMCA's emergency hospital despite the fact that she had then had only one day's experience in giving anaesthetic. The following year she was sent to the fishing community of Lockeport, Nova Scotia, where twenty-five people had died of Spanish influenza, when the local doctor himself came down with the disease. Following her graduation in 1919, Murray served briefly as an intern in a Boston hospital, attracted by its offer of salary and room and board and the opportunity to attend lectures by well-known Harvard medical specialists. Her dismay at the low level of medical care and personal attention given to the hospital's largely indigent patients prompted her to return to Halifax, where she was able to act as an assistant to a local surgeon, work as a demonstrator at the medical college, and treat private patients in her spare time.[13]

By comparison with other Canadian medical graduates of her era, Murray was 'rich in experience.'[14] In 1921, when her missionary career began, it was atypical for Canadian medical missionaries to begin their overseas service with *any* postgraduate experience.[15] Her years of experience as a student and new graduate were especially important, moreover, since they coincided with a period when new ideas about how to teach and practise modern, scientific medicine were taking hold, though not without conflict with other traditions. Indeed, such conflicts had been working themselves out in the medical school in Halifax in the years just prior to her arrival.

In 1910 the proprietary Halifax Medical College had been one of several Canadian institutions indicted for their shortcomings in Abraham Flexner's influential report on medical education in the United States and Canada. Prepared for the Carnegie Foundation, the report had subsequently served as the foundation's blueprint in its continent-wide campaign for medical school reform. As well as insisting on a model of medical training linked to laboratory-based research and clinical experience, the foundation required that assisted schools be part of a university.[16] Though instructors at the Halifax Medical College had resented Flexner's report, Dalhousie had acted promptly on its recommendations. Improved physical facilities and more endowed chairs had to wait until 1920, when foundation funding was provided, but within a year of the report's publication the Halifax Medical College had formally become the Faculty of Medicine at Dalhousie, with upgraded standards and entrance requirements.[17]

As several scholars have pointed out, in Halifax and elsewhere in North America a climate favourable to reforms in medical education had existed prior to the release of Flexner's report, albeit not necessarily in accordance with his precise blueprint – hence the resentment of medical faculty who regarded Flexner's criticisms as sweeping and unfair.[18] At the same time, the report 'had a galvanizing effect on public sentiment,' making the achievement of advances in medical training both more compelling and more feasible.[19] This new mood undoubtedly contributed to Murray's zeal for high standards of professionalism in the practice and teaching of Western medicine, especially when combined with the powerful work ethic and sense of Christian duty imbibed in her Presbyterian childhood.[20]

The fact that her medical training took place in a coeducational institution rather than a women's medical college was probably also significant for her future attitude towards missionary medicine and women's work for women. Only two women's medical colleges had been established in Canada in the late nineteenth century when professional medicine first opened to women, and both had ceased to exist by 1906; but like the more numerous women's medical colleges established in the United States in the last half of the nineteenth century, they had been vitally important in training the first generation of women medical missionaries, [21] whose particular mandate was, as noted, work among women, with their conversion to Christianity as the ultimate goal. Indeed, training medical missionaries was one factor in the support given for the establishment of women's medical colleges.[22] Though many of these colleges had ceased to exist in the United States even before 1900, the Flexner Report was an important factor in all but finishing them off. Such schools had frequently been proprietary rather than university affiliated, and associated with 'irregular' and holistic approaches to medicine – approaches increasingly deemed unworthy of support in the early twentieth century. Dr Mary Putnam Jacobi, a nationally prominent research- and publication-oriented American woman doctor, was already repudiating the notion of a distinct 'female' vision of medicine and a separate-spheres approach to training and practice in the late nineteenth century, despite the fact that her career as a student and instructor had begun in a women's medical college. As Regina Markell Morantz-Sanchez and Thomas Neville Bonner have shown in their studies of the history of women in medicine, the changes that took place around the turn of the century as 'the practice of medicine became a science' led not only to the demise of the separate schools but also to a sharp falling-off in the proportion of women taking up the study of medicine.[23] Florence Murray may not have been personally familiar with Jacobi's career or that of other women who won respect and acceptance for their good fit with the new, scientific milieu, but she seems to have been part of the new breed of women doctors who valued 'science' and 'standards' over sisterhood and female mentorship.

II

A primarily agricultural country that had been under Chinese cultural suzerainty for centuries, Korea was deemed a poor, ill-governed, and backward place even by comparison with other pre-modern societies in the late nineteenth century. This perception made modernizing Japan's increasing influence and its formal annexation of Korea in 1910 initially seem acceptable, even desirable, to the American Presbyterians who had pioneered Protestant missionary work in Korea in the 1880s.[24] In fact, Japanese rule increased the poverty of the rural masses, while the colonial administrative structure and educational system offered few opportunities for Koreans to advance.[25] In these circumstances and in the face of the colonial government's harsh responses to real or suspected dissident activity, missionaries sympathized with the plight of Koreans and were consequently suspected of disloyalty to the Japanese regime even before the March First Movement for national independence in 1919, in which Korean Christians played a prominent role.[26]

By comparison with their counterparts in other Asian countries, Protestant missionaries had enjoyed great success in winning converts in Korea, and under the leadership of a vigorous indigenous church, Christianity would ultimately become the second largest religion in the country.[27] But in the decade following the March First Movement, mission Christianity experienced external and internal challenges. Communism was a powerful rival ideology for nationalist-minded Koreans.[28] Despite the failure of the independence movement, many Korean Christians demonstrated a new self-confidence and assertiveness, and as a result, some grew impatient with the paternalism that had characterized the missionary presence in the early days.[29] At the same time, missionary institutions providing higher education and professional training (and occasionally serving as gates to further opportunities abroad) attracted modernizing young men, non-Christian as well as Christian, who saw in them a route to upward personal mobility and national regeneration.[30] One group of Protestant nationalists, described by Kenneth Wells as 'self-reconstruction nationalists,' rejected any immediate and militant steps for ending Japanese rule and instead worked for 'improvement of individual morality, knowledge and expertise' as steps that 'would inevitably transform society and finally secure independent statehood.'[31] Regarded by left- and right-wing nationalists at the time and by some historians subsequently as compromisers and collaborators,[32] these self-reconstruction Protestant nationalists seem to have been the Koreans with whom Murray had the closest affinity. Their values and pragmatic strategies were consonant with the way that she practised and taught medicine in Korea.

Her biggest challenge during her first term (1921–7) was learning to adapt her medical values and modes of practice to the unpropitious environment of her church's mission in northern Korea. Like their American Presbyterian mentors, the Maritime missionaries had offered Western medical services from the time of their arrival (one of the three 'founding fathers' had been a doctor as well as an ordained missionary). But they had done so sporadically, seeing medicine only as a subordinate part of their evangelistic task and hence not giving priority to acquiring appropriate buildings or equipment.[33] Even in 1921, when Murray arrived, the facilities and professional standards that she had learned to regard as the minimum necessary for practising medicine were almost entirely absent in the mission's hospital in the city of Hamhung, northern Korea, to which she was posted. The opening chapter of her published memoir graphically described her first tour of the hospital and its grim condition inside and out: 'Outside the back door I was horrified to see a bedpan with its contents setting on the ground together with a pail of blood-stained dressings and a pan full of pus. All were swarming with flies. My heart sank. How could I ever maintain decent standards under such conditions? There would be plenty to do all right, but conditions must be improved. *This would be a teaching job as well as a medical one.*'[34]

Written in retirement and for publication, Murray's memoir avoided openly blaming Dr Kate McMillan, the hospital superintendent and the mission's pioneer woman doctor, for the conditions Murray saw there. She had been more forthright at the time, however, in expressing criticisms in private correspondence to her family. Indeed, within a month of her arrival in Korea she was writing to her brother Foster, then a medical intern in Halifax, to express her dismay about conditions at the hospital. Even more disturbing than the lack of modern conveniences, professionally trained nurses, and sanitary standards was the easy tolerance of such conditions evident in the attitude of Dr McMillan and her Korean assistant, Dr Pak. 'The way they do things horrifies me,' she told Foster. 'I feel like I did in Boston when I saw the patients experimented on and was helpless to prevent it or do anything better for them ... I am very glad I am to go to Yong Jung for awhile. I do not see how I could work here under the circumstances. If I could speak enough to do anything independently it would be different, but to assist with work like that!!'[35] Contributing to Murray's dismay over the quality of the work she was observing was the fear that, over time, it would become her way of practising too. Significantly, later that autumn she asked her mother to forward copies of her Canadian medical journal 'to help keep me from going to seed.'[36]

Murray's temporary appointment to Yong Jung, Manchuria, to replace Dr Stanley Martin, a young male colleague who was about to go on health leave, gave her a reprieve from conditions in Hamhung as well as an opportunity to work in a hospital that seemed better administered and equipped than the one in Hamhung, despite its remote location. But things went less smoothly in Yong Jung after Dr Martin's departure, and soon her fear of falling behind in her profession returned to haunt her:

There is nothing like medicine for interest when you can dig right in ... and investigate your cases from both the clinical and laboratory side. One of the hard things out here is one is too busy to go into cases properly and has no one who can do lab work for one so one gets careless. I feel that after a year or two out here I shall be no good for anything else. It is impossible to spend enough time at the language to learn it properly and do a couple of operations every day and see thirty or forty out cases besides and attend the cases in the wards and superintend the dressings done by careless and ignorant dressers and still have enough time to do any of it as well as it ought to be done. And then you are disgusted with yourself for not doing things properly and you long for a blood count or a lab report or an x-ray plate and there is no one to do it and you haven't time yourself if you had the apparatus.[37]

Allotting increased hospital responsibilities to Korean medical personnel as a way to get more time for language study and her own work was not an option, in Murray's view, for while they were 'very competent' in some things, these individuals had yet to see what a 'decent hospital' was like. 'If they pattern their hospitals on the mission hospitals or the Japanese ones,' she wrote, 'they will fall a long way short of good scientific work.'[38] Her criticism of Japanese hospitals probably referred to those in

Korea, since she had not then seen any in metropolitan Japan, and as will be shown below, she would later send staff members there to see 'good' work and would sometimes go herself.

As for mission hospitals, the one that inspired her strongest disapproval in this period was the East Gate Hospital for Women in Seoul, an American Methodist institution run by Dr Stewart and Dr Rosetta Sherwood Hall, the latter an 1889 graduate of the Woman's Medical College of Pennsylvania.[39] Murray voiced her criticism of East Gate and its doctors in the context of a trip that she made to Seoul in December 1922 as part of a mission committee to inspect medical facilities there and place orders for supplies prior to rebuilding the hospital at Hamhung, to which she was slated to return. The Hamhung hospital had closed some months earlier following the sudden death of Dr McMillan and would not be allowed to reopen until renovations brought it up to standards acceptable to the colonial government.

In a long letter to her father, Murray expressed her disapproval of what she had seen of the work of the two women doctors at East Gate: with plenty of funds at their disposal, trained Western nurses, and two young Korean women doctors, they had only four in-patients in total. Yet because of their insistence on serving female patients exclusively, they had refused to affiliate with Severance Union Medical College and Hospital, an ecumenical mission institution in Seoul, despite the fact that it was 'packed to the doors and short of funds.' Their policy of treating only women patients would be justifiable, Murray wrote, if they did their work well and in sufficient volume, but that was far from being the case. Rather, they had made the term 'woman doctor' a byword for inferior standards, a situation she was determined to alter:

After having seen these two and Dr. McMillan and their institutions I am not surprised that missionaries, medical and non-medical alike, ask me if I can do surgery ... These people have established the standard expected of women doctors. I understand now why Dr. Martin wasn't enthusiastic about turning his hospital over to me when he first heard I was coming to Korea ... my little job seems to be to transform Hamheung [sic] Hospital from what it was into one of the best and most flourishing mission institutions in Korea and incidentally demonstrate to the missionary community that women doctors are not necessarily cantankerous and inefficient.[40]

Murray faulted the two American doctors for their failure to keep abreast of new medical developments in the West, as well as for persisting in a separate-spheres approach in the face of Severance's much greater needs. Named for Standard Oil magnate L.H. Severance, who had provided funds to establish the training hospital following an appeal from Dr Oliver Avison, a British-born Canadian serving under an American Presbyterian board, the college had graduated its first class of doctors in 1908.[41] While only a scaled-down version of Avison's 'ideal of medical education ... the University of Toronto,'[42] Severance was nevertheless the only mission facility in Korea staffed and equipped to provide training to Korean medical students at a level that brought government accreditation. As such, Murray believed, it ought to have first claim on the Western-trained missionary doctors and nurses and the ample resources she had seen at East Gate.

She was not, of course, unusual in favouring mergers and centralization. Such trends were a part of her era's 'search for order' in religious, as well as secular, affairs. Indeed, L.H. Severance had chosen to make medical work in Korea the object of his largesse after hearing a speech by Avison on 'Unity in Medical Missions.'[43] In 1932 the Rockefeller-initiated *Re-Thinking Missions: A Laymen's Inquiry after One Hundred Years* would recommend moves towards centralization and the creation of a few good, up-to-date medical institutions in the Asian mission fields whenever feasible as a way to help to return medical missions to the pre-eminence they had enjoyed in the nineteenth century. Writing with particular reference to China, the author of the *Inquiry* would declare that 'the trend toward union of women's hospitals with general hospitals is logical' and that limiting nurses only to women patients was 'inefficient and unnecessary.'[44] The Peking Union Medical College, an institution funded by the Rockefeller Foundation, undoubtedly served as a model of what the modernizing laymen had in mind. Its resources had reportedly made it 'one of the best-ordered and best equipped medical schools and hospitals to be found anywhere in the world,'[45] and it treated and trained both sexes.

But setting aside the question of efficiency, was there, in fact, a compelling need for separate, female-run medical services for Korean women in order to entice them to accept Western medical care, as was still thought to be necessary in India (even by the *Laymen's Inquiry*)? The answer seemed to depend on where within Korea such medical services were being offered, to which social classes, and when.

Traditional Confucian gender values in Korea called for female seclusion and strict segregation of the sexes, and taught the inferiority of women.[46] Early American women medical missionaries in Seoul, where the most important *yangban* families (the hereditary elite) lived, had emphasized respectable women's seclusion, and in an effort to win support among the elite, they accommodated, rather than challenged, seclusion practices. Dr Hall, for instance, made house calls on the royal Min family and talked of starting a night clinic for respectable women, who could not appear in public in daylight hours. The missionaries stressed that such women were reluctant to be treated by male doctors, whether Korean or Western.[47] Nor was the preference for treatment by their own sex confined to elite women. Grant Lee's account of the tandem growth of 'medicine and protestantism' in Korea speaks of large numbers of Korean women coming for treatment to the pioneer Western women doctors who began providing their services specifically to women patients in the last two decades of the nineteenth century.[48]

But this preference was evidently weaker and also less feasible to maintain in northern Korea, where *yangban* families had traditionally been rare. There the Koreans with whom the missionaries had readiest contact were the poor and uneducated, typically rural people.[49] Working in this northern setting, Murray seems not to have felt any strong local cultural imperative to restrict her medical practice to women.[50] Indeed, she clearly believed that the poor of both sexes should have access to affordable Western medical care. Thus in 1925, when Dr Hall of East Gate Hospital joined the McCully sisters, two elderly Canadian evangelistic missionaries, in urging Murray to restrict her practice to 'women's work for women,' she dismissed their suggestion in a joking fashion.[51]

Murray and the Koreans who became her interns or staff doctors – all but one of them male in the inter-war era – *did* practise separate-spheres medicine when it seemed necessary or feasible. It was the male doctors, for instance, who conducted medical examinations of applicants for the Hamhung mission's boys' high school.[52] But both Murray and her male colleagues treated patients of both sexes. And, significantly, they shared in teaching nursing students after the Hamhung hospital school of nursing was established in 1928.[53] When patients and hospital employees came from impoverished backgrounds, there was obviously less need for sensitivity to Confucian gender norms. The rural poor were a particularly important constituency, especially as Murray and the hospital's Korean Christian staff established and consolidated contacts with Christian communities and groups of enquirers outside Hamhung through evangelism and public-health work.[54] While they often came to the mission hospital only as a last resort and not necessarily as an exclusive choice, patients from such backgrounds were willing to take a chance on Murray and her institution regardless of their sex.[55] Meanwhile, as modernization and

Western influences took hold in Korea, there was some loosening of traditional gender norms even among the more affluent and respectable,[56] and this too made it more feasible to practise and teach medicine in a general hospital setting.

Murray's rejection of a separate-spheres approach to missionary medicine in Korea also reflected changes taking place in North American society in the inter-war era with regard to feminism and women's roles. Marriage, followed by family and full-time home-making responsibilities, was, of course, still the norm even for highly educated women. But among the small proportion of such women who did not marry, or who continued working after marriage, there were some who were no longer satisfied to build professional careers around the needs of women and children. In *The Grounding of Modern Feminism* Nancy Cott identified an unwillingness to be confined in this regard as one characteristic of the small band of 'modern' feminists who emerged in the 1910s as a group with a more radical and broad-ranging agenda than that of mainstream social or maternal feminists.[57] Similarly, in *Beyond Separate Spheres* Rosalind Rosenberg wrote about a generation of social scientists who differed from their first-generation sisters in their unwillingness to be confined to a world of women. Those of Margaret Mead's era, she observes, 'rejected the public side of feminism, with its ideology of female uniqueness and its organizational focus on female interests.'[58] There are important ways in which Murray differed from the groups and patterns described by Cott and Rosenberg, particularly in her ongoing adherence to conventional religious and moral values and social norms and in her assumption that marriage necessarily terminated a woman's professional career. Yet in her unwillingness to be confined to a 'women's sphere' in terms of clients and colleagues, she shared common ground with them. Cott's exploration of 'professionalism and feminism' is particularly helpful for charting the ironic development whereby a feminist ambition to become a professional woman in the 1910s evolved in the inter-war era into a professional identity so strong that it left conventional feminist concerns behind.[59]

If a decline in rigid gender segregation in inter-war Korea, especially among poor and Westernizing groups, made eschewing a separate-spheres approach seem feasible to Murray, it was this 'modern' desire to be fully professional, to achieve the highest possible level of efficiency in scientific medicine within the context of an Asian medical mission, that made a women-only work world unattractive. The paragraphs that follow deal with her pursuit of scientific missionary medicine in the years prior to her repatriation to Canada in 1942.

III

Returning to Hamhung in 1923 to reopen the mission hospital after her visits to East Gate and other sites in Seoul, Murray experienced a variety of setbacks rather than the rapid achievement of her stated goal of demonstrating what a good woman doctor could do. Early in 1924 a breakdown in health that seems to have been a combination of specific physical problems and emotional strain resulted in her being sent to the Peking Union Medical College.[60] When doctors there found no evidence of tuberculosis (the official diagnosis of missionary doctors in Seoul), she used the opportunity for professional development, taking a brief course in ophthalmology.[61] Once back in Hamhung, she returned to the challenge of building up her hospital's facilities, a task that involved a struggle for such conveniences as running water and electricity and a bathtub, as well as for the most basic medical equipment.[62] What *had* changed – and this was a change that would become more pronounced in later years – was that Murray was learning to be less critical of Western and Korean co-workers and to make small compromises when local customs conflicted with her Western notions of good hospital administration.[63]

During her second and subsequent missionary terms, Murray worked for and publicized various technological and procedural advances, including the installation of x-ray equipment – still a rarity in South Hamkyung province in the early 1930s – and the development of systematic laboratory work.[64] The latter emerged as a particular source of pride in a 1930 circular letter to supporters of her work: '[O]ut of about twenty-five mission hospitals in Korea our hospital was one of four that had a laboratory report sufficiently complete to be of use to a research worker who was preparing a paper for the medical journals. The other three are much larger institutions than ours so it was gratifying to be able to come up to their standard.'[65] As it became clear that tuberculosis was the biggest public-health problem in the region, Murray established the first on-site facilities in the province for caring for tubercular patients and occasionally tried surgical techniques such as those publicized by Norman Bethune.[66] In 1937 the hospital opened a new wing, and in August 1939, despite the tense international situation that was making many missions prepare for the departure of Western staff, Murray was authorized to draw up plans for a wholly renovated hospital plant.[67]

Paralleling these advances in the hospital's physical infrastructure were the steps taken to train staff and, to the extent possible, to develop specialities. A young man was hired to become the hospital's x-ray and laboratory technician as work in these areas grew.[68] A greater concern, of course, was with the training of nurses and interns. Murray's work with the former will be briefly described before we turn to the latter and the relationships that most clearly took her beyond gender norms in the West and in Korea: those with male interns and colleagues.

In Canada procedures for systematically training a staff of qualified, respectable women as hospital nurses had begun in the late 1800s and had taken shape in the early twentieth century as an essential part of the process of developing modern, scientific, hospital-based medicine.[69] It was not surprising, therefore, that Murray should have abandoned her predecessor's ad hoc approach to training assistants in favour of developing a full-fledged nurses' training school at the mission hospital, with the first class of three students graduating in 1932. To an even greater degree than in Canada the establishment of a nurses' training program in colonial Korea had to overcome the early reluctance of respectable families to let their daughters enter such programs. Even male church leaders in Hamhung were at first surprised that nursing students could be '*nice* girls.'[70] As in Canada too, some young nursing students were unwilling to risk their reputation for respectability by caring for male patients, a problem that Murray resolved in the manner that Halifax's Victoria General Hospital had done, by training a few male nurses.[71] Beginning with girls who were elementary school graduates, Murray was gradually able to draw in some high school students. Along with a public ceremony after six months to grant caps to probationers and another after three years, when black bands on these caps and the granting of pins signalled the young women's new status as graduate nurses, the higher education of some entrants helped to raise the status of hospital nursing.[72] The colonial government did not recognize the mission's nurses' training program as official, despite the fact that it was a three-year course combining classroom instruction and practical experience, since most students were unable to pass qualifying examinations in the Japanese language. Nevertheless, Murray took great pride in her graduates, affirming that as a result of their skills and Christian character, 'nursing [in South Hamkyung province] rose in public esteem from a despised occupation fit only for those who would otherwise starve, to a respected vocation second only to that of teaching.'[73]

Like most of her colleagues in Korea and the West, Murray regarded nursing as normally women's work and the role of the physician as normally a man's. It evidently did not concern her that no Korean women were being trained as doctors anywhere within the country.[74] During her years as superintendent of the mission hospital at Hamhung, she had, as noted, only one woman doctor on staff, a Korean who came as an intern in 1938 following training in Japan.[75] Unlike Dr Rosetta Hall, who by 1925 had financed the medical education of several Korean women and was anxious to convert Murray to 'her pet scheme,' Murray showed no interest in providing such mentoring.[76] Even in the West, she believed, marriage effectively meant the end of a woman's medical career.[77] The loss in Korea, it followed, would be even greater, since 'every girl' got married.[78] That being the case, she told her father in 1925, 'I would rather put any money I have to spend that way into some man who will be likely to do something for his fellow country men and women than in training up a doctor who will just wait on her husband in the end after all.'[79] Murray felt no such concern about the fact that most of her nurses married (some left the training program while still students to go into arranged marriages), since, as in the West, such training was regarded as valuable in a woman's future family life.[80]

While the Korean men whom Murray took on as interns were not lost to the mission through marriage, they were often lost to it, ironically, by the very training that the Hamhung hospital was providing. As in other missions in East Asia, after a period of interning in a mission hospital, many doctors left for higher paying jobs elsewhere or opened their own private practices, while a small but significant number went abroad for specialized training.[81] Murray was quite distressed by the former phenomenon during her first term, especially when such men worked in direct competition with her hospital, and certainly by the latter if those who went abroad did not return to Korea.[82] Yet the departure of former interns or staff doctors for practice elsewhere in Korea was not seen as a loss in the way that women doctors who married were, for as she had told her father in the 1925 letter decrying Dr Hall's 'pet scheme,' male doctors could be expected to go on contributing Western medical skills to the larger Korean community for the duration of their working lives.[83]

Since she regarded the training of such young men as an investment in Korea's future medical well-being, Murray took great pride in her own skills as a teacher. Even when an intern came to her to do surgical work with no previous experience, she was confident that, with time, she could 'make a surgeon of him.'[84] If one of the most noteworthy aspects of her correspondence is the degree to which she wrote about details of her medical work (even in letters to recipients who were not in the same profession), what is even more striking is the extent to which, within such let-

Dr Florence Murray and staff of Korean doctors at Hamhung Mission Hospital, Korea, 1941. Dr Kim Hyo-Soon was the only other woman doctor to serve on the hospital staff.

ters, she referred to her own mentoring function, despite the fact that she was not in charge of a medical school and that the men who came to her as interns had their classroom years behind them.[85]

Murray's zeal for her tutorial role was potentially a recipe for tense cross-gender, cross-cultural relations, and during her first term that potential was often realized. Hers was not the only mission hospital in Korea where tensions developed when Western women doctors, imbued with a sense of their superiority as Western-trained *professionals*, tried to tutor young interns instilled with centuries of Confucian gender values and conscious of their own superiority *as men*.[86] But as Murray had acknowledged in an unusually frank self-assessment in 1924, she was a 'hard taskmaster'[87] in terms of her expectations of staff. That tendency inevitably exacerbated already potentially difficult relationships with male interns and added to the difficulty of retaining them. Inevitably, too, interns who were not Christian would have been unable to contribute as fully to the life and outreach of the hospital as she would have wished. Accentuating these sources of tension was the significance that Murray attached to racial difference when confronted with professional problems during the early years. If her tendency to 'orientalize' individual interns' shortcomings as practitioners was made known to them in the way that it was conveyed in letters to her family, it is small wonder that such men found her a difficult mentor during that first term.[88]

By contrast, Murray's correspondence during her subsequent terms in northern Korea reflects a decided shift to more positive relationships with such men. Undoubtedly part of this change was due simply to the fact that as she came to feel more at home in Korea and more confident in her own role, she felt less need to demonstrate her own authority and was thus less critical of others and more inclined to 'positive' orientalism.[89] But there also appears to have been an increase in mutual professional respect between Murray and her Korean male colleagues in the years following her troubled first term and a greater willingess on her part to facilitate their professional development.

In 1929 Murray was the first woman to be chosen president of the Medical Missionary Association of Korea.[90] While mission-employed Korean doctors were not a part of the association at this time, the fact that Murray's mainly male Western colleagues had selected her for the role would perhaps have raised her status in the eyes of her Korean colleagues, as well as served to boost her own confidence and provide a new outlet for her 'taskmaster' tendencies. Meanwhile, in 1928 she had arranged for a promising young doctor who had served in her hospital during her furlough to obtain medical experience in a tuberculosis sanatorium in Canada.[91] Occasionally, other men would be sent to North America to gain Western medical experience. More commonly they went for shorter periods to Japan or China for specialized postgraduate study. This was the case in 1939, for instance, with a former intern, who was to spend three months in Peking before taking over as 'our Eye, ear, nose and throat man' from the hospital's former specialist in this field, who was entering private practice.[92]

Murray's ongoing efforts to upgrade her own skills were evident in her return to the Peking Union Medical College for a brief postgraduate course in 1929 and in her willingness to use holidays (as well as furloughs) partly for professional development.[93] Meanwhile, as some Korean colleagues emerged as particularly valued *and* anxious to specialize, she tried to accommodate their professional interests within the hospital. Thus in 1930 she spoke of surrendering much of the surgical work to Dr P.K. Koh, who had joined her three years earlier, despite the fact that surgery was her 'first love'[94] and comprised 'most of the interesting cases.'[95] Arranging for the building of a three-storey brick house 'like the other hospital buildings' for the Korean staff doctor was another way of signifying that professional status was to be recognized and rewarded.[96]

That Murray cared personally as well as professionally about her male associates' well-being, especially if they were young and promising and determined to overcome such obstacles as their own ill health,[97] undoubtedly contributed to improved relations with them. But perhaps what counted most was her growing willingness to learn from and with them. In 1937 she was the only woman and the only Westerner in a local scientific society that developed when meetings of the hospital staff expanded to accommodate other doctors who had 'asked to come in with us on the scientific meetings.' There was perhaps some condescension, but mainly pride, as she told her family about being part of this tiny scientific community with 'nine Oriental gentlemen.'[98]

Murray's zest for her role as hospital superintendent during the 1930s is evident in her correspondence. It is thus unlikely that initiatives for sharing responsibility for hospital management originated with her. Despite her increasingly cordial and mutually respectful relationships with Korean and Western colleagues, she retained what one relative remembered as 'the habit of command,'[99] and was perhaps somewhat reluctant to relinquish her authority. Yet as deteriorating relations between Japan and the United States and Britain made it seem likely that missionaries would have to resign from positions of responsibility in Christian institutions and perhaps withdraw from Korea, it became expedient to make changes. By 1938 Murray was sharing internal hospital administration with newly created departmental committees.[100] As in other missions, a hospital board was also established, made up primarily of Korean Christians.[101] In March 1941, with most American missionaries already gone from Korea and war between the Allies and Japan increasingly likely, Murray prepared for the possibility of her own departure by acting on colleague William Scott's suggestion and asking a Korean to take over her role. Dr Koh, her former surgeon and a man whose professional and personal qualities she greatly respected, was asked to prepare to leave his post as professor of surgery at Severance Hospital and return to Hamhung as hospital superintendent.[102]

Nor was this to be scaled-down work in the absence of Western staff. In 1940 Murray herself had gone to Japan to arrange for advanced training in a tuberculosis sanatorium for the nurse whom she proposed to put in charge of the hospital's enlarged tuberculosis building.[103] That building project went ahead, while housing left vacant by departing Westerners was turned into new hospital space, with a former YMCA residence becoming the new maternity annex under Dr Kim Hyo-Soon, the capable woman doctor who had come as an intern in 1938.[104] Meanwhile, Murray urged Woman's Missionary Society officials and her sister Anna to continue sending x-ray film and other supplies notwithstanding the impending changes.[105]

When she had first seen the mission hospital in Hamhung in 1921, it had had approximately ten beds and its medical staff had consisted of Dr McMillan and one Korean doctor. When she left twenty-one years later, it had one hundred beds and at least six Korean doctors.[106] Along with ordained colleagues E.J.O. Fraser and William Scott and nurse Beulah Bourns, she had delayed her departure as long as possible. While the two men had been interned and Fraser briefly jailed following the attack on Pearl Harbor in December 1941, Murray and Bourns had been permitted to continue working in the hospital until the day they left Hamhung, reportedly 'the only persons so allowed in all Korea.'[107] In June 1942 the four Canadians were repatriated as part of an exchange for Japanese internees in the United States and Canada.[108] Despite the tense circumstances surrounding their departure and the difficulties that lay ahead for their Korean colleagues, Murray had good reason to believe that the type of medical practice she valued had taken root in Hamhung.

IV

At the end of the twentieth century we are less confident than Murray was that modern medicine has been an invaluable gift from the West to the developing and underdeveloped world. In light of its limitations, costs, and unintended consequences, her enthusiasm for transplanting Western scientific values, techniques, and technologies may appear naive and even culturally insensitive. Yet in our critical, sometimes guilt-ridden reflections about such transfers as an aspect of cultural imperialism, it is easy to lose sight of the fact that Western medicine *did* offer advances that many people in underdeveloped regions wanted, and continue to want, and that industrialized postcolonial societies have maintained and built upon.[109] Moreover, much of what Murray and like-minded medical missionaries were introducing was not high-technology medicine with all the vulnerability to maintenance and supply problems that follows in its wake, but rather basic antiseptic and aseptic techniques[110] and what might now be called lifestyle changes designed to effect improvements in local sanitation, nutrition, and maternal and childcare practices. Nor did they introduce these changes without regard for what was locally viable. Murray's work with tuberculosis patients is a case in point: she could teach patients and Korean medical staff the West's ideas about the value of fresh air, prolonged rest, isolation, and a proper diet, and occasionally intervene surgically with her handmade pneumothorax apparatus, but she was well aware that most sufferers were too poor to avail themselves of long-term care or isolate themselves from other family members in order to avoid spreading the disease. Hence her personal pleasure in the dramatic, immediate gains that came from successful surgery for other types of health problems, and that produced such grateful patients as the farmer who came in from his village on the anniversary of his operation to bring her a load of apples.[111]

In her desire to cure, Murray's concern was with Koreans generally rather than specifically with women, and in her wish to mentor, her students and proteges were typically young men. Despite her familiarity with such exceptional women as Kim Hyo-Soon, the able young intern who became her colleague in 1938, and Helen Kim, the first Korean woman to obtain a doctorate and preside over Korean women's higher education,[112] women in Korea were associated in Murray's thinking not only with inferior status, which her feminist consciousness recognized as unjust, but also with ignorance, conservatism, and 'tradition,' which her reformist agenda found inconvenient.[113] In the march to modernize a 'backward' society's medical practices, which was her priority, it was, in her view, more efficient to bypass 'tradition' than to accommodate it and work for gradual change from within, as the first generation of women missionaries and later Helen Kim sought to do.[114]

The failure to attend to the training of women has, of course, been a major criticism of third-world development programs in recent decades.[115] Yet it remains a subject for historical investigation whether a secular continuation of the 'women's work for women' pattern of the high missionary era would have produced better results than the ostensibly gender-neutral (but in fact usually male-focused) modernization strategies that became the norm in the inter-war and post-war eras in colonial and post-colonial societies. In this connection modern South Korea provides some ambiguous lessons. An 'economic miracle' in the last quarter of the twentieth century (recent setbacks notwithstanding), it is also a society where women have attained a high level of advanced education. And yet university training for Korean women has normally served primarily 'as a means ... to contract a more desirable marriage' rather than as a route to a career;[116] and the prestigious Ewha Womans University, which still educated more than half of Korea's college women in the early 1960s[117] and had numerous professional and graduate programs and research institutions in the late 1980s, was also known for its 'finishing school atmosphere.'[118]

Meanwhile, for a historian with an interest in women and religion what seems most remarkable in connection with Florence Murray and the practice and teaching of Western medicine in Korea is that in her case medical modernization meant rejecting a focus on women's work for women but not on evangelization and church work. Though the religious aspect of Murray's vocation has not been the focus of the present paper, there is abundant evidence to show that her hospital practice and public-health work regularly featured medicine *and* evangelism (a tendency all the more noteworthy since *Re-Thinking Missions* had been interpreted as actively discouraging the blending of the two tasks in the role of the modern medical missionary).[119] At the same time, there never seems to have been any doubt in her mind about what her *primary* task was: working to achieve the highest possible standards of Western medicine in the circumstances in which she was placed, both as a teacher and as a practitioner. Unlike the pioneer medical missionaries in her church's mission, she was a doctor first and an evangelist second. In post-war South Korea her priorities would remain essentially unchanged.

NOTES

Research for this essay was facilitated by a Canada Research Fellowship from the Social Sciences and Humanities Research Council of Canada and a King's College Research Grant. I am grateful to Marion Current, Mary Ann Dzuback, W.P.J. Millar, Horace G. Underwood, members of the 'Womprof' Group, and especially the editors of this collection for suggestions on ways to strengthen the article. Final responsibility for its content is my own.

1 Margaret I. Balfour and Ruth Young, *The Work of Medical Women in India* (London 1929), 112ff; Stanley G. Browne, Frank Davey, and William A.R. Thomson, *Heralds of Health: the Saga of Christian Medical Initiatives* (London 1985), 316–18. Unless otherwise indicated, this essay follows the convention of using the term 'medical missionary' only in reference to a doctor.

2 For example, in Canada, Ruth Compton Brouwer, *New Women for God: Canadian Presbyterian Women and India Missions, 1876–1914* (Toronto 1990), and Rosemary R. Gagan, *A Sensitive Independence: Canadian Methodist Women Missionaries in Canada and the Orient, 1881–1925* (Montreal 1992); and in the United States, Jane Hunter, *The Gospel of Gentility: American Women Missionaries in Turn-of-the-Century China* (New Haven 1984), and Leslie A. Flemming, ed., *Women's Work for Women: Missionaries and Social Change in Asia* (Boulder 1989). Even these books give only brief attention to medical missionaries, with the exception of one article in *Women's Work*, discussed below.

3 Dagmar Engels and Shula Marks, eds., *Contesting Colonial Hegemony: State and Society in Africa and India* (London 1994), part 3, and introduction, 11, for quoted phrase. See also Geraldine Forbes, 'Medical Careers and Health Care for Indian Women: Patterns of Control,' *Women's History Review*, 3, no. 4 (1994): 515–30.

4 For instance, Luise White, ' "They Could Make Their Victims Dull": Genders and Genres, Fantasies and Cures in Colonial Southern Uganda,' *American Historical Review*, 100, no. 5 (1995): 1379–402.

5 Karen Minden, *Bamboo Stone: The Evolution of a Chinese Medical Elite* (Toronto 1994); quotation at 3–4. See also Yuet-wah Cheung's brief sociological study, *Missionary Medicine in China: A Study of Two Canadian Protestant Missions in China before 1937* (Lanham, Md, 1988).

6 In Flemming, ed., *Women's Work*, 137–57.

7 The emergence of a new model of scientific medical education in early-twentieth-century Canada following late-nineteenth-century changes has been the subject of a number of recent articles focusing on specific settings. See, for example, R.D. Gidney and W.P.J. Millar, 'The Reorientation of Medical Edu-

cation in Late Nineteenth-Century Ontario: The Proprietary Medical Schools and the Founding of the Faculty of Medicine at the University of Toronto,' *Journal of the History of Medicine and Allied Sciences*, 49 (January 1994): 52–78; and Colin Howell,'Medical Professionalization and the Social Transformation of the Maritimes, 1850–1950', *Journal of Canadian Studies*, 27, no. 1 (spring 1992). A.B. McKillop's 'The Healing Science,' in his *Matters of Mind: The University in Ontario, 1791–1951* (Toronto 1994), 347–61, captures essential changes in the inter-war period.

8 Nancy F. Cott, *The Grounding of Modern Feminism* (New Haven 1987).

9 Grant Wacker, 'A Plural World: The Protestant Awakening to World Religions,' in William R. Hutchison, ed., *Between the Times: The Travail of the Protestant Establishment in America, 1900–1960* (Cambridge 1989), 274.

10 Adrian Hastings, *The Church in Africa, 1450–1950* (Oxford 1994), 552–3.

11 Wacker, 'Plural World'; William R. Hutchison, *Errand to the World: American Protestant Thought and Foreign Missions* (Chicago 1987), esp. chaps. 5 and 6.

12 Florence J. Murray, *At the Foot of Dragon Hill* (New York 1975), viii. As the father of dependent children, Robert Murray had been deemed unsuitable for an overseas appointment. On the founding of the mission, see United Church/ Victoria University Archives (UCA), William Scott, 'Canadians in Korea: A Brief Historical Sketch of Canadian Mission Work in Korea,' unpublished typescript, 1975; and A. Hamish Ion, *The Cross and the Rising Sun: The Canadian Protestant Missionary Movement in the Japanese Empire, 1872–1931* (Waterloo 1990), 31–3. In 1925 the mission passed into the control of the new United Church of Canada.

13 Murray, *Dragon Hill*, ix–xii; Dalhousie University Archives (DUA), Robert Murray and Family Papers, MS-2/535 (hereafter MFP), A–10, Murray to 'Dear Papa,' 3 March 1916, A–12, Murray to Father, 27 Oct. 1918, A-13, Murray to Father, 23 July 1919.

14 Enid MacLeod, *Petticoat Doctors: The First Forty Years of Women in Medicine at Dalhousie University* (Lawrencetown Beach, NS, 1990), 62.

15 Minden, *Bamboo Stone*, 93; Gagan, *Sensitive Independence*, 42.

16 Abraham Flexner, *Medical Education in the United States and Canada: A Report to the Carnegie Foundation for the Advancement of Teaching* (New York 1910), 320–1, 325; Charles Vevier, ed., *Flexner: 75 Years Later* (Lanham, Md, 1987), 3–4.

17 T.J. Murray, 'The Visit of Abraham Flexner to Halifax Medical College,' *Nova Scotia Medical Bulletin*, 64 (June 1985): 34–41; Sheila M. Penny, '"Marked for Slaughter": The Halifax Medical College and the Wrong Kind of Reform,' *Acadiensis*, 19 (fall 1989): 27–51; P.B. Waite, *The Lives of Dalhousie University*, vol. 1, 1818–1925, *Lord Dalhousie's College* (Montreal 1994), 202–3, 245–8.

18 Penny, '"Marked for Slaughter"'; Gidney and Millar, 'Reorientation.' See also William G. Rothstein, *American Medical Schools and the Practice of Medicine: A History* (New York 1987), 144–50.

19 Kenneth M. Ludmerer, *Learning to Heal: The Development of American Medical Education* (New York 1985), chap. 9 (quotation at 167).

20 The argument that Murray's religious upbringing strengthened, rather than attenuated, her concern for medical professionalism is developed in Ruth Compton Brouwer, 'Home Lessons, Foreign Tests: The Background and First Missionary Term of Florence Murray, Maritime Doctor in Korea,' *Journal of the CHA 1995/Revue de la S.H.C.*, new ser., 6: 103–28.

21 The Woman's Medical College of Pennsylvania, for instance, had sent eight graduates to mission fields in Asia by 1881; see Ellen J. Smith, 'Medical Missionaries, "Ourselves Your Servants for Jesus' Sake,"' in *'Send Us a Lady Physician': Women Doctors in America, 1835–1920* (New York 1985), 199. For Canada see Veronica Strong-Boag, 'Canada's Women Doctors: Feminism Constrained,' in Linda Kealey, ed., *A Not Unreasonable Claim: Women and Reform in Canada, 1880s–1920s* (Toronto 1979), 109–29.

22 Carlotta Hacker, *The Indomitable Lady Doctors* (Halifax 1984; orig. ed., 1974), chap. 6; Brouwer, *New Women*, 58; Patricia R. Hill, *The World Their Household: The American Woman's Foreign Mission Movement and Cultural Transformation, 1870–1920* (Ann Arbor 1985), 44, 129; Regina Markell Morantz-Sanchez, *Sympathy and Science: Women Physicians in American Medicine* (New York 1985), 98–9.

23 Morantz-Sanchez, *Sympathy and Science*, esp. 144 (for quoted phrase), chap. 7, and 242ff; Thomas Neville Bonner, *To the Ends of the Earth: Women's Search for Education in Medicine* (Cambridge 1992), esp. chap. 7. In Canada in 1921 only 1.7 per cent of doctors were women; see Mary Kinnear, *In Subordination: Professional Women, 1870–1970* (Montreal 1995), 76 and also 178.

24 Stewart Lone and Gavan McCormack, *Korea since 1850* (New York 1993), chap. 1; Wi Jo Kang, 'The Presbyterians and the Japanese in Korea,' *Journal of Presbyterian History*, 62, no. 1 (spring 1984): 35–50; Allen D. Clark, *A History of the Church in Korea* (rev. ed., Seoul 1971).

25 Carter J. Eckert et al., *Korea Old and New: A History* (Seoul 1990), 254–69.

26 Chong-Sik Lee, *The Politics of Korean Nationalism* (Berkeley 1963), part 3.

27 Lone and McCormack, *Korea*, 55; Donald N. Clark, *Christianity in Modern Korea* (Lanham, Md, 1986), xi.

28 Lone and McCormack, *Korea*, 78–82.

29 James Dale VanBuskirk, *Korea: Land of the Dawn* (New York 1931), 52–8; Scott, 'Canadians,' 87–95; Helen Fraser MacRae, *A Tiger on Dragon Mountain: The Life of Rev. Duncan M. MacRae, D.D.* (Charlottetown 1993), 169–70.

30 For the autobiographical account of one such young man with connections to Canadian Presbyterian missionaries, see Younghill Kang, *The Grass Roof* (New York 1931).

31 Kenneth M. Wells, *New God, New Nation: Protestants and Self-Reconstruction Nationalism in Korea, 1896–1937* (North Sydney, Australia, 1990); quotations at 16.

32 Wells, *New God*, 8, 18, 161ff; Lone and McCormack, *Korea*, 80–1.

33 Public Archives of Nova Scotia (PANS), Maritime Missionaries to Korea Collection, MG 1 (MMKC), vol. 2270, file 3, Robert Grierson, 'Episodes on a Long, Long Trail,' unpublished ms., n.d.; Scott, 'Canadians,' 66; Florence J. Murray, 'Medical Work in the Canadian Mission,' *The Korea Mission Field* (hereafter *KMF*), May 1941, 78. Copies of this and other articles cited from *KMF* may be found in PANS, MMKC, vol. 2287, various files.

34 Murray, *Dragon Hill*, 4; italics added.

35 PANS, MMKC, vol. 2276, file 1, 21 Sept. 1921.

36 Ibid., Murray to Mother, 3 Nov. 1921.

37 Ibid., file 3, Murray to 'Dear People,' 15 Aug. 1922. Interestingly, in his *Technology in the Hospital: Transforming Patient Care in the Early Twentieth Century* (Baltimore 1995), Joel D. Howell identifies blood tests and x-rays (as well as urine samples) as procedures that went from being unusual to purely routine in the period between 1900 and 1925 in U.S. hospitals.

38 PANS, MMKC, vol. 2276, file 3, Murray to 'Dear Folks,' 2 Oct. 1922.

39 Sherwood Hall, *With Stethoscope in Asia: Korea* (McLean, Va, 1978), 'Beginnings.'

40 PANS, MMKC, vol. 2276, file 3, Murray to 'Dear Father,' 27 Dec. 1922. Surgery was a speciality that was gaining status in North America by 1900, by which time 'a handful of women' in the United States had begun to demonstrate proficiency in it; see Morantz-Sanchez, *Sympathy and Science*, 233.

41 Allen DeGray Clark, *Avison of Korea: The Life of Oliver R. Avison, M.D.* (Seoul [1979]), chap. 7.

42 O.R. Avison, 'Some High Spots in Medical Mission Work in Korea / Part IV – A Medical School,' in *KMF*, 35 (July 1939); copy in PANS, MMKC, vol. 2287, file 7. Avison was himself a graduate of the University of Toronto medical school and had briefly taught pharmacology there.

43 Clark, *Avison*, 112–15.

44 William Ernest Hocking, comp., *Re-Thinking Missions: A Laymen's Inquiry after One Hundred Years* (New York 1932), 199ff and 267 (for quotations). For a brief overview of the controversies created by the efforts of John D. Rockefeller Jr to impose a corporate model on foreign missions through the wedding of ecumenism and U.S. big-business techniques, see Charles E. Harvey, 'Speer Ver-

sus Rockefeller and Mott, 1910–1935,' *Journal of Presbyterian History*, 60, no. 4 (winter 1982): 283–99.

45 Quotation in Browne et al., *Heralds of Health*, 312–13.

46 See, for example, Kim Yung-chung, 'Women's Movement in Modern Korea,' 75–102, in Chung Sei-wha, ed., *Challenges for Women: Women's Studies in Korea* (Seoul 1986), trans. by Shin Chang-kyun *et al.*

47 Hall, *Stethoscope*, 42; Martha Huntley, 'Presbyterian Women's Work and Rights in the Korean Mission,' *American Presbyterians*, 65, no. 1 (1987): 40, 42–3. See also Yung-Chung Kim, ed. and trans., *Women of Korea: A History from Ancient Times to 1945* (Seoul: 1976), chap. 18, esp. 204.

48 Grant S. Lee, 'The Growth of Medicine and Protestantism under Persecution: The Korean Experience,' *Korea Journal*, 29, no. 1 (Jan. 1980): 40–1.

49 'The Canadian Mission Number,' *KMF*, May 1941, 67; photocopy in PANS, MMKC, vol. 2287, file 228. See also Kang, *Grass Roof*, 174–5, 310–11.

50 Nor, clearly, had Dr McMillan done so during her years of practice there; see Murray, *Dragon Hill*, 1.

51 PANS, MMKC, vol. 2276, file 8, Murray to Father, 24 Aug. 1925.

52 Ibid., file 22, Murray to Alex, 15 March 1939.

53 Ibid., file 36, Annual Report for Hamhung Mission Hospital and Nurses' Training School, 1930, 2–3.

54 Ibid., 1, 15–18.

55 See, for example, Murray, *Dragon Hill*, 50, 184–5.

56 In Seoul, for instance, Professor Horace G. Underwood recalls that in the church that his missionary family attended in 1923 'the curtains to divide the men and women were still there but were left open'; letter to author, 3 June 1997. It is worth noting too that the March First Movement brought some educated young women into the public eye in a way that could scarcely have been condemned by nationalist-minded Koreans.

57 Cott, *Grounding*, esp. 37 and chap. 7.

58 Rosaline Rosenberg, *Beyond Separate Spheres: Intellectual Roots of Modern Feminism* (New Haven 1982), 209.

59 Cott, *Grounding*, chap. 7, esp. 239. 'In contrast to nineteenth-century women's small likelihood of distinction except in woman's rights or woman-oriented activities,' she writes, 'twentieth-century women stood out as individuals, for pursuits not obviously determined by sex nor undertaken for the advancement of their sex.'

60 UCA, Presbyterian Church in Canada, Board of Foreign Missions, Korea Mission Correspondence (KMC), box 8, file 118, William Scott to A.E. Armstrong, 19 Jan. 1924; Brouwer, 'Home Lessons,' 121–3.

61 PANS, MMKC, vol. 2276, file 6, Murray to Alex, 20 Jan., and to Mother, 9 Feb. 1924.

62 Ibid., file 7, Murray to Foster, 11 Dec. 1924; file 8, to Father, 19 Jan., to Foster, 21 Jan., and to Mother, 22 Feb. 1925.

63 I am grateful to Professor Horace G. Underwood for reminding me of the fact that the kinds of frustrations which Murray experienced were common to many first-term missionaries and that their criticisms routinely targeted senior missionaries as well as local people; letter of 3 June 1997. What was perhaps unusual in Murray's case was the extent to which her frustrations were related to her professional work.

64 Ibid., file 12, Murray to Alex, 27 Oct. 1929; file 13, to Alex, 5 June, and to 'Dear Friends,' 15 Sept. 1930; 'Our Korean Hospital,' United Churchman, 22 April 1931, 14.

65 PANS, MMKC, vol. 2276, file 13, Murray to 'Dear Friends,' 15 Sept. 1930.

66 Murray, Dragon Hill, 97–102, 186–90; Murray, 'The Tiger Year in Hamheung Hospital,' KMF, Sept. 1939, 184–86, and 'Skirmishes With Tuberculosis,' KMF, Oct. 1940, 147–49, 154; copies in PANS, MMKC, vol. 2287, files 190 and 191.

67 Ibid., file 22, Murray to Alex, 2 Aug. 1939; Murray, 'Personal Report of 1938,' United Churchman, 22 Feb. 1939, 12.

68 PANS, MMKC, vol. 2276, file 17, Murray to Alex, 10 April 1934.

69 Kathryn McPherson, Bedside Matters: The Transformation of Canadian Nursing, 1900–1990 (Toronto 1996), esp. chap. 2.

70 Murray, Dragon Hill, 161–3.

71 Ibid., 164; McPherson, Bedside Matters, 35–9.

72 PANS, MMKC, vol. 2276, file, 12, Murray to 'Dear Folks All,' 12 May 1929; Murray, Dragon Hill, 162–5.

73 Murray, Dragon Hill, 163–4, and 169 (for quotation). Prior to the establishment of the nurses' training program at Hamhung, there appears to have been only one such program run by Protestant missions in Korea; see World Missionary Atlas (New York 1925), 150.

74 Duck-Heung Bang, autobiographical entry, in Leone McGregor Hellstedt, ed., Women Physicians of the World: Autobiographies of Medical Pioneers (Washington 1978), 361; World Missionary Atlas, 150.

75 Murray, 'Personal Report of 1938,' United Churchman, 22 Feb. 1939, 12.

76 PANS, MMKC, vol. 2276, file 8, Murray to Father, 24 Aug. 1925.

77 Murray's assumption notwithstanding, many North American women doctors of her own and earlier generations continued to practise medicine after marriage. See Morantz-Sanchez, Sympathy and Science, 135–7, and Kinnear, In Subordination, 60, 61, 71. When she learned in 1930 that her sister Anna, a recent

medical school graduate, was planning to marry, Murray was horrified, commenting twice in the same letter that it would be 'her own funeral'; see PANS, MMKC, vol. 2276, file 13, Murray to Alexander, 26 April 1930.

78 PANS, MMKC, vol. 2276, file 8, Murray to Father, 24 Aug. 1925. Murray *was* correct in assuming that marriage in Korea was a near-universal phenomenon; see Laurel Kendall, *Getting Married in Korea: Of Gender, Morality, and Modernity* (Berkeley 1996).

79 PANS, MMKC, vol. 2276, file 8, Murray to Father, 24 Aug. 1925. For two pioneer Korean women doctors who clearly did much more than just wait on their husbands, see the autobiographical entries for Moon Gyung Chang and Duck-Heung Bang in Hellstedt, ed., *Women Physicians*, 267–9 and 361–3.

80 Murray, *Dragon Hill*, 165, 168; McPherson, *Bedside Matters*, 191.

81 PANS, MMKC, vol. 2276, file 9, Murray to Mother, 4 April 1926; file 11, Murray to Alexander, 4 Oct., and to 'Dear Friend,' 10 Nov. 1928.

82 Jung-gun Kim, ' "To God's Country": Canadian Missionaries in Korea and the Beginnings of Korean Migration to Canada' (EdD thesis, University of Toronto, 1983), chap. 2.

83 See also PANS, MMKC, vol. 2276, file 19, Murray to 'Dear People All,' 12 Nov. 1936. Here Murray explained that, though Dr Ahn, a valued former associate, now had his own private practice, she and he continued to consult each other and remained friends. During the 1930s Murray also lost the men whom she had trained as the hospital's druggist, business manager, and x-ray technician, as each one left for other opportunities. While she found these losses inconvenient, she accepted them with little complaint; see ibid., file 20, to 'Dear People,' 11 Oct. 1937; file 22, to Alex, 15 March, and to Father and Mother, 20 April 1939.

84 Ibid., file 23, Murray to Alex, 25 March 1940.

85 See, for example, ibid., file 15, Murray to 'Dear Alex,' 31 July 1932; file 17, Murray to Alexander, 1 June 1934; file 20, Murray to 'Dearest People,' 6 April 1937; file 22, Murray to Alexander, 9 April 1939. Since, as the last of these letters indicates, it was not unusual for students in government-run medical schools in Korea to graduate without any hospital experience, Murray's concern for her teaching function was understandable.

86 Huntley, 'Presbyterian Women's Work,' 41.

87 PANS, MMKC, vol. 2276, file 7, Murray to her father, 28 Aug. 1924.

88 See, for example, ibid., file 4, Murray to Alex, 16 June 1923, p. 8; and file 9, Murray to Mother, 24 March 1926. Murray's racialist discourse prior to and during her first term is discussed more fully in Brouwer, 'Home Lessons.'

89 Regarding the latter, see, for example, PANS, MMKC, vol. 2276, file 19, Murray to 'Dear People All,' 12 Nov. 1936. A tendency to 'positive' orientalism

sometimes developed as missionaries gained a better understanding of 'their' people and took pride in their accomplishments, especially in the face of adversity. As Nicholas Thomas has observed, while depictions of the cultural differences of an 'other' were (and are) almost invariably reductionist, they are not invariably hostile; see *Colonialism's Culture: Anthropology, Travel and Government* (Cambridge 1994), 26.

90 PANS, MMKC, vol. 2276, file 12, Murray to 'Dear Ones All,' 14 Feb. 1929; Personals column, *United Churchman*, 28 April 1930, 261.

91 PANS, MMKC, vol. 2276, file 11, D.M. MacRae to Murray, 24 Feb. 1928; and ibid., Murray to 'Dear Friend,' 10 Nov. 1928. The initiative had come from Dr Hong himself, who had asked ordained missionary MacRae to write to Murray in Canada and request her to make the necessary arrangements.

92 Ibid., file 22, Murray to Alexander, 9 April 1939.

93 Ibid., file 12, Murray to Alexander, 5 Sept. 1929; file 15, to Alexander, 27 April 1932; and file 23, to Father and Mother, 4 Jan. 1940.

94 Murray, 'Personal Report of 1938,' *United Churchman*, 15 Feb. 1939, 12.

95 PANS, MMKC, vol. 2276, file 13, Murray to Alex, 27 Jan. 1930.

96 Ibid., file 12, Murray to 'Dear Folks All,' 12 May 1929 (for quoted phrase) and 16 June 1929. In the latter, Murray noted that the local population was impressed by the significance of the fine house. The stark difference between the quality of missionaries' housing and that provided for indigenous mission workers had been a subject of reproach upon early missions in Korea, as elsewhere.

97 See, for example, ibid., file 9, Murray to Alex, 16 Oct. 1926; file 12, to 'Dear Folks,' 12 July 1929; file 17, to Alex, 10 April 1934; Murray, *Dragon Hill*, 98–9.

98 PANS, MMKC, vol. 2276, file 20, Murray to 'Dear Everybody,' 22 Jan. 1937 (first quotation); and ibid., 2 June 1937 (second quotation).

99 Telephone interview with Isabelle Johnston (Murray's niece), Toronto, 23 Feb. 1996. The phrase originated with Mrs Johnston's late husband.

100 PANS, MMKC, vol. 2276, file 20, Hamheung Station Report, 1937–8, 7.

101 Florence J. Murray, 'Medical Work in the Canadian Mission,' *KMF*, May 1941, 79; copy preserved in PANS, MMKC, vol. 2287, file 228.

102 PANS, MMKC, vol. 2287, file 228; also containing P.K. Koh, 'Korean Doctor Takes Over Mission Hospital,' in *KMF*, May 1941, 79, 80; see also ibid., vol. 2276, file 24, Murray to 'Dear Korea Folks at Home,' 1 May 1941, and Murray, *Dragon Hill*, 228.

103 PANS, MMKC, vol. 2276, file 23, Murray to parents from Komahura, Japan, 14 Jan. 1940.

104 Ibid., file 37, 'Report of the Interim Committee of the Korea Mission of the United Church of Canada,' August 1942, 1, 2, 12.

105 UCA, United Church of Canada, Woman's Missionary Society, Overseas Missions, Korea Correspondence, 1933–45, box 3, file 51b, Murray to WMS, 13 March 1941; PANS, MMKC, vol. 2276, file 24, Murray to parents, 15 May 1941.

106 PANS, MMKC, vol. 2276, file 37, 'Report of the Interim Committee,' 12; Murray, 'Medical Work,' *KMF*, May 1941, containing photograph of medical staff; copy in ibid., vol. 2287, file 228.

107 Ibid., vol. 2276, file 37, 'Report of the Interim Committee,' 4.

108 Ibid., 4–5; Murray, *Dragon Hill*, 238–40.

109 See, for instance, Soon Yong Yoon, 'A Legacy without Heirs: Korean Indigenous Medicine and Primary Health Care,' *Social Science and Medicine*, 17, no. 19 (1983): 1467–76. Cautioning against the recent tendency to 'romanticize' indigenous medical practices, the author calls instead for studies of ways to improve such practices and integrate them into modern state-run primary health-care programs.

110 For a brief explanation of these techniques for lay readers see McPherson, *Bedside Matters*, 86–8.

111 Murray, *Dragon Hill*, 97–108; PANS, MMKC, vol. 2276, file 12, Murray to Alex, 27 Oct. 1929, and file 20, Murray to 'Dear Folks,' 15 June 1937.

112 Helen Kim obtained a PhD from Columbia University in 1931, having previously graduated from Ewha Woman's College, an institution that began in 1886 under American Methodist sponsorship as the first Western-style school for girls. Kim became Ewha's first Korean president in 1939 and led it to university status after the Second World War, when she was easily her country's best-known woman at home and abroad; J. Manning Potts, *Grace Sufficient: The Story of Doctor Helen Kim* (Nashville 1964); Ewha Womans University Library, Seoul, Helen Kim Collection, Helen Kim, 'Personal History.'

113 It is significant that Murray used no male equivalent for the epithet 'ignorant old woman' (*Dragon Hill*, 111). Similar phrases were used by missionaries and modernizing Indian women in early-twentieth-century India, especially in reference to traditional midwives, who constituted an obstacle to the reform of childbirth practices; see Geraldine Forbes, 'Managing Midwifery in India,' in *Contesting Colonial Hegemony*, eds. Engels and Marks, 152–72.

114 Murray's zeal to train young women for Western-style nursing may seem an obvious exception to this statement, but again her primary goal was medical modernization rather than opening up opportunities for girls from humble backgrounds, though the latter was also a desirable outcome from her point of view.

115 Ester Boserup's *Women's Role in Economic Development* (New York 1970) was one of the first works to take up this theme.

116 In-Ho Lee, 'Work, Education, and Women's Gains: The Korean Experience,' in Jill Ker Conway and Susan C. Bourque, eds., *The Politics of Women's Education: Perspectives from Asia, Africa, and Latin America* (Ann Arbor, 1993), 77, 86.

117 Potts, *Grace Sufficient*, 149.

118 In-Ho Lee, 'Work,' 87. See also Ji-moon Suh, 'Commentary,' *Asian Women*, 3 (Winter 1996), 104, which claims that 'images of finishing schools' still cling to women's universities in Korea and that as a result 'women wanting to become professionals tend to choose coeducational schools over women's colleges.'

119 Hocking, *Re-Thinking Missions*, espec. 199–201. See PANS, MMKC, vol. 2276, file 16, Murray's letter of 23 Jan. 1933, for her disapproval of this aspect of *Re-Thinking Missions*.

Music and Marginality: Jean Coulthard and the University of British Columbia, 1947–1973

WILLIAM BRUNEAU

Jean Coulthard is among Canada's best-known composers of 'art,' or classical, music. Like many young Canadians, I came to know her work as a piano student in the little town where I grew up. In the early 1960s her pieces were optional for List D, 'Contemporary Music,' in the syllabus of the Royal Conservatory of Music of Toronto. My teacher, herself a graduate of that conservatory and then living in rural Saskatchewan, had little patience for anything composed after 1900. She made an exception for Coulthard's piano *Etudes*. It surprised me to learn that Jean Coulthard was not French Canadian and not a man,[1] and even more surprising was how tough this approachable music was to play. Said my teacher, 'You're understanding with your head. Please, please listen and understand with your heart.'

This advice came back to me more than thirty years later when, as a curious opera-goer, I attended the world premiere of Coulthard's *Return of the Native*.[2] This partially staged reading with piano accompaniment was presented in Vancouver in September 1993.[3] That sunny fall day I was taking a break from work at the Archives of the University of British Columbia, where my research on the history of the university kept me busy, and had repaired to the Koerner Auditorium, in Vancouver's Kitsilano neighbourhood. Listening to Coulthard's expansive music immediately opened mental windows and doors, and it made each listener want to 'understand with the heart.'

Here was important music, but written by a composer of whom few musical enthusiasts had much knowledge, a long-time professor at UBC, and a culturally significant Canadian – and I knew next to nothing about the music and little more about her. The program notes informed me that the work had its origins during a sabbatical in France in 1956 and was twenty-three years in the making. Why, I wondered, had it not been performed before? And who was Jean Coulthard?[4]

It turned out that her instrumental, orchestral, and vocal works are regular features of symphony and recital programs in Canada. Her music is heard often on the networks of the Canadian Broadcasting Corporation, in live concerts, and on commercial recordings. I soon discovered that her reputation in Europe has grown continuously stronger, particularly since the mid-1960s.[5] She is something of an icon in Canada's musical community, having stayed in this country rather than moving to London or New York.[6] Her record of productivity, especially since 'retirement' in 1973 from full-time university teaching, still encourages writers a third her age.[7] Yet despite her importance in Canada's art-music community, several of Coulthard's works for orchestra or large-scale vocal ensemble have yet to be performed.[8] In this respect, her fate is that of many a Canadian composer, but especially those working far from the Toronto-Montreal axis.[9]

If we think of the history of Vancouver and its region, Coulthard's life acquires yet other meanings. As a Vancouver native, she has witnessed the city's development across nine decades. Her life points to the larger histories of city, region, and country. For part of the British Columbia populace, culturally and politically knowledgeable, she embodies a style of life that they would like for their 'better' selves. Born in 1908, Coulthard links them to an imagined distant time of art-in-life, of gentler pastimes, of an easier Edwardian existence.[10]

This latter notion does not, of course, square very well with Canadian social history. The sheer toughness of Vancouver's frontier political economy was hardly an inducement to gentility, then or ever.[11] As in all of Canada's growing towns and cities after 1900, it was not easy to maintain a artist's 'place' in Vancouver, Victoria, or other British Columbia towns.[12] The few artists who found and kept their places did so by adopting a range of survival strategies. For Emily Carr it meant occasional travel to culturally enriching places, but also running a boarding house to earn a living.[13] For Gideon Hicks, early church musician and all-round musical entrepreneur in Vancouver and Victoria for a half-century between 1890 and 1940, it meant patiently working as a carpenter, then a piano tuner, and then a small-time manufacturer, before he established himself as a singing teacher and became president in 1939–40 of the Vancouver Music Teachers' Association.[14] As painter William Weston said, British Columbia artists slowly learned 'to rely absolutely on ourselves for what we felt like doing.'[15] In his case, that meant accepting lifelong servitude in the art-education bureaucracy of the Vancouver School Board.

Artists' difficulties have remained a persistent sub-theme of art history in this region of Canada, as in most. About the difficulties we know a good deal. But we know less, and understand even less well, the full range of strategies that they have employed in order to survive, and occasionally to flourish.

The experience of Jean Coulthard as a member of the University of British Columbia teaching staff from 1947 to 1973 is an example of one such artist's strategy. In her case, academic appointment at UBC was by no means the only necessary one. Other strategies included foreign travel, certificates and awards in music, and 'public relations' work of a kind peculiar to art music in Canada. Coulthard travelled to England and France (a dozen times between 1947 and 1973), partly because she would thereby acquire a lustre otherwise denied to home-grown talent. And like many Canadian artists, she took practical qualifications (but not necessarily university degrees) that gave her a kind of professional status – in her case, two music-conservatory diplomas by 1930. She joined the infant Canadian League of Composers in 1951–2 as a founding member of that organization, seeing in it the future of professionalized music in Canada. She maintained active participation in community boards (for example, the Vancouver Symphony Orchestra's board in the 1950s) and worked as an adjudicator at music festivals throughout western Canada.

On the other hand, she attended university only for a few months in the fall of 1925, at the newly opened Point Grey campus of UBC, leaving before her eighteenth birthday. Her parents thought that the demands of a good musical education were great, and after trying a term of literary and scientific study, Jean could only agree. It seemed unwise to do five hours of piano practice and still more hours of theoretical study, all the while preparing for labs and exams. Until her honorary doctorate sixty-two years later, Jean Coulthard never took another university course or received a degree.[16]

She wrote music: dozens and finally hundreds of works came from her pen during the UBC years. Fewer were published than written, although after 1965 every manuscript found its way into the Canadian Music Centre and its publication-on-demand service.[17] In nearly ninety years of productive life, Coulthard has been consistent, not to say ruthless, in exercising her intellectual and artistic powers. She has written her own music, no matter what the musical tastes of the day, no matter what the distractions in her working or family life. Her daughter reports, 'Mummy was simply not there at times, even when we spent days and weeks close together in hotel rooms and *pensions* on her sabbatical [1955–6].'[18] In brief, her example appeals to anyone who hopes to overcome the weakness of the Canadian cultural economy, to work, and to create, come hell or high water.

I mention 'public relations' among Jean Coulthard's strategies, but I could just as well have said 'social relations.' Her connections to the Vancouver and Canadian establishments have given her art a social and political basis absent from many artists' lives.[19] In the 1920s and 1930s she taught the children of the best families in town, was an established concert performer and broadcaster,[20] and with her husband after 1935, interior decorator–artist Donald Adams, built up yet another circle of acquaintances among Vancouver's upper middle class. Coulthard gives no evidence of intending to establish a network of influence, but neither did she discourage it. That network later helped to make careers for her composition students, especially those who came to her in the 1960s and early 1970s, ensuring that they would be heard on the Canadian Broadcasting Corporation and their works performed by good instrumentalists. These same connections would help to save her career at UBC in 1950–1.

The ironies of Coulthard's creative life are nowhere more striking than in her twenty-five-year career as a member of the Department (later School) of Music at UBC in 1947–73.[21] She taught and learned at the university in ways that hint at larger truths about musical and artistic life in Canada. She was ingenious in helping younger composers to acquire a solid basis in musical technique, artistically strengthened and encouraged to pursue their own paths. But her very success made it all the more obvious that she was a craftswoman and a kind of musical caregiver, and these characteristics were not as highly valued in the UBC academic music community of the day as were more traditional marks of professionalism – publication in scholarly journals, high office in academic societies, and the holding of advanced university degrees. At many turns in the story, we are compelled to see how Coulthard's gender and its social meanings help to explain the constraints placed on her, the marginality of her work, and why she chose the strategic survival devices she did.

One might think that UBC would have welcomed musical theory and practice as a feature of its arts program from its beginning in 1915. Music had been, after all, a core subject in the medieval university curriculum.[22] In a contrarian way universities have provided homes for disciplines and fields of study whose economic and social utility were doubtful. On both grounds one would have thought that music would have a lively presence in the UBC curriculum, and this from the university's very beginning.

Organized musical study came, however, to UBC only in 1946 with the opening of a Department of Music and the appointment of a professor, Harry Adaskin.[23] The reasons for its late arrival had partly to do with public belief that musicians were not professionals as were doctors and lawyers and partly with the prevailing view among Canadian university people that music lacked a scholarly basis, in contrast to English, history, and the much newer fields of home economics, nursing, and social work.[24] Even after the foundation of a Department of Music, it would be a decade and more before UBC took seriously the claims of musical study. Until the late 1950s the Department of Music was thought to satisfy community demand, but not to require much money. The department's professoriate remained small, its published research minute, and its curriculum immobile. Although none of this was especially surprising in a teaching staff of three persons, it tells us something of the context in which Coulthard taught and wrote in the greater part of her academic career.

Harry Adaskin (1901–1994), the department's head between 1947 and 1958, was an energetic and bumptious man. His journalistic dicta, his popular courses in music appreciation, his local concert performances with highly accomplished pianist and wife Frances Marr, and his public-relations campaigns for the funding of music at UBC (sometimes carried out on American and eastern Canadian tours) came close to dominating the formal and informal life of the tiny department. Adaskin came to the university in 1946 to bring music to the Faculty of Arts, chiefly because President Norman ('Larry') and Margaret Thomas Mackenzie and a clutch of influential Vancouver families wanted him. A $5,000 donation from a local businessman and a campaign by the Community Arts Council helped. On the other hand, Mackenzie's biographer suggests that 'Larry could certainly spot a good teacher. He brought in Harry Adaskin in 1946 to begin Music at U.B.C. because he knew Adaskin from University of Toronto days, when Vincent Massey had helped to establish the Hart House String Quartet. Adaskin was appointed at a salary of $5,000, just $200 less than that of Walter Sage, who had been at U.B.C. as head of History for years ... Larry had an exceptional talent for picking academics with real talent for communication.'[25] Adaskin himself said he was the equivalent of a lecturer at a old-time country fair, bringing difficult music to life. He came from Ontario and knew all the 'important' musicians. His long and successful career as violinist in the Hart House quartet and his very real contributions to public music in Toronto recommended him.[26] He loved to talk and had a salesman's touch when it came to persuading business people to 'cough up for the arts.' He seemed the perfect frontman for the new UBC operation.

If Adaskin was the frontman, then someone had to be behind. He quickly took up the courses in music appreciation, but never taught junior or senior music theory or music history. Adaskin saw his UBC work as having two sides: the popularization of great art and concert performances with his wife.[27] He clearly intended from the start that someone else would teach systematic musical theory – certainly not he.[28]

The thirty-nine-year-old Jean Coulthard was perhaps the only Vancouver musician in the immediate post-war period, and one of the few in Canada, who might appropriately serve in the UBC music department. Her mother, Jean Robinson Coulthard, had been a central figure in the formation after 1910 of the Vancouver Women's Musical Club, a remarkable soloist and pianist from the moment of her arrival in Vancouver in 1905, and an indefatigable teacher from the family piano studio in Vancouver's Shaughnessy neighbourhood. The younger Jean's training as a composer had taken her to London and the Royal College of Music in 1928–9 and then to New York's Juilliard School in 1944–5. Her chief teachers had been Ralph Vaughan Williams and Bernard Wagenaar, with occasional criticism lessons from Aaron Copland, Béla Bartók, Arnold Schönberg, and Darius Milhaud. By 1947 she had completed and begun to publish works in every genre – art songs, symphonic suites, sonatas for piano, for cello, for violin – and was moving into a period of even higher creativity.

Coulthard's physician father and musician mother, despite their early deaths, had left Jean and her sister, Margaret ('Babs'), a kind of social legacy that the university authorities could hardly ignore. By 1935 she enjoyed the support of leaders in business and the arts. These people – Jean Coulthard's circle – were not always especially well off. But just as an inherited title may confer psychological power but not necessarily wealth, participation in Vancouver's cultural elite bestowed a limited notoriety and a kind of power by association.[29] Mackenzie was not one to be ignorant of either the forces or these people, having been at the UBC helm for two years, and he needed all the community support he could get. He and Margaret Mackenzie may have known about Jean Coulthard even before Harry Adaskin arrived in 1946.

Despite her background – or because of it – Jean Coulthard found herself spending considerable time in 1947 and 1948 arranging piano tunings for the Adaskins' violin-piano recitals, informing dozens of returned veterans about first-year harmony and theory, and running interference when the Adaskin music-appreciation lectures produced students with gaps in musical knowledge. She was joined in 1949 by fellow composer Barbara Pentland, who taught the senior courses in composition. Coulthard played little part in deciding on teaching assignments or general curriculum either then or in the succeeding decade.

In a letter of 29 July 1947 from Don Adams to Arthur Benjamin, Coulthard's circumstances are pictured this way: 'Musically Vancouver seems to be getting along slowly but surely ... Of course the most important news as far as we are concerned is that our Jeannie is to be on the faculty at the university this fall. They are starting out in a small way with just Harry Adaskin and Jean as THE music department. I believe Jean is to teach Harmony, CTP [counterpoint] and Aural training to first and second year students. Later, of course it will involve third year students. She is very happy about it and will be able to drop her private class in piano.'[30] As it turned out, Coulthard came to teach that third-year course exactly twenty years later, at the age of fifty-nine. Her fate as an instructor was decided in the 1950s by the fact that she had clearly acquired so much musical knowledge which Harry Adaskin claimed as his special province. Unfortunately, there was room for only one Adaskin, or so he thought, and he was the head. His attitude is well illustrated in his single reference to Coulthard in two volumes of autobiography: 'For a few years, Fran [Frances Marr, Adaskin's wife] and I *were* the Music Department. But the university was growing and we gradually added Jean Coulthard – to teach composition to first and second year students – and Barbara Pentland to do the same for third and fourth year.'[31] It is surely extraordinary that between 1950 and 1973 three of the best-known women composers of the period in English Canada were concentrated in the departments at UBC and the University of Alberta (Violet Archer). Archer came to Alberta from 'away,' was Montreal-born, with an advanced education in the United States, and was quickly appointed professor and head of the theory and composition department. Pentland too came from 'away,' in her case Manitoba, France, and Toronto.[32]

One might think that in 1949, as Pentland took up the third-year course at UBC and began to build a reputation for demanding and disciplined teaching, she would move up the academic ladder, acquiring influence over the curriculum as she did so. But like Coulthard and Archer, she did not move up. Pentland had by this time written widely in

Women professors of music theory and composition, 1945

University or conservatory	Number of women with professorial rank[a]	Total in professorial rank
Indiana University	1 (professor of voice)	12
Yale University	0	14
Juilliard School of Music (New York)	6[b]	31[c]

Sources: Annual calendars of Indiana University, Yale University, and Juilliard School of Music.
[a]At Juilliard the professorial ranks were limited to the Juilliard Graduate School of Music, whereas conservatory instructors worked in the Institute of Musical Arts.
[b]Juilliard's faculty included the influential and unquestionably great piano teacher Rosina Lhevinne. Most women in Juilliard's faculty taught voice.
[c]No women taught musical theory or composition at any of these leading institutions.

every genre and category of art music. Like Archer, she and Coulthard had achieved international stature, both in the musical competitions of the period and through a mix of commercial and educational publications. In the world of musical practice, we might now say that they had acquired the equivalent of doctoral degrees in an 'applied' field.

They were exceptional too in being women who taught and created in the fields of musical theory and composition. Among three of the highest-ranked American university and conservatory music schools, consider the faculty numbers for the year 1945, shown in the accompanying table. Women were wholly absent from advanced theoretical instruction in these 'model' institutions in the United States.[33]

Pentland and Coulthard must have seemed threatening, not just exceptional and outside the norm, in a university planning to make music a serious academic study. They were readier for that great change than Adaskin was. In Pentland's case, however, things got worse after a whole generation of largely American musicologists and theorists took over the Department of Music in the 1960s. She finally resigned in 1963, horrified by what she considered an 'intolerable decline in academic standards.'[34]

To return briefly to 1950, it is useful to recall that Harry Adaskin disliked administration. He had difficulty reading a balance sheet. He was impatient with academic procedures and regulations, and showed little inclination to change his ways.[35] These characteristics made organized change in the curriculum difficult, if not impossible (had he been so inclined). Worse, when Adaskin came to think in early 1951 that his tiny, three-person department was inexplicably over budget, he decided instantly how to solve his problem. In a moment snatched between rehearsals, recitals, and lectures, he chose to fire Jean Coulthard.

The news came by memorandum. She was thunderstruck, and not a little frightened. Her young family needed her income, since husband Don Adams's interior-decorating business had not yet taken off. Besides, Coulthard required an academic base. She had firmly decided after her appointment in 1947 that she would become a full-time composer-instructor, no longer played in public, and had no ready way of regaining lost income as a piano performer and teacher. Coulthard could not possibly go back to studio teaching, which was much less well paid and far more exhausting. An academic appointment meant a great deal outside the university, not just inside it.

Her solution was to seek out Geoff Andrew, assistant to President Larry Mackenzie. Andrew and Mackenzie conferred. Meanwhile, over a ten-day period Jean Coulthard was in touch with old friends in the city. Her connections meant that without any particular effort, the UBC Board of Governors and the university's entire upper administration knew within two days that something had gone badly awry in the Department of Music. Mackenzie and Andrew took one look at the Arts and Music budgets and knew that Adaskin had misread the figures. Suddenly it appeared that there was a small surplus overall, and in light of healthy enrolments in her first- and second-year courses, there was no reason to let Coulthard's appointment lapse. Adaskin received one of Mackenzie's famous 'persuader' telephone calls in late May 1951, and the president's office immediately forwarded to Jean Coulthard a contract for the 1951–2 academic year. Thereafter contracts followed one another in an unbroken chain until her sixty-fifth birthday. But the easy friendship that Coulthard and Adaskin had enjoyed was subtly and permanently undermined by this unfortunate event.

The episode is a piece of micro-history, but it establishes at once the character of the UBC administration in the late 1940s – its wholly male hierarchy and its involvement with Vancouver's elite families. It shows how Jean Coulthard could be both weak and powerful at the same time, and it raises the question of gender in the university's social relations. The consequences of her being one of two women subordinates in the administration of a singularly eccentric and male head were clear enough in the 1940s. Afterward, those consequences, if less instantly visible, merely changed in social and practical coloration.

Through the late 1950s, after Adaskin's departure from the headship in 1958, Coulthard was as secure as anyone could be as a lecturer in a university without a collective agreement. On the other hand, she had little to say about new appointments in the Department of Music, particularly following Welton Marquis's appointment as head in 1958, after which the department grew quickly. Later, in the rapid curriculum changes of the mid and late 1960s, her influence was, by all appearances, slight. The records of the department and faculty curriculum committees show no input either from Coulthard or from Pentland. Coulthard ended her career as senior instructor with job security, but without having reached professorial rank and without appointment as composer-in-residence or anything resembling that status.[36]

By the 1960s two factors helped to ensure that Coulthard's relation with the Department (School) of Music would remain as paradoxical as ever. The first had to do with the sort of music that she wrote, and the second with forms of professionalization in North American music after the Second World War. By the late 1940s the musical hothouses of Toronto and Montreal had produced in John Weinzweig, Istvan Anhalt, Harry Somers, Norma Beecroft, Serge Garant, Jean Papineau-Couture, and others a school dedicated to the serialist, twelve-tone, or 'dodecaphonic' approach to musical composition. It would be a massive exaggeration to claim that these writers, along with Barbara Pentland, the best-known western Canadian exponent of serialism, imposed their views on all Canadian art music. But when the Canadian League of Composers was founded in Toronto in 1951, several of its members shared this approach to the problems of composition. Even after the foundation of the much more 'open' Canadian Music Centre in 1959, it was difficult for non-serialists (or later, for non-practitioners of *musique concrète* or whatever was the latest fad) to find publishers and performances in Canada. In the late 1960s the entire 'system' fell apart as the acceptable forms of musical composition multiplied. Then it became easier for Jean Coulthard and her like-minded colleagues to make their way.

Coulthard had been interested in the possibility of a music whose forms were in some way a historical outgrowth of musical languages 'spoken' from the times of Palestrina to Prokofiev. She thought and still thinks in several musical dialects at once: Palestrina's, Bach's, Debussy's, Stravinsky's, Bartók's, and yet others. By 1950, however, she had made her own dialect and had begun to write a literature in it. Coulthard's new language was sometimes tonal, and full of complex and emotionally charged colours. It delighted in experiments with rhythm. It was at home in the twentieth century in its fluid harmonic choices and its free movement away and towards recognizable keys and modulations. Yet her particular musical dialect and her open-minded and tentative approach to the musical languages around her were out of place in the academic musical world of the 1950s and 1960s.

It did Coulthard little good that studio music teachers loved her compositions, that publishers came to be 'hooked' on them, or that orchestras and festivals commissioned new works every year. It did her no more good that Michael Conway-Baker, Lloyd Burritt, Jean Ethridge, Frederick Shipitzky, Joan Hansen, Sylvia Rickard, David Duke, Chan Ka Nin, and several other successful composers came from her junior and senior courses, and went on to build their own dialects and write their own literatures.[37]

Once again, Coulthard was both strong and weak in the academy. Although the Royal Society of Canada produced a grant for her in 1955 and the Canada Council became increasingly supportive of her in the mid-1960s,[38] the official view was that she was in some unnameable sense 'a derivative composer.'[39] In the period before about 1965 UBC allowed (even if it did not wilfully intend to maintain) Coulthard's marginality. Perhaps the university was attracted by the new 'professionalism' embodied in the Toronto-Montreal axis, both in the composers at work in those places and in the schools of music growing up there. It may have seemed that Coulthard simply did not fit the patterns and practices of that new professionalism. Still more likely, however, she was the unfortunate victim of a strong circumstance: she was one of just a half-dozen Canadian women composers of any note, thus in a tiny minority. Further, she was a westerner, although a resilient one. It was easy for the Canadian League not to ask her to serve on its executive committee.

I have argued that Jean's tenacious views, her close attention to the quotidian business of undergraduate education, and her consistent path in musical literature may have cost her dearly in the academic politics of the 1960s. On the other hand, her stubborn unwillingness to jump onto the serialist, concretist, and abstract bandwagons of the day helped to keep her composing and teaching work alive, where others' finally died.

Yet a third development further underlines the two-sided relationship between this composing woman and her institutional home: the arrival of the Americans. Their appearance at UBC was necessary for the kind of professionalization in music training that the university thought it wanted. Although the central Canadian view of the musical profession had some influence over western Canadian universities, by comparison with the effects of the American model, that influence was extraordinarily slight. As Canadian university music departments diverged from English and European ways, they joined a North American stream, aiming to become attractive (even glamorous) comprehensive university music schools on the model of Indiana or Michigan.[40] UBC was not alone in its quest. In music departments and faculties in western Canada, the objectives of the 1960s and 1970s called for growth and for a measure of specialization. If one were to offer minors and majors in theory, in history (as McGill, in particular, did), in ethnomusicology (as several west-coast American universities did), in performance (as Indiana, Eastman, and many other American institutions did), then enough people in each specialization had to be hired to make them free-standing.

The difficulty at UBC was that, although more money became available after 1958, the first head after Adaskin, Welton Marquis, hired Americans and *musical generalists* above all.[41] He and his new appointees fashioned a 'diachronic' curriculum that mimicked the evolution of music from the medieval period onward, significantly downgrading the place of eighteenth- and nineteenth-century music. That music had been the core of the curriculum in the previous regime. The course of study now emphasized music from the eighteenth century and earlier, especially in first- and second-year studies. This was a clever answer to the question of what to do when your specialist professors have nothing else in common on which to build a bachelor of music program. On one line of argument, it was a curriculum for generalists, a program that both allowed and encouraged the kind of liberal education for which UBC sought to be known, and even renowned. The specialists could teach a very few senior courses that suited them, but not at the expense of the program's overall generalism.

Jean Coulthard, by contrast, knew much more exactly the sort of musician-scholar she wanted to be. Further, she had a clear – if idiosyncratic – idea of how to make composers, performers, and teachers, and she had a sharp appreciation of their likely roles in the societies of western Canada. She was not in the business of writing articles for musicological journals, although she supported those who did. Nor was she anxious to move towards electronic music, although she wrote in that medium more than once.[42] On the other hand, between 1968 and 1973 she composed several instrumental sonatas and sonatinas and brought out a half-dozen chamber works,[43] moving towards the crucially productive 'retirement' year of 1973 and its new set of songs, seven new piano preludes, experimental

Jean Coulthard composing at home in the early 1970s, towards the end of her UBC career.

chamber work (*Birds of Landsdowne*), and the great *Octet: Twelve Essays on a Cantabile Theme* for two string quartets.[44]

Coulthard's outlook made her an object of curiosity in an Americanizing department, for she had, in many respects, the outlook of an old-fashioned liberal in political-academic theory and practice. One is reminded of Bertrand Russell in many of Coulthard's arguments and calculations. Her anglophilism and francophilism, her fondness for the Canadian experiment in nation-building, her two Presbyterian minister grandfathers, her English training, her daughter's English sojourn, her many refresher trips to England and France – all of this distanced Jean Coulthard from a group of able, but uncomprehending and often American-born or American-educated colleagues at UBC. She never became publicly active in politics, except to support the Canada Council. Her colleagues might share one, two, or even three of these characteristics, but not more. Coulthard was thus not automatically or necessarily close to the 'new' department after 1958.

But it is important to emphasize her way of teaching and her uncontrived commitment to education as the nurture and care of composition students. Her pupils spent whole weeks and months learning composition technique in the Coulthard living room. Her approach was reminiscent of 'Oxbridge' and 'Red-brick,' not of Indiana and Juilliard. It was close to Gustav Holst's way of teaching in the University of Reading, England, in the 1920s.[45] But it was not quite Holstian either, for education seen as nurture would have been slightly beyond even his ken. Her way of teaching must have been the expression of the mother-teacher in educational practice. In the late 1960s, in large classes at UBC, her approach was seen as profoundly conservative and mildly boring.[46] In work with students, one at a time, Coulthard's educational theory and her careful nurture had powerful effects. A dozen of her protégés from the late 1960s and 1970s now are producing and highly creative members of the Canadian compositional community. Her practices were clearly minoritarian and exceptional in her department and university, and these kept her in a semi-marginal region to which she became accustomed.

Coulthard remained at UBC until the usual retirement age. After the mid-1950s, as her husband's interior-decorating business became successful, she might have chosen to leave the university. She did not do so, and she had her reasons. She may have been on the periphery of university politics and administration, but the evidence is she was not paralysed thereby. Her list of successful composer-students attests to her educational effectiveness, especially after 1963.

Her compositions between 1947 and 1973, especially the writing of the greater part of the opera *The Return of the Native,* show levels of creative energy uncommon in a university. Her international career fared well during her quarter-century at UBC, in part because of her academic status. While at the university, she became something of a fixture in the community's musical life, whether organizing symposia and festivals, guiding the development of the Vancouver Symphony Orchestra as a board member, participating in CBC broadcasts, or helping musical associations to find speakers and performers, both in Vancouver and far afield.

The evidence is that Coulthard was politically and administratively 'marginal' at UBC, despite her musical importance, and partly *because* of it. The reason that she could be important and marginal at the same time was, in part, ideological. Especially after the arrival of American-trained and American-born professors between 1958 and 1965, the department's world-view – the conceptual scheme from which it moved – changed significantly. In that scheme her output became part of the 'woodwork' of the department, sometimes respected, sometimes barely visible. As a caring teacher, as a woman in a world where only men were administratively important, as a determined creator in a department still finding its way, Jean Coulthard was most of the time simply not noticed.

NOTES

1 The expectation that only a man would be likely to write études, sonatas, and symphonies is weakening with each passing year. But see Patricia Taylor Lee, 'Discovering Jean Coulthard,' *American Music Teacher: Official Journal of Music Teachers National Association,* 45, 2 (October/November 1995): 16–19, 62–3, for Lee's discovery during research at the Library of Congress that 'Jean Coulthard' was neither French Canadian nor a man!

2 Jean Coulthard, *The Return of the Native: An Opera Based on the Novel by Thomas Hardy* (2 vols., Vancouver: Canadian Music Centre, 1979).

3 Concert Opera production of Coulthard, *Return of the Native,* Koerner Recital Hall, Vancouver, 23, 24, and 26 September 1993, Kaspar Productions, Bliss Johnston, director.

4 The primary evidence for the argument of this paper comes principally from two sources: the Coulthard Papers and a series of annotated and transcribed

interviews between William Bruneau and Jean Coulthard, 1994–7. The Coulthard Papers – thirty-eight boxes of records from the artistic, educational, and family life of Jean Coulthard and her immediate family and friends – are held in the University of British Columbia Archives (UBCA), Vancouver. The Coulthard Papers were further enriched in 1997 by the first of three planned manuscript donations, chiefly of annotated and rough musical scores of drafts of small-scale instrumental and vocal works from the period 1942–89. The tapes and transcripts of the Bruneau-Coulthard interviews are in the possession of the author, but are to be deposited in the UBC Archives on 1 July 1999.

5 David Duke, *Jean Coulthard* (3rd ed., Toronto: BMI, 1985) [information booklet].

6 E. Keillor, 'The Conservative Tradition in Canadian Music,' in G. Ridout and T. Kenins, eds., *Celebration: Essays on Aspects of Canadian Music* (Toronto: Canadian Music Centre, 1984), 49–56.

7 David Duke, 'Coulthard's Career Intensifies since Retirement,' *Music Scene*, 229 (January/February 1978): 4.

8 Notable among unperformed Coulthard works are the Second Symphony ('Choral: This Land,' 1966–7), the Symphonic Ode for Cello and Orchestra (1964–6), and *Excursion* (1940; the first ballet ever written in British Columbia, but not yet staged).

9 See Stephen Willis, 'Opera Composition,' in H. Kallmann, G. Potvin, and K. Winters, eds., *Encyclopedia of Music in Canada* (2nd ed., Toronto: University of Toronto Press, 1992), 968–9.

10 William Bruneau, 'With Age the Power to Do Good: Jean Coulthard's Latest Decades,' *Classical Music*, 19, 2 (June 1996): 14–19.

11 Robert A.J. McDonald, *Making Vancouver: Class, Status, and Social Boundaries, 1863–1913* (Vancouver: UBC Press, 1996), esp. chap. 4, 'Capital and Labour,' 90–119.

12 For a recent discussion of this point, see Maria Tippett's revealing and direct autobiographical work *Becoming Myself: A Memoir* (Toronto: Stoddart, 1996). Tippett is the author of a helpful biography of Emily Carr, and the parallels between Carr's and Coulthard's lives have much to do with becoming and being an artist-intellectual in a place with too little space for matters of mind and heart. However, Vancouver was little different in essentials from any city of the Canadian west at a similar stage of development. The typical British Columbian from the Victoria of 1930, say, would probably claim that the capital had cultural advantages just because of the presence of its permanent civil service. On the other hand, even the interior of British Columbia could make cultural claims. The Okanagan, a valley 250 kilometres east of Vancouver, was

often argued to be a hotbed of art and music unaffected by the boom-and-bust miseries of the city. See Jean Barman, *Growing Up British in British Columbia: Boys in Private School* (Vancouver: UBC Press, 1984), for a discussion of this point. When Jean Coulthard retired from full-time work at UBC, she founded an annual Composers' Music Festival, and significantly, she chose to do this in a tiny Okanagan town.

13 Maria Tippett, *Emily Carr: A Biography* (Toronto: Oxford University Press, 1979); Paula Blanchard, *The Life of Emily Carr* (Vancouver: Douglas & McIntyre, 1987); and Doris Shadbolt, *The Art of Emily Carr* (Toronto: Clarke, Irwin/ Douglas & McIntyre, 1979).

14 Bryan N.S. Gooch, 'Gideon Hicks,' in Kallmann, Winter, and Potvin, *Encyclopaedia of Music in Canada*, 604.

15 Quoted in Jean Barman, *The West beyond the West: A History of British Columbia* (Toronto: University of Toronto Press, 1991), 245.

16 UBCA, Congregation Files, Honorary Doctorates, Speeches, and Talks, Jean Coulthard, LL.D., June 1988, 'This Splendid University,' Speech to the Annual Congregation of the University of British Columbia (4 pages ms.). Coulthard recounted her few months as a student at UBC in 1925.

17 The Canadian Music Centre is a 'non-profit, non-governmental library and information centre for the dissemination and promotion of Canadian concert, operatic, educational, and church music. It was founded 1 January 1959 by the Canadian Music Council with grants from the recently formed Canada Council and CAPAC [Composers, Authors and Publishers Association of Canada Limited],' according to Patricia Shand's article on the centre, in Kallmann, Winter, and Potvin, *Encyclopaedia of Music in Canada*, 204. The CMC has offices in Montreal, Toronto, Calgary, and Vancouver. Among its services, it provides a circulating library of all scores written by everyone named an associate composer of the centre. Its recordings and educational publications are well known in musical circles in North America and abroad. Coulthard has been an associate of the CMC from its beginnings.

18 Interview, Jane Adams and William Bruneau, West Vancouver, 6 December 1993. It is a matter of more than passing interest that Coulthard used her steady UBC income to travel regularly to Europe, to buy clothes that satisfied her 'artist's passion for clarity and straightforward grace,' and to retain nanny-cooks who usually 'lived in,' between 1947 and 1975. Her husband paid for daughter Janey's elementary, secondary, and art-school education, largely in private institutions on both sides of the Atlantic. See UBCA, Coulthard Papers, box 4-20, Jean Coulthard, '[Auto]biographical Sketches I–VI' (manuscript), 1–6.

19 See David Duke, 'The Orchestral Music of Jean Coulthard: A Critical Assess-

ment' (unpublished PhD thesis, University of Victoria, Victoria, 1993),
13–17.

20 Glenn Colton, 'The Piano Music of Jean Coulthard' (unpublished PhD thesis,
University of Victoria, 1996), 2–3.

21 There is, of course, a curious irony in Coulthard's later life as composer and
artist, that is, that her 'retirement' has been at least as creative as any other
period in her life.

22 D.R. Leader, *A History of the University of Cambridge*, vol. 1, *The University to 1546*
(Cambridge: Cambridge University Press, 1991).

23 H.T. Logan, *Tuum Est: A History of the University of British Columbia* (Vancouver:
University of British Columbia, 1958), 199.

24 On the newer professions at UBC, see Lee Stewart's helpful *'It's Up to You':
Women at UBC in the Early Years* (Vancouver: University of British Columbia
Press, 1990), esp. chap. 3, 'In the Back Door: Nursing at UBC,' 31–42, and
chap. 4, 'The Proper and Logical Study for Womankind: Home Economics at
UBC,' 43–65. A lengthy narrative of nursing education at UBC is G. Zilm and
E. Warbinek, *Legacy: History of Nursing Education at the University of British Colum-
bia, 1919–1994* (Vancouver: University of British Columbia School of Nursing,
1994). For a far more explanatory treatment of women in the professions,
including university and school teaching, see Alison Prentice and Marjorie
R. Theobold, eds., *Women Who Taught: Perspectives on the History of Women and
Teaching* (Toronto: University of Toronto Press, 1991); and Mary Kinnear, *In
Subordination: Professional Women, 1870–1970* (Montreal and Kingston: McGill-
Queen's University Press, 1995).

25 P.B. Waite, *Lord of Point Grey: Larry Mackenzie of U.B.C.* (Vancouver: University
of British Columbia Press, 1987), 142, 164.

26 Harry Adaskin, *A Fiddler's World: Memoirs to 1938* (Vancouver: November
House, 1977); and G. Lazarevich, *The Musical World of Frances James and Murray
Adaskin* (Toronto: University of Toronto Press, 1988), 24–5.

27 Harry Adaskin, *A Fiddler's Choice: Memoirs 1938 to 1980* (Vancouver: November
House, 1982), 63–4.

28 Adaskin's attitude to musical theory would have been completely out of place
in the late 1960s and 1970s. By that time the 'great powers' of the North American academic community, especially musicologists active in the American
Musicological Society, had given music theory a high and powerful place in
the university. In terms of budget and political influence, it came behind only
ethnomusicology in the largest music departments of the continent. Well back
from those two fields one might find some hardy proponents of serious practical study (and this would include those who accepted the idea of a doctorate
in musical arts, that is, a practical doctorate in such areas as piano playing,

organ music, and so on). And finally, bringing up the rear, were those who still thought that music appreciation deserved a place in the academic community. Adaskin's resignation from the headship in 1962 was, in brief, a timely one.

29 See C.C. Hill, *John Vanderpant* (Ottawa: National Gallery of Canada, 1979), on the 'better' families, whose photographs Vanderpant routinely took; see also Michael Kluckner, *M[ary] I[sabella] Rogers, 1869–1965* (Vancouver: Author, 1987), on the doyenne of Vancouver society before 1950; Bruce Macdonald, *Vancouver: A Visual History* (Vancouver: Talonbooks, 1992); and R.A.J. McDonald and J. Barman, eds., *Vancouver Past: Essays in Social History* (Vancouver: University of British Columbia Press, 1986).

30 UBCA, Coulthard Papers, box 1, file 2, Don Adams, Vancouver, to Arthur Benjamin, London, 29 July 1947. Benjamin was an Australian conductor and composer who spent the war years in Vancouver, helping Coulthard to learn basic symphonic composition while there, and then in 1946 moved on to a successful career in London, England. Adams was writing to persuade Benjamin to press the case for the publication of Jean Coulthard's music by an English firm, Boosey and Hawkes.

31 Adaskin, *A Fiddler's Choice*, 64.

32 S.E. Eastman and T.J. McGee, *Barbara Pentland* (Toronto: University of Toronto Press, 1963), 58, 82.

33 The *Directory of Music Faculties in Colleges and Universities in the U.S. and Canada, 1994–1995* (Missoula, Mont.: CMS Publications, 1995) shows that in 1994–5 women accounted for an average of 4.5 per cent of all regular, permanent appointments in music at the University of Southern California, Indiana University, Yale University, the Curtis Institute, the New England Conservatory, the Juilliard School of Music, and the Mannes School of Music, seven of the ten most-reputed institutions of advanced musical education in the United States.

34 Eastman and McGee, *Barbara Pentland*, 81–2.

35 Adaskin, *A Fiddler's Choice*, 54–5, 63–8.

36 Evidence for Adaskin's attempted removal of Coulthard comes from interviews by Bruneau with Coulthard, Vancouver, 14 September 1994; and from the personnel record card for Jean Coulthard-Adams, in UBCA, Personnel Records Archive. Documents on the curricular history of the Department of Music are to be found in UBCA, Department of Music Fonds, files 2–4.

37 The biographical essentials for these composers and former Coulthard students are to be found in Kalmann, Winter, and Potvin, *Encyclopedia of Music in Canada,* or in individual biographical data sheets available through the Canadian Music Centre, Toronto.

38 The Royal Society of Canada offered research and sabbatical grants to
    Canadian university faculty members in the mid-1950s, using funds pro-
    vided by the repayment of French and British war debts to the Canadian
    government. For a record of these and Coulthard's numerous grants and
    prizes, see UBCA, Board of Governors Fonds, box 2, s.v. Coulthard, f. 2.
    From 1 July 1949 Coulthard's salary was $2,000 per annum, and in 1955,
    $3,400 per annum. Harry Adaskin made $5,000 in 1947 and $6,900 in
    1955. The official calendar of UBC shows that he had no formal academic
    qualifications.

39 See, for example, George Proctor, *Canadian Music of the Twentieth Century*
    (Toronto: University of Toronto Press, 1980), 48: 'The neoclassical works
    include ... [Coulthard's *Two Songs of the Haida Indians*]. Coulthard also uses
    parallel fifths to capture the essence of native poetry ... In addition, folk-like
    melodies and romantic expressiveness find their way into these songs,
    features no doubt *derived from one of her teachers, Vaughan Williams* [emphasis
    added].'

40 A. Walter, 'Growth of Music Education,' in Walter, ed., *Aspects of Music in
    Canada* (Toronto: University of Toronto Press, 1969), 247–87. See also the
    unsigned article on 'Universities' in Kallmann, Winter, and Potvin, *Encyclopae-
    dia of Music in Canada*, 1337–8.

41 Of forty-two regular, full-time academic appointments to the UBC Depart-
    ment of Music in 1946–73, no less than 82 per cent were either American-born
    or predominantly American-trained (that is, with graduate degrees taken at
    American institutions).

42 Consider, for example, her *Birds of Lansdowne* for violin, cello, piano, and pre-
    pared tape, commissioned by the CBC and first performed at the Shawnigan
    Festival near Victoria, BC, in 1972.

43 In 1969, the list included the Second String Quartet ('Threnody'), a
    revision of an earlier work; the *Pines of Emily Carr* (for alto, narrator, string
    quartet, piano, and timpani; libretto adapted from the journals of Emily
    Carr); and a Lyric Sonatina for bassoon and piano. All this work came out
    in a year during which Coulthard spent two solid months in Europe, taught
    two academic terms, and continued to develop a theory of composition,
    teaching at the same time as she arrived at a new and sharper view of
    musical form.

44 This and other central works are offered in the six long-playing records
    Anthology of Canadian Music 10: Jean Coulthard (Vancouver and Montreal:
    Radio Canada International, 1982).

45 M. Short, *Gustav Holst: The Man and His Music* (Oxford: Oxford University
    Press, 1990), esp. chaps. 2–3.

46 A teaching-evaluation form for a Coulthard course has survived from the winter of 1968–9 in the private papers of a former student, David Duke. It places Coulthard at 'less than average' as a classroom instructor, yet as 'kind and considerate of individuals.' She was characterized by students, in a number of anecdotal remarks, as 'fairly conservative but certainly competent.' I thank Dr Duke for providing me with a copy of this document.

PART II:

MULTIPLE REFLECTIONS

Three Women in Physics

ALISON PRENTICE

In the late 1930s Elizabeth Laird, Elizabeth Allin, and Allie Vibert Douglas appeared to be on rather different paths. Laird, a graduate in maths and physics from the University of Toronto in 1896, was relinquishing her role as head of a thriving physics department at the well-known Massachusetts college for women Mount Holyoke. She was now heading back to Canada and her home town of London, Ontario, where she would carry on her research in the physics labs of the University of Western Ontario. Allin, a Toronto maths and physics graduate of 1926 who had taught at Toronto since the completion of her doctorate in 1931, was still on an annually renewable lectureship, as were two others of the half-dozen women who taught physics regularly or irregularly at the University of Toronto in the 1930s. But by 1941 the three women lecturers would be promoted to assistant professorships, undoubtedly in recognition of their long service but also perhaps because their contribution was doubly valued when the Second World War depleted the ranks of the men. Douglas, who had been born in Montreal two years before Laird graduated from Toronto, was also in transition. She had studied at Cambridge's famous Cavendish Laboratory after her McGill University bachelor's and master's degrees, but had returned to Montreal and McGill to complete her doctorate in 1926 and teach in that university's physics department. Now she was moving to Queen's University in Kingston, Ontario, where she would combine teaching and writing in her preferred subject of astrophysics with her new role as dean of women.

What Laird, Allin, and Douglas had in common was not only physics, but the fact that they had aspired to university teaching and research careers in the field during what one commentator has described as the 'heroic age of atomic physics.'[1] Reviewing Ruth Lewin Sime's fascinating biography of Lise Meitner, M.F. Perutz suggests that this era began with Marie and Pierre Curie's discovery of radioactivity in 1896 and ended with the discovery of atomic fission, by Meitner and others, in 1938. The three Canadian women thus started their careers in a period not only of great excitement in physics but one in which some women played leading roles in a discipline that is now seen as among the most hostile to female participation.[2] All three were captivated by and sought graduate degrees in the field. But of the three, only Elizabeth Allin achieved a lifetime career in experimental physics in a Canadian university setting. Despite her obvious talents, Elizabeth Laird was among the many early-twentieth-century Canadian women who could become academics only by migrating to the United States. For Douglas, a Canadian career unfolded, but not in her chosen subject of nuclear physics. Instead, she moved first into the related field of astrophysics and ultimately into university administration.

What can the stories of these three individuals tell us about gender and physics in the academy during the first generations of women's presence in Canadian university faculties? At one level, it is true that individual stories can be suggestive only. Although biography has been a favourite genre in the history of science, critics have rightly pointed out that focusing on the stars has woefully obscured the efforts of vital supporting casts in all fields of scientific endeavour. Dwelling on the excitement of 'discovery,' moreover, has obscured the fact that successful science involves long periods of steady work – not just inspiration and genius.[3] Yet as Farley Kelly has argued for Australia, there is nevertheless a case to be made for biographical studies of women scientists. For one thing, it seems useful to balance a record biased by countless biographies of men; for another, we need women's stories as well as men's if we hope to develop a full picture of how science works.[4] I would add that we also need biographies of women in physics to understand how their careers were similar to, or differed from, those of other women scholars of their time and place. Was there anything special about the way in which early-twentieth-century women became involved in physics, compared to women in other academic disciplines?[5]

In his study of physics in Canada, Yves Gingras has explored changes in the meaning of the identity 'physicist,' noting first an emphasis on the individual researcher and later the emergence of a community of researchers. The development of graduate programs and the founding of the National Research Council and the Canadian Association of Physicists (originally the Canadian Association of Professional Physicists) between 1900 and 1960 were essential, he argues, to the ability of Canadian physicists to see themselves as a social group. They needed to create institutions around their sense of community, moreover, before Canadian research could really take off in the field.[6] Another way to look at women physicists, then, might be to query their membership in this social group: to what extent were they fully admitted to and seen to be part of the community 'Canadian physicists'?

The exploration that follows cannot provide full answers to these questions; nor does it cover all of Canada. It aims, rather, to put forward some tentative answers by looking at the careers of three women whose first degrees were taken at Toronto and McGill between the years 1896 and 1926. By focusing on three leading female physics graduates of these universities, I hope as well to demonstrate that women were deeply involved in university physics almost from its beginnings in Canada. A case might even be made that the development of the field depended quite heavily, during the important formative years of the early twentieth century, on women scientists' work.

The First Generation

Elizabeth Rebecca Laird stands almost alone in what we might characterize as the first generation of Canadian women in physics. Born in Owen Sound in 1874, she was one of four children. Elizabeth and her sister Annie were both interested in science and were mentored by a brother, George, who was already making a scientific career (at Brandon College) by the time Elizabeth was beginning to think about hers. After graduating from London Collegiate Institute, Lizzie and Annie (as they always called each other) made their way to the University of Toronto, where Lizzie enrolled in maths and physics and Annie took chemistry. Annie Laird's future was to be in the Faculty of Household Science at Toronto, eventually as professor and dean, until her death in 1939. For Elizabeth, who wanted to be a physicist, no such alternative route presented itself. Nor was her access to graduate study in physics assured. Despite coming first in her class three years in a row, the prestigious 1851 Exhibition Scholarship, which entitled the top graduate to funding for advanced study abroad, was awarded to the man who came second. As a *London Free Press* article about her career put it in 1967, this injustice occurred because Laird was a 'she' and not a 'he' and the terms of the scholarship specified the latter. Undoubtedly disappointed, Elizabeth Laird obtained a teach-

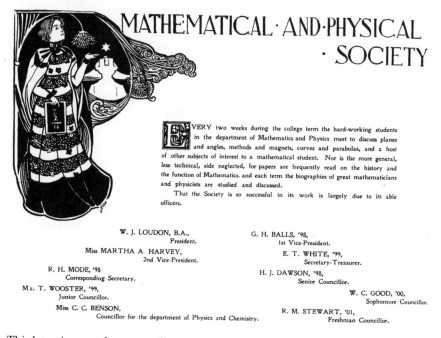

MATHEMATICAL · AND·PHYSICAL · SOCIETY

VERY two weeks during the college term the hard-working students in the department of Mathematics and Physics meet to discuss planes and angles, methods and magnets, curves and parabolas, and a host of other subjects of interest to a mathematical student. Nor is the more general, less technical, side neglected, for papers are frequently read on the history and the function of Mathematics, and each term the biographies of great mathematicians and physicists are studied and discussed.

That the Society is so successful in its work is largely due to its able officers.

W. J. LOUDON, B.A.,
President.

Miss MARTHA A. HARVEY,
2nd Vice-President.

R. H. MODE, '98,
Corresponding Secretary.

Miss T. WOOSTER, '99,
Junior Councillor.

Miss C. C. BENSON,
Councillor for the department of Physics and Chemistry.

G. H. BALLS, '98,
1st Vice-President.

E. T. WHITE, '99,
Secretary-Treasurer.

H. J. DAWSON, '98,
Senior Councillor.

W. C. GOOD, '00,
Sophomore Councillor.

R. M. STEWART, '01,
Freshman Councillor.

This late-nineteenth-century illustration suggests ambiguity about the presence of women in mathematics and physics, but there were in fact three women on the executive of the University of Toronto's Mathematical and Physical Society in 1898: Miss Harvey, Miss Wooster, and Miss Benson.

ing position at the Ontario Ladies' College in Whitby and began exploring other options.[7]

The one chosen was graduate work at Bryn Mawr, the American college for women that was not only working hard to achieve the same status as the top colleges for men but could give Laird the European fellowship denied her at Toronto. Fortunately, Laird's letters to her family about her time at Bryn Mawr and in Europe survive. Written chiefly to her sister Annie, these letters reveal much about one Canadian woman physicist's induction into her profession.[8]

The first thing that emerges from this correspondence is that, even with a fellowship, the decision to study abroad – let alone the planning of such an enterprise – was far from easy. Laird's father had died in 1897. By March the following year, when she was trying to make up her mind about the European fellowship, there was the care of her handicapped brother, James, to consider, as well as the future of Annie, who was currently looking after him. Elizabeth worried about claiming an unfair portion of the family's resources. She also wanted her sister and older brother to be involved in the decision. 'Now as to my plans – tell me what you really think – shall I plan to go or stay?' she asked her sister. 'I do not want to shirk my share.'[9]

Earlier there had been some anxiety about whether she even deserved the fellowship. In contrast to her feelings about the Toronto competition, when she had been confident of her right to the scholarship that had gone to another, she now expressed doubts. She was having 'strange experiences' and was unsure if she were 'glad or sorry.' Moreover, there was the problem of deciding where to go. As she pointed out in one letter, there were two good Swiss universities that accepted women as graduate students and Glasgow University in Scotland. Cambridge was also a possibility, but was too expensive. Laird was in communication with her former mentor at the University of Toronto as well as with her adviser at Bryn Mawr, and the former had mentioned 'a couple of places that seem to him best,' but he would not say 'directly' which would really be best for *her*. She was anxious to know what her brother George thought.[10]

Elizabeth Laird's earlier letters from Bryn Mawr had conveyed much more self-assurance. Indeed, so confident was she in her knowledge that she felt she had to put on an act in order not to insult a professor whose ideas about her work seemed absurd. 'He offers such impossible explanations I have to look grave as if I believed what he said.' In fact, she knew 'far more' about her experiment than he did. Laird was also quite confident in her ability to estimate the amount of reading that she should do for each of her instructors. She was focusing on the references that interested her, and some lectures did not seem to require any extra reading. At the same time, as she put it to Annie, 'Bryn Mawr exams ... cover the ground more fully than Toronto ones.'[11]

How Laird finally made her decision to go to Berlin is not clear. What is apparent is that she went well before the beginning of the fall term, in order to work on her German and perhaps so that George could accompany her. Her first letter to Annie from Berlin was written after his departure on 3 August 1898 and dealt both with their adventures on the journey and with her continuing search for a place to live. She noted that the flats were very different from Toronto ones and that she was trying for ground-floor accomodation within walking distance of the university.[12]

It was the end of September before Laird presented herself to the professor with whom she hoped to work. She called on him at his home.

'Screwed up courage and made bow before the Herr Professor Warburg. He was a little gruff at first, asked where I came from and called Canada a "province of England" much to my amusement.' Warburg warmed up when he discovered that Laird had considerable background in experimental work; the next task was to find an experiment for her, a problem that took much of October to solve. By November Laird had her own room at the lab, the occasional assistance of a lab 'servant,' and an experiment that was well under way, although it never seemed to work as well as she wanted it to.[13]

During this period Elizabeth was also attending lectures and colloquia at the university. In some classes she was often the only woman, but found this situation much less stressful than it had been at Toronto. There she had been forced to sit in the front row and be stared at 'by all the men' behind her. At Berlin she could sit anywhere, and she chose the middle of the lecture hall, where she felt much more comfortable. Laird also felt at home in the Berlin physics colloquia. When she looked back on the first one, for the benefit of her sister, the single problem she had to report was the bad air. 'Only the smoke! It seemed as if half the people smoked cigars.' She followed up with the information that at least Professor (Max) Planck was not among the smokers. She also commented on the liveliness of the colloquia, which she felt were quite different from the 'silent seminaries or journal meetings' that she had endured at Bryn Mawr.[14]

There was also a social scene to negotiate, and by early November Laird had begun to meet other students. By January she had been invited to attend a women's student-union meeting. Only twenty were present, but there was much excitement over the agenda; it reminded her of the 'Women's Lity [Literary] meetings' at the University of Toronto.

Still, social life was not the main focus for Laird, whose major goal was to learn more physics and successfully complete her experiment. At one stage, her efforts with respect to the latter involved learning how to blow glass, in order to get better tubing for her apparatus; at another point, she considered abandoning experimental work altogether and switching to a theoretical problem under the supervision of Max Planck. Finally, she negotiated with Warburg for a new experiment. Once again, Laird demonstrated considerable confidence in her own ability. By spring, in fact, she was so keen on Berlin that she contemplated staying to complete her doctorate, not realizing that the terms of her fellowship precluded such a transfer. She soon returned to the United States and a special fellowship at Bryn Mawr, where she conducted further experimental work for the PhD granted her in 1901.

Elizabeth Laird's willingness to move south of the border paid off. It is not clear if she attempted to find a job in Canada following the completion of her doctorate, but very soon she was one of three instructors in physics at Mount Holyoke College, and only a few years later the head of her department, a position she held until her retirement in the late 1930s. By then, the Mount Holyoke physics department could boast four faculty members, in addition to one 'trained mechanician' and a well-equipped laboratory.[15] Laird did not retire from experimental work when she left Massachusetts and headed home to Ontario, for very soon after her return to Canada, she embarked on a second, unpaid research career in the physics laboratories of the University of Western Ontario, work that she continued until 1953.

Although Elizabeth Laird appears to have been the first Canadian woman physicist of her era to make a lifetime career as a research-oriented academic, M.F. and G.W. Rayner-Canham's studies have revealed that she was not the only one to attempt to do so. McGill's Harriet Brooks, whose MA work there between 1898 and 1901 with Ernest Rutherford and subsequent research made important contributions to early-twentieth-century studies in radioactivity, eventually became convinced in her own mind that marriage and a career in physics could not be combined, and she abandoned the field when she married another scientist in 1907.[16] In the meantime, women were entering graduate study at the University of Toronto, and in 1913 Vivian Ellsworth Pound became the fourth candidate and first woman to complete a PhD in physics at that university.[17] After five years' lecturing at Queen's University (and a brief period in business) Pound, like Laird, found employment in the United States. She took a mathematics job at Buffalo, where she was eventually promoted to full professor and retired in 1955.[18]

The Second Generation

If Elizabeth Laird and her contemporaries either dropped out of physics or took up work south of the border, the next generation of women graduates began to be more visible in Canadian physics. When Elizabeth Allin studied physics at the University of Toronto in the 1920s and early 1930s, she was accompanied by five other women who also earned doctorates in the field. In order of the granting of their doctoral degrees, these were Mattie Levi Rotenberg, Elizabeth Cohen, Beatrice Reid Deacon, Florence Quinlan, and May Annetts Smith. That these six women, plus Vivian Pound, constituted nearly one-quarter of all students who earned physics

PhDs at Toronto during the first third of the twentieth century[19] is significant for two reasons. It reveals, first, how small the Canadian research community in physics still was. Second, it suggests the opportunities that appeared to be opening, in the inter-war years, to women interested in making careers in the field in Canada. But appearances were deceptive. As Margaret Rossiter has shown for the United States,[20] apparent encouragement of women in science did not translate into equality of opportunity.

The careers of three of the inter-war Toronto women physicists were undoubtedly complicated by their marriages. Although the marriage bar was perhaps a little less debilitating for these women than it had been when Harriet Brooks contemplated combining physics and marriage, most people still believed that women had to make a choice. Two of Toronto's women PhDs (Rotenberg and Deacon) nevertheless married before the granting of their doctorates; one (Smith) married soon after. One of the married women, Mattie Rotenberg, probably experienced additional prejudice because she was Jewish, a fact that may also have affected Elizabeth Cohen's career. Only two of the six women, Elizabeth Allin and Florence Quinlan, were able to secure what eventually became stable jobs teaching physics at the University of Toronto. Cohen, Rotenberg, and Deacon would also teach there for several decades, but only sporadically.[21] Quinlan took her doctorate some years after she began teaching physics at Toronto; she specialized in instructing household science and music students and may have had little time for research. For this or other reasons she was never promoted beyond assistant professor. Of the six women PhDs in this inter-war generation, therefore, only Elizabeth Allin was able to carve out a career in physics that involved teaching and research. That she was able to do so was the result of a whole series of factors. Oral-history interviews conducted with Allin in the early 1990s reveal many of these.[22]

To begin with, this daughter of a schoolmaster turned postmaster and merchant had an aunt and uncle who had attended university and were clearly influential in the choices that Allin made. Second, she loved mathematics as a young woman and, unlike her sisters, chose to go on to high school and university; here she turned to physics rather than mathematics because she wanted to be involved in the more practical of the two fields. In contrast to the situation faced by Elizabeth Laird, there were scholarships to support her studies and a lively crowd of graduate students, both male and female, accompanying her. Allin completed her Toronto doctorate in 1931, but soon won a fellowship year at Cambridge

Back Row: J. K. West *(3rd Year Rep.)*, Miss H. G. Gordanier *(1st Year Rep.)*, C. L. Bates *(1st Year Rep.)*, Miss A. Keast *(Rec. Sec'y)*, H. G. L. Watson *(4th Year Rep.)*, Miss W. D. Woolcombe *(2nd Year Rep.)*, J. C. Archibald *(Treas.)*.

Front Row: Miss E. J. Allin *(Cor. Sec'y)*, W. G. Macarthur *(Pres.)*, J. Satterly D.Sc. *(Hon. Pres.)*, A. R. Turnbull *(Vice-Pres.)*, Miss E. Cohen, B.A. *(Grad. Rep.)*

By 1926 the Toronto Mathematical and Physical Society could boast almost equal numbers of women and men on its executive. Elizabeth Allin (front row, left) was corresponding secretary; Elizabeth Cohen (front row, right) was graduate representative.

in 1933–4, where she encountered such luminaries as Ernest Rutherford, Max Born, and Marie Curie. Returning to Toronto to teach in a small department of some five or six professors, Allin survived the forced retirements that many women instructors, especially those who were married, suffered during the Great Depression. She even inched her way up from assistant demonstrator to lecturer, finally entering the professorial ranks in 1941, when her colleagues Florence Quinlan and another woman instructor with a master's degree, Kathleen Crossley, were also promoted to assistant professor. The war brought increased teaching and no time or money for non-military research, but at least some recognition and job security. As she later remembered it, the three new women assistant professors felt very lucky.[23]

It was only after the war that Allin was able to get back to her research in atomic spectroscopy. This work gave her a claim to membership in the growing Canadian physics community, but equally important was her active participation in the founding of the Canadian Association of Professional Physicists, which, Gingras suggests, was so central to the development of physics in Canada.[24] Allin was not only involved in the establishment of this national organization, but was proud to have been one of its first secretaries.

By the 1950s, however, a shift was becoming apparent which would alter Elizabeth Allin's situation dramatically, moving her from the centre of her disciplinary community to a more marginal position. Surrounded by other women physicists when she began her studies at Toronto and during her years of graduate work and early teaching, she was increasingly alone as a woman in her field. Florence Quinlan, who was considerably older than Allin, retired. Kathleen Crossley had no doctorate and could not hope to move up the ranks. Elizabeth Cohen, Mattie Rotenberg, and Beatrice Reid Deacon were sessional employees, only Cohen being able to achieve some sort of ongoing presence. Allin did have male friends; she also had women friends in other departments of the university. At some point she formed a lifelong domestic partnership with the botany professor Dorothy Forward. But there were no other women colleagues moving through the ranks in physics. Nor, during the 1940s, 1950s, and 1960s at least, were there many younger women coming along in her field.

It was Allin's friend Dorothy Forward who, in an interview conducted in 1974,[25] captured something of what it felt like to be an older woman scientist at Toronto during and after the post-war expansions. Forward attributed her feelings of alienation to the rapidly growing numbers of younger faculty members and the resulting generational conflict, saying nothing about gender. But she made it clear that things had changed for the worse.

Another Track

While both Elizabeth Laird and Elizabeth Allin made physics the focus of their entire university careers, Allie Vibert Douglas eventually abandoned the field. In her retirement, Douglas penned a family memoir that provides some fascinating details about her education and about this decision.[26] One of two orphaned children who had been raised by their maternal grandmother and two unmarried aunts, she was excluded as a young woman from some of the intellectual excitements that her brother, George, was able to enjoy, but their orphaned status made for close family ties by the time both were students at McGill University. Indeed, so strong were these ties that, shortly after grandmother Douglas died and George had signed up for war service in 1914, Allie too left her studies and, with the aunts, set up a household in England where her brother could join them when on leave. Finances were a concern, so Douglas put her mathematical skills to work at the British War Office, becoming 'head of the women clerks' in the Recruiting Branch, a demanding job that she held for the duration of the war. It was followed by a stint as registrar for the Khaki University, the institution set up in England for Canadian soldiers awaiting demobilization, before she returned to McGill to complete her bachelor's and acquire a master's degree in 1921. By the fall of that year Douglas was back in England for doctoral studies at Cambridge.[27] Once again, her aunts and later on her brother, who was doing graduate work in geology and engineering, were her companions.

It was at Cambridge that Douglas experienced the first major doubts about her proposed career in physics. Recalling these years, she juxtaposed a comment about women's anomalous status at this prestigious university and a statement about her lagging enthusiasm for her chosen field. As she noted, 'no woman could hold a Cambridge degree' despite the fact that 'she could acquire all the academic and resident requirements.' Douglas then went on to describe the concerns that she had developed about continuing her doctorate at Cambridge. 'As the months passed ... I became more aware of my own limitations and more doubtful that I would ever make myself into a research physicist.' Finally, she decided 'to forget the Cambridge Ph.D' and instead 'take full advantage of the rich offerings for widening one's horizon of interest' that the university offered.

Douglas's strength in, and possible preference for, the mathematical, rather than the experimental, side of physics may have been one reason for this decision. But her description of the explosive atmosphere in physics at Cambridge in the early 1920s suggests other possible causes. An argument that developed between the astrophysicist A.S. Eddington and the nuclear physicist Ernest Rutherford evoked metaphors of warfare. Eddington had been invited 'to expound his theory of electron capture in stars which led to a value for the opacity that differed from that found in laboratory discharge tubes.' This theory first provoked a 'lively' discussion, 'for the physicists were critical, maintaining that the opacity factor should not differ in the stellar gasses from that found in the laboratory.' Eventually 'Rutherford, like a mighty giant lusting for battle, entered the fray to deliver the final crushing blow. But Eddington's rapier met Rutherford's broadsword and neither gave an inch.'

In the end, Douglas felt that she had to choose between the two, and her choice fell on Eddington and astrophysics – but not before an aggressive new student had taken the wind out of her sails in physics. Determined and demanding, this young man pestered the authorities for 'none but the very best' laboratory equipment and got it. In a matter of months, he had solved the experimental problem that Douglas had been working on, using a method different from the one Rutherford had suggested to her. According to her recollections, it was at this point that Douglas decided that she was 'on the road to nowhere' and that neither her heart nor her talent lay in physics. Moreover, she had already been lured into a course in practical astronomy. Soon she made a complete shift to astrophysics, although the transition was not without strain. She remembered 'her nervous lack of self assurance' and Eddington's 'intense reserve.' Eventually, however, a research problem that aroused her curiosity also interested him; it ultimately led to the project which she completed for her McGill PhD.

Allie Vibert Douglas said little in her memoir about the social round at Cambridge. Cecilia Payne, who is mentioned several times, was a fellow student at Newnham College; as Cecilia Payne-Krapotkin she would later become a leading figure in astrophysics at Harvard. But Douglas's connection to Newnham and the other women scholars there was probably tenuous. Her major support in Cambridge remained her family, with whom she continued to live: one surviving aunt (the other died during the Cambridge period) and her brother, George.

In her memoir Douglas has little further to say about her career after the description of her move into astrophysics. We learn nothing about her final days at Cambridge or her transition to McGill. We must consult other sources[28] to discover that she conducted her research for the doctoral degree at Yerkes Observatory in the United States and that, after its completion in 1926, she continued to work for McGill, teaching both physics and astrophysics, always at the rank of lecturer. There must have been some dissatisfaction with this role or a wish to move on, for the late 1930s brought, first, an attempt to win the wardenship of McGill's residence for women, Royal Victoria College, and then a successful application for the deanship of women at Queen's University. From 1939 on, Douglas remained involved in astronomical societies, but devoted much of her intellectual energy to popular scientific writing and a biography of her Cambridge mentor, Arthur Eddington.[29] She combined these activities with work for women through the International Federation of University Women but especially as dean of women at Queen's.

Conclusion

The moves that Douglas made, first from physics to astrophysics but more importantly from a research-oriented career to one increasingly concerned with education and the promotion of women's interests in higher education, are suggestive. Were things tougher for a woman scientist at McGill in the 1930s than they were at Toronto? Or did Douglas foresee the changes that would eventually overtake Elizabeth Allin and her female colleagues at the latter institution? There is no doubt that the Second World War brought huge shifts that would affect women in physics. Evidence for these shifts is Elizabeth Allin's own history of her department, a text that devoted a passage to the inter-war women who earned doctorates in the field but had nothing to say about women's achievements in any subsequent period.[30] Certainly, women's share of Toronto PhDs in physics dropped radically after the mid-1930s. And as the physics department expanded following the war, the proportion of women on faculty dramatically declined. After Allin retired in 1972, there was no woman in a physics professoriate that had doubled in size several times since she had joined it.[31]

My sense of these transitions is that women were seen as worthy students and assistants in physics when research was just beginning in Canada and departments were small. There was so much exciting work to be done; by the 1920s and 1930s the National Research Council was provid-

Back Row: S. H. Standen, A. Douglas, K. McLeod, A. Morrisson, Wes. Fisher, B. Stannard, C. Penner, R. Pattison. Middle Row: G. Milne, L. Mundie, G. Thiessen, R. Sutton, T. Fox, R. Anderson, R. Fournier, K. Barnard, T. Stewart. Front Row: Dr. R. N. H. Haslam, Dr. E. L. Harrington, Dr. L. Herzberg, Dr. C. A. MacKay, Dr. G. Herzberg, Dr. B. W. Currie.

This photograph of the members of the University of Saskatchewan Physical Society in 1937 is suggestive of changes that would be even more pronounced by the post-war decades. Dr L. Herzberg is given prominence of place, but it could not be more obvious that she is the sole woman surrounded by many men.

ing funding; and helpers, even of the 'other sex,' were more than welcome. As physics grew and became more competitive with the advent of 'big science,' however, young men were increasingly attracted to the field, and women were either less welcome or simply massively outnumbered. As Margaret Rossiter suggests for the United States,[32] it would take a new, younger generation, the inheritors of feminist struggles for equality in the academy, to begin the pressure for more women in university physics.

If we look back at the careers of Elizabeth Laird, Elizabeth Allin, and Allie Vibert Douglas, we can see that all three faced obstacles because of their gender. For Laird these were straightforward: a Canadian woman of her generation, no matter how brilliant or how highly motivated, was forced to leave Canada if she wished to make a career in academic physics. For Douglas, opportunities opened up as the field developed. Her mentors were sufficiently impressed with her talents to see that she got to study with leading physicists in the English-speaking world. But her studies at Cambridge proved discouraging, and her interests shifted. Either because she then seemed to be on the margins of Canada's research agenda, or because it was impossible to promote any woman during the Great Depression, her career stagnated in the 1930s. In her middle forties Douglas shifted once again to focus on education, popular writing, and advocacy for women scholars. Of our three scientists, only Allin was able to achieve a career as an academic physicist in Canada. Yet even she was blocked during the decade when she was excluded from the professoriate. Nor were promotions after 1941 very swift in a career that was also limited by the heavy teaching loads of the 1940s and 1950s.

Laird, Douglas, and Allin were constrained in part by the general state of Canadian physics. At the turn of the century the only scholarship for graduate study abroad was British, and it was not available to women. When National Research Council fellowships were created in Canada in 1917, women appear to have been encouraged to compete for them and earn doctorates in physics. But as the physics community developed, it also created boundaries. Physicists referred to each other as 'men.' As one Canadian Association of Physicists brochure designed to alert bright high school students to the opportunities in physics saw it, the budding young physicist was not only a male, but a male who was narrowly focused to the point of obsession. 'Does he like to stay in the laboratory for weeks or years, realizing that his piece of experimental apparatus contains as many mysteries as the whole universe? Does he lose interest in an activity that becomes routine, and always want to be doing something new pushing into unexplored regions of knowledge? ... then he may well have been born a physicist.'[33] University men also expressed their reservations concerning women and physics. As Professor John Satterly of Toronto explained to the historian Frank Underhill regarding the latter's promising daughter, Betty, in 1943, even the brightest young woman might not want to put in the long years required for a doctorate. Teaching or marriage was probably on the horizon. And 'of course Father & Mother Underhill will want their girl to be happily married – She herself may want to also.' Would it be 'worthwhile slaving at Maths. Phys. & Chemistry' if all that labour were 'to be put on one side on entering the domestic life?' Of course, it wouldn't really be slavery, Satterly concluded; Betty was so bright.[34] There is no record of Betty Underhill's choice once she discovered that she had been the top student in her first-year honours science class.[35] But given such attitudes, it is perhaps not surprising that Elizabeth Allin and her female colleagues had difficulty developing a following of younger women in their field at the University of Toronto during and after the Second World War.[36]

The experiences of Canadian women in physics during the first half of the twentieth century were not unique. For all their brilliance and hard work, even Marie Curie and Lise Meitner were marginalized at certain stages of their careers.[37] Similarly, Canadian women who entered other scholarly fields in this period had to struggle for academic jobs and were excluded from the inner circles of scholarly power. Prior to the Second World War, women historians, for example, typically sought doctoral degrees in England or the United States; many left the country permanently when secure jobs proved virtually impossible to get in Canada. Indeed, things may have been harder for women historians than they were for physicists during the 1920s and 1930s. Douglas at McGill and Allin and her female colleagues at Toronto at least had work in physics; after the mid-1920s women historians, in contrast, were explicitly excluded even from lectureships at these universities, a prohibition that lasted until after the Second World War.[38] In general, there were more university jobs, however temporary or insecure, for women in the sciences than there were in the humanities or social sciences until the expansions following the war, probably because the sciences had more funding for assistantships in both teaching and research.[39]

Yves Gingras has described the controversies that developed following the founding of the Canadian Association of Professional Physicists in the late 1940s, when engineers forced the physicists to drop the word 'professional' from the name of their national society. Apart from legal concerns, promoters of what was to become the Canadian Association of Physicists gradually realized that there was a distinction to be made between the 'profession' and the 'discipline,' for the interests of physicists in industry and academic physicists were not necessarily the same. According to Gingras, entry into the 'discipline' was less restricted than into the 'profession.'[40] Yet it was during these post–Second World War debates over what constituted a physicist that women lost so much ground in the field. One wonders, then, whether the territorial battles between the engineers and the physicists were also a cause for women's declining position in physics. If there were anxieties about the viability of the developing physics research community, gender concerns could only have made matters worse.

Yet, as Rossiter's American research has shown, women were losing ground in all scientific fields during the 1950s and 1960s. Her findings confirm Dorothy Forward's insight that the problem was in part generational. Older women scientists were not respected by their younger male colleagues. But younger women also had trouble. They were not present in the sciences in the first place, were discouraged at some point in their studies, or hit glass ceilings once scientific careers were under way. According to Rossiter, it would take the feminist revolution that emerged from and followed these unfriendly decades to bring about even the small improvement in the climate for women that has occurred.[41]

We need similar explorations of the post-1940 period in Canada, where women continue to experience an especially chilly climate in physics, typically constituting no more than 15 per cent of all doctoral students in the field and an even smaller proportion of faculty.[42] What I hope this brief account of the early careers of Elizabeth Laird, Elizabeth Allin, and Allie Vibert Douglas has demonstrated is the complexity of the connections between historical time, national and institutional context, and personal choice that entered into the gendering of Canadian physics during its formative years. Women were not fully excluded; but neither were they fully integrated into the field. A count of all the women graduate students or former students who worked as research, teaching, and lab assistants or demonstrators at the University of Toronto between 1906 and 1931 produces a number approximately four times that of men who were professors during the same period.[43] From this fact and from the stories of the women physicists described in this paper, we can safely conclude that women's work was a significant factor in the early development of physics in Canada. At the same time, however, there was clearly a powerful bias preventing the advancement of nearly all these women or the addition of new, younger women to their ranks.

When asked how she remembered feeling about the physics department at Toronto when she was a student in the 1920s and early 1930s, Elizabeth Allin said that she and her friends felt so at home there, it was as if they had owned the place.[44] Unfortunately, this sense of total belonging may not have continued, even for Allin. Nor, I think, would many women physicists be likely to make such a claim today.

NOTES

The research for this essay was supported by the Social Sciences and Humanities Research Council of Canada. I owe special thanks to Alyson King, who found much of the documentation for Elizabeth Laird and Allie Vibert Douglas, and I am also grateful to Jim Prentice, Donald Wright, David Zimmerman, and the members of the University of British Columbia History of Education Group for their interest and helpful suggestions.

1 M.F. Perutz, 'A Passion for Science,' *New York Review of Books*, 20 February 1997, reviewing Ruth Lewin Sime, *Lise Meitner: A Life in Physics* (Berkeley: University of California Press, 1997).

2 Stephen G. Brush, 'Women in Physical Science: From Drudges to Discoverers,' *Physics Teacher* 23, 1 (January 1985), and M.R. Rayner-Canham and G.W. Rayner-Canham, 'Pioneer Women in Nuclear Science,' *American Journal of Physics* 58, 11 (November 1990), discuss the early women physicists. On the present-day problems of women in physics in Sweden and Great Britain respectively, see Else-Marie Staberg, 'Gender and Science in the Swedish Compulsory School,' *Gender and Education* 6, 1 (1994): 35–45, and Kim Thomas, *Gender and Subject in Higher Education* (Buckingham, UK: Society for Research into Higher Education and the Open University Press, 1990) and 'Physics, Gender, and Identity,' Paper presented to the workshop 'The Promised Land ... the Gendered Character of Higher Education,' Stockholm, August 1997.

3 On these questions, see Brush, 'Women in Physical Science,' and Carolyn Rasmussen, 'Science Was So Much More Exciting: Six Women in the Physical Sciences,' in Farley Kelly, ed., *On the Edge of Discovery: Australian Women in Science* (Melbourne: The Text Publishing Company, 1993), 107–8.

4 Kelly, *On the Edge of Discovery*, 3.

5 For comparisons and related studies, see Prentice, 'Scholarly Passion: Two Women Who Caught It,' in Alison Prentice and Marjorie R. Theobald, eds., *Women Who Taught: Perspectives on the History of Women and Teaching* (Toronto:

University of Toronto Press, 1991); 'Bluestockings, Feminists, or Women
Workers? A Preliminary Look at Women's Early Employment at the University
of Toronto,' *Journal of the Canadian Historical Association*, new series, 2 (1991);
'The Early History of Women in University Physics: A Toronto Case Study,'
Physics in Canada 52, 2 (March/April 1996); 'Elizabeth Allin: Physicist,' in Els-
peth Cameron and Janice Dickin, eds., *Great Dames* (Toronto: University of
Toronto Press, 1997); and 'Laying Siege to the History Professoriate,' in Bev-
erly Boutilier and Alison Prentice, eds., *Creating Historical Memory: English-
Canadian Women and the Work of History* (Vancouver: University of British
Columbia Press, 1997).

6 Yves Gingras, *Physics and the Rise of Scientific Research in Canada* (Montreal
and Kingston: McGill-Queen's University Press, 1991). Ruth Lewin Sime
has stressed how important Lise Meitner's sense of belonging to a physics
community was to her; see *Lise Meitner*, 12 and 95.

7 Mount Holyoke College Archives, Elizabeth Laird Papers, 'London Physicist
Acquainted with the Sting of Prejudice,' *London Free Press*, 21 April 1967. The
importance of the 1851 Exhibition Scholarship to the development of the sciences in Canada is explored in Gingras, *Physics*, 40–5. Between its founding in
1891 and 1914, six Toronto graduates were among the eighteen Canadians
whose physics studies abroad were financed by this British award.

8 University of Western Ontario, J.J. Talman Regional Collection, CA
90NLA1628, Laird Family Papers.

9 Ibid., letters dated 15 March, 29 March, and 4 May 1898.

10 Ibid., letter with no date and letters dated 15 March and 4 May 1898.

11 Ibid., letters dated 28 January and 22 Feburary 1898.

12 Ibid., letter dated 3 August 1898.

13 Ibid., letters dated 26 September, 4 October, 19 October, and 19 November
1898.

14 Ibid., letters dated 26 October, 2 November, 12 November, and 19 November
1898.

15 Mount Holyoke College Archives, Physics Department Records, series A, General Material, 'Department of Physics' (typescript). In spite of a busy teaching
and administrative career, Laird kept up with her research, spending two summers at Cambridge (in 1904 and 1909) and sabbaticals at the University of
Wurzburg and at Chicago and Yale. See Rayner-Canham and Rayner-Canham,
'Pioneer Women,' 1038.

16 M.F. Rayner-Canham and G.W. Rayner-Canham, 'Harriet Brooks – Pioneer
Nuclear Scientist,' *American Journal of Physics* 57, 10 (October 1989), and 'Can-
ada's first Woman Nuclear Physicist, Harriet Brooks, 1876–1933,' in Marianne
Gosztonyi Ainley, ed. *Despite the Odds: Essays on Canadian Women and Science*

(Montreal: Véhicule Press, 1990). Brooks's MA is dated 1901, as are her publications with Rutherford. These achievements were followed by studies at Bryn Mawr and Cambridge and two more papers, published in 1904. She taught for two years at Barnard College in New York and worked for another period with Marie Curie in Paris before her decision in 1907 to withdraw her application for a position at Manchester and marry.

17 The doctorate at Toronto was established in 1897 and the first PhD in physics granted three years later. See Gingras, *Physics*, 39, and Elizabeth J. Allin, *Physics at the University of Toronto, 1843–1980* (Toronto: Department of Physics, University of Toronto, 1981), appendix 3, 75.

18 *American Men [sic] of Science* (10th ed., New York 1961).

19 By 1933, thirty-two physics PhDs had been awarded at Toronto, of which seven had been granted to women. See Allin, *Physics*, 16 and appendix 3.

20 Margaret W. Rossiter, *Women Scientists in America: Struggles and Strategies to 1940* (Baltimore and London: Johns Hopkins University Press, 1982) and *Women Scientists in America: Before Affirmative Action, 1940–1972* (Baltimore and London: Johns Hopkins University Press, 1995).

21 Deacon, Rotenberg, and Cohen taught at Toronto off and on from the mid-1930s until the 1950s. We know most about Rotenberg, who worked in radio for some years and was also a powerful figure in Toronto's Jewish philanthropic community. May Annetts Smith's student card suggests much moving from place to place, but on at least one occasion, in 1955–6, she held a job teaching (agricultural) physics at Macdonald College for McGill. For more details and documentation, see Prentice, 'The Early History of Women in University Physics,' 94–6, and Allin, *Physics*, 16.

22 See Prentice, 'Elizabeth Allin: Physicist,' especially 266–71.

23 Ibid., 276.

24 Ibid., 277 and note 70. For an examination of the complex concerns, rivalries, and legal issues behind the early difficulties of the CAPP and the CAP, see Gringas, *Physics*, especially chapters 6 and 7.

25 University of Toronto Archives, B78–003, Dorothy Forward Interview, recorded in 1974.

26 Queen's University Archives, Allie Vibert Douglas Papers, Coll. 2303.9, 'Pilgrims Were We All.' All information about Douglas's career for which I provide no other citations comes from this source. Note that, although some published accounts of her life refer to Douglas as 'Alice,' her nephew has informed me that the name which appears on her birth certificate is in fact 'Allie' (interview with Patrick Douglas, fall 1996). She and her brother changed their surnames from Vibert to Douglas shortly before the First World War for reasons unknown; most of her writings were signed 'A.V. Douglas.'

27 It is interesting that, unlike Laird in the 1890s, Douglas could afford to study at Cambridge during the early 1920s. She and the family had perhaps been able to save money during the war; they may also have been wealthier than Laird's family.

28 'Publications,' 'Curriculum Vitae,' and 'Application for the Wardenship of Royal Victoria College,' in Allie Vibert Douglas Papers, Queen's University Archives; McGill calendars, 1926–39, McGill University Archives.

29 A.V. Douglas, *Eddington* (Edinburgh, 1956).

30 Allin, *Physics*, 16.

31 For the expansion of the department, see Allin, *Physics*, especially chapter 4, entitled 'The Years of Affluence, 1948–1969.' I cannot provide exact numbers of male and female graduate students; all faculty hirings during the expansionist period (and for many years after it) were men.

32 Rossiter, *Before Affirmative Action*, chapter 16.

33 Quoted in Gingras, *Physics*, 144.

34 National Archives of Canada, Frank Underhill Papers, MG 30, D 204, vol. 7, Satterly to Underhill, 4 April 1943. Many thanks to Donald Wright, who provided this reference.

35 Ibid., Satterly to Underhill, 14 June 1943.

36 See Prentice, 'Elizabeth Allin,' 278–80.

37 In Curie's case, there were problems after Pierre Curie was killed in an accident; Meitner was forced to flee Nazi Germany and never regained the status and supportive working environment that she had achieved, after many years, in Berlin.

38 Prentice, 'Laying Siege to the Professoriate.'

39 An examination of the distribution of female scholarly workers at Toronto in the decade between 1921 and 1931, for example, revealed ninety different women employed (for one year or more during that period) in the medical sciences and seventy in the other sciences, compared to thirty-four in languages and fifteen in the social sciences. Even the social and educational professions employed only seventy-four women during the decade. See Prentice, 'Bluestockings, Feminists, or Women Workers,' table 3, 245.

40 Gingras, *Physics*, chapter 7.

41 Rossiter, *Before Affirmative Action, 1940–1972*.

42 Between 1993–4 and 1995–6, women dropped from 15 to 14.2 per cent of full-time doctoral students in Canadian physics programs. 'Status of Women Supplement,' *CAUT Bulletin* 44, 4 (April 1997). In Britain, Kim Thomas also suggests that physics, 'with the possible exception of engineering [is] the last bastion of masculine [academic] exclusivity' Thomas, 'Physics, Gender, and Identity' 3.

43 Prior to 1921 twenty-six women were so employed, and between 1921 and
   1931, seventeen, a few of whom would also have been part of the earlier group.
   A total of eight men were on the faculty as professors at one rank or another
   between 1906 and 1931.
44 Quoted in Prentice, 'Bluestockings, Feminists, or Women Workers?' 256.

From the Science of Housekeeping to the Science of Nutrition: Pioneers in Canadian Nutrition and Dietetics at the University of Toronto's Faculty of Household Science, 1900–1950

RUBY HEAP

'The unfolding of the science of nutrition these past 30 years has been a fascinating one,' proudly observed Annie L. Laird, head of the University of Toronto's Faculty of Household Science, in a speech delivered in 1936 on the 'Status of Household Science in Canada with Special Reference to Nutrition and Health.'[1] As the title of Laird's speech suggests, the growth of the science of nutrition was closely related to the expansion of household science in Canada in the first decades of the twentieth century. As one of the architects of the first Canadian degree course in household science, established in 1902 at the University of Toronto, and then as faculty head from 1906 to 1939, Laird was herself a prime mover in the development of the field. She stands out, more particularly, as a leading promoter of dietetics, an important area of applied nutrition and one of the new women's professions that emerged in Canada during this period.

Interestingly, Annie Laird's major contribution to the emergence and growth of household science[2] has so far been largely ignored by English-Canadian historians who have written on the subject. This neglect can be attributed to the fact that they have generally focused on the 'household' dimension of household science. Published largely during the late 1970s and early 1980s, most studies bear in this respect the mark of the 'separate spheres' paradigm, which was highly influential at the time.[3] They contend that the main objective of the household science movement was to train women to perform their 'natural' duties in the 'private sphere,' that is, to make them better wives, mothers, and housekeepers, while men would pursue their main role as breadwinners in the 'public sphere.' Household science thus further entrenched gender-role stereotypes, thereby preventing women from gaining true equality with men in the public sphere.[4] The opinions expressed against female suffrage and women's paid work by Adelaide Hoodless, who is generally identified as the most devoted crusader for household science in English Canada at the turn of the century, have been amply quoted to support this view.[5]

In the meantime the 'scientific' and 'professional' dimensions of household science in Canada have been largely overlooked. Existing studies focus mostly on the 'professionalization' of housework and motherhood.[6] On the other hand, few historians have noted that the creation of university-based programs in household science carved an important niche for women interested in an academic career.[7] Little attention has been paid also to the links between the entrance of household science into academia and the development of the science of nutrition, as Laird's speech indicated. Finally, the professionalization of dietetics and its impact on university-based household science programs are usually mentioned only briefly in the existing literature, which tends to present school teaching as the only major outlet for graduates.

Significantly, the fledging history of women and science in Canada, which is now redressing the neglect of women scientists by women's historians as well as by historians of science in this country, has also neglected household science as an area of scientific work for women.[8] However, Margaret W. Rossiter's seminal work on American women scientists acknowledges the importance of home economics as a feminized field of science since the late nineteenth century and shows how the development of the science of nutrition opened avenues for women within departments of home economics in colleges and universities.[9]

In this light, the following essay will examine the careers of Annie Laird, Clara Benson, and Violet Ryley, three women whose names are closely linked to the early history of household science at the University of Toronto and to the development of nutrition and dietetics. Benson, Laird's long-time colleague at the Faculty of Household Science, where she taught food chemistry, was able to pursue a successful research career in nutrition, for which she gained wide recognition. Violet Ryley stands out as a leading pioneer in Canadian dietetics. She worked closely with Laird to establish a profession that attracted an increasing number of household science graduates eager to find employment in the early decades of the twentieth century.

Each of these women assumed different roles within the field of household science. In this respect, their careers correspond to the model elaborated by Margaret Rossiter in her study of university-based home economics departments in the United States between 1900 and 1940. According to Rossiter, the women attached to these departments could be divided into three groups: like Annie L. Laird, some made their mark as administrators and institution builders; others focused on research, which was the route followed by Clara Benson; finally, there were those who, along with Violet Ryley, chose to pursue careers mainly outside university walls, as teachers, demonstrators, or lobbyists.[10]

Furthermore, Laird, Benson, and Ryley were typical of the growing number of single women who, in the early decades of the twentieth century, wished to use their higher education to pursue careers in the public sphere instead of opting for marriage and motherhood. As single career women, they thus departed from the older and more widely known 'heroines' of household science in Canada, namely, Adelaide Hoodless and Lillian Massey-Treble. Household science offered them employment opportunities that allowed them, in turn, to perform pioneering work in the field and to open avenues for other aspiring women professionals.

Annie L. Laird, Institution Builder

Annie Louisa Laird's career constitutes a good example of the opportunities which the establishement of household science within academia could provide for an educated, determined, and enterprising woman. As head of the Faculty of Household Science at the University of Toronto for over thirty years, she was able to shape and orient the course of study, promote teaching and research in the nutritional sciences, and create employment opportunities for both staff and graduates.

Annie Laird was born in 1871 in Fergus, Ontario. She completed her high school education in Collingwood and London, where her father, a Methodist parson, conducted his ministry. Annie developed an interest in science, which she shared with her sister, Elizabeth, and her much older brother, who held a doctorate and was teaching physics at Brandon College in Manitoba. Both sisters enrolled at the University of Toronto, Annie in chemistry and Elizabeth in the maths and physics program.[11] A dutiful daughter, Annie Laird was to put her studies on hold in order to remain at her father's side and to take care of an handicapped brother; but following her father's death in 1897, she decided to pursue her higher education. Infused with a reformist spirit, she was concerned with the improvement of standards of living, especially with health and diet. The field of household science seemed to correspond to her interests and aspirations.

In the United States, the 'home economics' movement had expanded considerably during the last decades of the nineteenth century.[12] One of its most important dimensions, which is often overlooked, was that of nutrition research. The beginnings of modern nutritional science are linked to the work of German chemist Justus Liebig, who, starting in the 1840s, promoted the scientific study of food and human metabolism together with his numerous German and American followers.[13] At first, men dominated the field of nutritional science in the United States, but from the 1890s on, women began to take an active part in its development. Chemist Ellen Swallow Richards, who is considered the founder of home economics in North America, was a prime mover in this regard. The first woman to graduate from the Massachusetts Institute of Technology, which then employed her as an instructor in sanitary chemistry, Richards developed an interest in the scientific study of food and in the problem of nutrition for the poor. Through the establishment of demonstration kitchens, the publication of many popular works, and other various initiatives, she transformed nutrition into a national movement. She fostered the emergence of dietetics, which consisted of the efficient and scientific feeding of individuals in institutions such as schools, hospitals, factories, and prisons. Women were also becoming involved in the nutritional sciences through academic appointments in home economics at teachers' colleges and, more importantly, at land-grant agricultural colleges and state universities. This last group formed an increasingly strong contingent at the annual Lake Placid Conferences on Home Economics, inaugurated in 1899 by Ellen Richards, which culminated in the foundation of the American Home Economics Association in 1909, with Richards as its first president.[14]

While these developments were occurring, the Canadian household science movement was still in its infancy at the turn of the century. Certainly, the future looked promising in Ontario. Adelaide Hoodless and Lillian Massey had launched their promotional campaign, and the provincial government had taken important steps to introduce the subject into its elementary schools and to regulate the training of household science teachers. However, no institution of higher learning was offering courses in the area.[15] For Annie, then, the solution was to head south, as her sister, Elizabeth, had done to complete a doctorate in physics at Bryn Mawr. At the time three American establishments were recognized as providing university-level training in household science: the Pratt Institute in Brooklyn, Teachers' College in New York, and the Drexel Institute in Philadelphia. With Elizabeth at nearby Bryn Mawr, Drexel stood out as the obvious choice. In 1901, at age thirty, Annie left for Philadelphia to pursue her training, which she completed in 1902.[16]

That same year she accepted the position of senior instructor at the Lillian Massey School of Household Science in Toronto. Established in 1901, the school was an expansion of the earlier cooking classes inaugurated in the 1890s by Mrs Massey-Treble (then Miss Massey) at the Fred Victor Mission, built by her wealthy father. To train teachers in household science, Massey-Treble the next year inaugurated a two-year normal course with the support of the Ontario Department of Education.[17] But there was still an urgent need for qualified women to take charge of the Lillian Massey School. Massey-Treble wrote to the Drexel Institute, where she had already recruited the school's first principal. In 1903, one year after her arrival at the school, Laird took over the principalship.

Her rapid rise at the Lillian Massey School launched her impressive career in household science. Her influence in the field was soon felt. Indeed, Laird worked closely with Nathanael Burwash, the president of Victoria College and a fervent supporter of Mrs Massey-Treble, to establish in 1902 the first Canadian degree course in household science at the University of Toronto. The Lillian Massey School would make available its facilities for the various branches of household science, while the other subjects would be taught at the university.[18] The four-year course, which led to a bachelor of household science degree, was quite broad in scope and intent. While household science was its most important feature, it embraced, in the words of Burwash, 'the fundamental elements of a liberal education and is intended to be as complete and as severe, as a discipline, as one of the Honour Courses for the B.A. degree.'[19] Science subjects such as chemistry, physics, microbiology, and biochemistry thus formed the basis of the course, while studies connected with the humanities and the social sciences (history, literature, languages, economics, etc.) were included in each year to provide a sound cultural education. The fourth and final year would be focused on intensive laboratory work devoted to special problems related to household science.[20]

It is difficult to measure Laird's real input in the mapping of this first course of study. She was the only woman to sit on the drafting committee, composed of Burwash and science professors from the University of Toronto. Officially, Laird credited Burwash with being its prime architect, celebrating his broad vision of household science education and his promotion of high standards for those enrolled in the field.[21] Undoubtedly, one of her main concerns was to establish and maintain a course of university calibre.'There is no thought that the universities are to become

Annie L. Laird, professor and head of the Faculty of Household Science, University of Toronto, 1906–36. She was a charter member of the American Dietetic Association, founded in 1917, and was also co-founder and first honorary president of the Canadian Dietetic Association, 1935.

cooking schools,' she insisted.[22] As Laird was certainly aware, this kind of stigma was attached at the time to the home economics programs both in American agricultural colleges and state universities in the west and in urban schools of cookery and sewing in the east. Prestigious women's liberal arts colleges such as Bryn Mawr and Vassar had, in fact, dismissed home economics as unable to provide serious and profound training for intelligent women.[23]

Similar opposition had been expressed in Toronto. Indeed, between 1900 and 1902 members of the women's Alumnae Association of University College questioned the advisability of introducing household science as a university course, wondering if such a step would be in the best interest of women's higher education. Some envisaged the course as consisting of a 'limited amount of science and cooking,' while others felt that a 'course strictly for women would be treated with something like contempt and neglected.'[24] The discussion ended after the establishment of the degree course,[25] but one suspects that similar opinions continued to be articulated by those who promoted full equality between the sexes in higher education and who opposed, as a result, the idea of introducing university programs specifically designed for women.

At the same time, Laird could find inspiration in the vision and accomplishments of those American pioneers who had successfully introduced household science into academia. She corresponded with Ellen Richards, who encouraged her to maintain high academic standards for her program.[26] But it was Isabel Bevier, with whom Laird also corresponded, who seems to have espoused ideas and principles that were the closest to Laird's. A chemist of repute and head of the Department of Household Science at the University of Illinois since 1900, Bevier had established at this state university a four-year course aimed at giving women a liberal education with a basis of pure and applied science. She insisted on university standards for admission and wanted to promote the scientific side of household science. Significantly, she named her department 'household science' rather than 'home economics.' Bevier was particularly committed to research on food and nutrition. Although she thereby aroused the antagonism of the 'cooking and sewing school adherents,' who wanted practical advice for housewives and future homemakers, her department rapidly gained a strong reputation. At the 1904 Lake Placid Conference on Home Economics, the University of Illinois was cited, along with the University of Chicago, as offering the best academic program in the field.[27]

Like Bevier, Laird adhered to the principle of a broad liberal education for household science students.[28] Taking this stand also helped dispel doubts and concerns about the program's calibre and its claim to provide young women with a proper university education. It is clear, however, that Laird's interests lay with the scientific components of household science. She scored an important victory in 1902 when the committee charged with drafting the new degree course, on which she sat with professors of chemistry, agreed on the importance of including food chemistry for the training of future researchers and food analysts. In 1906, largely because of Mrs Massey-Treble's offer to erect a well-equipped building to ensure the success of the new course, the University of Toronto agreed to establish a Faculty of Household Science, with which was merged the Lillian Massey School. Laird, who had remained principal and an instructor at the school, was then given a university appointment and granted the rank of associate professor. Even more important, she became head of the new faculty. She worked closely with Mrs Massey-Treble on the plans for the projected building, which was opened in 1913. Laird was particularly proud to announce in the *University Monthly* that the whole south wing would be devoted entirely to the teaching of food chemistry, with laboratories at the disposal of the students, including one reserved for advanced students doing research. The study of food, she submitted, was 'perhaps the most important phase of Household Science.'[29]

Laird expressed more conviction on this issue with her close colleagues. In 1906 she wrote to Clara Benson: 'As you know, the nutrition side of the work appeals to me the most strongly and to my mind it is that side of the work that undoubtedly places the work on a University curriculum on a par with other scientific subjects.' Conversations with her sister had convinced her that the study of food at the university should include a proper balance of theory and experimental work. She reported with satisfaction that 'people from a distance, from other schools have told me that we give much more theoretical work to our ladies' classes than is given elsewhere.' But she also insisted that 'it is just as impossible to teach household science without laboratory work as to teach physics and chemistry without it.' Her views led her to disagree with Adelaide Hoodless, who favoured the practical over the theoretical and claimed that 'cooking classes should be simply such.'[30]

During Laird's thirty years as faculty head, the original course of study underwent many changes. As early as 1907 Latin and mathematics were added to allow students to enter the Faculty of Education and obtain a high school teaching certificate. The course then became an honour program in the Faculty of Arts leading to a bachelor of arts degree instead of a bachelor of household science.[31] The university was thus responding rapidly to the needs of those graduates who sought paid employment, since teaching was at the time the main professional avenue opened to them. With the support of Mrs Massey-Treble and the provincial Department of Education, the faculty was already training teachers for the elementary schools through its normal course, which, in the early years in fact attracted the largest contingent of students. Laird thought that the course was an effective way to make her Faculty 'widely and favorably known,' especially in the United States. But it lacked the full support of the university administration, which finally abolished it in 1912.[32]

On the other hand, Annie Laird was no doubt pleased with the other changes to the faculty's offerings, which put greater emphasis on science and fostered the development of research. According to her, many household science students were demanding more science, a trend that she more than likely encouraged.[33] The careers of Edna Wilhelmine Park and her sister, Ruth, illustrate the kind of influence that Laird could exert on students. Both interested in science, the two sisters enrolled in household science against the advice of their father. After graduation, Edna went on to complete a master's in education. She returned to the Faculty of Household Science as an instructor in 1919 and was encouraged by Laird to conduct research on the impact of proper nutrition on children's performance in school. As for Ruth, she pursued a successful career as head of nutrition and dietetics at the Montreal General Hospital. 'She [Laird] inspired all of us,' said Edna.[34]

In 1920 the creation of a master's program in nutrition was another important acknowledgment of Laird's scientific and professional goals. By now, household science at the University of Toronto clearly distinguished itself from the two other programs established as a result of Adelaide Hoodless's campaign, the first one offered by the Macdonald Institute of Home Economics, established in Guelph in 1904, and the second one dispensed at Sainte Anne de Bellevue by the School of Household Science, established in 1907 at Macdonald College, which was affiliated to McGill University. Both were originally designed to offer practical training to rural women, and the Macdonald Institute was also involved in the training of elementary school teachers. The two programs were therefore less academically and science oriented, although McGill would later move in that direction in the 1920s and 1930s.[35]

In 1915 *Maclean's* published an informative article on the many facets of household science at the University of Toronto and on the professional opportunities which the field offered. The author, Laura Bradshaw Durand, interviewed Annie Laird, Clara Benson, and Violet Ryley, as well as some household science graduates. Although Laird was reluctant to talk about herself, Durand was impressed by this woman 'with the gentle voice and manner associated with some strong and tenacious natures.' One graduate, now a dietitian, testified to Laird's love of science: 'She keeps in close touch with experimental science everywhere.' Indeed, Laird travelled frequently to Europe and the United States, often with Elizabeth, to keep abreast of the various developments in the nutritional sciences. However, she conceded to Durand: 'My sister *is* a very clever and distinguished scientist.' The dietitian interviewed by Durand strongly disagreed: '*Both* are true scientists,' she assured the latter.[36]

Lacking a graduate degree and absorbed by her heavy administrative duties, Laird could not, however, focus all her energies on research. She did conduct and supervise research projects on various problems related to nutrition, the content of food, and food preparation.[37] She also took part with Clara Benson and other household science colleagues in a project sponsored by the federal Department of Fisheries and Oceans. Laird was a sought-after lecturer in Canada and in the English-speaking world. She also attended some of the famous Lake Placid Conferences on Home Economics, and she followed in the footsteps of Ellen Richards and other household science pioneers by producing 'popular science' books on nutrition.[38]

Laird's accomplishments and boundless dedication to the field of household science led to many honours and rewards. In 1919 her alma mater, the Drexel Institute, conferred on her an honorary master of science degree. Two years later she was appointed to the University of Toronto Senate. Finally, in 1926, at age fifty-five, she was named full professor. The promotion, stated President Robert Falconer, was granted in recognition of Laird's 'efficient service to this University.'[39] She had made history as the first of two women to obtain a full professorship at the University of Toronto that year. Significantly, the other woman was her colleague Clara Benson.

In the meantime, Annie Laird was directing her energies to the realization of another major goal: the organization of dietetics as a new profession for household science graduates.

Toronto hospitals had already started to appoint Canada's first dietitians at the turn of the century. The Hospital for Sick Children led the way in 1908. Two years later one of Laird's graduates, Helen Reed, was appointed to the Toronto General Hospital. In 1913 Reed set up at the

Toronto General a dietetic intern program, whose first two graduates were also recruited from the Faculty of Household Science. During these pioneering years, the hospital dietitian's main responsibilities were to teach student nurses, instruct patients and outpatients such as diabetics, and prepare and administer therapeutic and special diets. The need to incorporate into the hospital the advances of the emerging science of nutrition was by now acknowledged.[40]

The Great War provided Annie Laird with a golden opportunity to promote the vital importance of food as a therapeutic and cost-effective agent in the treatment of sick and wounded soldiers, and thereby to boost the emerging field of dietetics in Canada. In 1915 the federal government assigned the medical care and rehabilitation of returning soldiers to a new civilian body, the Military Hospitals Commission. Two years later the commission asked Annie Laird and the Faculty of Household Science to prepare standard menus for a month. She pressed instead for the appointment of dietitians capable of treating patients and planning meals in a scientific and economical way.[41] The MHC agreed to appoint a 'general organizing dietitian,' who would supervise the management of food services throughout its hospitals as well as a staff of appointed dietitians. The position went to Violet Ryley, a former student of Laird's, who was at the time superintendent of the University of Toronto's dining hall. As we shall see, Ryley's work during the war would stimulate the growth of hospital and commercial dietetics in the 1920s.

The next challenge was to establish the occupation as a full-fledged profession. A major step in that direction was the creation of an association that would improve the standards of practice by raising the qualifications of dietitians. As a charter member of the American Dietetic Association, established in 1917, Laird had already played a vital role in the professionalization of American dietitians. Her election as vice-president of the ADA in 1931 is a clear indication of her influence. Meanwhile, Canadian dietitians had been allowed to join the ADA on an individual basis. As their numbers grew and the range of their activities expanded into the private and public sectors, many, starting with Annie Laird, felt the necessity for a national association in Canada. Already provincial organizations had been established in Quebec, Ontario, and British Columbia. Laird had played a key role in the formation of the Ontario Dietetic Association in 1926. As honorary president of the ODA, she then mobilized the various forces favouring an autonomous Canadian association. An ADA proposal, which would have imposed compulsory membership of all ODA members in the American body, precipitated events in

1934. Laird was firmly opposed to this proposition, reminding her colleagues that they 'should not be dictated [to] by a foreign organization.'[42] A nation-wide consultation concerning the possible creation of a Canadian organization resulted, and in due course a founding meeting was held in Ottawa in 1935, with Laird as chair.

The Canadian Dietetic Association would promote, encourage, and improve the status of dietitians in this country by establishing and raising standards of training. Significantly, the first requisite for active membership was a bachelor's degree with a major in food and nutrition from a recognized university. One should not underestimate the importance of this clause. It was based on the conviction, firmly held by Laird, that the 'really scientific dietitian' needed considerable knowledge in biology, physics, and chemistry, which she could only obtain at a university.[43]

As a sign of gratitude for her contribution to the profession, Annie Laird was chosen as the CDA's first honorary president. The creation of a national dietetic association was her last major accomplishment. In 1936 health problems forced Laird to step down as head of the Faculty of Household Science, and she died three years later. By then, reported Clara Benson, over a thousand students had graduated in household science; half of them were employed, the majority in the field of dietetics.[44] Benson's statistics are a strong tribute to Laird's efforts and success as an institution builder.

Clara C. Benson, Researcher in Food and Nutrition

By using her foresight and leadership skills to develop the science of nutrition at the University of Toronto, Annie Laird had allowed a highly qualified woman like Clara Benson to pursue a successful career as a researcher and to help build and strenghten, by the same token, the reputation of the Faculty of Household Science.

Benson's career is emblematic of the experiences of a generation of women who, having obtained graduate degrees in chemistry in the late nineteenth and early twentieth centuries, found in the growing departments of household science a niche in which to do research and publish. Despite their growing numbers, these women had difficulty finding employment as research chemists. Few were accepted in industry, and fewer still on the regular faculties of PhD-granting institutions. They had therefore to seek opportunities in fields outside the normal disciplines of organic, inorganic, and physical chemistry. Biochemistry, which was born from agricultural chemistry and physiological chemistry, proved to be the area most open to women scientists, whose contributions to the field are impressive.[45]

Clara Benson also chose this area. Born in 1875, the daughter of Judge Thomas Moore Benson, she attended high school in her home town of Port Hope. In 1899 she obtained a BA at the University of Toronto, with honours in physics and chemistry, winning the same year a graduate fellowship to pursue further studies in chemistry at the university. In 1903 she became the first Canadian woman to obtain a doctorate in this field. Her research area and her first publications were in physical chemistry.[46] The same year, however, Benson accepted from the provincial Department of Education a position as assistant to Edith Curzon, an instructor in science at the Lillian Massey School of Household Science. Curzon's background was in the natural sciences, in which she had graduated in 1889 from the University of Toronto. Interested in household science, she had left her job as an analyst at the university's School of Practical Science for her current position at the Lillian Massey School. There she inaugurated a course in food analysis, at a time when food chemistry was not yet taught in Canada.

On becoming Curzon's assistant, Benson agreed, for her part, to move from one field of chemistry to another. The transition was accelerated by Curzon's sudden death from drowning the same year. Chosen to take over as main instructor, Benson struggled to learn quickly the different subjects taught by her predecessor, including bacteriology, physiology, and food analysis. Fortunately, she was coached by male professors from the University of Toronto, including Archibald Byron Macallum, the father of biochemistry in Canada.[47] This highly prominent scientific researcher seems to have acted as a mentor to Benson, or at least as a supportive senior colleague. According to her, he was greatly interested in household science. He took part in the discussions leading to the creation of the new degree course in household science and to the introduction of food chemistry at the University of Toronto. In 1905 all the science classes taken by household science students were moved from the Lillian Massey School to the medical building of the University of Toronto. The Department of Physiology, headed by Macallum, then took Benson on as a lecturer; there she taught physiology, bacteriology, and food chemistry to the department's students.[48]

In 1906 Benson was appointed associate professor of physiological chemistry in the new Faculty of Household Science. Six years later she moved her headquarters to the now-completed household science building. President Falconer gave her full control of her own laboratories and further agreed to credit all her research to the Faculty of Household Science: 'The main object to bear in mind is, in accordance to your own words, that your heart will be in the Household Science Building.'[49] Interestingly, Benson in 1901 had supported a motion submitted to the Alumnae Association of University College to the effect that 'domestic science on the university curriculum was at present unpractical.'[50] One wonders if her anticipation of the many hurdles that she would probably face as a researcher in a male-dominated field had led to her decision to further her career in a 'women's faculty.'

Whatever factor dictated this move, Benson engaged from then on in productive research in the nutritional sciences. In 1915 she enthusiastically described the field of nutrition as being of 'wide scope and in a very lively state of existence.'[51] A few years later, Benson joined a group of women and men scientists who launched a series of long-term and ground-breaking investigations into fish and fish products for the Biological Board of Canada, created by the federal government in 1912, which reported to the Department of Fisheries and Oceans.[52] The team conducted its research at the board's Atlantic Station, located in St Andrews, New Brunswick. Over the years, Benson would became a distinguised authority on the biochemical study of blood and tissues of fish.[53] In 1919 she also worked for the Biological Board through a special research committee composed of herself, Annie Laird, and representatives from Macdonald College and the Macdonald Institute. The committee studied and submitted reports on methods for preparing fish and on the comparative nutritional merits of various species.[54]

The Great War and its aftermath proved to be a challenging and fruitful period for Clara Benson. Details about her war activities are scarce, but we know that, along with many women scientists at the time, she provided her services to the war industry. She was able to apply the methods of food chemistry to the chemistry of explosives, setting the accepted techniques for analysis in munitions laboratories. She even trained a few women to carry these out.[55] The end of the war would bring important rewards. In 1919 Benson became head of her own Department of Food Chemistry at the Faculty of Household Science. The same year she was the only female founding member of the Canadian Institute of Chemistry. Finally, from 1920 to 1937 Benson is reported as working for the Food Research Commission of the National Research Council of Canada, established in 1916.[56] That A.B. Macallum served as the first chair of the NRC from 1917 to 1920 may account for Benson's association with the council.

Her work in nutrition, combined with her academic position and her status as a single woman, enabled her to integrate with considerable success into the mainstream of male-dominated science. She conducted her research in the United States and Germany as well as in Canada. She belonged to influential scientific organizations, including the Canadian Institute of Chemistry, the American Association of Biological Chemists, of which A.B. Macallum was a founding member, and the American Chemical Society, which honoured her fifty-year membership following her retirement in 1949. Benson was also accepted as a fellow of the American Association for the Advancement of Science and as a member of the Royal Canadian Institute. Her strong research record would secure her a listing in the various editions of *American Men of Science* (though she was neither American nor a man).

Benson's recognition by male scientists did not keep her away from household science or from women's organizations. For a long time she acted as secretary of her faculty, a responsibility that she carried until her retirement. She belonged to professional bodies such as the University of Toronto's Women Club and the American Home Economics Association. She was also an activist on behalf of women. She devoted many years to the YWCA, where she served as a member of the National Executive Committee and as chair of the foreign and world fellowship committees.[57] As president of the University of Toronto's Women's Athletic Club from 1922 to 1945, Benson struggled hard for the construction of a women's athletic building. Victory finally came in 1959, and her name was given to the new building as a tribute to all these years of effort.[58] She was also concerned with women's rights. Her early comments on the advisibility of introducing household science at the university suggest that she then feared the repercussions of separate programs for women. Her review of Olive Schreiner's *Women and Labour*, published in 1912 in the *University Monthly*, is revealing as well. In the opening paragraph, Benson states: 'It is a book which the worker for women's rights will read with satisfaction, and which will furnish thought for those who would set a woman on a pedestal and keep her there – with nothing to do.'[59]

Her own career, marked by many firsts, could serve as a source of inspiration for aspiring women scientists. According to Edna Park, Benson, like Annie Laird, exerted a profound influence on students. Park described her as 'full of fun,' but also as a 'hard taskmaster in the labs in Chemistry.'[60] In 1915 Benson explained to *Maclean's* reporter Laura Bradshaw Durand that commercial chemistry was a growing field in Canada which would soon employ many of her students. 'Dr. Benson is san-

Clara C. Benson, in 1903, was the first Canadian woman to obtain a doctorate in chemistry. She was a professor of food chemistry in the Faculty of Household Science at the University of Toronto from 1906 to 1949. She was also co-founder of the Canadian Institute of Chemistry in 1919 and both a member of the Royal Canadian Institute and a fellow of the American Association for the Advancement of Science.

guine of the future,' reported Durand.[61] Armed with her doctorate and her eventual position as head of the Department of Food Chemistry, she was able to supervise several students in various research projects in food chemistry and encourage them to pursue careers in the nutritional sciences.

In 1949 Clara Benson retired at age seventy-four. She was named professor emeritus, and a year later she was honoured as a pioneer in household science by over two thousand alumni, who presented to the University of Toronto a scholarship bearing her name.[62] Eight years later, the *Varsity Graduate* would applaud Clara Benson as the 'grande dame' of the University of Toronto.[63] Still active, she lived to be eighty-nine.

Violet Ryley, the 'Dean' of Canadian Dietitians

While Annie Laird and Clara Benson were pursuing careers at the University of Toronto's Faculty of Household Science, Violet Ryley was playing a leading role in shaping the field of dietetics outside the walls of academia. Indeed, she took up the work began by Laird in organizing nutrition work in the early decades of the twentieth century.

Born in 1884 in Bethay, Ontario, Violet Ryley later settled with her family in Toronto. After graduating from Jarvis Collegiate Institute, she enrolled at the Ontario College of Art but had to quit for health reasons. On the advice of Dr Helen MacMurchy, who had taught at Jarvis before engaging in public-health reform, Ryley enrolled in the two-year normal course at the Lillian Massey School of Household Science, from which she graduated in 1907. Because she did not have a university degree, she probably could not envisage an academic career in household science. However, she soon formed a lifelong association with Margaret Eaton, which would have a decisive impact on the course of Canadian dietetics. Like Lillian Massey-Treble and other women of Toronto's upper class, the wife of retail giant Timothy Eaton was concerned about the poor living conditions of many of the city's workers and new immigrants. She therefore asked Ryley to design and run a kitchen in what was called 'shack town,' in the St Clair vicinity, to teach English and Scottish immigrant women how to prepare nutritious and economical meals. Ryley agreed to take part in this project.[64]

Her community work likely led to her decision to pursue a career in dietetics, which would enable her to apply the knowledge that she had acquired in the field of nutrition. She faced serious constraints, however. At the turn of the century, hospitals were the most important employers of dietitians, and only American hospitals at the time offered postgraduate internships in dietetics. Ryley therefore headed for the New York City Hospital to pursue her training. She then worked briefly as a dietitian at Albany's General Hospital, where she was put in charge of the dining hall.[65]

Violet Ryley's early ties with the Lillian Massey School of Household Science soon brought her back to Toronto and to her first major challenge as a pioneer in Canadian dietetics. In 1910, on the recommendation of her former teacher, Annie Laird, Ryley became superintendent of the University of Toronto's dining hall. The position had been created in 1907 when Laird had advised President Falconer that the appointment of one of her students as superintendent would help to solve the problem of the large-scale feeding of students.[66]

Recorded accounts all attest to Ryley's outstanding work at the University of Toronto. The quality and productivity of the food service increased considerably. This success can possibly be attributed to Ryley's commitment to introduce at the dining hall the latest methods in labour management and efficiency. She was a fervent admirer of Frank G. Gilbreth, the author of *Theories on Motion Study and Individual Efficiency*. F.W. Taylor's *Shop Management* and Harrington Emerson's *Twelve Principles of Efficiency* were also major sources of inspiration. Ryley was firmly convinced that these theories could be successfully applied to a dietary routine, where labour proved to be a highly costly item.[67] Laura Bradshaw Durand, who interviewed Ryley at the dining hall for her article on household science, observed in *Maclean's*: 'System, from what I could gather in a morning's visit, is the key to her success.' The dining hall's recorded daily output was certainly impressive – the average attendance was 200 students (all male) in 1909; six years later Ryley and her staff were serving more than 1,400 meals.[68]

The First World War marked an important turning point in Violet Ryley's career. As we have seen, Annie Laird's ability to seize opportunities that could promote the field of nutrition and dietetics led in 1917 to Ryley's appointment as general organizing dietitian for the Military Hospitals Commission. The MHC had no hesitation in offering this challenging position to her. The director of the MHC was struck, in fact, by her knowledge of the various theories on scientific management and labour efficiency, which had also made a deep impression on him.[69]

As general organizing dietician, Ryley was given full responsibility for food, food service, and food costs at over thirty-nine military hospitals across Canada. She was also to select and appoint dietitians. The major problem she faced from the beginning was an acute shortage of practitioners. In 1917 there were only about six or seven hospital dietitians in Canada. With the help of Annie Laird, Ryley set out to build her staff through short training courses. Laird established a one-year special course for dietitians at the University of Toronto; for her part, Ryley instituted a four-month training program which focused on institution management and cost accounting. The recruits would provide their services to the military hospitals in return for their training and their room and board. They were recruited among household science graduates from the University of Toronto, Macdonald Institute, and Macdonald College. Some forty-five dietitians and pupil-dietitians worked in MHC hospitals under the supervision of Violet Ryley from 1917 to 1918, at which time the active treatment hospitals were transferred to the Department of Militia and Defence.[70]

Ryley took advantage of her high-profile wartime position to press upon her medical supervisors and military superiors the vital importance of hospital dietitians. The superior service offered by the Dietary Branch of the MHC easily demonstrated, she argued, the 'absolute value of the scientific system' that it had organized. Each dietitian, she insisted, was also trained to use 'modern scientific methods' in every branch of her work in military hospitals.[71] Because there was a 'great deal of misunderstanding' regarding the work of the hospital dietitian, Ryley also firmly outlined what she considered to be this emerging professional's legitimate scope of practice. Many dietitians, she explained, were at present teaching and supervising nurses in the diet kitchen. She eagerly promoted the more-prestigious and challenging model of the 'modern executive Dietitian,' who was not only a teacher of diet but above all an administrator who had the right to expect that the employees in her department would carry out 'her ideals and spirit.' More important, Ryley claimed for this professional full authority in the performance of her duties. She was thus calling for a redefinition of powers in the hospital.[72]

For Ryley and other pioneers in the field, the hospital dietitian could engage in a threefold set of activities: the training of nurses, student dietitians, and medical students; the administration of food services; and the therapeutic treatment of patients, in accordance with the doctor's prescription. The 1920s witnessed a rapid expansion of hospital dietetics along these lines. Internship programs spread across the country. Dietetics departments were also established, which opened the position of chief or head dietitian. As a result, an increasing number of household science graduates found employment as health professionals.[73]

During the post-war years Ryley embarked on her most celebrated venture: the development of commercial dietetics in Canada. At the end of the war she remained briefly as chief dietitian for the federal government's veterans' hospitals, but then tendered her resignation in 1920. The following year she became the first dietitian to be employed by a North American hotel, the Bigwin Inn on Lake Muskoka. Ryley's staff was largely composed of university students, many of whom were in household science. She thus innovated once again by introducing in-service training for dietitians in the hotel industry.[74]

However, it was Ryley's close relationship with Margaret Eaton which helped to launch commercial dietetics on a large scale. Following the death of her husband in 1907, Mrs Eaton had taken an increased interest in the management of his stores, particularly the food service. In order to attract and keep the customers shopping, Eaton's had expanded in this area since the 1880s. A coffee room had given place to a small restaurant in the basement, which was relocated in 1901 to more spacious quarters on the third floor.[75] After the war Mrs Eaton decided to enlarge and improve the quality of the food service. In 1923 she took the first step by appointing Violet Ryley as dietitian and manager. The two women then worked closely together on the planning of the Georgian Room Restaurant, which opened in 1924 with the capacity to seat 450.

Over the years, Eaton's restaurants were organized in Toronto, Montreal, and Hamilton by Ryley and her assistants, most of whom were household science graduates. She was then appointed general supervisor of Eaton's food service departments, a position she maintained for more than twenty-six years. During this period Eaton's restaurant services expanded across Canada, managed by some thirty dietitians and employing a staff of over eight hundred. When Ryley left Eaton's in 1949, the field of commercial dietetics had grown considerably. Household science graduates were finding employment as managers of lunch rooms, cafeterias, and restaurants in large retail establishments, hotels, and business institutions such as banks and insurance and utility companies.[76]

In 1936 Annie Laird had already paid tribute to Violet Ryley for the 'tremendous success' that she had made of commercial dietetics.[77] The two women had maintained close ties over the years as they worked together in establishing the foundations of the dietetic profession. In 1917 Ryley had joined Laird as a charter member of the ADA, which also elected her second vice-president. In 1935 she once again joined Laird, this time as a charter member of the CDA. Following her former teacher, Ryley would also act as its honorary president. Later in her career she would also promote dietetics and the nutritional sciences as a member of several advisory bodies, including the National Nutrition Committee of the Canadian Red Cross and the Advisory Commitee on Food Technology at the Ryerson Institute of Technology.[78]

Violet Ryley died in 1949, soon after her retirement from Eaton's. According to the official historians of the CDA, she was 'a legend in her own time,' as 'she touched the lives of more dietitians in the country than any other person.'[79] Many of these individuals were household science graduates from the University of Toronto whom Ryley had trained or assisted directly or indirectly since her days as superintendent of the dining hall.

Conclusion

In 1927 Annie Laird gave an address that she entitled 'Household Science – A Profession.' Instead of calling for the 'professionalization' of housework and motherhood, she focused instead on the different occupational avenues open to household science graduates. Dietetics was clearly her first choice, but she also discussed teaching, food analysis, journalism, and demonstration work. Marriage and 'homemaking' came last, Laird reminding her audience that 'one should not overlook the fact that many college women marry.'[80]

Her address illustrates the importance of examining much more closely the scientific and professional dimensions of the household science movement in Canada. Laird clearly did not consider the University of Toronto's Faculty of Household Science primarily as a training school for future wives and mothers or as a vocational institute for school teachers. Her main agenda as head of the faculty for more than thirty years was the development of the science of nutrition and of this field's applied component, dietetics. Her close associates, Clara Benson and Violet Ryley, largely shared this vision and these goals. As a result, these enterprising women created career opportunities for themselves and helped to open new avenues of professional employment for household science graduates in educational, medical, governmental, commercial, and business settings.

Margaret Rossiter has suggested that, of the women attached to American departments of home economics in the early decades of the twentieth century, it was those who engaged in research who enjoyed the most prestigious careers.[81] Certainly, Clara Benson's strong research and publication record contributed to her reputation within the male-dominated world of science. One wonders, in fact, if she would have been as productive in a department of chemistry, where women were either absent or employed in subordinate positions. It can thus be argued that the University of Toronto's Faculty of Household Science constituted a positive space for single women interested in science as well as a professional career. Rossiter has also observed that home economics was the only place where female faculty members could hope to be promoted and to secure important administrative positions in universities. Laird's and Benson's careers confirm that this was indeed the case at the University of Toronto. Similarly, many of Laird's graduates found positions as department heads in colleges and universities, not only in Canada but also in the United States and abroad.

There is, however, the other side of the coin. Despite their pioneering contribution to the development of the field of nutrition and dietetics in Canada during the early decades of the twentieth century, Annie Laird, Violet Ryley, and even Clara Benson have been largely overlooked in the historical record.[82] The identification of the Faculty of Household Science as a 'woman's faculty,' which deprived it of the status granted to units considered more 'academic' and more 'scientific,' was in part to blame. That Laird was never given the official title of dean and that it took some twenty years before she and Benson (who held a doctorate) received their full professorships clearly indicate this lower status. In addition, the gendering of nutrition and dietetics as a result of their close association with the applied field of household science tended to undermine the importance of the scientific work produced by women in those two areas.[83]

During the period covered by this study, the Faculty of Household Science suffered serious material constraints which can probably be attributed to its status as a 'women's faculty.' Laird's early correspondence and reports testify to the faculty's underfunding and its overburdened staff.[84] Financially weak, it could hardly expand or improve its laboratory facilities or attract strong scholars committed to research.[85]

Finally, another factor that may help to explain the invisibility of women's work in nutrition at the University of Toronto was the increasing professionalization of the field. This process, which was related to rapid developments in biology and chemistry in the first half of the twentieth century, as well as to the growing importance of food chemistry in industry, especially after the Second World War, fostered the entry of men in the field and an increased focus on university research. As I have shown elsewhere, the professionalization and masculinization of the nutritional sciences were some of the major factors that led to the eventual closure of the Faculty of Household Science in the late 1970s and the transfer of the 'food sciences' to the male-dominated Faculty of Medicine.[86] One unfortunate consequence of these developments has been to obscure the early contribution and achievements of Annie Laird, Clara Benson, and Violet Ryley.

NOTES

I would like to thank Amber Lloydlangston, a doctoral candidate in history at the University of Ottawa, for her research assistance, as well as Alison Prentice for her useful comments on an earlier version of this article.

1 University of Toronto Archives (hereafter UTA), Faculty of Food Sciences, A75–0008.

2 Many different terms have been used to identify this field and the movement that led to its creation in the late nineteenth century: home economics, domestic science, domestic economy, household arts, and so on. I will use here the term 'household science' since this was the name given to the first degree course offered by the University of Toronto in 1902 and to the faculty established in 1906.

3 For an effective review of the development and influence of this paradigm, see Susan M. Reverby and Dorothy O. Helly, 'Converging on History,' in Helly and Reverby, eds., *Gendered Domains: Rethinking Public and Private in Women's History* (Ithaca: Cornell Univerity Press, 1992), 1–24.

4 Although most studies point out that the middle- and upper-class urban women who endorsed the movement also wanted to resolve the 'servant problem' by ensuring the training of working-class girls as domestic servants, the growth of domestic science is still linked primarily to the promotion of 'woman's sphere' in the home. See, for example, Diana Pederson, '"The Scientific Training of Mothers": The Campaign for Domestic Science in Ontario Schools, 1890–1913,' in Richard A. Jarrell and Arnold E. Roos, eds., *Critical Issues in the History of Canadian Science, Technology and Medicine* (Ottawa: Tornhill, 1983), 178–94; Robert Stamp, '"Teaching Girls Their God Given Place in Life": The Introduction of Home Economics in the Schools,' *Atlantis*, 2, 2 (spring 1977): 18–34; Terry Crowley, 'Madonnas before Magdalenes: Adelaide Hoodless and the Making of the Canadian Gibson Girl,' *Canadian Historical Review*, 67, 4 (1986): 520–47; and Marta Danylewycz, Nadia Fahmy-Eid, and Nicole Thivierge, 'L'enseignement ménager et les "Home Economics" au Québec et en Ontario au début du 20e siècle. Une analyse comparée,' in

J. Donald Wilson, ed., *An Imperfect Past: Education and Society in Canadian History* (Vancouver: Centre for the Study of Curriculum and Instruction, University of British Columbia, 1984): 67–119. A.B. McKillop refers to these studies in his recent history of higher education in Ontario and comes to largely similar conclusions; McKillop, *Matters of Mind: The University in Ontario, 1791–1951* (Toronto: University of Toronto Press, 1994), 139–41.

5 Cheryl MacDonald acknowledges the popularity of this view in her biography *Adelaide Hoodless: Domestic Crusader*, published in 1986 (Toronto and Reading: Dundurn Press). In her foreword she states that both 'academics and feminists' portray Hoodless as 'a sinner against the feminist cause, an ultraconservative whose desire to maintain middle class standards of living did nothing to advance the women's movement.'

6 See the studies cited in note 4.

7 A notable exception is Alison Prentice, who has observed that the Faculty of Household Science 'employed by far the largest number of women at the rank of lecturer and above at the University [of Toronto] prior to 1921'; Prentice, 'Bluestockings, Feminists, or Women Workers? A Preliminary Look at Women's Early Employment at the University of Toronto,' *Journal of the Canadian Historical Association*, 1991, 241. In her master's thesis Kerrie J. Kennedy also makes this point, although she focuses more on the 'household' dimension of the movement; Kennedy, 'Womanly Work: The Introduction of Household Science at the University of Toronto' (MA thesis, University of Toronto, 1995).

8 Marianne Gosztonyi Ainley, ed., *Despite the Odds: Essays on Canadian Women and Science* (Montreal: Véhicule Press, 1990), which remains to this day the most important collection on Canadian women scientists, features no article on the contributions of women in the field of household science, including nutrition. Ainley and Tina Crossfield provide a brief sketch of Clara Benson in their short article 'Canadian Women's Contributions to Chemistry, 1900–1970,' *L'Actualité chimique canadienne/Canadian Chemical News*, April 1994, 16–18.

9 In her more recent study, Rossiter observes that 'by far the most numerous and the highest-ranking women scientists employed in the faculties of the nation's top universities in the 1950's and 1960's were those concentrated in the highly but not totally feminized area of home economics'; see her *Women Scientists in America: Before Affirmative Action, 1940–1972* (Baltimore and London: Johns Hopkins University Press, 1996), 165. Rossiter explored the emergence and growth of home economics in her first book, *Women Scientists in America: Struggles and Strategies to 1940* (Baltimore and London: Johns Hopkins University Press, 1982). Similarly, Rima D. Apple has recently shown how the

gendering of the science of nutrition in the United States between 1840 and 1940 allowed some women to pursue a scientific career at a time when other areas of science were closed to them; Apple, 'Science Gendered: Nutrition in the United States, 1840–1940,' in Harmke Kamminga and Andrew Cunningham, eds., *The Science and Culture of Nutrition, 1840–1940* (Amsterdam and Atlanta: Rodopi, 1995), 129–54.

10 Rossiter, *Women Scientists in America: Struggles and Strategies to 1940*, 201–2.

11 See Alison Prentice, 'Three Women in Physics,' in this volume.

12 Two informative histories of the American home economics movement have been written by one of its pioneers, Isabel Bevier. See Isabel Bevier and Susannah Usher, *The Home Economics Movement* (Boston: Whitcomb & Barroes, 1906), and Bevier, *Home Economics in Education* (Philadelphia, London, Chicago: J.B. Lippincott Company, 1928). A good account can also be found in Rima D. Apple, *Mothers and Medicine: A Social History of Infant Feeding, 1890–1950* (Madison, Wis.: University of Wisconsin Press, 1987).

13 See Rossiter, *Women Scientists in America: Struggles and Strategies*, 65–6. See also Kamminga and Cunningham, *The Science and Culture of Nutrition, 1840–1940*, 1–9.

14 Rossiter, *Women Scientists in America: Struggles and Strategies*, 68–9. On the life and career of Ellen Swallow Richards, see Robert Clarke's stimulating biography, *Ellen Swallow: The Woman Who Founded Ecology* (Chicago: Follett Publishing Company, 1973), especially 126–40. An earlier biography was written by one of Richards's associates, Caroline L. Hunt; see *The Life of Ellen H. Richards* (Boston: Whitcomb and Barrows, 1912).

15 Robin S. Harris, *A History of Higher Education in Canada, 1663–1960* (Toronto and Buffalo: University of Toronto Press, 1976), 284–6. In French-speaking Quebec some female religious orders had already introduced *l'enseignement ménager* in their programs of study. On the history of household science in that province, see Nicole Thivierge, *Histoire de l'enseignement ménager-familial au Québec, 1882–1970* (Québec: Institut québécois de recherche sur la culture, 1982).

16 Margaret Lang and Elizabeth Upton, eds., *The Dietetic Profession in Canada* (Toronto: The Canadian Dietetic Association, 1973), 2.

17 Ibid., 1; Clara C. Benson, 'Household Science; Chiefly of Lillian Massey Treble School,' UTA, Faculty of Food Sciences, B92-0039.

18 UTA, Senate and Senate Committee Minutes, A68-0012, vol. 8, 12 December 1902; Land and Upton, *The Dietetic Profession in Canada*, 1.

19 N. Burwash, 'Views of Prominent Educators on Household Science,' *Lillian Massey School of Household Science and Arts Calendar, 1903–1904*, UTA, Faculty of Household Science Alumni Association, B80-0024.

20 Edna W. Park, 'A Brief History of the Development of Household Science in the University of Toronto' (n.d.), 1, UTA, Edna Park Papers, B82-0004.

21 Annie L. Laird, 'Speech Given at Alberta, 1936,' UTA, Faculty of Food Sciences, A75-0008.

22 Quoted in Edith Child Rowles, *Home Economics in Canada: The Early History of Six College Programs: Prologue to Change* (Saskatoon: University of Saskatchewan Bookstore, 1964), 26.

23 Bevier and Usher, *The Home Economics Movement*, part 1, 14–15. Similarly, the Association of Collegiate Alumnae, which gathered women from these elite colleges, was reluctant to promote a movement with 'home' in its name. Home economics, it was feared, would threaten the association's efforts to ensure full equality between women and men. See Emma Seifrit Weigley, 'It Might Have Been Euthenics: The Lake Placid Conferences and the Home Economics Movement,' *American Quarterly*, 26 (March 1974): 92–4.

24 Minutes of the Alumnae Association of University College, 1902, 14, quoted in Kennedy, 'Womanly Work,' 81.

25 Ibid., 81–2.

26 Richards to Laird, 26 November 1906, National Archives of Canada (hereafter NA), Canadian Home Economics Association Records, MG 28, I 359, vol. 31, file 2.

27 Lita Bane, *The Story of Isabel Bevier* (Peoria, Ill.: Chas. A. Bennett Co., 1955), 73, 74, and 53. See also Apple, 'Science Gendered,' 144–5. In 1906 Bevier reported to Laird on the work performed in her department. The director of the University of Illinois's College of Agriculture also wrote to Laird, informing her that Bevier's department 'has been maintained on a strong scientific basis and has the cooperation and support of all scientific departments in the institution.' See Isabel Bevier to Annie Laird, 26 November 1906, and Eugene Davenport to Laird, 28 November 1906, UTA, Faculty of Food Sciences, A75-0008.

28 Household science graduates, she declared in 1927, 'should be able to take their place in the world as educated women, not merely as experts in household science'; Annie L. Laird, 'Address 1927: Household Science – A Profession,' 2, UTA, Faculty of Food Sciences, A75-0008.

29 A.L. Laird, 'The New Household Science Building,' *University Monthly*, 11, 9 (July 1911): 428.

30 Laird to Benson, 10 August 1906, UTA, Faculty of Food Sciences, A75-0008.

31 Annie L. Laird, 'Address, 1927, with Much History and Some Statistics,' 3–4, UTA, Edna Park Papers, B82-0004. According to Laird, Nathanael Burwash felt that it would be unwise to shut household science graduates out of the Faculty of Education and thus consented to this major change.

32 A.L. Laird, 'Normal Work in Household Science in the Lilian [*sic*] Massey
    School (February 1910),' UTA, Faculty of Food Sciences, A75-0008; Laird to
    Falconer, 9 February 1910, UTA, Office of the President, A67-0007, Correspon-
    dence of Robert Falconer. One of the main issues seems to have been the cost
    encountered by the Department of Education in maintaining this course; Fal-
    coner to Laird, 8 February 1912, ibid. Through various agreements with the
    Department of Education, the faculty, however, maintained its involvement in
    the training of teachers for the provincial school system.

33 Laird, 'Address, 1927, with Much History and Some Statistics,' 4.

34 Transcript of oral interview with Edna W. Park by Barbara Byers, 3 May 1974,
    2, UTA, Edna Wilhelmine Park, B74-0043.

35 Only in 1919 did McGill University agree to introduce a degree course leading
    to a bachelor of household science. The first two years were offered in the Fac-
    ulty of Arts and Sciences and the last two at Macdonald College. See Harris, *A
    History of Higher Education in Canada*, 285–6. For developments at McGill, see
    also Margaret Gillett, *We Walked Very Warily: A History of Women at McGill*
    (Montreal: Eden Press, Women's Publications, 1981), 347–53.

36 Laura Bradshaw Durand, 'The Latest Science – Housecraft,' *Maclean's*, 1915;
    reprinted in Lang and Upton, *The Dietetic Profession in Canada*, 72.

37 These research projects were recorded regularly in the annual reports of the
    president of the University of Toronto.

38 These included *Milk and Milk Products, Flesh Food and Their Value*, and *Food: A
    Factor in National Progress*, all published by Grolier in the 1920s in the series
    Book of Popular Science. She also co-wrote with Edna W. Park *The Household
    Science Book of Recipes: Individual and Large Amounts for Home and School* (Tor-
    onto: University of Toronto Press, 1923). These works had an important edu-
    cational value, since they discussed the latest findings in the nutritional
    sciences, such as the importance of minerals and vitamins in the human diet.

39 Robert Falconer to Annie Laird, 14 June 1926, UTA, Office of the President,
    A67-0007, Correspondence of R.A. Falconer.

40 Lang and Upton, *The Dietetic Profession in Canada*, 11, 16. For a recent study on
    the history of dietetics in Quebec and Ontario, see Nadia Fahmy-Eid et al.,
    *Femmes, santé et professions: Histoire des diététistes et des physiothérapeutes au Québec et
    en Ontario, 1930–1980* (Montréal: Fides, 1997).

41 'Violet Ryley, 1884–1949,' 2–3, Archives of Ontario (hereafter AO), T. Eaton
    Company Archives, Violet Ryley Papers, F 229-162-0-1378.

42 Meeting of the ODA executive, 18 May 1934, Minute book, 1929–35, part 2,
    AO, Records of the Ontario Dietetic Association, F 4168.

43 For the events leading to the creation of the CDA, see Lang and Upton, *The
    Dietetic Profession in Canada*, 27–32. Laird's determining role in the creation

of the CDA is confirmed by Edna Park, who stresses her 'strong, strong leadership' in these events. See Transcript of oral interview with Edna W. Park, 22, UTA, B74-0043. For Laird's views on the training of dietitians, see her 'Qualifications of Dietitians,' UTA, Faculty of Food Sciences, A75-0008.

44 Clara Benson, 'Report on the Faculty of Household Science,' in *Report of the President of the University of Toronto*, 1939, 31; 'Home Economics in Ontario: Data Required for Home Economics History,' 3, UTA, Edna Park Papers, B82-0004. Of the 50 per cent of graduates who were employed, 20 per cent were in dietetics, 18 per cent in teaching, and 12 per cent in other fields.

45 Jane A. Miller, 'Women in Chemistry,' in G. Kass-Simon and Patricia Farnes, eds., *Women of Science: Righting the Record* (Bloomington and Indianapolis: Indiana University Press, 1990), 311, 315–16. See also Carole B. Shmurak and Bonnie S. Handler, '"Castle of Science": Mount Holyoke College and the Preparation of Women in Chemistry, 1837–1941,' *History of Education Quarterly*, 32, 3 (fall 1992).

46 Her thesis dealt with the 'rates of reaction in solutions containing ferrous sulphate and potassium iodide and chromic acid.' Two articles based on this research appeared in 1903 in the *Journal of Physical Chemistry*. See the *University of Toronto Monthly*, 4 (January 1904): 117.

47 On Macallum's prestigious career, see Gordon Young, *The Development of Biochemistry in Canada* (Toronto: University of Toronto Press, 1976), 5–7.

48 On Benson's early days at the Lillian Massey School and at the Faculty of Household Science, see Clara C. Benson, 'The Beginnings of Household Science,' 'Teaching of Food Chemistry,' and 'Household Science: Chiefly of Lillian Massey Treble School,' undated documents, UTA, Edna Park Papers, B82-0004. Macallum would teach household science students in the early years of the faculty.

49 Falconer to Benson, 7 February 1912, UTA, Office of the President, A67-0007, Correspondence of R.A. Falconer.

50 Minutes of the Alumnae Association of University College, 1901, 7; quoted in Kennedy, 'Womanly Work,' 78.

51 C.C. Benson, 'Recent Work in Nutrition,' *University Monthly*, 15, 3 (January 1915): 135.

52 In 1937 the name was changed to the Fisheries Board of Canada. See Young, *The Development of Biochemistry in Canada*, 60.

53 'Report of E.E. Prince, Secretary-Treasurer of the Biological Board of Canada, Dominion Commission of Fisheries, to M. Lapointe, Minister of Marine and Fisheries,' 16 August 1923, NA, Records of the Department of Fisheries and Oceans, RG 23, vol. 1467, file 769-1-2 [3]. Prince reported to the minister that Benson was 'regarded as the most distinguished authority on this matter.'

54 'Report of Fisheries Branch,' Department of the Naval Service, Canada, *Ses-*

sional Papers, 1921, no. 40, 11. See also Kenneth Johnstone, *The Aquatic Explorers: A History of the Fisheries Research Board of Canada* (Toronto: University of Toronto Press, 1977), 86.

55 Cathie Breslin, 'Dr. C.C. Benson, First Professor of Food Chemistry,' *Varsity Graduate*, March 1958, 26.

56 Philip C. Enros, *A Bibliography of Publishing Scientists in Ontario between 1914 and 1939* (Ottawa: HSTC Publications, 1985), 30.

57 Minutes of the National Executive Committee, 3 April 1919, NA, Records of the YWCA, MG 28, I 198, vol. 10; Minutes of the World Fellowship Committee, 3 February 1941, ibid., vol. 57.

58 *Varsity Graduate*, December 1959, 50.

59 Clara C. Benson, Review of 'Woman and Labour' by Olive Schreiner, *University Monthly*, 12, 4 (February 1912): 147.

60 Transcript of oral interview with Edna W. Park, 2.

61 Durand, 'The Latest Science – Housecraft,' 73.

62 Toronto *Globe and Mail*, 25 March 1964, 2.

63 Breslin, 'Dr. C.C. Benson, First Professor of Food Chemistry,' 26.

64 'Violet Ryley, 1881–1949,' 1. Ellen Swallow's famous experimental kitchens, designed to supply a similar service to the American urban poor, could provide inspiration and guidance.

65 Ibid., 2. See also Lang and Upton, *The Dietetic Profession in Canada*, 6.

66 Lang and Upton, *The Dietetic Profession in Canada*, 20. Ethel Eadie was the first household science graduate to hold the position of superintendent. Ryley took over after Eadie's departure two years later.

67 'Violet Ryley, 1884–1949,' 3.

68 Durand, 'The Latest Science: Housecraft,' 76–7.

69 'Violet Ryley, 1884–1949,' 3.

70 Ibid., 3–4; Violet M. Ryley, 'How the Dietitian May Be of Assistance to the M.O. In Charge of T.B. Sanatoria,' Department of Veterans' Affairs, MHC, *Bulletin of the Association of Medical Officers Caring for Tuberculous Soldiers in Canada*, no. 5 (n.d.), 32, NA, RG 38, vol. 371, file: MHC, Care of Tuberculous; 'Report of the Department of Soldiers' Civil Re-Establishment,' 1919, Canada, *Sessional Papers*, 1920, no. 14, 61–4.

71 Ryley, 'How the Dietitian May Be of Assistance,' 33; 'Report of the Department of Soldiers' Civil Re-establishment,' 64.

72 Ryley, 'How the Dietitian May be of Assistance,' 33; Minutes of the Conference of Medical Superintendants Caring for Tuberculous Soldiers in Canada, 27 May 1918, Department of Veterans' Affairs, MHC, *Bulletin of the Association of Medical Superintendants Caring for Tuberculous Soldiers in Canada*, no. 10, NA, RG 38, vol. 371.

73 Upton and Lang, *The Dietetic Profession in Canada*, 10–17.

74 Ibid., 29.

75 See Joy L. Santink, *Timothy Eaton and the Rise of His Department Store* (Toronto: University of Toronto Press, 1990), 96, 146, 270.

76 For a detailed account of Ryley's years at Eaton's, see Florence Stacey, 'Commercial Dietetics in Canada,' T. Eaton Company Archives, Restaurant and Dietetics, AO, F 229-162-0-1353. See also Lang and Upton, *The Dietetic Profession in Canada*, 22–5.

77 Annie L. Laird, 'Speech Given at Alberta, 1936, with Some History,' UTA, Faculty of Food Sciences, A75-0008.

78 'Violet Ryley, 1884–1949,' 7.

79 Lang and Upton, *The Dietetic Profession in Canada*, 22.

80 Annie L. Laird, 'Address, 1927, Household Science – A Profession,' UTA, Faculty of Food Sciences, A75-0008.

81 Rossiter, *Women Scientists in America: Struggles and Strategies*, 201.

82 Even Benson, whose work was highly praised by her male peers, is given only five brief lines in a scholarly study on the history of biochemistry in Canada. The author also states that 'few original contributions of a biochemical nature have been published from the department [of food chemistry, at the Faculty of Household Science].' See Young, *The Development of Biochemistry in Canada*, 24.

83 It seems that Laird, Ryley, and other charter members of the Canadian Dietetic Association were eager to separate dietetics from household science, since they decided, like their American counterparts, to choose this name for the new organization and to dismiss suggestions such as the 'Canadian Association of Household Science Graduates' and the 'Canadian Home Economics Association.'

84 See Laird correspondence and reports in UTA, Faculty of Food Sciences, A75-0008. Lillian Massey-Treble had even to cover the salaries of some staff members in the early years of the faculty.

85 Edna Park also discusses the impact of the faculty's early difficulties on its staff and facilities. See Transcript of oral interview, 11–12.

86 See Ruby Heap, 'To Save "Women's Sphere": The Struggle over the Closure of the Faculty of Household Science at the University of Toronto in the 1970's,' paper presented to the 1994 conference of the Canadian History of Education Association, St John's, Newfoundland.

War and Peace: Professional Identities and Nurses' Training, 1914–1930

MERYN STUART

Conventional wisdom holds that female nurses who went to war between 1914 and 1918 were self-denying 'mothers of the world' who would save it from the barbarism of war. The image was a convenient and powerful one for the Canadian Red Cross, the emerging welfare state, and contemporary nursing leaders, who all had reasons to enhance this imagery to further their own goals. Because of this feminized symbolism, a direct relationship between nurses' war efforts, women's suffrage, and state registration for nurses has frequently been postulated.[1]

When one examines the lives and careers of particular nurses, however, a much more complicated picture emerges.[2] They did not necessarily go to war for reasons portrayed in the often romanticized rhetoric. Some did go for patriotic reasons, but they also went for adventure, for travel, and for a good time. I argue in this essay that many First World War nurses parlayed the heroic, dutiful image and their unique front-line experience into new careers in public-health nursing, and because of the prominence of this emerging field of practice, university education became a limited, although ultimately compromised, reality for these women. I focus on the stories of public-health nurses such as Marguerite Carr-Harris to illustrate the wider realities of the 1920s.

The war was not the only reason for the space that nursing found in that decade. The social context of university-based nursing education included the struggle for state registration and standardization of nurses' training by the nursing leadership,[3] the maternalist politics of the new woman of the 1920s and 1930s,[4] post-war concern over the poor health of army recruits, and the Canadian context of the welfare state, within which medical doctors and emerging male civil servants looked to the state to provide health and welfare services. Public-health projects aimed at mothers and children were initiated all over Canada in the teens and early twenties, sponsored by provincial governments, the Red Cross, and other philanthropic groups.[5] University certificates in public-health nursing were initiated in 1920 at the University of Toronto (and at five other universities across Canada) because of the huge demand for nurses in this field and because of the new roles emerging for single women in paid work. This was the beginning of a full-fledged professional university degree for nurses.[6]

By 1930, however, the heyday for public-health nursing was over, and just three university schools of nursing in Canada offered degrees: British Columbia, Western Ontario, and Alberta.[7] At the University of Toronto an integrated, basic baccalaureate program was delayed until 1942, when it was finally accepted that some nurses required higher education to be considered professional.[8] Although the war had created many of the social conditions necessary for public-health nursing to flourish, this momentum was not enough after 1930 to expand the certificate programs to full baccalaureate recognition within universities. In the 1920s and 1930s the expectation of a return to traditional feminine roles and the perception that the work of nurses was essentially a vocation, not a profession, were both incompatible with university degrees for nurses.

Ideology and Reality: Nurses and the First World War

Patriotism, femininity, piety, and duty to others came together in the image of the First World War nurse. A well-known, international Red Cross poster used for the recruitment of nurses depicts a seated female figure, robed and veiled, with the Red Cross sign on her cap, gazing heavenwards while she cradles a tiny wounded soldier on a stretcher. Literary critic Sharon Ouditt calls the image in the poster (titled 'The Greatest Mother in the World') 'a bizarre intersection of the madonna and child, and the Pieta.' She argues that recruitment appeals in England emphasized 'humility, unselfishness, the importance of giving generously and wholeheartedly, grudging nothing.'[9] Reminiscences of a Canadian nurse, appearing in the 1920 *Canadian Nurse Journal*, exemplify a spiritual view and also echo the poster's imagery: 'The Resuscitation Ward! Who, having been there could forget it. Sister and orderly working side by side with eyes that blurred and hearts that ached over the stretcher with its bundle of khaki, mud, and the questioning face of a soldier ... Here one saw the soul of the man and was proud and satisfied. The thought so often came: surely "this is holy ground."'[10]

Many feminist scholars argue that war must be understood as a gendering activity, one that ritually marks the gender of all members of a society whether or not they are combatants.[11] For example, roles for women other than nursing during wartime were seen by many as inappropriate and even insulting to the 'true' soldier. Some feminists believe that women symbolized qualities that fended off the barbarism implicit in war. Ouditt states that the values expressed were more 'spiritual than practical and they appeal to the self-denial promulgated by Christianity, to patriotism and to a general subservience to patriarchy.'[12]

Anne Summers's work on British military nursing points to reasons why it had such enormous appeal for women, and she gives us a detailed account of the origins and development of the regular Army Nursing Service. According to Summers, 'the archetypally feminine functions of caring, mothering, serving and housekeeping were given a setting of high drama, and elevated into the means by which women could achieve unequivocal public honour.'[13] The setting of high drama is indeed evident when one examines the careers of some Canadian nurses using their diaries, letters, reminiscences, and other primary sources.

During the war 3,141 nurses joined the Canadian Army Medical Corps (CAMC), and 2,500 went overseas. Forty-six died as a result, of wounds received during bombing, drowning at sea, or diseases such as dysentery and malaria.[14] Many more were undoubtedly changed physically and emotionally. Nurses went to war in large numbers, after enlisting in cohorts from the same schools of nursing, shortly after graduating. They were a self-selected, highly motivated group of women who wanted adventure and experience in a very public arena.[15] They were also seeking freedom from the tedium and boredom of hospital schools and hospital nursing. Many have retained pictures and descriptions of their striking uniforms, replete with brass buttons and scarlet collars, which became treasured keepsakes.[16] Even contemporary fiction, such as Radclyffe Hall's story of a woman ambulance driver who was filled with the 'fire of a desperate regret' after the war's adventures were over, speaks to a yearning for freedom from the constraints of being a traditional woman in 1918.[17]

The military nurses' accounts of their war experiences often reveal the good times rather than the horrors. They knew how to have fun with each other and with the military medical officers. Fraternizing with non-commissioned men was strictly forbidden, although Nursing Sister Wilhemina Mowat revealed that her 'first kiss in the Army' had been delivered by an orderly when she was carrying a tray of sterile instruments in the operating room. She also disclosed that she had got six weeks of leave after breaking her ankle, not in the line of duty, but by falling over a stool while dancing with another nurse! She vividly described her leave, with its trips and opera visits and good food.[18] Nursing Sister Ada Gillespie also described her six days of sightseeing in London and dinners with medical officers just after her experience on the torpedoed ship that had brought her to England.[19]

The Nurses' Work during the War

The initial overseas assignment for Canadian nurses who served with the CAMC Nursing Service was generally in English military hospitals – either the Queen Alexandra Military Hospital or St Thomas's. From there they were dispatched to one of several destinations, including the English emergency stations at Boulogne, Canadian camps at Salisbury Plains, or France, Italy, Salonika, Egypt, Russia, Mesopotamia, India, and East Africa. In each of these areas, they did duty in various types of hospitals or casualty clearing stations, ambulance trains, and hospital ships.[20] According to several accounts of the nursing service, the assigning of nurses to the various stations was the responsibility of Matron-in-Chief Margaret Macdonald, who, in the five years of war, distributed 2,500 Canadian nurses to the various hospitals.[21]

Nurses took on responsibilities that they had never faced before the war. Some learned how to give anaesthetics; others became masseuses, physical therapists, or dieticians. They learned to set up a tent hospital quickly, to assess the critically wounded, and to manage huge wards of sick men with little help. As a result, and because their devotion to the sick and wounded was such an inspiration to the nation, it was frequently said that their courage 'matched that of the greatest heroes of the war.'[22] Because of the unexpected number and types of casualties, nurses (and physicians, especially surgeons) were often under extreme stress and hardship. Number 3 Canadian Stationary Hospital, a casualty clearing station during the German offensive of March 1918, was thus described:

The Operating Room was a scene of greatest activity and gravely wounded cases predominated. The admissions rose rapidly. On the 21st of March, 276 were received; on the 23rd, 1064; on the 26th, 1622; the 27th, 1932, and on the 28th the record was 2333. It became necessary to place two patients in one bed, and one on a mattress under the bed. Day and night, work in the Operating Room went on without cessation. At first, four teams (A surgeon, Sister, and two orderlies constituting a team) by day and 3 by night, and later there were at least a dozen teams in operation continuously. To successfully cope with the greatest emergency, almost super-human effort was required and be it recorded, the Nursing Staff rose to the occasion in majestic fashion.[23]

Yet not all nurses were in such emergency situations at all times. The war record of Alfreda Atrill, the first Winnipeg General Hospital graduate to go overseas in 1914 with the first contingent of the Canadian Expeditionary Force, illustrates the wide range of duties assigned to nurses at the front.

Atrill's responsibilities included clerical work in the matron-in-Chief's executive office and sickbay duty on transport to England, caring for cases of flu and tonsillitis. Subsequently she took charge of storage and inventory of all equipment at one hospital, did relief duty in two wards, and special duty with gangrene cases. She was then made sister in charge of the largest ward in the Queen Alexandra Military Hospital, Westminster, which was situated in the dining room and tea verandas of the Golf Hotel. She originated the fresh-air and sunlight treatment of gas gangrene cases. One year later she was put in charge of a ward at Outreau, France (General Hospital No. 2), and soon after was transferred to Salonica, where she served on duty in malaria tents and dysentery lines and was then recommended for charge duty in sanitation arrangements. She was also put in charge of the eye and ear hut, made the assistant night nurse responsible for a hospital of 100 beds, and assigned duty as the sewing sister, at which time she made one hundred (sleeping?) bags and blackout curtains. The next stage in Atrill's military career took her back to England, where she did relief duty at Basingstoke on the 'incorrigible ward'; after that she served on a hospital ship to Canada, where she had a brief furlough before returning overseas in 1918. In March that year she received a diploma for completing the special remedial course and was put in charge of special massage and remedial work at Palace Hospital. According to her war record, Alfreda Atrill gave 2,200 treatments while in the Remedial Department. She returned to Canada in August 1919, and in October resumed civic duties as a public-health nurse in the Child Welfare Division in Manitoba.[24]

The war fostered a national alliance that gave Canadian nurses a sense of identity and a belief that their numbers constituted a powerful sort of movement, ensuring nursing a visibility that had not been possible before

First World War nursing sisters relaxing at Orpington, England, site of a Canadian military hospital. Ada Gillespie is standing at the back (first left) in the white apron.

the war. Military nurses, and through them, civilian nurses, now had an international recognition that was unparalleled and had been created in part by their commissioning to officer rank (which American and British nurses had not received) and by the awarding of medals to them, in particular, the Royal Red Cross.[25]

The New Woman, Public Health, and Maternalist Politics: Marguerite Carr-Harris

Intractable social problems such as poverty, women's working conditions, prostitution, prisons, sick babies, maternal mortality, and urban decay were all exacerbated by the years of war. Maternal solutions to these problems characterized the approach of many educated, reform-minded, Anglo-American women who were born in the 1860s, 1870s, and 1880s. Mariana Valverde and many other feminist scholars have analysed women's agency in the formation of state social policy, exposing the complicated interplay of moral reform, social purity, and the social gospel.[26] Canadians such as Nellie McClung, Charlotte Whitton, and Alice Chown, as well as well-known Americans among whom were Miriam Van Waters, Jane Addams, Florence Kelley, Lilian Wald, and Eleanor Roosevelt, joined 'ordinary' nurses such as Marguerite Carr-Harris and Ellen La Motte, an American who pioneered tuberculosis nursing, fought the opium trade in the East, and was a published author about her war experiences.[27] They lived lives that had no precedent. They were career-minded, ambitious, and independent, and they stayed out of conventional wife-mother roles. They often lived with an extended family or in settlement houses or domestic relationships with other like-minded women. Even Eleanor Roosevelt, married to the American president and a mother of five, wielded a great deal of political power in her own right and led another life with her women friends and lovers.[28]

Marguerite Carr-Harris was just such a middle-class, well-educated, unmarried woman who was armed with a semi-religious passion for helping to make the world a better place within her vision of the needs of the empire. She was born in Ottawa in 1879, the third in a family of six children. Her father, Robert Carr-Harris, was a prominent civil engineer and professor. Her mother, Ellen Fitton, had participated in all the privileged activities of Ottawa's upper-class society.

Marguerite's mother died in 1890, the year her daughter was twelve and began a diary of her life detailing her devotion to her father. Carr-Harris attended Kingston Ladies College and played on the Kingston ladies' hockey team. In 1896 her father remarried. Now almost twenty, Marguerite attended Queen's University for two years, studying humanities, but left without graduating.[29] Her father's inherited money was now gone, and his second wife was to bear six children. Undoubtedly because she was 'redundant' and needed to earn a living, Carr-Harris went to the prestigious Presbyterian Hospital in New York in 1904 to train as a nurse. She worked off and on in the never-secure position of private-duty nurse to the rich (also visiting the Grenfell Mission in Newfoundland) until the war began and she joined the CAMC. She was sent overseas in 1915 and saw active service for four and a half years, returning in July 1919, after being decorated by the king for her bravery under a bombing attack at the Canadian hospital in Étaples.[30]

Carr-Harris's family was concerned because 'she could not make up her mind' about marriage on at least two occasions, although she lived an active social life in France, New York, and Toronto. She had clearly been bored with life and discouraged with nursing[31] before she went overseas, so it must have seemed a godsend when she received her telegram to report for duty in 1915. By 1920, when the Ontario Board of Health was looking for nurses, she was ready. Her special interest was parent education, and she had the desire for adventure and the independence to make her an ideal candidate.

Like Carr-Harris and Alfreda Atrill, most military nurses were well suited to public-health work because they were accustomed to being on their own, in public and dangerous places, with men, on troop ships and trains all over Europe.[32] They believed that they were more alert and self-confident than nurses who had stayed at home, and furthermore, they had focused on the prevention of disease and illness in often ill-equipped places. One nurse saw herself as 'adjunct both to the Medical Officer's skill and the soldier's courage.' She also distinguished herself from her civilian sisters: 'Military nursing follows no laws, abides by no rule, is governed by no precedent that is not honoured in the breach and disregarded coolly when the occasion, expediency and necessity require. A broad-minded, progressive intelligence, a quick imagination and a supreme disregard for that "aseptic conscience," so necessary in civil nursing, are essential factors in successful Military Nursing.'[33] As Nursing Sister Marjorie Heeley put it, 'We had freedom to use our own initiative ... we had lived in a man's world.' This freedom was lacking in hospital and private-duty nursing positions.[34] In the latter, conflict resulting from class inequality flourished; the nurse was often 'superior' to the domestic servants in the home but 'inferior' to her patient.

Public-health nursing was a way to get ahead, to achieve status in the profession. Harriet Meiklejohn, one of the first nurses hired by the Ontario board, confessed that she had entered the field in order to 'advance' herself.[35] It was also a way to express inculcated values of Christian social justice within a feminine, nurturing occupation that was considered appropriate for single women. In tones similar to the rhetoric of the war, Miss E. MacPherson Dickson, inspector of Ontario training schools in 1923, extolled public-health nursing: 'More Christian service can be given in these new fields because they are more arduous, rougher, more democratic than the average case of private nursing. These new public services seem nearer to the firing line, nearer to the point of greatest suffering, and of greatest need for service, where one can spend oneself most freely.'[36]

The Rural Child-Welfare Project and the Ontario State

In May 1920 Dr John McCullough, chief medical officer of the Provincial Board of Health, told his minister that he was looking for 'natives of Ontario' for the position of provincial public-health nurse. The regulations pertaining to the nurses stipulated that applicants must be graduates of a 'recognized training school,' possess two years of high school or its equivalent, be eligible for membership in the Graduate Nurses' Association of Ontario, and provide letters of recommendation from the secretary of the training school alumnae and a physician. A 'certificate of health' was also required.[37]

By June 1920 eight nurses had been hired, each at a salary of $1,500.00 per year. In addition, the Ontario Red Cross announced its intention to pay the salaries and expenses of a further eight nurses, allowing two to go to each of the eight districts in the province. McCullough made it clear that the board controlled the duties of the nurses; the Red Cross would only pay the salaries.[38] In October the Board of Health sent the sixteen nurses to northern and rural parts of the province to 'educate' mothers, in an attempt to lower the unacceptably high infant mortality rate. This was in fact a kind of natural field experiment, called a 'demonstration,' because it was entirely new to the delivery of public-health programs.[39]

And what would the nurses be doing in their districts? As McCullough explained to the minister of labour and health, they would 'endeavour to interest newspapermen, clergymen, physicians and prominent men and women in establishing a *Community Health Centre* and in securing a public health nurse to carry on maternal and child welfare work, medical inspection of schools and general public health follow-up in neighbourhoods. [emphasis mine].'[40] Clearly, an expanded function – 'general public health and follow-up' and 'community health' – had replaced the focus on infant mortality that many members of the board had insisted should dominate. There is no direct evidence that the new minister and the United Farmers government (elected in October 1919) had influenced this more general direction. However, it seems likely that, given their commitment to a more equitable system, they wished to provide basic health care to those who had none. Certainly, Premier E.C. Drury was aware of the program: in 1920 he invited Marjorie Heeley, who was demonstrating in Barrie, to come up onto the platform during a political rally to talk about the work that she and the board were doing.[41]

Although 'all but one' of the nurses had previous public-health experience, McCullough and his advisers decided that a three-month 'intensive' course in child hygiene was necessary. An outline of the course reveals as much emphasis on generalized public health as on child hygiene. The nurses spent one month at the Toronto Hospital for Sick Children, under paediatrician Dr Alan Brown's 'direction,' learning 'pediatrics' and the 'organization of baby welfare clinics.' In addition, they were taught 'ear, nose and throat nursing' at the hospital, and Dr Gallie, an obstetrician, taught prenatal nursing care, confinement care and technique, and post-confinement care. The remaining course work included public-health administration, tuberculosis, venereal diseases, communicable diseases, social service, statistics, economics (child-labour laws), and sanitation.[42]

Ontario's public-health nurses received higher salaries than most other nurses – and indeed, higher salaries than most women professionals, other than physicians and lawyers. Fifteen hundred dollars a year ($125 a month) compared favourably with the income of the private-duty nurse, who could not expect to earn more than $70 a month (often less) and whose work could not be guaranteed for twelve months. (Most superintendents of schools of nursing in the best hospitals could expect to earn $1,000 a year and never more than $2,000.) In addition, public-health nurses were given their living expenses – $50 a month – which generally allowed them to stay at a good boarding house or hotel.[43] They often had the use of the board's cars, which in the 1920s lent prestige and status to the nurses and their work. They were not required to wear uniforms but often worked in 'tweed suits,' or other comfortable clothing.

Nor were they expected to do menial cleaning tasks related to their work. In fact, in an effort to keep the prestige of the project – and that of the nurses – high, they were actively discouraged from undertaking work which would lower their image from that of a 'health teacher.' For example, when Nurse Olive Gipson wrote to say that she had undertaken to scrub the clinic room in Rockland, her supervisor, Miss Knox, told her to get 'a woman' to clean it and send the bill in to the central office.[44]

The outdoor life of public-health nursing appealed to many, anxious to be freed from the confinement of hospital walls. Many were reportedly anxious to go to the north because they sought adventure. Nurse Edna Squires wrote in 1923 that she was 'glad of the excitement' of being stuck with her car in a storm on a winter night. Another nurse, Ina Grenville, wrote blithely of crossing thin ice on a sleigh in the course of her work. And in 1923, Marguerite Carr-Harris wrote of her joy at being in the countryside: 'Driving through these glorious hills with none but the wild animals to disturb you is a real feast of the soul.'[45]

In October 1920 Carr-Harris was sent with another nurse to Health District Seven, which comprised 90,000 square miles in the extreme northwestern part of Ontario. The towns and villages were often joined only by railway lines; no roads connected them, merely 'wild land.' One-fifth of the area was organized into municipalities (a total of 56,000 people), but the population of unorganized settlers, mostly outside the towns and villages, was unknown. Many lived in very isolated conditions. The people were primarily of British, Scandinavian, and eastern European origin. Carr-Harris's mission was to serve the whole district. However, she began her demonstration in the town of Kenora.[46]

Her work was to consist of 'demonstrating' public-health nursing through the following rather daunting list of activities: obtaining lists of all births within the previous two years; visiting all 'registered' babies and expectant mothers at home; making a special effort to find 'unregistered' babies; giving mothers 'council [sic] and demonstrations in all matters pertaining to health, sanitation, hygiene and healthful living'; gathering all information possible on cases of tuberculosis, 'mental deficiency,' communicable diseases, and bad sanitary conditions and reporting all such findings to head office; directing and coordinating the work of voluntary agencies and workers in the event of epidemics, carrying out bedside nursing 'in cases of absolute emergency,' and teaching by demonstration a member of the family; holding clinics for pre-schoolers; and inspecting all school children after getting permission from the local Board of Education. She was to send daily and monthly reports back to head office and also make visits to the surrounding towns and villages.[47]

Despite the fact that they were fifteen hundred miles from Toronto and lacked any real supervision from their superiors, the nurses' operat-

Marguerite Carr-Harris at approximately age fifty, after her public-health nursing adventures.

ing 'regulations' cautioned them against suggesting treatment or diagnosis to their patients – indeed, even against 'advancing opinions.' Family physicians were to be notified in writing after the nurse had made the first visit, and future visits were to be deferred pending his reply. Nurses were also forbidden to give 'material relief' to their patients.[48]

The focus on 'health education,' however it was delivered by the nurses, would not erase the effects of poverty or replace the lack of expert care in the treatment of morbidity and the prevention of mortality. The program was a facile solution to the serious problem of a lack of permanent resources for immigrant settlers in northern Ontario and the poor in the south of the province, as well as the tensions created by rural depopulation.[49] Nevertheless, through the strategies of socializing with isolated mothers and organizing clubs and parties, as well as utilizing every opportunity to teach about health, the nurses were effective in showing people that someone was at least interested in their well-being. Carr-Harris noted in one of her many reports: 'To be able to say to a mother living away back in the bush, 'the government have sent us to see how you and your children are getting along, and if we can be of any service to you,' invariably brought not only willingness to show the children but an eagerness to get all they could out of the visit.'[50]

Perhaps because of her new-found autonomy, the public-health nurse was by now characterized as an elite member of her profession. These nurses had unlimited scope, and there seemed to be much to do. According to Ethel Johns, the first director of the School of Nursing at the University of British Columbia and editor of the *Canadian Nurse* from 1933 to 1943, the public-health nurse's mission was different from that of the institutional nurse. As she put it, 'You are going out as leaders; you are not tied to routine duties like your sisters in the hospitals; you are not harassed with 1001 petty interruptions; you have time to think and read and plan, and, above all, you have the opportunity to break new ground.'[51] George Weir, an influential educator and architect of the welfare state, explained: 'as a travelling evangelist and teacher of health ... no patriot could ask for greater opportunity to serve his country than is given to these young public health missionaries and teachers in rural and urban Canada.'[52] The issue of how to educate these 'missionaries,' however, was a large part of the nursing and medical discourse by 1918.

The War and Higher Education for Nurses

The war had provided the impetus to raise the numbers as well as the standards for applicants to hospital nursing schools, the only places where women could obtain a nursing education in 1918. Unprecedented numbers applied for admission to the large and prestigious Toronto General Hospital in 1914 and 1915 (1,912 in 1915, compared with 1,323 in 1913).[53] After the war many nursing superintendents, especially those from the large, urban schools, raised their standards of admission. For example, Jean Gunn, the superintendent of the Toronto General Hospital from 1913 to 1941, increased the school's minimum entrance requirement from one to three years of high school in 1923.[54] Untrained or partially trained women had been a sore point with the nursing leadership during the war. There were complaints that the military accepted some women whom the nurses believed were unfit for overseas duty because they had not graduated from a recognized training school with appropriate entrance standards. There was no relationship between the military nursing service and civilian nursing organizations, the former being controlled by the medical officers of the CAMC. Most superintendents, like Jean Gunn, were not veterans, although they supported the war effort at home by actively working with the Red Cross.

Throughout the early twentieth century, nursing leaders had collectively and vigorously campaigned to increase public awareness of the necessity for standardized and comprehensive professional training. Higher education in universities was always part of the plan. In 1918, in an attempt to standardize training in Toronto, nine of the eleven hospital schools centralized some of their lectures in the medical building at the University of Toronto. Although it represented only the lending of classroom space, this move was considered by Gunn to be a first step to full association with the university.[55]

However, no matter how standardized, Ontario hospital schools did not prepare nurses for the post-war work of reconstruction and health teaching that was believed to be needed in the wake of the discovery of Canadians' poor state of health. A special nurse, fitted to be a health reformer, was needed, and universities were seen to be the best site for the preparation of this new public-health worker because they could provide the courses in bacteriology, sanitation, adminstration, social service, and educational methods. Nursing leaders knew that this was so, and in 1918 they surveyed every university president in Canada about his plans for nursing education.[56] Although most (including the University of Toronto's Robert Falconer) were indifferent or non-committal, one important report in Ontario recommended that nursing education for 'reconstruction' must 'look to universities for leadership and aid.'[57]

This was a strong endorsement for public-health nursing to be located in an academic setting. Such nursing was practical, utilitarian, and similar to other professional programs, such as social work, engineering, and public-health medicine, all programs that Ontario universities, especially the University of Toronto, supported in principle after the devastation of the war.[58]

In 1920 formal preparation in public-health nursing was available in Canada at only one university – Dalhousie in Halifax. However, courses were to begin that year at four other universities, including Toronto and Western Ontario.[59] Provincial branches of the Canadian Red Cross had decided to fund the education of public-health nurses as part of their peacetime activities, after active lobbying by nurse leaders. This move gave nursing a 'foot in the door,' so to speak, in its quest for higher education within a university setting.

In June 1920 the Senate of the University of Toronto passed a recommendation establishing the Department of Public Health Nursing.[60] It was to be administered as a separate department, with no official status or Senate representation, under the sponsorship of the School of Hygiene in the Faculty of Medicine and financed by the Ontario Red Cross Society. The Department of Public Health Nursing was also affiliated with the Social Service Department, which taught the 'Medical Social' class and provided lecture-room and reading-room accommodation until 1926, when Nursing moved into the newly constructed School of Hygiene building.[61] By 1923, when Red Cross funding expired, approximately 130 nurses had graduated from the one-year certificate program, and the attrition rate was extremely low. According to Kathleen Russell, the director of the program, an enrollment this large was 'unprecedented in the history of new departments in the university.'[62]

The demand for public-health nurses in Ontario exceeded the supply that either Toronto or Western Ontario could provide. In her 1921–2 annual report Russell stated that 45 per cent of her graduates had found jobs in Toronto and another 45 per cent throughout Ontario. These figures were constant for most of the 1920s, when demand from both boards of health and the Victorian Order of Nurses was high. And the graduates were all women; no men appear as students of the University of Toronto program in the 1920s and 1930s.

However, the university refused Russell's recommendations to develop a degree program or to award the nursing staff academic status or the department Senate representation when the Red Cross funding expired. A long period of experimenting with a four-year diploma program in conjunction with the Toronto General Hospital and of seeking autonomous school status, as well as a building, finally ended in 1933 when the Rockefeller Foundation gave funding for five years for a separate school of nursing. The Ontario government also provided money towards renovations when it was clear that the university and outside interests were supportive. In 1939 the Rockefeller Foundation decided to provide an endowment of $250,000 for the school, and its future was secure.[63]

It is clear, however, that the public-health nursing program was never really intended to lead to a generic degree or to full professional status for all nurses. At this time, nursing leaders, including Russell, did not support degree programs for nurses except for those in public health, teaching, and administration. For her 'the most significant issue was the separation of nurses' education from hospital service,'[64] not the acquisition of a degree. In fact, reconciling the caring, practical, feminine content of the nursing curriculum with more-masculine, scholarly, scientific goals proved to be a barrier to baccalaureate education for all nurses.[65]

Hospitals were definitely not interested in degree programs since they did not hire graduate nurses in any numbers until after the Second World War. Student nurses staffed hospitals; there was no need for a university-educated bedside nurse in the 1920s, unless she was in patients' homes, away from the supervision of physicians and head nurses. When Marguerite Carr-Harris obtained a baccalaureate degree in 1929 from Teacher's College at Columbia University, it was undoubtedly meant to provide her with advanced credentials in either public health or nursing education.[66]

Conclusion

British historian Susan Kent concludes that after the First World War, people 'sought a return to the traditional order of the prewar world, an order based on natural biological categories of which imagined sexual differences were a familiar and readily available expression.'[67] After the war a powerful ideology of motherhood and a re-emphasis on separate spheres for men and women augmented the political and economic restructuring. Images of femininity, nurture, and the family were invoked to restore the balance of the militarism and barbarism of war and to protect society's faith in the social order. A gendered social environment slowed nurses' ambitions to a crawl by 1930.

The war had created expectations about new and adventurous roles for women, and had roused public-health reformers and demobilized mili-

tary nurses to join with the Red Cross, boards of health, and philanthropic organizations to save the health of Canadians. However, although
university education for public-health nurses developed as a response to
these trends, universities were unwilling to give degrees to nurses because
of the status of nursing as a menial, if romanticized, occupation. As for
nursing leaders, they were ambivalent about degrees because they did not
see them as a goal for all nurses, and they wished to maintain the caring,
practical aspects of nursing the sick. Women's professional identities had
changed, but there were strings attached.

NOTES

The research on which this article is based was supported by Associated Medical
Services Inc. and the Hannah Institute for the History of Medicine.

1 See, for example, Veronica Strong-Boag, 'Making a Difference: The History of
   Canadian Nurses,' *Canadian Bulletin of Medical History* 8(2) 1991: 244, and Alison Prentice et al., *Canadian Women: A History* (2d ed., Toronto: Harcourt
   Brace, 1996), 146, 244.
2 There is very little documentation on the First World War and Canadian nursing, either primary or secondary, despite the fact that nurses were the only
   women in formal military roles and at the front. There were no men in the
   military nursing service. The few primary sources are scattered all over Canada
   in various archives, public and private, military and civilian. There is one valuable, but strictly narrative, account of the development of the Canadian nursing sisters' corps: G.W.L. Nicholson, *Canada's Nursing Sisters* (Toronto:
   Samuel, Stevens and Hakkert, 1976). On the use of sources, see Ruby Heap
   and Meryn Stuart, 'Research Note: Nurses and Physiotherapists: Issues in the
   Professionalization of Health Care Occupations during and after World War
   One,' *Health and Canadian Society* 3 (1995): 179–93. For autobiographies, see
   Ellen La Motte, *The Backwash of War: The Human Wreckage of the Battlefield as
   Witnessed by an American Hospital Nurse* (New York: G.P. Putnam's Sons, 1916),
   and Mabel Brown Clint, *Our Bit: Memories of War Service by a Canadian Nursing
   Sister* (Montreal: Barwick, 1934). The latter is the only published contemporary Canadian account by a First World War nurse. For work that is particular
   to Canadian military nursing in the war, see M. Leslie Newell, '"Led by the
   Spirit of Humanity": Canadian Military Nursing, 1914–1929' (Master of science
   in nursing thesis, University of Ottawa, 1996).
3 Leaders considered that the examination and registration of nurses (accomplished in Ontario in 1922) was an essential aspect of the drive for the recogni-

tion and professionalization of an occupation then viewed by the public and many physicians as barely better than servitude.

4 See Carroll Smith-Rosenberg, 'The New Woman as Androgyne,' in Smith-Rosenberg, *Disorderly Conduct: Visions of Gender in Victorian America* (New York: Alfred A. Knopf, 1985). See also Estelle Freedman, 'The New Woman: Changing Views of Women in the 1920s,' *Journal of American History* 71 (September 1974): 372–93, and her fascinating biography of a 'new woman,' *Maternal Justice: Miriam Van Waters and the Female Reform Tradition* (Chicago: University of Chicago Press, 1996). Van Waters was a social worker and reformer who was superintendent of the Massachusetts Reformatory for Women from 1932 until 1957.

5 For a description of one such demonstration, the Massachusetts-Halifax Health Commission, see Kathryn McPherson, 'Nurses and Nursing in Early Twentieth Century Halifax' (MA thesis, Dalhousie University, 1982), chapter 4, 86–101.

6 For an example of analysis regarding the necessity for university education, see a report on the future of the School of Nursing at McGill University, in which the director, Bertha Harmer, recommended two nursing degree programs because, without degrees, nurses would be at a disadvantage; Survey Committee of 1930–31, Recommendations of Survey Committee, School of Nursing, McGill University Archives, RG 64, C10, box 5.

7 Rondalyn Kirkwood, 'The Development of University Nursing Education in Canada, 1920–1975: Two Case Studies' (PhD thesis, Department of Adult Education, University of Toronto, 1988), 159.

8 Degrees were generally believed to be desirable for public-health nurses, teachers, and administrators only, until the 1960s.

9 Sharon Ouditt, *Fighting Forces, Writing Women: Identity and Ideology in the First World War* (London and New York: Routledge, 1994), 20–1.

10 Nursing Sister L.E. Denton, 'What Went Ye Over to See?' *Canadian Nurse* 16 (August 1920): 367. This was typical of the kind of article published during and immediately after the war. No pieces critical of the conflict could be found in the *Canadian Nurse*, but see La Motte, *Backwash of War*, for a highly critical contemporary American nurse's account.

11 Margaret Higonnet, Jane Jenson, Sonya Michel, and Margaret Collins Weitz, eds., *Behind the Lines: Gender and the Two World Wars* (New Haven: Yale University Press, 1987), 8.

12 Ouditt, *Fighting Forces*, 21.

13 Anne Summers, *Angels and Citizens: British Women as Military Nurses, 1854–1914* (London: Routledge, 1988), 6.

14 Nicholson, *Canada's Nursing Sisters*, 98.

15 See the article by (anonymous) 'Nursing Sister C.A.M.C.': 'Military Nursing,' *Canadian Nurse* 13 (August 1917): 482–90. She discusses the work and also the 'great adventure,' patriotism, and travel inherent in the military nurse's experience.

16 Many of the first-person accounts discussed below include a description of the uniform.

17 Radclyffe Hall, *Miss Ogilvy Finds Herself* (London: William Heinemann Ltd, 1934).

18 See Wilhemina Mowat (Mowie) Waugh, 'White Veils, Brass Buttons and Me': Memoirs of a Nursing Sister in World War 1 in the CAMC, 1915–1920,' Brandon General Hospital Archives, uncatalogued.

19 Ada V. Gillespie, CAMC, First World War diary, in the possession of her family (photocopy in author's possession).

20 Unsigned paper entitled 'The Development of Canadian War Nursing Service,' McGill University Archives, RG 64c. 7, folder 21, Military Nursing Service, W.W.1.

21 Ibid.

22 Letter from Matron Macdonald to Mr Landon, 1922, National Archives of Canada (NA), MG 30, E 45, Macdonald Papers.

23 NAC MG30 E45- File: History of the Nursing Service/Memoranda; Article: NO. 3 Canadian Stationary Hospital, p. 4–5. This was presumably written by Matron Margaret Macdonald, since these records are from her papers and were notes collected for a history of the nursing service which she never completed.

24 Alfreda Atrill, 'War Memories of Miss Alfreda J. Atrill' in a collection of unpublished papers titled, *The Development of Canadian War Nursing Service.* See also Mabel Clint, *Our Bit*, pp. 54–68, for a description of the nurses' difficulties with dysentery, flies, and other sanitation problems in Greece on the Island of Lemnos. One matron and a nursing sister died there in 1915.

25 An example of the visibility was the national War Memorial, erected in 1926 in the Hall of Fame in the Canadian Parliament buildings. See Kathryn McPherson, 'Carving Out a Past: The Canadian Nurses' Association War Memorial,' *Histoire Sociale/Social History* 29 (1996): 417–29, for a cogent analysis of the imagery and ideology behind the lobbying for, and successful erection of, the Memorial.

26 Mariana Valverde, *The Age of Light Soap and Water: Moral Reform in English Canada, 1885–1925* (Toronto: McClelland and Stewart, 1991). The literature on maternalism and the welfare state is large internationally, especially in the last five years. A special issue of *Gender and History*, Autumn 1992, is devoted to this topic. For the most helpful Review Essays, see: Felicia Kornbluh, 'The New Literature on Gender and the Welfare State: the U.S. Case,' *Feminist Studies*, 22

(spring 1996): 171–97; Jane Lewis, 'Women's Agency, Maternalism and Welfare,' *Gender and History* 6 (April 1994): 117–23; and Renate Howe, 'Gender and the Welfare State: Comparative Perspectives,' *Gender and History* 8 (April 1996): 138–42. For critical Canadian perspectives on the state and public health and children's issues, see Mary Louise Adams, 'In Sickness and in Health: State Formation, Moral Regulation and Early VD Initiatives in Ontario,' *Journal of Canadian Studies* 28 (winter 1993–4): 117–30, and Mariana Valverde, 'Families, Private Property and the State: The Dionnes and the Toronto Stork Derby,' *Journal of Canadian Studies* 29 (winter 1994–5): 15–34.

27 Ellen La Motte wrote one the first 'blueprints' for the establishment of tuberculosis nursing programs in the United States, *The Tuberculosis Nurse* (New York: G.P. Putnam Sons, 1915), before going to war. As a prolific writer, she influenced North American public-health programs, which were obsessed with routing tuberculosis. Her life and work are analysed in Marie Lanser Beck, 'The Early Career of Ellen Newbold La Motte (1873–1961), World War One Nurse, Author and Anti-Opium Crusader, 1902–1925' (MA thesis, History, Shippensberg University, 1992).

28 Her life is insightfully explored in Blanche W. Cook, *Eleanor Roosevelt*, vol. 1, 1884–1933 (New York: Viking, 1992).

29 Her student record is in the Queen's University Archives. None of her relatives whom I interviewed knew (or remembered) that she had ever attended Queen's.

30 Carr-Harris was named for 'good work' (also called 'mentioned in dispatches') during the bombing of the hospital in 1918; see 'History of the Nursing Service,' chapter 6, NA, MG 30, E 45. This is undoubtedly why she received the Royal Red Cross.

31 Evidence for this interpretation is contained in a letter that she wrote to her aunt from France on 19 August 1912, in the possession of May Sharpe.

32 For an example of danger, see Ada Gillespie's diary on the experience of being evacuated from a boat about to be torpedoed. For being in public places unescorted, see Mowat's memoirs about a trip to Belgium on a troop-filled train.

33 Anonymous nursing sister, 'Military Nursing,' 482.

34 Interview with Marjorie Heeley Whitney, 12 August 1986.

35 Letter, H. Meiklejohn to Beryl Knox, Archives of Ontario (AO), RG 62, F 1b, box 475.

36 'Report of the Inspector of Training Schools in the Province of Ontario' 1923, 9. This report is to be found among the public-health nurses records in AO, RG 10, 30 A1, box 11, file 8a.

37 'Regulations' (typescript, n.d., 1920?), AO, RG 10, 30 A1, box 4, file 8.

38 The announcement of the funding, along with the names of the nurses sponsored, is to be found in Canadian Red Cross Society, Ontario Division, *Bulletin*,
no. 2 (1 April 1921), 1, AO, RG 10, 30 A1, box 4, file 8. Their support was
reported to be part of the Society's 'peacetime' effort to encourage public-
health nursing.

39 For an analysis of the whole project, see Meryn Stuart, 'Let Not the People
Perish for Lack of Knowledge: Public Health Nursing and the Ontario Rural
Child Welfare Project, 1916–1930' (PhD thesis, University of Pennsylvania,
1987).

40 Memorandum to the Minister of Labour and Health from McCullough,
14 June 1920, AO, RG 62, B 1b, box 439, file 2.

41 Interview with M. Heeley Whitney in September 1986.

42 'July, August and September, 1920' (typescript), AO, RG 10, 30 A1, box 4, file
8. The nurses were each given a copy of the list of courses that they had
completed.

43 Information about private-duty nursing salaries is found in John Gibbon and
Mary Mathewson, *Three Centuries of Canadian Nursing* (Toronto: Macmillan
Co., 1947), 164. Superintendents' salaries are provided in Marjorie Mac-
Murchy, *The Canadian Girl at Work* (Toronto: T. Nelson, 1920), 44.

44 Letter, Gipson to Knox, 7 November 1920, and Knox's reply, AO, RG 62, F 1b,
box 474.

45 Letter, Squires to Mary Power, 3 January 1923, AO, RG 62, F 1b, box 475; Grenville to Knox, n.d. (1922?), ibid., box 481; Carr-Harris to Power, 19 October
1923, ibid., box 478.

46 The population and mileage estimates are taken from a hand-drawn map and
notes in Carr-Harris's own writing, to be found in AO, RG 10, 30 A1, box 1, file
14. It took more than eighteen hours to cross District Seven by train.

47 'Outline, Plan of Work for Provincial Board of Health Nurses,' AO, RG 10,
30 A1, box 8, file 15.

48 The regulations are in 'Outline, Plan,' 3–4.

49 On rural depopulation, see W.R. Young, 'Conscription, Rural Depopulation
and the Farmers of Ontario, 1917–1919,' *Canadian Historical Review* 53 (1972):
289–319. For a modern account of the medical personnel problems of the
north, which the welfare state has been unable to resolve, see 'Medical
Bureaucracy a Source of Affliction in Town of Rainy River,' *Globe and Mail*, 2
January 1989, A1; this town of 850 was unable to find a second physician. Molly
Ladd-Taylor is critical of the influence of women's movements on the state,
arguing that 'the welfare system we have today is in many ways a legacy of the

parochialism of the maternalist network'; *Mother-Work: Women, Child Welfare and the State, 1890–1930* (Urbana and Chicago: University of Illinois Press, 1994), 203.

50 'General Report of Work ... in District No. VII,' 4, AO, RG 10, 30 A1, box 8, file 14. Many of the nurses' names became 'household words.' See, for example, a mention of public-health nurse Rose Hally in Alice Marwick, *The Northland Post: The Story of the Town of Cochrane* (Oshawa: Maracle Printing Co., 1950), 261. Carr-Harris's files contain some letters from mothers and children which indicate that she was a friend and source of help to them.

51 Ethel Johns, 'Ideal in Public Health Nursing,' *Canadian Nurse* 14 (March 1918), 911.

52 G.M. Weir, *Survey of Nursing Education in Canada* (Toronto: University of Toronto Press, 1932), 124.

53 Natalie Riegler, 'The Work and Networks of Jean I. Gunn, Superintendent of Nurses, Toronto General Hospital, 1913–1941: A Presentation of Some Issues in Nursing during Her Lifetime' (PhD thesis, University of Toronto, 1992), 371.

54 Ibid., 370. Gunn was involved in almost every nursing and Red Cross Society initiative in Ontario between 1913 and her death in 1941. She was also president of the Canadian National Association of Trained Nurses between 1917 and 1920 and the second vice-president of the International Council of Nurses between 1925 and 1933, among her numerous committee memberships, nationally and internationally.

55 Ibid., 269–70.

56 For the implications of the war on health, see W.H. Hattie, 'Some Medico-Sociological Problems Arising Out of the War, '*Canadian Nurse* 12 (November 1917): 682–9. For the survey on university education, see Helen MacMurchy, 'University Training for the Nursing Profession, '*Canadian Nurse* 14 (September 1918): 1284–8.

57 MacMurchy, 'University Training,' 1288. This was Justice Hodgins's *Report and Supporting Statements on Medical Education in Ontario,* published in 1918.

58 See A.B. McKillop, *Matters of Mind: The University in Ontario, 1791–1951* (Toronto: University of Toronto Press, 1994), 562.

59 For a summary of Red Cross support to schools of nursing, see Barbara Tunis, *In Caps and Gowns: The Story of the School for Graduate Nurses, McGill University, 1920–1964* (Montreal: McGill University Press, 1966), 122.

60 See Kirkwood, 'The Development of University Nursing Education,' 58–140, for the following analysis and description of the University of Toronto school.

61 Evidence for the relationship with Social Service is found in the University of Toronto's 'President's Report, Report of the Director of the Social Service Department,' 1921–2, 62, University of Toronto Archives (UTA).

62 'Department of Public Health Nursing Annual Report, 1922–23,' 1, UTA, A83-0041, Faculty of Nursing. Quoted in R. Kirkwood, 'Blending Vigorous Leadership and Womanly Virtues: Edith Kathleen Russell at the University of Toronto, 1920–52,' *Canadian Bulletin of Medical History* 11 (1994): 180.

63 See Kirkwood, 'Blending Vigorous Leadership,' 190–1, for a complete description and analysis of this period.

64 Ibid., 196.

65 For this problem of dissonance, see Kathleen Russell's article, 'The Canadian University and the Canadian School of Nursing,' *Canadian Nurse* 24 (December 1928): 627–30.

66 There are no letters or other personal documents to tell us why she studied for a degree. She was fifty years old when she graduated, and she apparently never worked for pay afterwards. There is some evidence that she kept house for relatives and travelled with wealthy women as their companion. She also became a Rosicrucian and spent much time in California. She died at the Veteran's Hospital in Montreal in 1961.

67 Susan K. Kent, *Making Peace: The Reconstruction of Gender in Interwar Britain* (Princeton, NJ: Princeton University Press, 1993), 140.

The Feminine Face of Forestry in Canada

PEGGY TRIPP-KNOWLES

Forestry as a profession has been a male bastion for most of its almost century-long existence in Canada. This bias has been the result in part of the history of forest work, which required stamina, strength, and relocation away from urban centres. Remnants of this reputation are still evident in forestry education, with such professional rituals as 'lumberjack' competitions. In recent decades, however, women have been accessing forestry education and careers in increasing numbers.

As a woman university educator in a professional forestry faculty, I have pondered this gendered history of forestry juxtaposed with the present role of women. What is the feminine face of forestry in Canada? To explore this question I present the results of three very different avenues of investigation. First, I offer a thematic presentation of the personal voices of several women reflecting on their own experiences in forestry. They comment on their initial motivation to study this field, the existence of and reaction to barriers, and their views about the role of women in forestry. Second, I have summarized the scholarly and popular literature as an overview of the topic. Finally, a statistical analysis of women graduating with forestry professional degrees provides a quantitative perspective.

Personal Voices

I introduce the personal voices with my own history to clarify both the choice of themes presented and my motivation to examine this issue. My connection with forestry as a profession originates from my appointment in 1980 to a tenure-stream faculty position in forestry. At the time I was unaware of the fact that I was the first woman with such an appointment in Canada. That position followed an undergraduate specialization in psychology (after I had failed a science program), work experience in social-science research, and graduate work in evolutionary biology using forest trees as organisms of study.

This circuitous career path was compounded by a major directional change after more than a decade of successful professional academic work. I experienced a crisis of conscience about the value of my forest-science research. In the course of a sabbatical I agonized over an increasing sense of conflict between myself as a woman and myself as a forest scientist. The difficult decision to close down my research laboratory was the culmination of my deliberations.[1] The major source of tension for me was focused beyond the level of gender interaction in the workplace to the core of underlying assumptions: I was unable to conduct research without condoning what I felt was inappropriate domination of the forests by overzealous harvesting and my own unavoidable contribution to environmental degradation with laboratory chemical wastes. In other words, the eco-feminist in my soul was screaming for expression. I made a directional change in my professional life by closing my lab, developing ties with Women's Studies, and designing more interdisciplinary teaching and research. The present analysis of the role of gender in forestry is a manifestation of that shift in direction.

To introduce the themes that surfaced in my own career history, I first focus on examining the early motivation that led to an eventual association with forestry. My experience indicates a lifelong sense of connection to the forest, which created a desire for such a career, starting with a narrative about a pine tree in grade three. Later, in a high school guidance course, I was directed away from exploring a career in forestry to the more 'appropriate' topic of dental hygiene. Ironically, this incident occurred in the very same year that the first woman graduated from forestry at the University of Toronto.

The second theme addresses barriers experienced by women in forestry. I use the term 'barriers' as broadly defined; some interviewees preferred 'challenges.' My experience leads me to interpret the attainment of my position as an accomplishment gained in spite of the educational system, rather than because of it. My initial attempt to study at the graduate level was denied because I was married to an in-progress graduate student, a status that implied to the psychic admissions committee that I would leave town before my own completion date. Several years and special-interest courses later, my application was successful. Is this strategy of persistence in the face of barriers or challenges a common theme among women in forestry?

Another personal recollection pertains to a social barrier that I experienced as a young woman faculty member in forestry. One social event involved playing a hockey game followed by drinking at a local strip bar. I recall this incident with mixed feelings. I recollect a sense of comfort at being accepted by my peers, along with the discomfort of sports and drinking as a recreational activity.

As a final theme, I ask the question that I have often pondered, 'Have women had an impact on forestry?' My personal speculation is 'Indirectly, yes,' as evidenced by the simultaneous rise of the feminist and environmentalist movements over the past three decades. However, this potential (and some would say tenuous) connection among environmentalism, feminism, and forestry is an indirect association. Have the women in forestry had a *direct* impact on the profession? From my perspective the answer to this question is 'Not appreciably,' since there are still small numbers of women in the profession and of those, very few rise to positions of power.

I have asked four women to contribute reflections on their own histories, addressing these themes. The personal voices are those of women with strong, and in some cases long-lasting, connections to forestry. Since it is uncommon to find women with high-profile forestry positions, anonymity is impossible. More to the point, however, it is undesirable. These women are essentially pioneers in forestry in Canada, and they merit documentation and acknowledgment as such. Two criteria were used to select the women for this project: a successful career in forestry in Canada, with an emphasis on educating professional foresters at the university level, and/or a forestry background with expertise in feminist analysis. Three of the four contributors are currently associated with the forestry profession, and two of these are in educational settings, while the third is associated with industry. One of the interviewees has a forestry background and is at present working in an advocacy role for women. Of the four contributions, three are based on personal interviews that I conducted and the fourth (Winifred Kessler) on a thematically organized autobiographical sketch. When questioning the contributors, I asked them to focus on the themes listed above: initial motivation, barriers or challenges encountered including coping strategies, and opinions about women's impact on forestry.[2]

To introduce the contributors briefly, I begin with Marie Rauter as a well-established career forester, currently president and CEO of the

Ontario Forest Industries Association. In 1965 she was the first woman to graduate from the University of Toronto with a forestry degree and one of the first women forestry graduates in Canada. After undergraduate training, she pursued a master's degree in forest genetics, secured a research position in that field, and subsequently worked with a governmental agency in forest policy development before shifting to her present position in industry.

The second contributor, Winifred Kessler, is a professor and the chair of forestry at the University of Northern British Columbia. She is the first woman in Canada to head a professional forestry academic unit. Her undergraduate and graduate work was conducted in the United States, in zoology and in wildlife and rangeland management respectively. Her career path included a faculty appointment at the University of Idaho. She served as a U.S. Forest Service ecologist in Alaska and Utah and then as a policy analyst in Washington, DC. Her present academic position brought her to Canada.

Sandy Smith is a professor of forestry at the University of Toronto. She was hired in 1988, becoming the first and only woman to hold a tenure-stream appointment at the Toronto Faculty of Forestry since its founding in 1907. Although Sandy was unaware of it at the time, the original funding for her position had been provided to the university by the provincial government as an 'equity' package to increase the proportion of women in academia. Ironically, the undergraduate program in forestry was terminated soon afterwards (in 1993) by the university administration. Sandy's undergraduate degree was in agriculture and her graduate specialization in forest entomology. Postdoctoral studies followed her PhD, and she subsequently assumed her current faculty position.

Gwen O'Reilly enrolled in the undergraduate forestry program at Lakehead University, from where she graduated in 1981. Thereafter she conducted a research project for the master's program and held a research position in a forest genetics project until 1991. Since that time she has had a long-standing front-line position in women's advocacy and in that context has developed expertise in feminist analysis.

With these brief introductions, I turn my attention to the first thematic question about initial motivation to study forestry. Most contributors' responses indicate an undercurrent of social pressures influencing early choices, including family expectations, awareness of the existence of programs, and stereotypical perceptions of the role of the professional forester. All contributors exhibited an unquestioned motivation to study beyond the high school level and a passion for studying a discipline within the biological sciences, but not necessarily forestry. There was a split in the motivation to focus on application, with some respondents initially attracted to the applied biological sciences and some to the natural biological sciences.

To sharpen the focus, the first contributor, Marie Rauter, had a confident determination to study forestry at university. She was initially unaware of, then unperturbed by, the fact that women had not previously enrolled in forestry at the University of Toronto.

I didn't know what I was getting myself into, and when I discussed forestry with my counsellor in high school, he thought it was peculiar, but arranged for me to get a calendar and see the dean ... and so ... when I looked at the calendar, I thought ... 'They've got Devonshire House as the men's residence, but I don't see a women's residence!' When I met with the dean I asked ... 'I've got some questions about the calendar ... Where is the women's residence?' ... And he said, 'We've never had any women in the forestry program before.' But I wasn't going to let that get me down ... I don't think I even took an extra gasp. I just continued with my next question and just thought, 'Well, okay, where do we go from here?'

Winifred Kessler was similar in her confidence, but in her case she was determined to pursue her interest in wildlife and the outdoors.

I chose Zoology because this major would fit my interest in wild creatures while providing a suitable pre-med course of study. Why pre-med? I assumed that as a physician, I would be able to limit my practice to 2 or 3 days a week, thus freeing up ample time to pursue my interests in wildlife and the outdoors. At the time, I hadn't a clue that careers in wildlife biology and management even existed. If the school counselors were to be believed, my career choices consisted of nurse, teacher, legal secretary, or dental hygienist – none of which appealed to me.

As it turned out, Winifred did not go to medical school because opportunities for studying wildlife management materialized.

As young women, both Winifred and Sandy shared a passion for studying a biological field other than forestry. Sandy knew that she wanted to pursue an applied biological science, so she chose agriculture, since 'I didn't know that forestry existed when I came out of high school.' Even if she had been aware of the forestry program at the University of Toronto, the city of Toronto itself would have been out of reach. Sandy, who grew up in a very small southern Ontario town, recalled that her parents 'would have been very concerned if I said I was going to Toronto to university ... it was bad enough going to Guelph.'

Gwen's attraction to forestry had a strong undercurrent of wanting to study and work out of doors. She held a popular perception of the forestry profession that included a cabin in the woods and 'the romantic notion of living in the bush.' From her home town of Guelph, Gwen initially applied for and was accepted in a biology program both at Guelph and at Lakehead in Thunder Bay, but was turned down for forestry. In the meantime she visited and enjoyed Lakehead University and its surroundings, and decided to pursue forestry by waiting a year to reapply. Fortunately, a helpful guidance counsellor got her on a waiting list, and she was accepted without delay.

Responses to the second theme, focusing on barriers or challenges encountered by the women, indicated that obstacles were pervasive, but the reactions to them varied. Winifred's strategy in the face of barriers was one of confident persistence and patience. She summarized her general reaction with the following reflection on the themes that have characterized her career: 'Seize all opportunities! Persevere in the tough times! When obstacles arise, blaze new trails around them.' One example will illustrate her strategy:

With the master's degree in hand, I was keen to work in the field. My applications earned only rejection letters, in which it was cordially but firmly noted that field positions were not open to female candidates. Today we would cry 'discrimination!' But such outright exclusion was normal and socially acceptable at the time. I responded by looking for a PhD opportunity. My objective was to make myself so well and uniquely qualified that prospective employers couldn't afford to pass me up, despite my gender.

In general, Winifred reported that the gender barriers she encountered, particularly recently, were minimal.

By this time [after her appointment to the University of Idaho], gender had pretty much ceased to be an issue in the natural resource fields. It's true that I worked mostly with men, but this was never a problem. I'd grown up with brothers, and my positive experiences with my professor-mentors gave me a high comfort level for working with men. Besides, my unique combination of academic and practical experience made me significantly better qualified than most of my male peers.

Marie revealed a similar assertive perseverance in her reaction to challenges, as the above-mentioned anecdote about her initial enquiry of the university dean attests. Once enrolled in the forestry program, she was the only woman for the entire four years of training. She described her classmates as 'not knowing what to do' with her and playing pranks on her during classes. In one incident the other students took advantage of Marie's habit of taking her shoes off during class by surreptitiously placing them on a light fixture, beyond her reach. She recollected this event with affection and a smile, and proceeded to emphasize the protectiveness with which the other students treated her. 'I never tried to be "one of the boys." Through the four years, many of us developed close friendships – friendships that have lasted through the years.'

In considering the topic of gender barriers in forestry, Marie preferred the term 'challenges.' According to her, the perception of events as barriers is a matter of interpretation that was never a component of her mindset. Rather, she attributes career success and collegial respect to a positive outlook on life, in contrast to a negative attitude or blaming male students and professors.

Furthermore, she regards herself a humanitarian rather than associating with any particular group. The increasing societal focus on 'minority' concerns (including women and ethnic minority members) has a drawback, according to Marie.

When you think about political correctness, you are being forced into thinking about differences instead of thinking about what is the calibre or quality of the best thing that I want [referring to interviewing young people for forestry jobs] ... I find that there is more discrimination today in all ways than there was when I was in public school ... [At that time] I didn't feel that I was discriminated against because I was a female ... One thing that I have always been against is tokenism. I can remember when I moved from research into policy with government, I had no sooner been ensconced in my new job, when someone from the Human Resource Department paid me a visit to ask about my desired career path – being a promotable female. After my anger subsided, my response was that once I had proven myself in my current job, I would entertain other positions – but I expected that any promotion would be because of my accomplishments, not my gender.

Like Marie, Sandy reported a lack of experience with what she would interpret as barriers in her own career in forestry. She was, however, aware and concerned about obstacles, particularly those surrounding family issues, about which she has valuable experience. Our initial discussion took place in Sandy's kitchen at the end of her maternity leave after the birth of the second of her two sons. Barriers that women face in forestry, according to her, include the conflict between the location of work, traditionally in the north with continual relocation, and the need for more stationary residence for family commitments involving partners and/or children. 'I think the thing is ... not to give up your career for a family. I still firmly believe that, even after having a family. I think you should be able to do both with the right support network. I'm in a situation where I can do that ... I am glad I did career first and then a family ... but that's a personal thing ... not everyone can have that.'

Gwen's consideration of obstacles was one of insight into the larger societal meanings of barriers against women in forestry. Recollecting her university experience evoked mixed reactions. Mastery of the knowledge base and skills of the discipline were welcome challenges. Gwen also reminisced warmly about the camaraderie among her close-knit male and female student peers. On the other hand, she recognized the 'damage to my self-esteem over the four years of university.' Gwen was particularly articulate about this problem, which she associated with her role as a woman in forestry.

In retrospect, there was a lot of submerging. You had to be tough to cope ... you had to be one of the guys ... you had to drink like one of the guys ... and still keep your marks up ... And I always felt really disadvantaged when they [male peers] made a sexist comment and I would try and counter them with the limited language and analysis that I had at the time. They would say, 'You sound like a feminist,' and I would say, 'I'm not a feminist ... but ...' And some of my professors would bug me. [One of them] would always make comments about breasts, ... and [another] had a particular fondness for objectifying women.

The reaction of classmates to the accidental loss of field photographs by a women's work crew during Gwen's first summer work experience had an enduring impact.

[Our] male classmates believed that I had lost the photos on purpose so we wouldn't have to do the work. In retrospect I wonder if [they] felt that as a girl I ... wasn't up to this, and this was my solution ... So that was one of my first real introductions to what it meant to be a woman in forestry ... After that I decided that I liked the work in the bush, but I would feel more competent in a research position ... I felt like I would have more ... credibility ... That was a world where women had a sense of control ... that men own the bush. As long as it was a physical venue where strength or courage ... was the most desirable trait ... then men would always have the most credibility in those situations.

Gwen's developing interest in women's issues, feminism, and lesbianism was another focus of tension as she moved through her educational career from senior undergraduate level to graduate work and then on to a research assistant position in forestry.

It was probably during my senior year and then when I went on into graduate school that I had been getting involved in feminism ... reading a lot of stuff ... thinking a lot about sexism. At the time I was also coming out as a lesbian, so that was a whole other area of my life ... People knew that I was a feminist, and people also knew that I was a lesbian ... I was doing some television work ... and there was a certain amount of overt homophobia that would go on ... I really felt like an outsider ... There was this increasing alienation.

From this sense of alienation in forestry, Gwen moved to a new career promoting social change and economic justice for women. Her life in forestry contributed to the matrix of experiences motivating her to work towards equity goals and feminist ideals. 'Feminism is really the place where I got my ability to analyse politically ... and what feminism does is that it connects everything ... I feel more comfortable with feminism than forestry. [With forestry] I don't really feel authentic. I really think that that is what gets stolen when you create a kind of status quo that exclusively belongs to men ... that women can't own it.'

Gwen's uncomfortable experiences in forestry underscore the tenacity of obstacles in the profession. Since she was the youngest interviewee, one might have expected a smoother pathway if 'all the battles had been won.' This, unfortunately, was not the case. An analysis of the responses of the interviewees according to age indicates that, while the barriers persist, there may have been a shift from structural ones, such as the lack of precedents for women in forestry programs or jobs, to more subtle attitudinal obstacles.

Like the women's strategies for coping with barriers, their opinions about the third theme, women's impact on forestry, were diverse. There was an overall acknowledgment that there are relatively few women in the profession. Within this framework, the views expressed formed a continuum from the sentiment that women had little direct impact on forestry as a profession to the notion that the few women involved have made a substantial and positive contribution.

Marie considered the paucity of women in higher-level forestry positions:

That's what disappoints me with many of the females. They graduate, they work for a couple of years ... and then they just drop out of sight ... and if you take a look at how many have graduated over the last few years, they're not represented in forestry jobs today. Perhaps they don't have a commitment to a career ... If women have a shortcoming in the general sense, it is probably insecurity, a lack of confidence in their own capabilities. I have been fortunate throughout my career [in] having confidence in my capabilities and support from those around me, including my professional peers.

In spite of this paucity of women in the profession, Marie has high esteem for their contributions to forestry. She cites particularly accomplished women who have had responsible positions within the forestry community, including a president of the Canadian Pulp and Paper Association; a spokesperson within the business community who has a undergraduate forestry degree as well as a joint master's degree in law and business administration; and a forest programme developer for the Ontario Ministry of Natural Resources. Marie summarizes her regard for the significance of women in forestry and details the achievements of exemplary women in the profession:

Given that there are relatively few women in the field, they have made a tremendous contribution to forestry, science, education and policy throughout Canada. Their influence on forestry in Canada is substantial at present and will continue in the future. Examples include: a policy analyst who participated in the programme development for forest certification; a research scientist with the Canadian Forestry Service; an internationally respected forest ecologist with Wildlife Habitat Canada; and a member of the Canadian Pulp and Paper Association, who was instrumental in developing the educational course used by school boards across Canada.

Sandy expressed the expectation that more women in forestry would alter the profession, but that the nature of the change would be impossible to know in advance. In answer to the question 'Will women change forestry?' she responded:

Yes. If there [are] enough of them, they will, because any new group that comes in will change it. At U. of T. [University of Toronto] it is very international. Our forestry program is not a traditional one ... although it started that way and has been up until the mid-80s ... because of the international component of the profs that are involved ... We've had three or four out of fifteen or twenty profs, 15 to 20 per cent [who were from outside of Canada]. If you got that of women I'm sure they'd change it. It's just the perspective because people bring in a background that is a little different.

Prior to its recent closure, the undergraduate program in forestry at the University of Toronto had a higher proportion of women students than was found at other institutions. Sandy recalls that often up to 50 per cent of the students were women, and she attributes this high representation in part to the location of the program in Toronto, close to home for much of Ontario's population. Many women students who for financial, cultural, or emotional reasons wanted to study close to their parental home found that a Toronto location made that possible.

Our faculty has always been atypical because of Toronto, because of where we are ... That was one of our arguments to prevent the suspension of the undergrad program ... was that we're a door through which some groups will come into the forestry program that otherwise won't come into it. International students and women might be more apt to come into the profession through us than through other faculties across the country. That was our argument, but they didn't buy it. [The decision to close the program prevailed.]

Gwen's experience with issues of social change has given her a global perspective on the impact of women on forestry:

I have a real hard time juxtaposing [women and forestry]. When I think about forestry now, I think about corporations ... My sense of forestry is that it is controlled by corporate influences ... the same way I see most other things in the world, especially resource-based economies ... that it's controlled by corporate interests and that there's a very similar set of circumstances that go with that and that is ... lip-service to development ... lip-service to reforestation ... increasing government policies [that are] increasingly giving corporate interests a freer hand in taking forests for their own use ... and not providing any particular regulatory power ... Individual people are losing control ... particularly women ... [So] I have a hard time thinking about women and forestry impacting in a particular way. The women who have entered industry have been co-opted ... The size and nature of industry is too large for women to have an impact ... That is one thing I have learned from my feminist organizing around social change and economic justice ... is that you can't enter into that without your own agenda ...

The issue is ... who becomes just token representatives? ... It doesn't matter if they are strong women or not ... they go to a meeting and their agenda is completely overlooked ... they're not listened to ... they can't make any valuable contribution.

From the personal narratives of these four women and my own, it is apparent that the professional careers of women in forestry are diverse. While commonalities exist among the experiences of the five of us, differences are also conspicuous. In an attempt to contextualize our collective stories further, my journey took me to the literature on women in forestry.

A Look at the Literature

My first impression of the collective literature on the topic of women and forestry was its paucity. I have examined the scholarly works in both the forestry and women's studies professional journals, as well as in popular magazines. The works analysed can be divided into three distinct categories: acknowledgment of women's participation in the forestry profession, description of the special connections between women and forests in third-world countries, and eco-feminist critique of the industrial forest management paradigm.

The highlighting of women's participation in traditional forestry practice coincides with the goals of the liberal feminist movement. That is, the 'system' (in this case, the forest management 'system') is considered generally sound, but the under-representation of women is seen as a problem. Thus the thrust of these papers is to encourage more women to enter the field. Examples of works in the literature with this focus include almost all the articles in an entire journal devoted to and called *Women in Natural Resources.* Unfortunately, its circulation is limited. The majority of articles in this category are personal accounts of the rewarding lives of women professional foresters[3] or historical accounts of all the women who have influenced a regional or national forestry initiative.[4] The introduction to a conference entirely devoted to women's contributions to forestry promotes the high quality of research conducted by the participating women in order to 'help break down stereotypes and encourage other women to pursue excellence' in the profession.[5] The literature in this category has seen few Canadian contributions, tends to be somewhat dated, and is found mainly in the forestry professional literature.

Items in the second category are woven together by the common thread of women's contributions to forest use, deforestation, and afforestation (planting trees) in third-world countries. In forestry jargon these studies are called social forestry or community forestry. Journal articles focus on such topics as the significance of women's participation in local land-use projects, the role of women as fuel-wood collectors, and women's access to international funds. International aid is often highlighted in these works, with many papers evaluating the impact on women of funding for remediation of environmental and economic problems.[6] This literature tends to be more recent, with some Canadian content, and has a wider, interdisciplinary scope beyond forestry, extending into anthropology, geography, and women's studies journals.

Finally, there is a third category that I have called 'eco-feminist critique.' It includes papers that criticize the founding assumptions of industrial forest management. They link women with nature and consider that patriarchal domination of both is a major contributor to global crises in general and to over-exploitation of forests in particular. For example, one author describes herself as unwilling to 'support an industry that is based on the exploitation of both the forests and people.'[7] In another example, the work of a women's collective in cultivating a tree farm is documented.[8] And the feminist scientist Vandana Shiva coins the term 'maldevelopment' in her paper critiquing the impact of colonial forestry practices in India.[9] My own paper in this area examines the discipline of forest genetics and points to perceived masculine biases.[10] This category of literature is the most recent and is found exclusively in professional or popular women's periodicals and books. Of the three themes, eco-feminist critique was represented by the fewest papers, and the authors were all women, chiefly from the former British colonies of India and Canada.

In sum, the literature contains few contributions from practising foresters, the activity in which the majority of women working in the profession are employed. Even where it exists, this literature does not reflect very strongly the experiences of women in forestry. Is the situation the same for the culture of professional forestry education? A quantitative analysis of the data on women's enrolment in forestry education assists us in constructing answers to this question.

Professional Forestry Education in Canada

A forester gains professional status in Canada by acquiring a bachelor of science in forestry (BScF) degree or by writing equivalent exams offered

TABLE 1
Dates of establishment and present status of professional forestry programs in Canada

University	City	Program initiation	Program status/ date of closure
New Brunswick	Fredericton	1908	ongoing
Moncton	Edmunston	1985	ongoing
Laval	Quebec City	1910	ongoing
Toronto	Toronto	1907	1993
Lakehead	Thunder Bay	1971	ongoing
Alberta	Edmonton	1970	ongoing
British Columbia	Vancouver	1921	ongoing
Northern BC	Prince George	1993	ongoing

Sources: Initial data drawn from George Garratt, *Forestry Education in Canada* (Sainte-Anne-de-Bellevue: Canadian Institute of Forestry, 1971), 22. Additional data supplied through personal communication with the universities listed.

by provincial forestry accreditation organizations. At present the degree is offered as a four-year program in seven universities across the country. Table 1 shows the dates of establishment and present status of the Canadian programs. Where do women fit into Canadian professional forestry education? Two different types of evidence address this question. First, I have examined the language used in documents about forestry education, and secondly, I have gathered statistical data of the ratios of graduates by gender from selected forestry degree programs in Canada.

Over the past four decades, language depicting the image of a forester as masculine has gradually given way to a more gender-neutral standard. As an example of the ubiquitous portrayal of a forester as male up to the 1960s, I quote from a 1960 description of forestry training: 'If the forestry schools are to turn out men who will provide leadership at all levels, they must offer programs that go far beyond vocational training.'[11]

A 1971 document has much more inclusive language, with such terms as 'forester,' 'professional,' and 'student,' rather than 'man.'[12] Gender bias, however, is evident in the use of the masculine pronoun, as seen in this description of the importance of the fieldwork component of forestry education: 'The value of this experience ... is dependent upon ... the extent to which he is exposed to a range of activities.' As late as the mid-1980s this use of the masculine pronoun for a forestry student was still evident in the offerings of at least one university calendar.[13] But since then gender-neutral language appears to be the rule, not the exception.

The increasing incidence of such language coincides well with the

growing profile of women in forestry education, as revealed by graduation statistics. Table 2 lists these figures from forestry programs at three
Canadian universities.[14] It is noteworthy that 1960 and 1965 mark the
graduation of the first two women foresters in this data set. The proportions slowly rise in the 1970s, with a substantial, albeit minority, female
profile apparent throughout the 1980s and 1990s.

A comparison of the last two columns – that is, the percentage of
females who dropped out with that of males who did so – indicates that,
on average, proportionally more women leave professional forestry education than men. This outcome can be interpreted as evidence that barriers against women in forestry still exist. Both the statistics and some of the
evidence drawn from the interviews discussed earlier support the theory,
drawn from the literature on women in science, that women in non-
traditional professions are disadvantaged throughout their careers.[15]

The numbers of women professors in forestry education in Canada are
nevertheless gradually increasing, an informal reading of current trends
suggests. According to Ursula Franklin, the University of Toronto feminist scientist, one has to 'look to the margins' to find women instructors
in forestry.[16] But women have long made up a small, but consistent proportion of sessional or contract instructors, lab demonstrators, and professors in related disciplines such as botany.[17] And the majority of forestry
faculties in Canada now have at least one woman member, while the
University of British Columbia and the Université de Moncton have relatively high proportions of female faculty members.

Conclusion

This snapshot of women and forestry suggests that the profession is at a
pivotal stage with respect to gender. The personal voices represent a
diversity of impressions about the impact of women on forestry, but they
do paint a coherent picture of a profession with very few women in high-
profile or long-standing positions. But the graduation data show an
increasing number of women. This trend may indicate that forestry is at a
turning point and on the brink of incorporating considerable numbers of
women into the profession.

A second conclusion involves the background of the women in my
interview sample who are working in professional forestry education. Not
one of the three of us (Winifred, Sandy, and myself) has a professional
forestry undergraduate degree. My familiarity with the relatively few
women in Canada in professional forestry education suggests that we are

TABLE 2
Gender analysis of the numbers of professional forestry graduates from three Canadian universities, 1907–1995

Individual university				Totals of the three universities		
Ratio of women/men graduates						
Year	Toronto	British Columbia	Alberta	% graduates female	% female drop-outs[a]	% male drop-outs[b]
1907–20	0	–[c]	–	–	–	–
1921–59	0	0	–	–	–	–
1960	0	1:32	–	3	0	36
1961–4	0	0	–	–	–	–
1965	1:25	0	–	4	0	31
1966–70	0	1:na[d]	–	–	–	–
1971	1:45	0:53	0:na	1	0	8
1972	3:46	0:37	0:na	4	25	24
1973	0:43	0:42	0:na	0	100	35
1974	4:45	5:66	0:33	6	−79[e]	16
1975	1:43	0:59	0:38	1	75	37
1976	2:47	5:73	2:53	11	44	26
1977	5:56	11:70	10:65	12	40	20
1978	4:42	11:50	13:53	16	36	27
1979	14:53	14:75	6:38	17	7	17
1980	18:53	6:67	8:39	17	29	1
1981	14:38	11:39	7:33	23	41	20
1982	21:43	15:49	7:35	25	33	16
1983	14:44	2:66	7:36	14	47	28
1984	11:44	20:65	5:18	22	40	40
1985	12:47	18:63	7:29	21	−56	20
1986	12:37	14:69	8:45	18	12	20
1987	5:34	6:52	8:44	13	37	11
1988	8:23	7:52	3:33	14	33	−24
1989	5:29	4:26	6:34	14	42	27
1990	6:13	12:36	7:22	26	−53	18
1991	2:19	9:53	6:33	14	−38	−138
1992	3:18	8:41	4:34	14	26	14
1993	4:11	14:52	9:25	23	−23	−16
1994	6:14	16:70	11:35	22	−12	−95
1995	4:6	10:42	9:25	24	47	43

[a]This figure was calculated as follows: for each of the three universities individually, the number of female drop-outs was calculated by subtracting the number of female graduates from the number of females who had enrolled four years earlier (in the first year of that cohort's program). The numbers of female drop-outs were summed across all universities and then divided by the sum of the number of female enrollees across universities and multiplied by 100 per cent.
[b]This figure was calculated analogously to 'a' using the data for males.
[c]A dash indicates that calculation of that value was inappropriate (e.g., the program did not exist that year at that university).
[d]na = not available.
[e]A negative value indicates that more students joined the ongoing program than dropped out (usually with a forestry technology background).

representative; many women in forestry education come to the profession from related disciplines. We may therefore conclude, first, that forestry is relatively tolerant of diverse backgrounds and, second, that as in many other professions, women have made successful inroads into the discipline 'from the margins.' Given time, these few women in professional forestry education are likely to encourage women students to complete professional degrees and pursue related careers, eventually making women's profile in forestry more visible.

At the same time, the existence of a feminist critique of industrial forestry agendas is significant. This critical voice is yet a whisper, seen here in the very recent literature as well as in the personal voice of the youngest interviewee and my own. However, its existence is noteworthy since feminist critique is playing an increasing role in influencing other disciplines. I would earmark this component of women's influence on forestry as worth watching as a harbinger of a greater contribution in the future.

NOTES

1 Peggy Tripp-Knowles, 'Androcentric Bias in Science: An Exploration of the Discipline of Forest Genetics,' *Women's Studies International Forum* 17 (1994): 1–8.

2 I wish to thank Winifred Kessler, Gwen O'Reilly, Marie Rauter, and Sandy Smith for their autobiographies or interviews, their patience and collaboration at all stages of this manuscript, and their permission to use their personal voices.

3 Sample papers include Richard Pardo, 'Can a Woman Be a Forester?' *American Forests* 84 (1978): 22–5; Diana Starr, 'Why I Want to Be a Forester,' *American Forests* 73 (1967): 6; Deborah Yarrow, 'Straight Talk,' *Journal of Forestry* 91 (1993): 60.

4 Lee Pendergrass, 'Dispelling Myths: Women's Contributions to the Forest Service in California,' *Forest and Conservation History*, January 1990, 17–25; Elaine Enarson, *Woods-Working Women* (Tuscaloosa, Ala: University of Alabama Press, 1984).

5 R. Max Peterson, 'Women in Natural Resources,' in S. Kossuth and N. Pywell, comps., *Current Topics in Forest Research* (USDA Forest Service General Technical Report 5E46).

6 Sample papers include William Grigsby and Jo Ellen Force, 'Where Credit Is Due: Forests, Women and Rural Development,' *Journal of Forestry* 91 (1993): 29–34; Louise Fortmann, 'Women in Subsistence Forestry,' *Journal of Forestry* 84 (1986): 39–42; Irene Tinker, 'Women and Community Forestry in Nepal,' *Soci-*

ety and Natural Resources 7 (1994): 367–81; Cathy Nesmith, 'Gender, Trees and Fuel: Social Forestry in West Bengal, India,' *Human Organization* 50 (1991): 337–48.

7 Priscilla Boucher, 'In Search of a More Complex Telling: Challenging the Dominant Story of the Forest Industry,' *Canadian Woman Studies* 13 (1993): 42–4.

8 Kate Millet, 'All Spruced Up,' *Ms Magazine* 16 (1988): 30–1.

9 Vandana Shiva, 'Colonialism and the Evolution of Masculinist Forestry,' in Sandra Harding, ed., *The 'Racial' Economy of Science* (Bloomington: Indiana University Press, 1993), 303–14.

10 Tripp-Knowles, 'Androcentric Bias.'

11 Forestry Education in Canada, *1960 Joint Forestry Convention, Chateau Frontenac, October 23–28* (Quebec: Canadian Institute of Forestry, 1960) 67.

12 George Garratt, *Forestry Education in Canada* (Sainte-Anne-de-Bellevue: Canadian Institute of Forestry, 1971), 47.

13 Lakehead University calendar.

14 Registration and graduation data were obtained directly from the respective universities.

15 Peggy Tripp-Knowles, 'A Review of the Literature on Barriers Encountered by Women in Science Academia,' *Resources for Feminist Research* 24 (1995): 28–34.

16 Ursula Franklin, personal comments, Massey College, May 1996.

17 As a historical example, Mrs Fernow, the wife of the first forestry dean at the University of Toronto (1907–19), 'contributed to the more formal work of the Faculty by teaching German to the forestry undergraduates' (J.W.B. Sisam, *Forestry Education at Toronto* [Toronto: University of Toronto Press, 1961], 31). See, as well, M. Gosztonyi Ainley, ed., *Despite the Odds: Essays on Canadian Women and Science* (Montreal: Véhicule Press, 1990).

PART III:

COLLECTIVE CASE STUDIES

'Medettes': Thriving or Just Surviving? Women Students in the Faculty of Medicine, University of Toronto, 1910–1951

W.P.J. MILLAR AND R.D. GIDNEY

While a good deal is known about the pioneer generation of women medical students in Canada, those who came later have received far less attention, and generalizations about them tend to be based on singular examples or isolated reminiscences. Moreover, almost nothing is known about the conventional career patterns that followed graduation.[1] In this essay we present a group portrait of the women who attended one medical school, in this case at the University of Toronto, during the first half of the twentieth century.[2] Contemporaries, christening them 'Medettes,' pronounced them a 'thriving minority.'[3] Using a large volume of routinely generated student records,[4] we want to assess the soundness of that observation by examining their socio-economic and academic backgrounds, their progress through medical school, and the ways in which they resembled or differed from their male peers. Though the evidence is much less satisfactory, we will also consider the records of their professional careers in order to trace the patterns of their lives after graduation.

Perhaps their most obvious characteristic is their scarcity (see figure). Of the 114 students entering first year in 1910, only 1 was a woman. Since at the time both the Queen's and Western Ontario medical schools barred female entrants, she was the sole woman in first-year medicine across the province in that year. By 1914, however, 10 women were enrolled in the first year of the program at Toronto, and during the war that figure increased sharply, reaching over 30 by 1918. But this high point was not to be matched until the waning years of the Second World War, when over 25 women entered medicine each year between 1943 and 1945. After both wars first-year female enrolments quickly dropped back to a more normal level.

Enrolments in first year
1910-1951

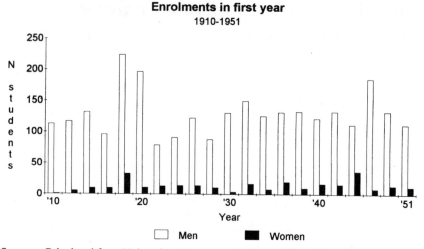

Source: Calculated from University of Toronto Archives, Office of Admissions, A69-0008/178-95.

Focusing upon the years 1920 to 1940, Veronica Strong-Boag has characterized such fluctuations in the numbers of women in medical and other 'male-dominated' professional university faculties in Canada as a 'critical decline.'[5] But to choose such dates confounds the issue, given the unusually high enrolments of women during wartime. Moreover, even by this measure, Toronto did not suffer any significant decline.[6] And eliminating the effects of wartime conditions produces a rather different picture. In 1926–7, after much of the large post-war enrolment had graduated, the proportion of women in the *entire* student medical body rose to its highest level in nearly a decade. Nor was there much of a drop even during the depths of the Depression. Rather than decline, it would seem that, at Toronto at least, female enrolment during the inter-war years stabilized at the level it had reached by the early 1920s.

The women embarking upon a medical course, like their male peers, were not enrolling in 'graduate' work – building, that is, upon an undergraduate education. Over the entire forty-year period, the vast majority of both male and female students came directly from high school with an Ontario Department of Education matriculation certificate.[7] Thus the high school remained the gatekeeper to a medical education (as it was to other professional schools) because it was the guardian of the matriculation certificate. And since Toronto admitted *all* applicants who held that certificate, this fact brought opportunity: upon graduation from a high school system that for decades had been open to them, women acquired the same right to university entrance as their brothers.

It has become an accepted truism that women applicants faced the obstacle of quotas on the number who would be admitted to medical school.[8] Both male and female physicians reminiscing about their student days frequently mention arbitrary limitation. Dr Marjorie Davis, for example, a future head of surgery at Women's College Hospital, who enrolled in medicine at Toronto in 1933, recalled that 'they kept the admission rate on women to about 10% of any class. Our class I think ended up with 9 or 10 women. It started out with one or two more, but ... you suddenly lost some and some dropped back and some joined you from [other courses] ... So it ran at about 10% and it ran at that for years.'[9] Yet the evidence suggests that, at least until after the Second World War, there was no formal quota for women, or for any other group, at Toronto.[10] The proportion of women among all entrants to first year varied from 3 to 14 per cent: thus, although the *average* intake resembled a fixed quota of 9 or 10 per cent, the numbers differed each year in a manner that suggests the effects of individual quirks and abilities, the vicissitudes of the economy, or some factor other than the deliberate attempt of university authorities to limit the number of women medical students.

The qualitative evidence makes the case even more strongly. On several occasions during the inter-war period, members of the faculty protested that large classes of first-year entrants were making it impossible for them to offer a high-quality, modern, small-group medical education in laboratories or, above all, in clinics and hospital wards. Yet nothing was done to keep numbers down to something approaching the 'ideal' class size of 80 to 100 in each of the clinical years, an ideal that was predicated on a small first-year intake. Despite many faculty proposals to limit the annual number of entrants into first year, the university's Board of Governors, encouraged by the political authorities of the province, refused to countenance any such departure. The faculty indeed was forced to concur in the view that the university had a moral obligation to accept all qualified applicants: 'we have a definite matriculation standard which gives any Ontario student who has it, no matter how long he took to obtain it, the right to register.'[11] For most of our period, in other words, all qualified applicants to medicine at Toronto, whether male or female, were guaranteed access. The numbers of women who intended a medical career undoubtedly reflected many factors that encouraged, or impeded, their progress into the profession.[12] But formal discrimination by means of limiting the size of the female intake into medical school was not one of them.

What mattered greatly, however, was socio-economic background. From the outset it is clear that we are dealing with a relatively privileged group – privileged in terms of family background and social standing, religious affiliation, and previous schooling.[13] For most of the period, the female students' fathers were more likely to work as professionals or in business, supervisory positions, or the burgeoning white-collar sector than were the fathers of male students. Thus from 1910 until after the Second World War, we generally find that the proportion of women from professional and business families was above 70 per cent – sometimes well above – while in contrast, the percentage of men from similar social backgrounds remained at much more modest proportions. As well, more female than male students came directly from the family farm. Women were much less likely to have fathers who were artisans or skilled craftsmen, factory workers, or labourers, although, like male students, the proportion of women who came from such families rose modestly between 1910 and 1951. However, the numbers of females from working-class families did not rise above 10 per cent until the 1940s, though for males that point had been reached in the 1920s.[14]

A high proportion of women, in sum, began their medical studies with the advantages of family support and financial backing, and the cultural background that could sustain support for women's higher education in a prestigious, and largely male, domain. Marjorie Davis, for example, had the financial aid of an older sister who taught school, an important contribution during the Depression for the daughter of a farmer in modest circumstances.[15] Marion Hilliard's family provided security and encouragement, and her father, if not enthusiastic at first about his daughter's medical ambitions, readily supported her in enrolling at Victoria College in science.[16] There were certainly women who did *not* have such advantages; on the whole, however, female medical students belonged to a relatively privileged sector of society.

They were also more likely than men to be residents of the city of Toronto, at least through the first half of our period – again, reflecting the tendency of women university students in Ontario and elsewhere in Canada to be disproportionately drawn from the immediate vicinity of the university.[17] Parents were less inclined to send their daughters to study in distant institutions; throughout their years of medical studies, many of the Toronto women lived at home, where parental support and surveillance presumably continued. Moreover, women medical students were always younger than their male peers: their average age of 19.8 years at entry into the course in 1910–14 dropped steadily to 18.2 by 1951, compared to the overall average of 20.6 years in 1910 and 18.6 in 1951 – statistics that might also explain why parents who lived in the same city would be more amenable to sending a girl to medical school. Both these characteristics of age and geographical origins tended to recede towards the norm by the late 1930s. Overall, however, women who entered medicine at Toronto were likely to be younger than the men, and the daughters of professionals and businessmen who lived in Toronto or of farmers with ambitions (or ambitious daughters) taking advantage of the provincial university's accessibility to anyone who could jump the matriculation hurdles.[18]

Another telling indication of their generally privileged position is the kind of schooling that many of these women received before they entered medical school. From 1920 to 1929, 16 per cent of incoming women had some sort of private school background (compared to 9 per cent for other students), and in the 1930–2 cohort almost a third (29 per cent) had received some private education. Through the 1930s the number of women who received at least a modicum of private schooling remained at over one-quarter of those who enrolled in medicine, and the percentage continued high until after the Second World War. In contrast, only 11 per cent of the total first-year cohort in 1935 had a private school education; in 1938 the figure was 18 per cent.[19] When set in conjunction with the other traits of women medical students that we have discussed so far, the impression of relative privilege persists.

Yet one would not want to make too much of this point. For all that they tended (not unlike their male peers) to be drawn from families who could afford, and supported, their children's higher education in medicine,[20] women students had to prove their own academic merit. Each one had to acquire, as the minimum entrance qualification, a matriculation certificate, a requirement that in itself proved a tight-meshed sieve for several generations in Ontario. And getting into medical school was only the first step: each woman had to survive the rigours of a medical education that the faculty deliberately made difficult for all entrants, especially in the preclinical years.[21]

More women than men entered the medical program with academic qualifications above the minimum – with, for example, one or two years of arts or even a university degree. The actual numbers of all entrants with superior academic backgrounds remained small, however. More telling is an analysis of the marks received on the Department of Education matriculation examinations. In the 1920s women tended to have as high averages as men, and higher English marks as well; in science, however, they tended to do worse. Over the next decade the marks of women entering with senior matriculation were slightly lower than those of the total cohort, especially in science; their English marks had also dropped. By the mid-1930s, moreover, about 20 per cent of the men were taking their final matriculation examinations in one year, the shortest time possible, while women were stretching them out over two years or more and yet still passing with lower averages. In wartime the gap narrowed. The 1943 female entrants had a somewhat better record. Like the men, they now were likely to have taken senior matriculation in one year – possibly a result of wartime pressures – and fewer had failed any subjects. But their English and especially science marks were still lower. In sum, for most of this period the previous academic records of those women entrants coming directly from high school tended to suffer by comparison with their male peers.

The pattern of their academic careers in medical school also differed from that of the male students. The first year of the program tended to be the most difficult for the student of either sex to pass without being required to write one or more supplementary examinations, or even to repeat the entire year's work: failure rates for the first year's final examinations always topped those of other years, and at times reached truly heroic proportions (46 per cent in 1937–8). Throughout the 1920s and 1930s women generally had a higher failure and repeat rate than men.[22] Moreover, women who had to redo their first year's work were also more likely to drop out of the course at some point. Between 1910 and 1937, 46 women, or 15 per cent, repeated their first year, and of the 41 we can trace, 23, or 56 per cent, failed to graduate. Such a result was not unique to women; the consequences of failing first year were well known to the faculty and constituted one of their strongest arguments against allowing failures to take the year over again.[23] However, the percentage of women students who never graduated seems to have exceeded that of men.

Among those who did graduate, women had a somewhat poorer academic record than men – far more of them had to write supplementary examinations at some point in their program. Like the men, on the other hand, women had far more difficulty in the first half of the course (which stressed the basic and medical sciences) and less in the clinical years, when the winnowing process had been virtually completed.

Not all students began their medical studies at Toronto in the first year of the course. From the second decade of the century on, a growing number, including some women, entered at an advanced level from other universities or after one or two years of science studies at Toronto, for example, into second-year medicine or higher. And an increasingly significant sector of the medical student body enrolled in the prestigious 'combined course in Arts and Medicine': the 'Biological and Medical Sciences,' or 'B and M,' as it was familiarly known.[24] This course, designed to offer an even heavier component of the scientific subjects deemed essential for the best medical education, led to a medical degree after seven years, an extra year beyond the regular program (four years of the B and M course, followed by the last three of medicine).[25] We do not know precisely how many enrolled in the course. In 1931 the faculty's curriculum committee noted that 136 students had transferred from B and M to fourth-year medicine over the previous ten years, which worked out on average to 10 per cent annually of the total in fourth year;[26] a more accurate figure, calculated after the course was well established, would have been 14 per cent. There may have been an even higher percentage in the 1930s. Women, however, formed only a small proportion of these students, a fact that is perhaps telling about their previous academic preparation: as we have noted, they tended to have weaker backgrounds and lower marks in science. But at least a handful of women did in fact enter medicine from B and M: between 1921 and 1940 they constituted a quarter of second-year female medical students, and over 74 per cent of them graduated, a much greater proportion than among those in the regular course. They included such well-known individuals as Dr Marjorie Davis and Dr Marion Hilliard, whom we have already mentioned; Dr Jessie Gray, who had a distinguished academic and professional career and became head of surgery at Women's College Hospital before Dr Davis; and many others who subsequently had illustrious careers.

These women were outstanding achievers in a challenging endeavour, and their success was heartening but not necessarily typical. What of the first-year women students we started with: how did they fare through the rest of the medical program? One way to answer that question is to ascertain how many actually graduated. We have calculated the number of graduates, and the time they took to complete the course, for all entrants at several points in time over the period 1922–3 to 1951–2 by tracking the entering class through class lists, convocation programs, internship lists, and other sources. The results show that, until the Second World War, a lower proportion of female than male entrants graduated. For whatever reasons – and we can only speculate about these – large numbers of women did not finish their professional education, and certainly not to the extent that men did. Even in the relatively prosperous decade of the 1920s women medical students dropped out of school much more often than their male peers. During the next decade the prospect of graduation for many entrants and for women especially grew fainter. Financial difficulties during the Depression were certainly one cause,[27] and women may have felt those pressures more keenly because families were less inclined to support a daughter's than a son's expensive education. As well, the introduction of more-rigorous examinations probably contributed to a higher drop-out rate.[28] Whatever the causes, the results were unfortunate. Of all the women who entered between 1933 and 1936 (a total of 43), only 36 per cent graduated.[29] In one particularly unlucky cohort, the entry class of 1934, only 1 of 7 women is recorded as graduating. The comparable figure for *all* students in 1934 is 69 per cent.

Moreover, the women who managed to graduate often took longer than their male peers to complete the course. During the inter-war period, because students were allowed to repeat any year they had failed, from an eighth to a fifth of the students who graduated took an extra year or more to do so. But on average, women graduates required substantially longer time to complete their degrees. Again, one likely cause was higher rates of failure and/or other academic problems along the way, though the economic constraints of the Depression were probably also an important factor in the extremely low graduation rates of the 1930s.

The final hurdle in a medical education was the hospital internship taken by almost all graduates after their six-year course. Like the stories of quotas for entrance to medical school, tales abound, and perhaps not without some reason, of the difficulties for women in getting or keeping an internship, of discrimination on the wards and in the dressing rooms, and of the necessity to look far afield for a position.[30] Men did not have to face as many difficulties (unless they were Jewish),[31] but for both sexes there was often no position in Ontario. In 1926, for example, 43 per cent of the graduates looking for a hospital internship were intending to go to the United States.[32] In the university registrar's papers a number of 'class lists' have survived which give the addresses of the graduating classes in medicine from 1928 to 1942,[33] and from these we can estimate how many women took up an internship and where. Of the 115 women listed 64, or 56 per cent, did at least one year's internship in Toronto; 13 per cent took a year at a hospital in the United States.

About half, then, were able to find positions in the city, a good number of these at Women's College Hospital and the Hospital for Sick Children (which together provided for 34 per cent of women interns in Toronto). The overall average is somewhat misleading, however, since through the inter-war period there came to be more positions open in Toronto and at other Ontario hospitals, and therefore less necessity to leave the province.[34] Thus of the 1938 graduating class in medicine at Toronto, 32 per cent of the men went to U.S. hospitals for internships, as against 3 of the 8 women (38 per cent). Thirty per cent of the men took positions in Toronto; 38 per cent of the women did so. Since the numbers of women are so small, the percentages in this case must be used indicatively only. Nevertheless, if we take as another example the interns of 1935, we find 60 per cent of the men in Toronto, compared with 63 per cent of the women. The other women took positions elsewhere in Canada. Not a single one went to an American hospital, while 13, or 13 per cent, of the men did so. Finding an internship in Toronto, or even elsewhere in the province, could be difficult. But it is not clear that it was any more difficult for women than for men.

But what of a woman's professional life after her medical education? Though the available sources are flawed,[35] enough evidence survives to indicate the successes that some women graduates achieved, the compromises and accommodations sometimes made between career and family life, the extraordinary opportunities available to some women doctors, and the satisfactions of professional life that some of them may have experienced.

Between 1910 and 1930, 16 of the approximately 120 women whose post-graduation records we traced followed a path established by many of the pioneer women doctors – they went out to India or China as medical missionaries, often for a lifetime of service.[36] Some were continuing a family tradition: Janet McClure, for example, daughter of a Presbyterian medical missionary, sister of Robert McClure, a future moderator of the United Church who worked in the China mission himself, and wife of Dr Leslie Kilborn, MB 1921, who laboured side by side with her for twenty-five years on the mission field;[37] or Flora Gauld, who went off as a medical missionary with her sister, a graduate of the nursing school at Toronto's Hospital for Sick Children, to Formosa to join their mother, a missionary there for thirty years.[38] However, at least among those we traced, fewer of the graduates of the 1930s or later chose such a career.

Perhaps a third of the earlier graduates practised medicine at some point after finishing medical school. If that proportion seems low, it may reflect simply the limitations of the records; at any rate, the proportion rises as we move through later years. *All* the 1940s entrants who graduated and whom we traced seem to have practised medicine at some point in their lives. And the proportion of this group who married and continued in the profession was substantially higher.

Balancing work and family responsibilities is a common theme indeed, and it underscores the episodic and discontinuous nature of training and experience. In the 1920s the first woman medical student at Toronto to marry and have a child during the program dropped out for a year; she returned, however, and went on to work at the postgraduate level in the Department of Anatomy. Another such example twenty years later was a woman whose parents were Finnish working-class immigrants to northern Ontario; while still studying medicine, she married a fellow student and 'took time off from her interning' to produce a daughter, but she returned in 1952 to finish the year while her husband worked as an anaesthetist at Sunnybrook and her mother-in-law babysat.

A more common choice for the timing of marriage in the first half of the century was after graduation. But to combine marriage and a career was to be, as Mary Kinnear has termed it, 'a person in conflict,'[39] perpetually juggling family and professional life against the model of the normal male career path. Over the entire period about half of our graduates married, and of these, half again lack any record of practising after marriage. To continue to work after marriage, as Veronica Strong-Boag has argued, was unconventional for middle-class women until the Second World War; to some extent, that situation may have been true immediately after it as well.[40] Though a study in the 1920s of American women graduates showed that the large majority of them continued to practise after marriage,[41] and there is no reason to think that Toronto graduates would be different, there were undoubtedly some, especially in the early years, whose lack of professional records after marriage reflects reality. That pattern provided a justification for the opinion frequently expressed by university administrators and others that male students should be given preference. And it fits the conventional sensibilities of early-twentieth-century Canadian society, epitomized in the explanation of one woman graduate, married in 1920 to a Rockefeller Foundation employee whose job took him all over South America, where her three children were born (each in a different city): she 'worked with the Anglo-Saxon community' in each place they settled, but she 'never practised medicine ... my first job was as a married woman.' More important, and perhaps belying this rationalization, was the fact that 'I didn't have a licence.'

Nevertheless, there are enough examples hinted at in our sources that one must assume a certain measure of success in performing that balancing act. To achieve it might require sacrifices. One woman, for example, graduated in 1938 but temporarily retired to marry and raise a family; she kept her medical skills honed with voluntary work in hospital clinics, and in 1952 she returned to polish up her formal education with an internship at Women's College Hospital. As we have noted, however, sentiments changed over the years, and there is some evidence that a growing number of women graduates were both practising physicians *and* married.

Wartime offered opportunities to both single and married women for novel and sometimes extraordinary work, not only in the armed forces but also in residency and specialist training positions that might not have been available to them under normal circumstances.[42] A member of the class of 1922 became the first woman doctor to enlist in the Canadian navy. Another went to England in 1938 for postgraduate training at the University of London, enlisted in the Canadian army while there, and became the first woman physician to serve overseas. Captain Jean Newman, MD 1931, left a Windsor practice to enlist in the Royal Canadian Army Medical Corps and by 1945 ended up in England training as an anaesthetist.[43] Deborah Glaistor served on the staff of Canadian hospitals in England and western Europe in 1944–5, while her husband was also overseas in the armed forces – she was 'one of the few Canadian women to receive this appointment.'[44]

Opportunities opened up on the home front as well. Marjorie Davis, for example, jumped at the chance to be resident in surgery at Toronto General Hospital under Dr William Gallie, the chief of surgery and dean of the Faculty of Medicine, when, in 1942, 'all the younger [male] surgeons had gone to the war and he was short of any person to be the resident who had any degree of training.'[45] Anna Hardman, a graduate of the class of 1931, stayed home in Chatham while her doctor husband went off to war, but inherited their joint practice to manage by herself.[46] When a situation became available in Haliburton County at the start of the Second World War after the male practitioner enlisted, Agnes Jamieson realized 'a lifelong ambition to be a country doctor'; she was still there in 1946, attending to 'backwoods farmers, woodcutters, trappers, and villagers' through winter storms and rugged conditions, according to the *Toronto Telegram,* which did not fail to note the diminutive size of a woman 'doing what was considered a man's job, but what she has proved to be a woman's job too.'[47]

There are glimpses in these records of peacetime careers that ranged from urban or small-town general practice to hospital and university teaching and specialization. One woman who graduated in 1935 practised in Niagara Falls for four years as the first and only female physician in the city, before joining the staff of Toronto General Hospital. Another, a graduate of 1929, had a fifty-year career in psychiatric medicine at Toronto Psychiatric Hospital and elsewhere. As Mary Kinnear found for Manitoba women doctors, there was a marked tendency to work in an institutional setting – hospital, school clinic, research laboratory – rather than to set up a private practice; the attractions of regular hours and reasonable pay, not to mention the greater possibility of fitting in work with family life, were no doubt factors, as she suggests.[48] Thus Women's College Hospital and the Banting Institute, for example, particularly in the early years, provided professional homes for many distinguished women doctors among our alumnae. Nevertheless, there was also a tendency for private practice to become more common among the later University of Toronto graduates. Many of them established their own practices, often lasting their lifetimes, in Toronto or in smaller centres. A 1923 graduate, for example, had a general practice in Simcoe for twenty-five years after postgraduate training and marriage. Many others pursued careers far from their alma mater, in other provinces and countries, drawn away by marriage or, like male graduates, by the opportunities of the developing Canadian west or the United States.

Finally, it should be noted that the apparent failure of some women to continue in medical studies did not always indicate departure from professional education. We do not know what happened to all our 'dropouts' from medicine, but some at least simply switched to other professional fields.[49] Two examples from the 1935 entry cohort will suffice for illustrative purposes. One went through to the end of second-year medicine and then disappeared from the class lists. But her records show that she then completed a pass arts degree, became a social worker, and in 1951 was still involved in her professional career in nursery-school work. Another had to repeat her first year in medicine and subsequently dropped out of the course. But she went on to get a BA and an MEd at Toronto. Because the records do not always catch such students, it is important to remember that there were always some, like these, who graduated into professional work lives, though of a different kind.

Rather like their male counterparts, female medical students exhibited, in the aggregate, modest changes over the space of forty years, but also much stability. However, the Second World War does seem to mark something of a divide in this respect. There was a modest diversification in social and economic background for both men and women, but this change was more pronounced among female entrants after the war. Those enrolling for the first time in medicine between 1949 and 1951, for example, were somewhat less likely to come from professional or business families than at any previous time, and the proportion of those from working-class families rose to its highest level ever. About half the women still came from Toronto, though that was now true of all entrants. They still tended to be a little younger than the men, but the gap had narrowed from nearly a full year's difference in 1910, on average, to just four months in 1951. There were other slight indications of a changing social composition as well. The proportion of Catholic and Jewish women tended to rise over time; the number who had attended private schools fell slightly. In sum, the result of these small changes is that women as a group tended in the post–Second World War era to be assimilated more closely than in previous years to the socio-economic profile of the entire student body; that is, they were coming to resemble the men.

The sharpest point of contrast between male and female entrants at mid-century, however, lies in their academic records. Women entrants in 1951 constituted a group of outstanding academic achievers. On the whole, their grade thirteen averages were much higher than those of the entire cohort; their average marks in both science and English were also higher. Four of their number (out of 11) were in fact taking four sciences at that level, and obtaining good marks, compared with the more usual two sciences for both men and women. And they maintained that lead through the course of their medical school careers. Seventy-five per cent of the women graduated six years later, compared with a figure of 69 per cent for all; if one includes in these calculations all those who would eventually graduate, the difference grows substantially: 92 per cent of women did so, compared with 81 per cent of men. By contrast, in the United States over the period 1950–9, 92 out of every 100 freshmen in a *four-year* medical course graduated. Given the disproportionate failure rates at the premedical stage in Toronto, the statistics show that these women were achieving a higher rate of graduation than all students in the United States, while Toronto men were significantly lower.

Almost certainly this stellar record resulted from the introduction of entry quotas for women students. During the Second World War, the Faculty of Medicine began to institute procedures for limiting the number of entrants, first by a series of annual resolutions approved by the administration and then in 1945–6 by official university policy.[50] Entrants were selected from a much larger pool of qualified applicants, many of whom would be rejected on one ground or another. In this process, we suggest, women lost their equal footing at the doors of the provincial university, and their entry numbers began to resemble the quota that persists in communal memory. From a high of 20 per cent or more of first-year students during the war, the number of female entrants dropped abruptly, and it stabilized at 10 per cent annually, or very close to that figure, over the next decade and a half.[51] Given these circumstances, it is not surprising that, in the immediate post-war years at least, women medical students had superior application records compared to the men, or that they had superior performance records throughout the course itself.

The nature of women's professional education during the first half of the twentieth century, and the quality of their experience, cannot be measured by numbers alone. Many aspects resist quantification altogether. What does it mean, for example, to be one of a handful of women in a male-dominated professional school? As Marion Hilliard remarked about her experience in the 1920s, 'The pioneer work had been done by the time I went to medical school ... of course the girls had to sit in the front row and you could hardly say we were welcomed – but we certainly were not outcasts.'[52] During the First World War, on the other hand, in anatomy classes female students had been relegated to a small room 'without any proper facilities,' while the men dissected in a well-equipped laboratory. Such anecdotal evidence is essential to give meaning to the statistical record; yet the latter can also help to illuminate some aspects of women's medical education, such as the varying nature of opportunities for them. Women crowded into the medical school during both wars, for example, as space was opened up by the departure of male students for war service and by the demand for more doctors. But as Strong-Boag puts it, only 'the most intrepid and well-armed penetrated such male monopolies as medicine, law, engineering, and theology' during the inter-war years,[53] and that pattern would appear to have been true after the Second World War as well.[54] Fewer women had the opportunity to contest a male preserve, and perhaps those who did had to work harder. Many of those who enrolled in medicine, often coming from relatively privileged backgrounds, supported by familial resources, or simply possessing individual pluck and merit, seem to have accommodated themselves to inconveniences and inequities, acquired an education, and gone on to practise their profession. Many others, perhaps entering with poorer academic records or lesser resources, encountered difficulties of a more or less serious nature. Over the course of these years, however, women became an accepted, if not always advantaged, part of university life. Indeed, despite its limitations, our evidence suggests that, for most women studying medicine at the University of Toronto during the first half of the twentieth century, the reality of their student experience lay somewhere *between* 'thriving' and 'just surviving.'

NOTES

1 For Ontario, an overview of developments in medical education may be found in A.B. McKillop, *Matters of Mind: The University in Ontario, 1791–1951* (Toronto: University of Toronto Press, 1994), esp. 74–7, 132–6, 347–52; and R.D. Gidney and W.P.J. Millar, *Professional Gentlemen: The Professions in Nineteenth-Century Ontario* (Toronto: University of Toronto Press, 1994), esp. 153–9, 324–5, 356–9, 362–8. The latter includes a section on the education of the pioneer generation of women medical students and a guide to the literature about them. On women in medicine in Manitoba, see Mary Kinnear, *In Subordination: Professional Women, 1870–1970* (Montreal and Kingston: McGill-Queen's University Press, 1995), esp. chap. 3. For women's medical education generally, the most recent account is Thomas Neville Bonner, *To the Ends of the Earth: Women's Search for Education in Medicine* (Cambridge, Mass.: Harvard University Press, 1992).

2 For more detail on the composition of the largely male student body, the nature of the program, student academic careers, and the policies and politics of the medical faculty and the university, see R.D. Gidney and W.P.J. Millar, 'Medical Students at the University of Toronto, 1910–40: A Profile,' *Canadian Bulletin of the History of Medicine* 13 (1996): 29–52, and 'Quantity and Quality: The Problem of Admissions in Medicine at the University of Toronto, 1910–1951,' *Historical Studies in Education* 9, 2 (fall 1997): 165–89.

3 *Varsity*, 9 Nov. 1938, 2.

4 Two of the most important sources for this study, located at the University of Toronto Archives, are the complete set of applications to enter the Faculty of Medicine between 1910 and 1951 (University of Toronto Archives [UTA], Office of Admissions, A69–0008/178–195, Applications to the Faculty of Medicine, 1910–51) and the academic records of all graduates, 1910–29, numbering about 2,600 (UTA, Faculty of Medicine, A86–0026/001–004, 1890–1929, Student Record Cards; these are not complete for the period before 1910, and the last set belongs to the graduates of 1929). To follow students through their course of studies, we have also consulted the name lists of students enrolled in the faculty each year, which were printed annually in the university calen-

dars. Altogether, 523 women entered first-year medicine between 1910 and 1951.

5 Veronica Strong-Boag, *The New Day Recalled: Lives of Girls and Women in English Canada, 1919–1939* (Toronto: Copp Clark Pitman, 1988), 23: the proportion of women in medical studies in Canada between 1920 and 1940 fell from 2.14 per cent of undergraduates to 1.97 per cent.

6 At Toronto, the female proportion in 1920–1 was 7.96 per cent; in 1940–1, 7.89 per cent.

7 For more detail, see Gidney and Millar, 'Medical Students,' 32. Until well into the century, other professional faculties in the university also accepted high school matriculants; see, for example, Sara Z. Burke, *Seeking the Highest Good: Social Service and Gender at the University of Toronto, 1888–1937* (Toronto: University of Toronto Press, 1996), 125.

8 See, for example, McKillop, *Matters of Mind*, 135; Paul Axelrod, *Making a Middle Class: Student Life in English Canada during the Thirties* (Montreal and Kingston: McGill-Queen's University Press, 1990), 90; Strong-Boag, *New Day Recalled*, 67; Kinnear, *In Subordination*, 63–6.

9 *Oral History Interviews*, University of Toronto, Faculty of Medicine (Hannah Institute for the History of Medicine), Dr Marjorie I. Davis, vol. 8 (typescript), 7. See also ibid., Dr William B. Spaulding, vol. 41, 86.

10 Quotas may have existed at other institutions. For our discussion on this point and for documentation for the following paragraph, see Gidney and Millar, 'Quantity and Quality.'

11 University of Toronto, *President's Report*, 1938, Report of the Dean of the Faculty of Medicine, 32.

12 Such as informal counselling against entry; see, for example, Axelrod, *Making a Middle Class*, 91; Kinnear, *In Subordination*, 62; 'Kicking Down Doors,' Toronto *Star*, 30 Mar. 1995. A graduate of 1948 recalled that her father had opposed her 'unladylike' desire to enter medicine, but the rest of her family had encouraged her.

13 This tendency held for women university students generally. See Axelrod, *Making a Middle Class*, 29; Judith Fingard, 'College, Career, and Community: Dalhousie Coeds, 1881–1921,' in *Youth, University, and Canadian Society*, ed. Paul Axelrod and John G. Reid (Kingston: McGill-Queen's University Press, 1989), 27–35; Nicole Neatby, 'Preparing for the Working World: Women at Queen's during the 1920s,' in *Gender and Education in Ontario: An Historical Reader*, ed. Ruby Heap and Alison Prentice (Toronto: Canadian Scholars' Press, 1991), 336.

14 The figures for women are three-year averages, since the small number of cases in any given year would provide misleading percentages.

15 *Oral History Interviews*, Davis, 1, 5.

16 See Wendy Mitchinson, 'Marion Hilliard: "Raring to Go All the Time,"' in *Great Dames*, ed. Elspeth Cameron and Janice Dickin (Toronto: University of Toronto Press, 1997), 228.

17 See Fingard, 'College, Career, and Community,' 27, 33–4; Chad Gaffield, Lynne Marks, and Susan Laskin, 'Student Populations and Graduate Careers: Queen's University, 1895–1900,' in *Youth, University, and Canadian Society*, ed. Axelrod and Reid, 8.

18 Not surprisingly, given the religious complexion of Ontario society, the vast majority of applicants belonged to one of the three major denominations – Presbyterian, Methodist (after 1925, United Church), or to a lesser extent, Anglican. The applications also give father's nationality, but increasingly over time it was recorded as 'Canadian' rather than any more revealing designation.

19 Only in 1951 were these positions reversed: the figure for all entrants then stood at 28 per cent, while for women alone it was 24 per cent.

20 During the Depression the effects of social class were markedly revealed in the even greater proportion of women from professional and business families and the reduction in working-class entrants generally.

21 For a more extensive discussion, see Gidney and Millar, 'Quantity and Quality.'

22 Though in some years no woman repeated, but a few men did; so that this would not appear to be a consistent or intentional policy aimed at women.

23 UTA, Faculty of Medicine Council Minutes, A86–0027/021, 15 Sept. 1933, 244, 'Repeaters.' Of 22 repeaters in the 1932–3 entry cohort, 9 (41 per cent) graduated.

24 *Calendar*, 1925–6, 393. A former University of Toronto medical student remembered it as an elite course that produced distinguished physicians: *Oral History Interviews*, Dr Allan Walters, vol. 45, 50.

25 From 1935 until the demise of the B and M course during the war, it took eight years, including the last four in medicine.

26 See UTA, Faculty of Medicine, Office of the Dean, A86–0027/008, Curriculum and Examinations, 1922–32, 27 Jan. 1931, 352.

27 Gidney and Millar, 'Quantity and Quality.'

28 Ibid.

29 The proportion might be as high as 48 per cent if it were possible to trace all those who would have graduated during the war. By the fifth and sixth years of the medical course, the failure rate was virtually zero.

30 See, for example, Deborah Gorham, '"No Longer an Invisible Minority": Women Physicians and Medical Practice in Late Twentieth-Century North America,' in *Caring and Curing: Historical Perspectives on Women and Healing in*

Canada, ed. Dianne Dodd and Deborah Gorham (Ottawa: University of Ottawa Press, 1994), 190, 206n25; *Oral History Interviews*, Davis, 28.

31 Jewish students usually went to the United States to intern, although at least one landed an internship at Toronto General Hospital in 1931, according to the lists in UTA (see note 33). We have found no cases of Ontario-born blacks applying to medical school.

32 *University of Toronto Monthly* 26, 8 (May 1926): 373.

33 UTA, Office of the Registrar, A73–0051/226/010, Medical Graduates, 1928–42. The list for 1930 is missing. A few graduates (both male and female) had to write supplementary examinations, and it is possible that they did not take up their internship positions.

34 See the *Journal of the Association of American Medical Colleges* 4, 2 (April 1929): 185. In the previous seven years, 37 per cent of University of Toronto graduates went to the United States; at McGill 37 per cent of the 1928 class did so; 22 of 43 graduates in 1928 at Queen's intended to go to the United States. But compare Toronto *Star*, 15 Mar. 1938: about 15 per cent of Toronto graduates were taking up internships in the United States (UTA, Faculty of Medicine, A79–0023/061, series IX, 'Clippings,' 954).

35 UTA, Department of Graduate Records, A73–0026. The records do not exist for every graduate, and those that do are uneven at best – some, for example, mention simply the place and date of internship, others give only the addresses of offices over the years, and still others amount to detailed career descriptions. We have tolerable records for about one-quarter of the women who graduated up to the end of the Second World War.

36 For an analysis of the careers of some medical missionaries who graduated from the University of Toronto, see Karen Minden, *Bamboo Stone: The Evolution of a Chinese Medical Elite* (Toronto: University of Toronto Press, 1994), 88–92; see also Ruth Compton Brouwer, *New Women for God: Canadian Presbyterian Women and India Missions, 1876–1914* (Toronto: University of Toronto Press, 1990), appendix B.

37 For a biography of Robert McClure and a brief mention of his sister, see Munroe Scott, *McClure – The China Years of Dr Bob McClure* (Toronto: Canec Pub. and Supply House, 1978).

38 See the fictionalized account in Jean Little, *His Banner Over Me* (Toronto: Viking, 1995).

39 Kinnear, *In Subordination*, 160.

40 Strong-Boag, *New Day Recalled*, 42–3. See also Joan Sangster, 'Doing Two Jobs: The Wage-Earning Mother, 1945–70,' in *A Diversity of Women: Ontario, 1945–1980*, ed. Joy Parr (Toronto: University of Toronto Press, 1995), 99–107, and Kinnear, *In Subordination*, 156–9.

41 UTA, Faculty of Medicine Council Minutes, A86–0027/019, 8 Dec. 1926, 240.

42 Similarly, see the comments on wartime opportunities for women in another professional field, in Alison Prentice, 'Three Women in Physics,' in this volume.

43 *University of Toronto Monthly*, May 1945.

44 *University of Toronto Monthly*, Oct. 1944, and UTA, Department of Graduate Records, A73-0026.

45 *Oral History Interviews*, Davis, 20.

46 *University of Toronto Monthly*, Oct. 1942.

47 *Toronto Telegram*, 3 Feb. 1940, and *Charlottetown Patriot*, 9 Feb. 1946, in UTA, Department of Graduate Records, A73-0026.

48 Kinnear, *In Subordination*, 61, 70.

49 Or completed medical studies elsewhere. Winifred Blampin, for example, began at Toronto, but was one of the first women graduates in medicine at McGill; see Margaret Gillett, *We Walked Very Warily: A History of Women at McGill* (Montreal: Eden Press Women's Publications, 1981), 297.

50 For more detail see Gidney and Millar, 'Quantity and Quality.'

51 One male member of the Toronto faculty who was intimately familiar with its selection procedures maintained unequivocally that a quota system was indeed in place from the post-war years onwards: *Oral History Interviews*, Dr Jan Steiner, vol. 43, 51–3, 59, 107.

52 Quoted in Anne Rochon Ford, *A Path Not Strewn with Roses: One Hundred Years of Women at the University of Toronto, 1884–1984* (Toronto: Governing Council, University of Toronto, 1985), 39. A more positive perspective is offered by Enid Johnson MacLeod on her experience at Dalhousie in the 1930s: 'I enjoyed medical school, due mainly to a class of very understanding and kind men who were exceptionally considerate and helpful.' See her *Petticoat Doctors: The First Forty Years of Women in Medicine at Dalhousie University* (Lawrencetown Beach, NS: Pottersfield Press, 1990), 5. See also Gorham, '"No Longer an Invisible Minority,"' 205n16.

53 Strong-Boag, *New Day Recalled*, 53.

54 See McKillop, *Matters of Mind*, 555–6.

Professionalization among the Professed: The Case of Roman Catholic Women Religious

ELIZABETH SMYTH

In her 1995 work *Women on the Margins* Natalie Davis writes that she chose her three subjects 'so I could see what differences religion made in women's lives, what doors it opened for you, what doors it closed, what words and actions it allowed you to choose.'[1] One of these subjects was Marie Guyart, who, as Mother Marie de l'Incarnation, disembarked in New France in 1639. Guyart's shipboard companions were other women religious: the Augustines de la Miséricorde de Jésus, whose work was in hospitals, along with the members of her own community, the Order of St Ursula (Ursulines), whose work was in education. Their arrival on this continent began a three-century tradition of Catholic women living dual professional lives: as professed women religious who defined their existence as a response to a call from God and as members of the emerging professions in the secular world in such fields as education, health care, and social service. While religious life offered them the means to undertake professional work outside their convent walls, it also served as an acknowledgment that women maintained a separate (but not equal) role within the Catholic Church.

This essay explores the opportunities for dual engagement in professional life and work which communities of women religious presented to those who embraced the Roman Catholic faith. It examines the impact that state regulation and the resulting demands for professionalization had upon vowed women. Drawing examples from communities of Canadian women religious, the essay explores the tensions that resulted from the integration of professional duties with a vowed life. I develop the discussion in four sections. The first explores the roots and development of women as professional workers within the Catholic Church. The second

examines what happened as women religious became professional workers in the secular world, and it illustrates the tensions that resulted within
their religious domain. The third section documents the shifts that have
occurred within communities of women religious in their roles as professional workers in the religious and secular worlds. It analyses the current
debates on the future of religious life as a dual profession, including
papal pronouncements surrounding the movement for professional status in the one arena which has been denied to Catholic women by their
church: ordination to the priesthood. The essay concludes with analysis
of what the case of professionalization among the professed contributes
to our knowledge of the impact of women upon the professions.

My interest in this topic grows from my research on the variety of roles
that women have played in education: elementary, secondary, tertiary,
and professional. I was educated in Roman Catholic schools in which
women religious were present in all aspects of leadership – as principals,
consultants, and authors of textbooks. As an adult researcher, I was surprised to discover that, in most histories of women's involvement in the
professions of education, social service, or health care, treatment of the
role of women religious fell into two categories. The first was neglect:
authors simply ignored them. The second category was dismissive, with
authors employing such infamous lines such as 'and the good sisters
taught/ nursed/ ran orphanages.' Such commentary frequently followed
litanies of every male – priests and bishops who were members of religious orders or who were ordained for a diocese, or laymen – who held
any type of administrative or nominal role in the enterprise. Why was this
the case? The answer lies in the intersection of several conflicting lines of
authority and orientation.

For most of their existence, women religious embodied the tension
that existed for women within the patriarchial Catholic Church. First, the
roles assigned to vowed women were separate and unequal to that of
vowed men. While the church labels the oppression of women as repre-
hensible in such documents as the 1988 apostolic letter *Mulieris Dignitatem*
(The Dignity of Women), which condemns 'those who seek to justify
structures that unjustly oppress women,'[2] it is apparent that the Vatican
does not view itself as leading such a structure. Secondly, for most of their
existence, women religious saw their role as one of silent serving. Many
communities viewed the vow of obedience as embodying humility and
thus did not campaign for public recognition for their achievements or
for a more active voice in ecclesiastical decision-making. Thirdly, as the
archives of their communities are private sources, access for historians

seeking to analyse the roles of women religious was restricted. It has only been within the recent past, most significantly with the renewal of religious life stimulated by the Second Vatican Council,[3] that women religious, both themselves and collaboratively with secular historians, have begun to study their historic and historical roles.

For historians examining the roles of women within the professions, the case of women religious illustrates the complexity of professionalization. In historical and contemporary times women religious have lived dual professional lives: as vowed women through their lives in religion and as members of the professions through their work in the secular world. How these two segments of their lives interact with each other reveals much about women's experience in the professions.

Religious Life as a Women's Profession

The history of women as professional religious within the Roman Catholic Church can be viewed as a series of role transformations, institutionalizations, and struggles as women carved out a meaningful way to heed a call from God. In the early Christian church women played many public roles, most significantly in the office of deaconesses (sacramental assistants to bishops) or as members of the order of widows (women over sixty who had been married, had lived good lives, and gave themselves over to prayer and care for the sick). Yet as Christianity changed from a movement to an institution, women church workers found their status diminished. By the end of the fifth century the offices of deaconesses and widows were in decline,[4] eroded by the growing church patriarchy. What emerged in their place was the Christian adaption of vowed virginity, which was a means for women to create a life engaged in charity, sharing community with other women, and being independent of the influence of fathers, husbands, or male guardians. Yet, like Christianity itself, vowed virginity became institutionalized, a result in large part of the male clergy's successful quest to formalize and regulate the lives of women. Over the next seven hundred years the lives of vowed virgins became more controlled. This control reached its zenith with the declaration of Pope Boniface VIII in 1298 on the role of nuns:

Nuns, present and future, to whatever order they belong and in whatever part of the world, shall henceforth remain perpetually enclosed within their monasteries; so that no nun tacitly or expressly professed in religion shall henceforth have or be able to have the power of going out of these monasteries for whatsoever reason or cause, unless perchance any be found manifestly suffering from a disease so great and of such nature that she cannot without danger or scandal, live together with others ... that so, altogether withdrawn from public and mundane sights, they may serve God more freely and diligently preserve for Him in all holiness their souls and their bodies.[5]

The lifestyle choices for Christian women were once again narrowed. For those who wished to gather together to pray and do good works, unencumbered by the roles of wife and mother, they now had to live as nuns, enclosed by convent walls and a highly regulated prayer life.

The cloistering of women did not eliminate the attempts to serve God through serving the poor and engaging in the work of education, social service, and health care. These works necessitated experimentation with life outside the convent walls, and numerous examples can be found of short-lived attempts by women to establish structures that would enable them to carry out works of charity in the secular world. Until the seventeenth century this story is not one of widespread success. Angela Merici, a fifteenth-century Italian woman, established the Company of St Ursula (Ursulines) as a community of uncloistered educators, living under promises and not vows. Yet after her death, in some countries Merici's company became a cloistered order. The story is frequently repeated until the seventeenth century, when Louise de Marillac (1591–1660), a French widow, and her spiritual adviser, Vincent de Paul, were in the vanguard of a movement creating a new role for women in the Roman Catholic Church: that of the sister.

Although the terms 'nuns' and 'sisters' have become interchangeable, both in the vernacular and among women religious themselves, they have quite different meanings. Canon law, the set of guidelines that governs the Roman Catholic Church, codifies the difference between the two according to the type of vows they take, how they live, and the works in which they participate. Although both nuns and sisters vow poverty, chastity, and obedience, their vows fall under different classifications in canon law. The vows of nuns are solemn and permanent; those of sisters are simple. Nuns live in a cloister, with their work driven by prayer and contemplation. Sisters live in a separate and private space that is not enclosed, and their orientation is described as a combination of prayer and good works. While sisters do spend a portion of their day in prayer, they are also involved in works outside their convent walls: in education, health care, and social service. Because of their engagement in these areas of work, which have come to be known as the active apostolate, and their intersection with the growing opportunities for professional engagement in the secular world, this essay focuses on the lives and work of sisters.

In their study of the origins of the professions in nineteenth-century Ontario, Gidney and Millar describe these occupations as 'a sacred calling, a sacred duty, a commitment not only to service of others but to the larger social good.'[6] By this definition, women religious can be seen as constituting a profession. The vows that a woman takes when she is admitted to a religious community illustrate this point. For example, even today a woman who becomes a member of the Sisters of Charity of Halifax vows, in a public ceremony before God and her community, 'poverty, chastity and obedience according to the Sisters of Charity of St Vincent de Paul' as a means of carrying out a life of service to God and neighbour. She requests that the superior of the community 'accept these vows that I may participate in the life and mission of the Church as a member of this congregation.'[7]

The life cycle of a sister was and remains one of dual formation: as a religious and as a professional. Although the individual responses of religious communities to the directions of Vatican II and the decline in the numbers of religious vocations have modified them in terms of their length and the site of their delivery, the discreet stages in the formation of a religious have remained constant. When a woman approached a community of women religious for admission to membership, there was a formal and canonically regulated set of stages through which she progressed. Each was marked by changes in habit, in duties, and in community involvement. The first stage was the postulancy. As a postulant, the woman dressed in a modified secular dress and frequently continued in her pre-postulant work or education. At the end of a six-month to one-year postulancy, if she was deemed suitable by the leadership of the community and she herself wished to continue, she received the community habit in a formal ceremony. Many communities held these events in public spaces – churches or community chapels. The candidate, often dressed in wedding attire, received the community habit and became a novice.

The habit was the outward representation of the woman's stage in religious life. In some communities the novice wore a white veil within the convent walls. As she progressed through her noviciate, she took a series of vows in ceremonies held before the community and in some cases before the public at large. Changes were made to the habit to mark her growth as a religious. Some communities presented the sister with an ornamental crucifix at the time of her first vows. Initially, it would be worn inside the habit; it was worn on the outside when she became a community sister – a fully vowed member of the community.

The noviciate was a period of apprenticeship and education as the candidate was formed into a sister. The mistress of novices was the sister charged by the community with the task of transforming the novices into women religious. Her sense of formation and the direction that she received from the community leadership shaped the noviciate experience. The 'canonical year' – the name is taken from the ecclesiastical rules that govern it – was a mandated part of the noviciate experience. The term is somewhat of a misnomer since its length varied throughout the nineteenth and twentieth centuries, yet its intent remained the same. It was a time of prayer, study, reflection, and work within the closed world of the community. The novice withdrew from the world, from her family (with whom contact was limited); from her employment in the secular world (leaving her career as a teacher, nurse, or social worker), and from the larger community itself, to focus on becoming a sister. As well as their directed studies in theology, community history, and the constitutions and vows, the novices were assigned chores within the community and performed many of the household tasks.

After their canonical year the novices resumed their work outside of the community, but were still separated to a degree from the community sisters. Frequently they were housed in separate wings or in separate buildings. While the community prayed as a whole, the novices ate, slept, and took their recreation in separate areas. It is important to note that provisions were made for sisters who were in the beginning stages of their professional careers to have opportunities for assistance in their work. There are many instances of young sisters reporting the great help that they received from teaching principals and senior nursing and social-service sisters in their early secular careers. Yet balancing the demands of the life of a vowed religious and that of a woman working in one of the emerging professions created tensions and challenges, individually and collectively, within many communities of sisters.

Reconciling a Vowed Life with Growing Professionalization of 'Women's Work': The Example of Teaching Sisters

The tensions associated with the dual engagement of sisters as professional workers in the church and in the secular world can be documented in many ways. Communities of sisters paid high prices for their success. As one historian has commented, 'The need and desire for sisters to teach and care for the sick ensured them a welcome everywhere. But bishops and parish priests were not inclined to view this work as professional. Indeed, they tended to see it as a voluntary expression of natural womanly instincts.'[8] From the perspective of the Vatican, until the early twentieth century sisters' status as professional church workers remained somewhat ambiguous. Yet both the state and the church escalated their demands on these women to establish their credentials as both religious and secular working professionals. This pressure is clearly illustrated in the case of the teaching sisters who were members of the Congregation of the Sisters of St Joseph of Toronto.

The Sisters of St Joseph had their origins in seventeenth-century France. In 1851 five sisters, led by Mother Delphine Fontbonne, came to Upper Canada at the invitation of the bishop of Toronto, Armand de Charbonnel. In their native France and since 1836 in the United States, the Sisters of St Joseph had dedicated their lives to the service of God through the education of children and young women, through social service among the poor, elderly, and prisoners, and through the provision of health care in the homes of the poor and in hospitals. In each of these areas they saw their work as filling a void, meeting a need not addressed by other agencies or institutions. They carried this tradition to Canada, education and health care being their key focuses.

For young women seeking to serve God and neighbour as a teaching or nursing sister, St Joseph's was only one of many options. This community was attractive because it was diocesan in orientation. Simply put, this means that, in the majority of instances, a woman who became a member would undertake her noviciate and spend her career in her home diocese. Many women sought to enter communities that they knew, and since the Sisters of St Joseph served in numerous schools and hospitals, for a majority of these women, a sister was by definition a Sister of St Joseph.

The sisters who taught in the government-inspected and publicly funded schools needed to possess government certification. Throughout the nineteenth century the leadership of the Toronto community took steps to ensure that their members were adequately qualified as teachers. As I have written elsewhere,[9] even before the passage in 1907 of the Ontario Act Respecting the Qualification of Certain Teachers, the *Annals* of the Sisters of St Joseph reveal that the community leader had reviewed both prospective and present members of the community, assessing their credentials and their potential to gain qualifications. Unlike their contemporaries in other parts of the country, communities of women religious based in Ontario did not generally create their own teacher-training institutions. Instead, their members usually attended the public institutions of the province in their various incarnations: normal schools, teachers' colleges, and faculties of education.

Being a vowed religious and a teacher was exhausting and demanding work. Days were very full: early rising for morning mass, journeys to their places of work, meals taken in community, evening prayer, community recreation (which often meant stitching and mending). Life was highly regulated, with little time for personal reflection. Summer 'vacation' often meant study: many sisters acquired additional teaching qualifications or their university degrees through part-time study. When their summer study sessions ended, they might act as relief workers in the other community enterprises to free up community members to take their annual retreats, or they might participate in the cooking and canning 'bees' to prepare fruits and vegetables produced on community farms for the winter.

The teaching sisters were highly sought after by local school boards and parishes, for they were 'teachers plus.' Sometimes they worked for less pay than lay teachers. Even more significant, they also gave fully of themselves to prepare pupils for reception of the sacraments and to serve the parish community in other roles: as sacristans who cared for the altar, organists, choir leaders, and teachers in Saturday catechetical classes. They often worked seven days a week. A late-nineteenth-century incident demonstrates the costs that such lives exacted. In 1886 the Sisters of St Joseph withdrew their teachers from a school in Brockton, Ontario. Two letters related to this action give a snapshot picture of the challenges that these women faced. Explaining their decision to the parish priest, Toronto archbishop John J. Lynch wrote, 'The Sisters of St Joseph have to their great sorrow undertaken more than they can well accomplish. A number of the Sisters are sick, some from overwork and exposure in begging through the country for the poor.'[10] This letter documents another type of work in which the sisters engaged: undertaking 'begging missions.' They travelled in pairs to parishes throughout the diocese. They would stay in ordinary households and visit families, soliciting donations for the community's schools, orphanages, seniors' homes, and hospitals.

The second of this pair of letters sheds additional light on the question of costs. In it Archbishop Lynch writes to Mother Superior Antoinette that her community's work in the 'service of neighbour' – that is, in teaching and funding the other charitable enterprises of the community – is taking away from the sisters' formation and prayer life. Lynch says, 'and there is another very serious difficulty very injurious to your community, that is, as your novices are so engaged in teaching and in other works that there is very little time for recollection and religious services ... many are sickly from over work and naturally break down under it.'[11] The archbishop obviously saw that the demands placed upon the sisters by their jobs as teachers and their membership in the collective charity of the community were making their lives as professed religious difficult. As the century turned, these difficulties grew.

Since education became a focus of community enterprise, leadership teams were determined to ensure that the women they accepted were well qualified, meeting not only the spiritual criteria but the standards of the state. Once a woman became a member of a religious community, the decision to acquire credentials and where those credentials would be used was made by the leadership team of the community, the mother superior and her council. This was common practice across communities. Typically, sisters were told in the form of a published list detailing who would be stationed where. Less frequently, they might be called to the superior's office and asked how they would feel about being sent to an area or about taking on certain studies. It is important to note that the criteria used by the leadership team in decision-making was to match the needs of the community and its enterprises with the skills of the members. Sisters were not set up to fail.

Thus until the mid-twentieth century, for Catholic women who wished to engage in professional work as both church workers and members of secular professions, the choice of life as a vowed woman religious offered the path to achieve both goals. As Marta Danylewycz has argued, becoming a religious held out a legitimate alternative to 'marriage, motherhood and spinsterhood.'[12] It provided both the religious and the secular credentials to engage in work that was not typically open to secular women. As women religious, sisters were able to rise to positions of power and influence in the educational, health care, and social service sectors. They served as university presidents, hospital chief executive officers, and directors of social service. Yet as the societal conditions in which they operated changed and as the role of women in the secular world evolved, the lives, spheres of influence, and enterprises previously dominated by women religious radically shifted.

Professionalization and Women Religious: Facing the Twenty-First Century

It is not hyperbole to state that the last half of the twentieth century has

As professional qualifications changed, many women religious annually updated their credentials. Among the women pictured in this photograph of music educators are members of the Congrégation de Notre Dame, Daughters of Wisdom, Holy Cross Sisters, Sisters of Charity 'Grey Nuns,' Sisters of St Joseph, and Ursulines.

seen more transitions in the lives of women religious than all the years of their previous history combined. The impact of changes in both canon and civil law that governs the status of women religious as professional church workers and professional workers in the secular world has been enormous. During the papacy of Pius XII there began a scrutiny of their lives and works. The World Congress on the States of Perfection (1950), followed quickly by a General Congress of Religious (1950), an International Congress on Teaching Sisters (1951), and an International Congress of Mothers General (1952), met to review the current state of religious life. The issues of the orientation of ministry, admission, and credentials of members and the nature and execution of decision-making were focuses of discussion. The age of religious reform had begun. The deliberations and decisions of Vatican II would be catalysts of further change.

The impact of Vatican II on the lives of women religious has been the subject of much debate and analysis.[13] For those sisters engaged in professional work in the secular community, one of the key elements that derived from the implementation of *Perfectae Caritatis: The Decree on the Up to Date Renewal of Religious Life* was an evolving understanding of the vow of obedience. As a result of the changes introduced by Vatican II, obedience no longer means verbatim adherence to the directions of community leadership. Key decisions, such as those concerning employment and career direction, now involve the individual sister as well as the superior and her council. Similarly, the sisters can more freely request the support of their community in furthering their own professional education. Thus personal and professional interests, not only community need, are the determinant of professional deployment. In some communities sabbaticals for renewal of religious life, as well as for career growth, are features of community life.

A second significant feature that has emerged from the Vatican II reforms is the recognition among women religious themselves that they are significant players within a historical continuum. Responding to the call to search out 'the primitive inspiration of the institute,'[14] they were and are finding their roots. Armed with the tools of feminist scholarship, they continue to discover a history of independent women, frequently at odds with the institutional church.[15] Many now view their founders as women who challenged the barriers of their times. They see their history as one of like-minded women who, banding together in the name of social justice, sought to establish flexible structures to support their initiatives. From these past roots, women religious draw encouragement and strength. They have also discovered that religious life is itself cyclical. It has witnessed periods of both expansion and decline.[16]

Vatican II also challenged the perceptions that many women religious (and indeed, Catholics generally) had about the goals and orientation of their lives in religion. They abandoned many of the features that had characterized religious life in the pre–Vatican II church, such as living in large institutions, leading a highly regulated prayer life, paying strict adherence to the religious rule, and most visibly, dressing in a religious habit. As they did so, many sisters and nuns found themselves asking what made them women religious. For a good number, attempting to answer that question brought them into conflict with themselves, their communities, and in many cases their male ecclesiastical superiors.

Yet the reforms of Vatican II came at a time when the demographics of religious life were already shifting. Statistics compiled for Canadian religious communities by their own central administrative unit bear this observation out. The data contained in *The Census of Religious Sisters in Canada*, which were collected in 1965 (before the issuance of the Vatican II document on religious life, *Perfectae Caritatis*), present a remarkably complete picture of the state of 98.4 per cent or 65,248, of the approximately 65,948 women religious in Canada.[17] The study reveals several key points: women religious had a high degree of professional qualifications; their major endeavours were in education and health care; their members were aging; they were failing to attract new members.

The *Census* reported data on women religious who were members of some 183 institutes and categorized the work of these communities as belonging to seven major fields: contemplatives (or nuns), missionaries, hospitallers (those engaged in health services), educators, educator-hospitallers, social workers, and domestic helpers. Even in the early sixties, many of these communities had very small numbers of members. This characteristic arose from the fact that, for most of the nineteenth century, any group of women who had an idea for a community and who could obtain the support of the local bishop or priest (or vice versa), could gain status as such. Table 1 presents the distribution in enterprises of women religious in Canada. An analysis of these data reveals that a large majority of women religious in Canada – 87.3 per cent in fact – were sisters active in ministries of education or health care. Secondly, contemplatives – those women religious who could be classified as nuns – represented less than 3 per cent of the total. Numerically, this category was smaller than that of women religious engaged in the domestic service to priests and seminarians.[18]

TABLE 1

Functions and number of institutes in Canada in 1965

	No. of institutes	%	No. of members	%
Contemplatives	18	10.2	1897	2.9
Missionaries	8	4.3	2566	3.9
Hospitallers	13	7.1	3836	5.9
Educators	80	43.6	30855	47.2
Educators/hospitallers	33	18.0	22301	34.2
Social workers	16	8.7	969	1.5
Domestic helpers	15	8.1	2824	4.3
Totals	183	100.0	65248	100.0

Source: Lessard and Montminy, *The Census of Religious Sisters of Canada*, 295.

TABLE 2

Numbers of women religious, 1940–65

	1940	1945	1950	1955	1960	1965
Number	43,994	47,799	51,646	55,949	59,712	61,885

Source: Lessard and Montminy, *The Census of Religious Sisters of Canada*, 345.

TABLE 3

Variation in the number of women religious at five-year intervals, 1940–65

	1940–5	1945–50	1950–5	1955–60	1960–5
Numerical variation	3,805	3,847	4,303	3,763	2,173
Percentage of variation	8.6	8.0	8.3	6.7	3.6

Source: Lessard and Montminy, *The Census of Religious Sisters of Canada*, 345.

Perhaps the most revealing statistics are those that pointed to the problems of attracting women to the religious life. As table 2 illustrates, the number of Canadian women religious rose between 1940 and 1960. Yet these figures were somewhat misleading. The authors of the *Census* reported a 'quick drop in the annual increase' between 1960 and 1965, a drop that had significant implications for an aging community. The data reported in tables 2 and 3 show that, while the number of women religious appeared to be rising, the percentage of variation had declined

TABLE 4
Percentage by age cohort, 1965

	Less than 30	More than 60
Contemplatives	11.88	29.04
Missionaries	17.89	16.94
Hospitallers	10.48	30.43
Educators	18.25	24.37
Educators/hospitallers	18.20	26.74
Social Workers	30.40	11.20
Domestic Helpers	12.14	26.64
Total	17.30	25.10

Source: Lessard and Montminy, *The Census of Religious Sisters of Canada*, 327.

over the fifteen-year period between 1950 and 1965. The authors went on to report that, when the variation was examined over the twenty-five-year period between 1940 and 1965, the percentage of variation was 40.6.[19] Further, the *Census* contains age-profile tables for women religious under thirty and over sixty (see table 4). In the accompanying text, the leadership of religious communities was alerted to the problems that were appearing on the horizon – indications that some sectors were reaching 'the fatal point where 30% are 60 or over.'[20] These statistics are telling. The communities classified as oriented to contemplation, domestic service, and hospitallers were reaching a critical state. The authors of the *Census* pointed out that the institutes devoted to social work were 'few in number and are definitely younger,' while the oldest and the largest institutes devoted to education or care of the sick had 'the lowest rate of recruitment.' Most revealing, perhaps, was the insight that religious were 'entering into competition with lay persons in the labour market and will do so more and more in the future.'[21] Communities were advised to undertake strategic planning in the education and assignment of their members in order to come to terms with these facts. Further, they should pay even closer attention to the education of their members, since the authors suggested that it was the key to their further success.

The data presented in the *Census* on the academic qualifications of women religious deserves note. 'One of the most important indicators of the changes taking place in the world of sisterhoods is certainly the tremendous efforts they are making to raise their academic qualifications. On the one hand, the aspirants who come with a better schooling have

TABLE 5
Proportion of occupations in 1991

Occupation	Percentage
Service to the congregation	28.62
Retired (fully)	19.60
Retired (partially)	17.60
Work in school	13.14
Service to the church	9.57
Work in hospitals	6.07
Social work	3.91
Other occupations	1.49

Source: Canadian Religious Conference, *Statistiques des congrégations religieuses du Canada*, 26.

the opportunity to continue their studies and on the other hand, a goodly number of older Sisters are attending university or specialized schools.'[22] These conclusions were based on the academic qualifications reported: 31 per cent of the sisters had at least a bachelor's degree, and 21.6 per cent of that group possessed 'a Doctorate, a Licentiate or Master's degree.'[23]

What emerges from the *Census* is an image of Canadian women religious as a cohort of the best-educated professional women in the country. Concentrated in the fields of education and health care, religious communities offered much to new members. Yet women were increasing not coming forth in the numbers they once had. The authors of the *Census* would soon see dramatic evidence of their conclusions. Between 1967 and 1972 the number of women presenting themselves as postulants and novices declined by 80 per cent.[24]

Almost thirty years after the *Census* was compiled, the data collected for the 1991 *Statistiques des congrégations religieuses du Canada* document just how profoundly the state of women religious in Canada has changed. This report listed 152 communities of women religious with 30,707 members, a decline of some 47.1 per cent from the record high established in 1967. The occupational profile had also been transformed (table 5). While the occupational classes are quite different from those used in the *Census*, what is apparent from the 1991 statistics is the extent to which the types of service in which women religious are engaged have changed. In the first place, the occupational profile is dominated by retirement. Secondly, work related to the administration of the communities themselves occupies a significant portion of the workforce. Many factors have contributed to this change in profile, not the least of which is the fact that communities of women religious are not attracting women in the same numbers as they once were. Lack of entrants, not departure, is the major cause of the numerical variation, for at the highest point of departures, the number of women who left communities represented 1.72 per cent of the total number of women religious in Canada.[25]

Many scholars have hypothesized about the reasons for these dramatic shifts. The professionalization of women's work plays a central role in some of these theories. The authors of the *Census* highlighted the fact that women religious had to compete with laypeople for positions. Those areas of neglect and need which communities of women religious were founded to address were falling under the umbrella of secular authorities. As a result of the professionalization of the female workforce and the subsequent increase in status and financial remuneration, these areas of work were becoming attractive to (and possible for) laypeople. Women could work as nurses and teachers and in social service without requiring the resources of a community of like-minded and similarly focused women to provide for them the structures within which to perform such tasks. Because there were now reasonable wages attached to such services, women no longer needed to live in community and share meagre resources in order to work in these areas.

Scholars also point to the links between industrialization and entry into religious life. There are more women religious in less-developed societies because of the lack of options that exist for women. A recent article has stated, 'Industrialization influences the number of nuns [*sic*] available ... it is only within the more industrialized nations that the necessary occupational structures arise to provide women opportunities for social advancement that seem more attractive than the chances for social mobility available in Catholic social orders.'[26] Yet what is missing from these hypotheses is attention to the very core of the professed woman: the concept of vocation. Women religious identify their lives as a personal response to serve God and their neighbours. How the present-day institutional church views this vowed life will now be discussed.

Within the Roman Catholic Church the future of religious life has been the subject of much study and debate. In October 1994 Pope John Paul II convened a synod of bishops to examine 'The Consecrated Life and Its Role in the Church and in the World.' Significantly, the majority of bishops are not members of the religious communities that the synod set out to discuss. Even more important is the fact that the majority of religious are women, and because of their exclusion from the priesthood (the initial credential for ascension to positions of decision-making and governance within the church), women were present only as observers and not as voting members of the synod. The resulting documents and papal letters have produced no real consensus or plans of action to move religious life into the twenty-first century. As well, papal pronouncements have discouraged, rather than encouraged, women who seek a more equal role within the Roman Catholic Church.

The institutional church traditionally held three roles for women – single, married, and religious. It has stated categorically that, because of their sex, women are denied access to the sacrament that would start them on the road to leadership of the universal church, the priesthood. Pope John Paul II argues in support of the feminine rather than feminism since he believes 'a certain *contemporary feminism* [emphasis in original] finds its roots in the absence of true respect for woman.'[27] Further, in an apostolic letter issued on 22 May 1994 and entitled 'On Reserving Priestly Ordination to Men Alone,' the pontiff concludes, 'I declare that the Church has no authority whatsoever to confer priestly ordination on women and that this judgement is to be definitively held by all the Church's faithful.'[28] For him the issue of women's ordination is closed, and this view *should* be held by all members of the church.

It is curious that one should make a pronouncement which is impossible to enforce. For among the international leadership of women religious, the future of religious life involves discussion of how to enhance the role of women in the church. The issue of ordination is a part of this discussion. One of the most widely respected and widely cited women religious who have reflected on these questions is the former president of the Leadership Conference of Women Religious, Joan Chittister. This American Benedictine sister has not been silenced by the papal directive. Chittister argues, 'Religious congregations stood as bulwarks against ignorance, illiteracy, disease, abandonment and secularism ... Unless and until we turn our corporate energy to the specific issues and social questions of this age, educating the world to their importance, advocating for change and modeling fresh responses to ourselves, the question of why we bother to go on together is a valid and imperative one.'[29] At a time when Pope John Paul II is calling for a return to the traditional enterprises (especially education) – and indeed, traditional accoutrements (especially the dress) of religious life, Chittister is asking for the examination of religion from a feminist perspective. She writes:

We must form both women and men for feminism. Every novitiate in this country must teach the status of women worldwide, the theological inconsistencies that ecclesiastical chauvinism breeds, the danger to the globe of institutionalized machoism, and the loss of credibility to a church that preaches equality but does not practice it. Of all the issues facing religious life, feminism is surely the most veiled and the most dangerous because it brings us most in conflict with the flow of history. We can as church and congregations, all close our eyes, sink into our albs or become the female part of a patriarchal system if we will, but if we do it will not be long before religious life will die of its own sexist disease.[30]

Chittister is representative of a segment of women religious who are challenging current papal statements, especially those that have at their core a nostalgia for a past form of religious life. She questions the use of these models as images for religious life in the twenty-first century and calls for religious to act as agents of change, as advocates for 'the prophetic rather than the obedient, for the pastoral rather than the ecclesiastically proper.'[31] Such statements embody the tension lived by women religious today as they seek to find a place for themselves within the institutional church that will allow them to realize their dual roles as professional church workers and as advocates of both societal and ecclesiastical change.

Conclusion

Until the mid-nineteenth century, for women of the Roman Catholic faith, entry into religious life gave access to careers and an independence that few of their contemporaries possessed. It offered them status, power, and authority as women who were professional workers in both the religious and the secular worlds. By banding them together in communities, it also provided a means of living an independent life, sustained by the products of their work. Yet there were tensions inherent in women's entry into religious life and engagement in the professions. Roman Catholic women who sought the actualization of gospel values through affiliation with the institutional church have frequently had their initiatives reshaped and reoriented by it. As a result, religious communities became institutions themselves and often found that they were increasingly removed from the aims of their founders and from those whom they sought to serve.

Religious communities have provided for Catholic women a means to live their lives as a dual professionals: as professional religious and as workers in professions. A woman who entered religious life followed a formation process, serving an orientation and an apprenticeship period, and after a suitable period of evaluation by community members, was recognized by the community with the external symbols and the rights and privileges of full membership. The religious community was the means of providing the resources for a woman to progress through the ranks and gain employment in a community enterprise, thereby becoming a professional worker in the secular world. In contemporary society, as dual professionals, women religious are living unresolved tensions as they attempt to reconcile articulated ideas with actions; traditional enterprises with emerging needs; the change-oriented values of their founders with a nostalgic longing on the part of some Catholics to return to their recent past. How these tensions work themselves out will be apparent during the next decades as women religious prepare once again to change, to renew, and to alter in the search for a meaningful way to actualize their professional secular work as professed women of God.

NOTES

The author acknowledges the Social Sciences and Humanities Research Council of Canada for its role in supporting the research reported here. She thanks the archivists of many communities of women religious for their assistance in accessing the documents analysed in this study. The author also thanks Dr Veronica O'Reilly CSJ, Dr Patricia Byrne CSJ, and the members of the Women in the Professions Research Network for their feedback on the many drafts of this essay.

1 Natalie Z. Davis, *Women on the Margins: Three Seventeenth Century Lives* (Cambridge: Harvard University Press, 1995), 3.
2 Richard Leonard, *Beloved Daughters: 100 Years of Papal Teaching on Women* (Ottawa: Novalis, 1995), 55–6.
3 The Second Vatican Council (1962–5) will hereafter be referred to as Vatican II.
4 See, for example, Elisabeth S. Fiorenza, *In Memory of Her: A Feminist Theological Reconstruction of Christian Origins* (rev. ed., New York: Crossroads, 1995); Jo Ann K. McNamara, *Sisters in Arms: Catholic Nuns through Two Millennia* (Cambridge: Harvard University Press, 1996); Mary Augusta Neal, *From Nuns to Sisters* (Mystic, Conn.: John XXIII, 1990).
5 Boniface VIII, *Periculoso*, as quoted in Neal, *From Nuns to Sisters*, 21.
6 Robert D. Gidney and Winnifred P.J. Millar, *Professional Gentlemen: The Profes-*

sions in Nineteenth-Century Ontario (Toronto: University of Toronto Press, 1994), 8.

7 Marguerite Keenan SC, personal communication, 25 May 1996.

8 McNamara, *Sisters in Arms*, 614.

9 See Elizabeth Smyth, 'Writing Reveals our Mysteries,' in Beverly Boutilier and Alison Prentice, eds., *Creating Historical Memory* (Vancouver: University of British Columbia Press, 1997); E. Smyth '"Christian Perfection and Service to Neighbours": The Congregation of the Sisters of St Joseph in the Archdiocese of Toronto,' in Elizabeth Muir and Marilyn Whiteley, eds., *Changing Roles of Women within the Christian Church in Canada* (Toronto: University of Toronto Press, 1995), 38–54; E. Smyth, "Much Exertion of the Voice and Great Application of the Mind": Teacher Education within the Congregation of the Sisters of St Joseph of Toronto, Canada, 1851–1920,' special joint double issue of the *History of Education Review* and *Historical Studies in Education*, no. 3 (1994): 97–113; E. Smyth, '"Congregavit nos in unum Christi amor": The Congregation of the Sisters of St Joseph in the Archdiocese of Toronto, 1851–1920,' *Ontario History* 74 (September 1990): 225–40.

10 Archbishop Lynch to Father J. McCann, 16 November 1886. Archives of the Archdiocese of Toronto, LB05.071, 58.

11 Archbishop Lynch to Mother Antoinette CSJ, 16 November 1886, ibid.

12 Marta Danylewycz, *Taking the Veil: An Alternative to Marriage, Motherhood and Spinsterhood in Quebec, 1840–1920* (Toronto: McClelland and Stewart, 1987).

13 See Patricia Wittberg, *The Rise and Decline of Catholic Religious Orders* (Albany, NY: SUNY Press, 1994), as a recent example.

14 'Perfectae Caritatis,' 28 October 1965, in A. Flannery, ed., *Vatican II: the Conciliar and Post Conciliar Documents* (Northport: Costello, 1975), 612.

15 The Sisters Servants of the Immaculate Heart of Mary of Monroe, Michigan (IHM), for example, have labelled their historical project 'Claiming Our Roots: IHM Interdisciplinary Feminist History Project.' Their seventeen working assumptions include the statement that, 'in practice, a range of feminist ideologies exist, but feminist approaches to history accept as a starting point that patriarchy exists in society and in its institutions, including churches.' The influence that this project will have, especially through international organizations such as the History of Women Religious Conference (HWR) and its Internet discussion group Sister-L, remains to be seen.

16 See especially the work of sociologist P. Wittberg, 'Previous Decline Periods in Religious Orders: Social Movement Perspectives,' in *The Rise and Decline of Catholic Religious Orders*, 178–205.

17 M. Lessard and J.P. Montminy, *The Census of Religious Sisters of Canada* (Ottawa: Canadian Religious Conference, 1966), 274.

18 It is ironic to note that during his 1984 visit to Canada, Pope John Paul II canonized the founder of one of these religious communities.

19 Lessard and Montminy, *The Census of Religious Sisters of Canada*, 345.

20 Ibid., 328.

21 Ibid., 378.

22 Ibid., 377.

23 Ibid., 342.

24 Canadian Religious Conference, *Statistiques des congrégations religieuses du Canada* (Ottawa: Canadian Religious Conference, 1991), 28.

25 The highest number of departures, which occurred in 1972, was 823; the total number of women religious for that year was 47,965; ibid., 28.

26 H.R. Ebaugh, J. Lorence, and J.S. Chafetz, 'The Growth and Decline of the Population of Catholic Nuns Cross-Nationally, 1960–1990: A Case of Secularization as Social Structural Change,' *Journal for the Scientific Study of Religion* 35, no.2 (1996): 182.

27 John Paul II, *Crossing the Threshold of Hope* (New York: Knopf, 1995), 217.

28 John Paul II, 'On Reserving Priestly Ordination to Men Alone' (apostolic letter, 22 May 1994), 8.

29 Joan Chittister, *The Fire in These Ashes: A Spirituality of Contemporary Religious Life* (Kansas City, Mo.: Sheed & Ward, 1995), 167.

30 Ibid., 166.

31 Ibid., 172.

Who's Accounting? Women Chartered Accountants in Nova Scotia

CYNDY ALLEN WITH MARGARET CONRAD

Nova Scotia–born Christine Ross was North America's first female 'professional' accountant. In June 1898 she wrote and passed the examination introduced two years earlier as a requirement by the Association of Certified Public Accountants in the state of New York. Despite misgivings, and after considerable delay, the ACPA's New York Board of Regents voted on 21 December 1899 that she be granted 'the full CPA certificate.' Ross had been an accountant for nearly a decade before taking the CPA examination, and she continued to practise in New York after her certification.[1] Ross provides a dramatic contrast with the progress of women in the accounting profession in her native province. It was not until 1956, more than half a century after her certification, that Newfoundland-born Janet C. Dawe became the first woman to be admitted to the Institute of Chartered Accountants of Nova Scotia on the basis of training, examination, and registration in that province.[2]

Prior to the 1960s accountancy in Canada and elsewhere was a profession dominated by men. Women often worked as 'bookkeepers' and 'clerks,' but they were systematically excluded from the highest professional ranks. Over the past thirty years they have entered the profession in increasing numbers, but they have not reached the rank or remuneration levels of their male counterparts in chartered accountancy, the most prestigious of the professional associations in the accounting field. This essay briefly outlines the evolution of women's status in the accounting profession in Canada and focuses on Nova Scotia as a case study of the current condition of women in chartered accountancy.

We became interested in this topic because of Margaret Conrad's work on Ellen Fairclough, Canada's first female federal cabinet minister, who was also one of the country's first female accountants.[3] In 1995 Margaret hired Cyndy Allen to research the history of female accountants in Canada, and she became curious about the contemporary status of women in the profession. Indeed, Cyndy's life course was dramatically altered by her brief foray into accounting history. She decided to do her master's thesis in sociology at Acadia University on female chartered accountants in Nova Scotia,[4] and she then landed a research job with the Bank of Montreal. Both authors have had a long-standing interest in exploring the status of women and other marginal groups in the largely male-dominated arenas of business and political life in Canada.

Accounting for Women

Accountancy has had a long history spanning over seven thousand years, but its modern form is rooted in the fifteenth century, when the Italians adopted the double-entry accounting system and established the first association to regulate the activities of accountants. In the nineteenth century the expansion of accounting operations relating to banking, bankruptcy, and taxation in the industrializing market economies of the North Atlantic world offered lucrative opportunities for people who 'kept the books.' Like many other skilled workers, accountants hoped to control entry into their field of expertise and the standards under which they worked so that they could reap the rewards of the industrial age.[5]

The founding of accounting associations in Scotland (1853) and England (1870) served as both a stimulus and a model for developments in Canada. Concerned that British associations might try to control accounting throughout the empire, Canadian accountants formed their own provincial associations, beginning in Ontario and Quebec in 1879. Each association took the name 'chartered accountant' (CA) following the British model. In 1900, two years before a national association (the Dominion Association of Chartered Accountants) was founded,[6] Nova Scotia became the fourth province (after Quebec, Ontario, and Manitoba) to establish an institute of chartered accountants.

As these institutes gained in public esteem and legal privileges, non-members began to form competing organizations with different entrance and training requirements. Canadian accounting history offers a confusing array of legally constituted associations, including the Certified General Accountants' Association, Certified Public Accountants, Certified Management Accountants, Accredited Public Accountants, and the Guild of Industrial, Commercial, and Institutional Accountants. As the competition for prominence mounted, education became one of the most effective tools for establishing ascendancy. Their increased emphasis on university-based education, first required by the Institute of Chartered Accountants of Ontario in 1921, eventually gave CAs the edge in maintaining their dominance in the field of 'public accounting.' As distinguished from 'management accounting,' public accounting is typically defined as 'adding credibility to financial information by conducting an audit and presenting a signed public opinion on the adequacy of information.'[7]

The increasing reliance of Canadian governments on monies from corporate and personal income taxes following their introduction during the First World War contributed to the demand for professional accountants. However, until the 1930s 'full-time' accountants, chartered or otherwise, were relatively rare in the business world. With the onset of the Depression, bankruptcies skyrocketed, resulting in the introduction of legislation that required accountants to act as 'unbiased' third parties in establishing the financial state of corporate enterprises.

As happened in many other professional groups, the men who pioneered in the field tried to exclude women and minorities from their ranks. The Institute of Chartered Accountants of Ontario voted in 1896 to ban women from membership on the grounds that 'the employment of women clerks was detrimental to the value of male labour.'[8] Even in accounting jurisdictions where formal measures were not taken, women were clearly unwelcome. The question of the status of female accountants was raised at the annual meeting of the Dominion Association in 1913 but was relegated to a committee that seems never to have submitted a report.[9] Table 1 underscores the impact that professionalization had on the status of women in accounting. In 1891 women made up 13 per cent of those defined as accountants and auditors, but thereafter their relative and absolute numbers declined. As in many other professions, a gendered hierarchy emerged in accounting whereby men had exclusive access to the high-status and high-paid positions, while women were relegated to the ranks of poorly paid bookkeepers and cashiers.[10]

Although the granting of female suffrage at the federal level in 1918 marked a turning point for the status of women, equal access to positions of 'privilege,' including membership in professional organizations, continued to be contested. The Institute of Chartered Accountants of British Columbia voted to admit women members in 1919 but, following a reorganization two years later, denied admission to Mary Ellen Crehan, who

TABLE 1

Canadian accountants, auditors, and financial officers, 1891–1991[a]

Year	Total	% Males	Males	% Females	Females
1891	10,244	87	8,931	13	1,313
1901	3,563	99	3,501	1	62
1911	2,697	96	2,600	4	97
1921	1,468	98	1,432	2	36
1931	17,623	97	17,052	3	571
1941	34,379	91	31,384	9	2,992
1951	30,879	95	29,354	5	1,525
1961	30,670	95	29,121	5	1,549
1971	103,015	85	87,360	15	5,655
1981	155,315	68	106,190	32	49,125
1991	234,045	53	123,685	47	110,360

Source: Dominion Bureau of Statistics/Statistics Canada, 1915–96.

[a]The census definition of 'accountants' changed periodically between 1891 and 1991, but the figures provide a reasonably reliable guide to the general numbers and gender break-down in what was perceived as the 'profession' over time. People concerned with manage-rial activities in banks and investment and financial institutions since 1971 have not been included in the category of 'accountants, auditors, and other financial officers'; Statistics Canada, *Standard Occupational Classification 1980*, Cat. no. 12-565E (Ottawa: Minister of Supply and Services, 1981), 56.

was a qualified candidate. She subsequently took her case to the Supreme Court of British Columbia, which decided in her favour. Women in Saskatchewan (Irene Patterson) and Nova Scotia (Florence Herkins) passed their chartered accountancy exams in 1922, but their names failed to appear on membership lists. As late as 1929 Charlotte N. Howell, who had successfully completed CA requirements in May of that year, was denied registration in the province of Quebec.[11]

Howell's status was held in abeyance until the decision on the Persons Case was handed down by the Judicial Committee of the Privy Council in Great Britain, the final court of appeal for Canadians until 1949. Initiated by five women in Alberta, the Persons Case was designed to test a nine-teenth-century law that denied women equality with men in rights and privileges and was still being used to prohibit the appointment of women to the Senate. The Privy Council's decision, announced on 18 October 1929, recognized the personhood of women and opened the way to women's entry into all avenues of public life. In 1930 Charlotte Howell in

Quebec and Helen Burpee in Ontario were registered as CAs, the first women to achieve their status through training and examination rather than by proclamation or court action.[12]

It proved difficult for women to acquire in practice the equality that they had won in theory. Comfortable in their exclusive enclaves, men continued to throw roadblocks in the path of women who tried to rise above their status as bookkeepers and clerks. The progress of women in most professional fields was slow and even retrograde in the period from 1921 to 1961, and accountancy was no exception. Despite the expansion of the field during the Depression and the Second World War, women never represented more than 9 per cent (in 1941) of those involved in all accounting and auditing activities in this period, and their representation fell back to 5 per cent following the war. Female CAs were so rare that they elicited comment.

Beginning in the 1960s the expansion of jobs in accounting, increased female labour-force participation, and feminist efforts to break down barriers against the entrance of women into fields hitherto dominated by men combined to bring more women into the profession. By 1991 they constituted nearly half (47 per cent) of those who worked as 'accountants, auditors, and other financial officers.' In this respect, accountancy differs from professions such as engineering and architecture, where women are still a tiny minority. The number of women in accounting, however, masks other gender inequalities that characterize the field.[13] Not only are they less likely than men to be chartered accountants – only 20 per cent of CAs are women – but they are rarely elected to partnerships in prestigious firms – only 9 per cent of partners are women – and are more likely to work part-time and in small firms than men.[14]

It is in this context that Janet C. Dawe's achievement in winning admission to the Institute of Chartered Accountants of Nova Scotia in 1956 must be viewed. In 1901 when the chartered accountants in the province formed an association, there were only 10 licensed practitioners, none of them women. In 1970 all of the 21 new CAs were men, but by 1995 women made up 42 per cent of graduating CAs. While the ICANS lagged behind many other provincial associations in admitting its first female member, its conservatism was typical of the profession.[15] Sluggish economic conditions in the Atlantic region, which reduced the demand for chartered accountants and prolonged the dominance of the few men at the top of the profession, served only to accentuate trends that were played out everywhere across the nation.[16]

Accounting for Women in Nova Scotia

There were 247 female CAs registered with the Institute of Chartered Accountants of Nova Scotia in 1996. To assess perceptions of their current status in the accounting profession, a survey was sent to these women and to an equal number of men selected by a systematic random sample from a pool of 1,056 male CAs registered in the province.[17] Surprisingly, the survey generated the same response rate (58 per cent) from both women and men, producing 143 replies from each group. To explore in more depth some of the responses gleaned from survey data, interviews were conducted with 10 CAs (5 women and 5 men).

The survey was divided into three sections. The first was designed to determine the personal characteristics of the respondents, such as gender, age, and career development; the second elicited perceptions relating to work and gender around job assignments, salary differentials, choice of specialties, and commitment to career; and the third consisted of three open-ended questions that gave the respondents an opportunity to describe their individual experiences in the accounting profession. The main thrust of the study was to evaluate perceptions of gender differences in opportunities for advancement in the field of chartered accountancy.

The majority (81 per cent) of the chartered accountants surveyed had received their initial designation in Nova Scotia and most (83 per cent) were employed by an accounting firm; the balance were either self-employed, unemployed, or retired. Over 95 per cent had a university degree, a requirement introduced by the ICANS in 1970. The respondents ranged in age from 25 to 76, with a mean age of 36.5 and a median of 30 years; the mean age of women (33.5, ranging from 25 to 54) was considerably lower than that of men (39.6, ranging from 25 to 76), reflecting the recent entry of women into the profession.

As table 2 reveals, nearly half (45 per cent) of the respondents worked in public accounting, while 28 per cent were employed in industry. Smaller portions worked in government, education, and other sectors. Eighty-two per cent (85 for men and 80 for women) classified their position as managerial; only 4 per cent indicated that there was no differentiation between management and junior positions in their organization (see table 3). The rest, 14 per cent, were recently hired juniors. The high incidence of management positions reflects the small size of most accounting firms in the province and the fact that CAs are often hired in management positions in industry and government.

TABLE 2
Percentage of respondents in fields, by gender

	Total	Female	Male
Public Accounting	45	42	50
Industry	28	27	29
Government	12	17	8
Educational	7	6	7
Non-profit	3	4	1
Other	5	4	5

TABLE 3
Distribution of women and men in management and junior positions[a]

	Males	Females
Management	85% (109)	80% (106)
Juniors	15% (20)	20% (27)

[a]In the tables that show management and junior respondents separately, a small group of 4 per cent which falls into neither category has been excluded.

Most respondents (81 per cent) were currently married, with men (83 per cent) only slightly more likely than women (79 per cent) to be in such a relationship. Perhaps as a function of age and changing social values, managers (83 per cent) were more likely than juniors (70 per cent) to be married. Most (60 per cent) of this sample of Nova Scotian chartered accountants had children, with managers (63 per cent) more likely than juniors (40 per cent) to be parents. While 73 per cent of male managers were fathers, only 53 per cent of female managers were mothers, reflecting age differences and perhaps confirming the qualitative evidence which suggests that women tended to postpone having children for the sake of their careers. Significantly, 41 per cent of male managers, but only 18 per cent of female managers, had three or more children.

Children seem to pose a greater problem for female than for male CAs. One thirty-five-year-old female respondent noted: 'I wanted to be partner and was told if I planned to have a family I couldn't be partner – subsequently [I was] laid off' (no. 20).[18] A male partner who was interviewed for this study also underscored the conflict between career and children for women: 'There is always the uncertainty that after her baby is born that she will change her mind and want to stay at home,' he concluded (interview G). Another male interviewee, a partner in a small firm, offered this perspective: 'I don't know what you would do in a small firm if someone had a baby in January ... it is very difficult to replace that skill level for a three- or six-month period. Right or wrong that has to be the bias' (interview H). As these responses suggest, the current generation of female CAs is perceived as having parental obligations that men apparently do not share, and such perceptions, as we shall see shortly, have an impact on the status of women in the profession.

The assignment of complex and/or prestigious jobs provides junior CAs with experience that is essential for promotion. When presented with the statement 'Women and men in Chartered Accountancy are given the same types of job assignments,' 90 per cent of those who responded agreed that they were (see table 4). When the responses are controlled for gender, differences appeared. Nearly 16 per cent of female and only 2 per cent of male CAs believed that men were given the better assignments. Although there was virtually no difference between managers and juniors in their perceptions of the effects of gender on job assignments, gender again made a difference. Fifteen per cent of female managers and 3 per cent of male managers believed that men were given better job assignments, compared to 20 per cent of female juniors and no (0 per cent) male juniors.

Older respondents recognized that, despite continuing biases against women, conditions had improved. A forty-nine-year-old woman working in industry noted: 'In 1967 there was a salary differential between male and female students and sex was a factor in assigning audits – I expect this is no longer the case' (no. 241). If there is discrimination against women in the 1990s, it tends to be more subtle. One twenty-six-year-old woman working in public accounting noted: 'Although women are given [the] same job assignments ... it is easier for men in social business situations, since most owner managers are male as well as senior management in corporations or non profit organizations' (no. 255). A thirty-three-year-old female manager in public accounting indicated that, although one job assignment is 'not necessarily better than the other ... some job assignments are based on gender' (no. 141); and a male partner confirmed this tendency, reporting that 'men and women are given different assignments, not based on better but rather [better] suited' (no. 191). In some cases, decisions on female assignments were described as motivated by

TABLE 4

Access to opportunities and rewards by gender and by management status

Men and women in chartered accountancy are:		Percentage						
		Total	Female	Male	Female manage-ment	Female junior	Male manage-ment	Male junior
A Given the same types of job assignments	Men given better assignments	9	16	2	15	20	3	0
	Same	90	83	97	84	80	96	100
	Women given better assignments	1	1	1	1	0	1	0
B Encouraged to develop the same industry specialties	Men encouraged for better positions	13	20	6	19	27	7	6
	Same	86	79	94	80	73	93	94
	Women encouraged for better positions	1	1	0	1	0	0	0
C Have the same opportunity to make partner, given equal job performance	Men have a better opportunity	52	71	33	68	76	29	50
	Same	46	29	63	31	24	67	45
	Women have a better opportunity	2	1	4	1	0	4	5
D Paid comparable salaries for the the same responsibilities and performance	Men are paid more	15	25	7	26	14	8	0
	Same	84	75	93	74	86	91	100
	Women are paid more	1	0	0	0	0	1	0

'benevolence'; that is, women were being given lighter assignments because of perceived familial obligations. Some women objected to being placed on what they identified as 'the mommy track' – a slower career path for women with children – or wished that they had been given the opportunity to make the decision rather than have their superiors make it for them (interview A and surveys 240, 101, 113, and 182).

Another statement in the questionnaire was designed to elicit perceptions concerning specializations within the field (see table 4). The consensus of most accountants (86 per cent) was that men and women were encouraged to develop the same specializations. Thirteen per cent agreed that men, and less than 1 per cent that women, were encouraged to develop more-prestigious specializations. Again a difference emerges when we examine the responses by gender. Seventy-nine per cent of women and 94 per cent of men thought that men and women were encouraged to develop the same industry specializations.[19] Interviews supported the view that sex segregation occurs in the field of chartered accountancy. A married, twenty-nine-year-old male vice-president of finance gave the example of men being encouraged to specialize in insolvency while women were directed to tax work, but he believed that there was 'no difference in prestige level' between the two specialties (no. 156). One thirty-seven-year-old female accountant asserted that a woman would more likely become a partner by specializing in tax accountancy (no. 264). A female manager interviewed for this study added: 'I think more men go into management consulting ... there seems to be just recently a bit of rumbling [that] tax is something that might be better for women in terms of managing personal and professional life' (interview A).

Respondents were also asked whether they agreed that 'women and men have the same opportunity to make partner in a CA firm, given equal job performance' (see table 4). Fifty-two per cent of respondents agreed that men, and only 2 per cent that women, had a better opportunity to become a partner; the rest concluded that women and men had equal opportunity to do so in a chartered accountancy firm. Broken down by gender, 71 per cent of women and 33 per cent of men thought that men have the edge over women in the pursuit of a partnership. One's position in a firm seems to influence perception. Forty-nine per cent of managers and 63 per cent of juniors believed that men had a better opportunity to become a partner. While 68 per cent of female managers believed that men had a better chance of a partnership, only 29 per cent of male managers agreed; for female juniors the agreement was 76 per cent and for male juniors 50 per cent. This perception on the part of 71 per cent of women and nearly one-third of the men that there are obstacles to women acquiring partnership suggests that women are disadvantaged in achieving the highest ranks in chartered accountancy.

Survey respondents perceived family responsibilities as the primary factor inhibiting women's advancement in partnership elections. One thirty-six-year-old female manager in industry with two pre-school children asserted that there was a 'lack of flexibility in public firms for women raising a young family' (no. 201). A twenty-seven-year-old married women with no children made the same point: 'The negative experiences stem mainly from working in a public accounting firm. In many ways the firm is quite rigid and slow to change. Human resource skills are poor. The most disheartening experience has been the realization of the fact that although nearly half of the new CAs and CA students today are women, a small percentage of senior managers and partners in a CA firm are female. Women have to sacrifice much more than men. A woman cannot be devoted to both family and career (nor can a man in most cases) and advance to partner in a public firm' (no. 14). A thirty-six-year-old male public accountant with two pre-school-aged children declared: 'This is an interesting questionnaire. However, it presumes, I think, that success is partnership in a big firm. I think it takes a certain type of person to become a CA partner – a hard driving, focused person willing to make huge sacrifices in terms of family life, quality of life, low pay in the years leading up to partnership [and] low control over one's destiny' (no. 285).

Like many professions, chartered accountancy has a workplace culture that makes it difficult for people with family responsibilities to prevail in the competition for partnership positions. A thirty-three-year-old female senior manager in public accounting with one pre-school-aged child noted: 'I believe that the long hours required to make partner, and to work as a partner, cause many women to leave public practice. This is because the bulk of the child rearing responsibilities fall to women, and it becomes a difficult juggling act. Personally, I have taken myself off the partnership track, and will be looking for a part-time work situation within the firm in the next couple of years. Only very recently have firms provided this type of opportunity. It is a welcome change, and one that will help firms retain their women managers through their childbearing years' (no. 271).

A female junior suggested that the male perception that women will choose a career path that allows them to combine family and career, like the assignment of tasks in an accounting firm, results in male managers second-guessing their female employees: 'I haven't experienced any discrimination, but when you look at the number of women partners and the number of men, it's obvious. [Partnership] depends a lot on the partners in the firm. [Some] are of the old school [that] "women should stay at home and raise kids" ... they have the ingrained attitude that "well, she's going to get pregnant and leave"' (interview B). A thirty-seven-year-old woman without children working in government summed up the feeling of many women: 'The firms still tend to reflect a lifestyle that many male and female CAs are turning away from (partners expect long, long hours and reward the toil rather than the results). [I h]ave observed that the women are seriously disadvantaged in terms of childbearing and the demands it involves and the impact it has on "the partnership track"' (no. 50). The question relating to partnerships elicited a strong reaction on the part of many women, who resented the culture of the workplace that requires accountants to sacrifice a satisfying family life to attain success.[20]

Studies show that access to opportunities and rewards is one of the best predictors of strong organizational commitment.[21] If women feel that they are not given equal access, morale may suffer and commitment give way to thoughts of leaving the firm. Decreased organizational commitment seems to be closely linked to the presence or perceived presence of non-merit criteria for pay increases and promotion. In response to the statement 'Women and men are paid comparable salaries for the same responsibilities and performance,' 84 per cent of respondents agreed, while 15 per cent believed that men, and 1 per cent that women, were paid higher salaries (see table 4). When gender was examined, more women (25 per cent) than men (7 per cent) thought that men were paid the higher salary. Although a majority of both managers and juniors believed that salaries were equal, more managers (17 per cent) than juniors (8 per cent) agreed that men were paid more. The gap in perception between management and junior levels points to difficulties that women face as they rise in the organizational hierarchy, and probably reflects current realities. At the junior levels the difference between the lowest and highest paid employees is smaller than at the management level, where individuals with the same job classification can receive different remuneration based upon perceived attributes and skills. It seems that when more discretion is allowed in the awarding of salaries, women are more likely to be disadvantaged.[22]

Although studies have yet to be done to explain fully the lower salaries paid to women, it is likely that the predominance of men at the management level (91 per cent) biases perception of meritorious performance in favour of men. Since many of the male managers came of age before

TABLE 5
Ability to generate new business by gender and by management status (percentages)

	Total	Female	Male	Female manage-ment	Female junior	Male manage-ment	Male junior
Men better	37	40	33	37	43	32	40
Same	62	58	67	61	57	68	60
Women better	1	2	0	2	0	0	0

female participation in the field of accounting skyrocketed in the 1980s and 1990s, they may have values that disadvantage women. Men who have stay-at-home wives or wives whose income is seen as supplementary to the family economy may regard women as less deserving of salaries equal to men and, despite the recent attention focused on equal pay, continue to be resistant to the concept. One thirty-five-year-old married woman with no children, working in industrial accounting, 'was told that her performance was superior yet found out male co-workers made more money for the same performance.' When she confronted the partner, she was told that she 'would have to learn to live with it' (no. 20).

Within the changing field of accountancy, the generation of new business is an increasingly important part of the CA's job. The statement 'Women and men are equally able to generate new business effectively' attempted to delve into gender differences in this aspect of professional life. As table 5 indicates, 62 per cent of those surveyed thought that women and men were equally effective in generating business for the firm, while 37 per cent thought that men, and 1 per cent that women, were more effective. There was little difference between women and men and between management and juniors on this issue, but women were more likely than men to perceive how gender worked to their disadvantage. A twenty-eight-year-old female public accounting manager outlined the problems she faced: 'Almost 100 percent of my clients are male, and it is easier for a man to get close to these clients (golf, hockey games, etc.) than it is for a women. And this definitely impacts our careers because part of our performance appraisal is based on generating new business, and men meet clients socially a lot of the time and women aren't given these opportunities' (no. 184). A thirty-five-year-old single woman working in the educational field stated: 'In the CA firms, I found I was generally treated equally until it came to promotions. I was told once that a male counterpart had been promoted because he was perceived to be able to bring in more business because he was an avid golf player. His work was no better than mine and we brought in the same amount of business' (no. 205).

Men tend to see factors other than gender as having the greatest impact on an accountant's ability to generate business. One male manager noted that 'the ability to generate new business in a lot of cases is more a function of age than gender, i.e., if you're fifty you will generally gravitate to accountants you know in your age range' (no. 196). A male partner agreed that women faced obstacles in their efforts to generate business but concluded that conditions would improve with time: 'Yes there seem to be problems, [making it] harder for women to generate new business [because of] the general feeling in the business world. There are still a lot of people out there that find it difficult to accept women in higher positions. The woman probably has to work a little harder. This will continue to change as more women enter the industry' (interview G).

As table 6 shows, responses to two statements relating to perceptions of organizational commitment suggest that most (88 per cent) thought that women and men were equally committed to their work. While there was little difference between women (89 per cent) and men (86 per cent) on this matter, 18 per cent of juniors thought that men were usually more committed, while only 7 per cent of managers were so inclined. One female partner noted that 'women who want to become partners are as committed if not more so [than men]' (interview J). A male partner also refused to accept a gendered notion of commitment: 'Women can be just as aggressive and work just as [many hours] as men and are as committed to getting the job done' (interview I). Another female manager maintained that part-time work was no indication of a lack of commitment: 'I would be as committed to my clients and to the work I do for those three days a week as I am now for five days a week' (interview A).

The final statement on the questionnaire was designed to discover how CAs felt they were perceived by management. Management perceptions (and beliefs about management perceptions) are important to examine because managers decide on assignments, remuneration, promotions, and partnerships. As table 6 indicates, 65 per cent of the respondents concluded that management viewed men as more committed, 34 per cent believed that men and women were perceived equally by management, and 1 per cent agreed that women were perceived by management as more committed to their careers. Perhaps not surprisingly, this question

TABLE 6
Commitment and perceptions of commitment by gender and by management status (percentages)

	Total	Female	Male	Female management	Female junior	Male management	Male junior
Men more committed	9	7	11	5	17	9	20
Same	88	89	86	92	79	87	80
Women more committed	3	4	3	3	4	4	0
Men perceived as more committed	65	78	52	75	87	51	65
Same	34	22	47	25	13	48	35
Women perceived as more committed	1	0	1	0	0	1	0

produced the greatest gap between male and female respondents. Only 22 per cent of female, compared to 47 per cent of male, accountants thought that men and women were perceived by management to be equally committed to a career in chartered accountancy. Gender and rank both influence beliefs about management perceptions. Majorities of all groups believed that managers thought men were more committed, but female juniors were most convinced (87 per cent), followed by female managers (75 per cent), male juniors (65 per cent) and then male managers (51 per cent).

A twenty-six-year-old single woman employed in public accounting asserted: '[T]he perception exists with some partners that females will leave as soon as they start a family and are less committed' (no. 263). A thirty-eight-year-old woman with two children highlighted the double standard that in her experience still prevailed: 'Occasionally, personality conflicts arise between auditors and clients. When I experienced one of these, I was taken off the audit and not assigned to any more, which led to my termination as a result of not enough chargeable hours. When a similar thing happened to one of my male counterparts (also a student, who was physically ejected from the client's premises) all the "old boys" had a great laugh and [it] didn't affect him at all' (no. 229). A female manager also thought that there was a double standard operating in the profession: 'I think there definitely is a perception out there by men in more senior positions, men from perhaps a different generation, that women are leaving the profession to go home and raise their families ... I have looked at people who have left this office and have gone elsewhere, and I can't name anyone who is at home full-time raising their family. Men leave to go to other jobs, but yet there is that perception that women are going to go [back home]' (interview A).

This question points to a major problem in terms of the perceptions of management's treatment of women. While 88 per cent of all respondents agreed that women and men were equally committed to a career in chartered accountancy, only 34 per cent said that management perceived women and men as equally committed to their careers. Interestingly, male managers were the least likely group to agree that they do in fact hold such beliefs. Whatever the facts of the situation, the interviews suggest that female CAs feel disadvantaged by the views believed to be held by management about their commitment to the profession.

Client perceptions are also important in chartered accountancy, and complaints from clients have been used as a reason to exclude women from career advancement. When respondents were asked to comment on the statement 'Women and men are equally acceptable to clients to perform on work engagements,' 82 per cent agreed that men and women were equally acceptable, while 18 per cent thought that men, and 1 per cent that women, were preferred. Gender and rank did not affect the result significantly. About 80 per cent of chartered accountants agreed that men and women were equally acceptable to clients, while about 20 per cent of respondents in all categories claimed that men were preferred.

Despite the high incidence of acceptance of female accountants, there are still clients who prefer to work with men, and comments written on the questionnaire and our interviews lead us to think that this is a more significant problem than the percentages given above would suggest. A male partner stated: 'There are certainly some males who find it difficult to accept financial advice from a woman sitting on the other side of the desk. They much prefer it coming from a man [although] it might be the same advice ... There are ... not as many as there used to be. I can see a decline' (interview G). A thirty-seven-year-old female senior manager in a public accounting firm asserted that 'initially being one of the first two females in our office was difficult as some "prejudice" against women existed and had to be overcome by "proving" our abilities. There are still some older clients who prefer to deal with a man' (no. 234). One married woman with two children working in public accounting stated that there 'are definitely many instances where clients were looking for the "man" on the job ... If I went to a new client with a male colleague, it was normally assumed that the male was in charge' (no. 35). A female manager revealed that one client was so deeply opposed to having a female accountant that the firm operated on the assumption that it could not send a woman there 'to be beat up on' (interview A). A thirty-one-year-old female staff accountant in a public accounting firm added that 'being a female in the profession ... made it extremely difficult to obtain the respect and recognition of some clients and the older male CA population' (no. 237). She claimed that she had to 'work twice as hard' as the males with whom she had articled. In some cases, partners were as difficult as clients. One female staff accountant noted: 'we did have one of the old partners with company X. His attitude was recognized by the other two partners as just his way, and was never given any credence at all. He would never choose me to be on his jobs. That was supposed to be my punishment for being a female in his firm, but I was just as pleased not to have to work with him' (interview D).

Conclusions

There was a marked tendency on the part of respondents to the survey to conclude that women and men had the 'same' career experiences in the field of chartered accountancy. On questions relating to job assignments, industry specialties, remuneration, career commitment, and even the ability to generate new business, most respondents believed that men and women faced similar challenges and opportunities. At the same time, a majority of respondents agreed that men had an advantage over women when it came to achieving partnerships in accounting firms, and women were in general more likely than men to believe that men were advantaged in the various ways. It may be the case, as a number of respondents suggested, that the 'glass ceiling' with respect to partnerships will disappear with time; but it is equally possible that chartered accountancy, which remains a highly competitive and rigidly hierarchical profession, will continue to develop gendered structures to keep women in subordinate positions.

The responses to the survey and interview questions point to the likelihood that the latter trend will prevail. A high proportion of the respondents, most of whom believed that women were as committed to their jobs as their male counterparts, thought that managers were more likely to see men as having the greater career commitment. Given this perception, it is not surprising that women are reluctant to embrace the competitive race to the top of the professional ladder. Interviews and comments written on the questionnaire show that the respondents also believed that women more so than men were disadvantaged by family responsibilities. Together, the perceptions that management is biased against them and that women have more family responsibilities than men make it highly likely that women more than men will opt for part-time or less-demanding full-time jobs which offer them more flexibility in juggling paid work and family responsibilities, both of which are structured to their disadvantage. These findings are not surprising and reflect the 'catch-22' that many women experience in the paid labour force. As Mary Kinnear notes in her historical study of five professions in Manitoba, 'professional women share with all working women disadvantages vis-à-vis their male counterparts in terms of governance, pay, and demands on their time.'[23]

The professions as we know them today were predicated on a gendered world in which women and men were scripted to play different and complementary roles in society. Indeed, the very questions that we asked of the respondents indicate that professionals are valued for being ambitious, single-minded, and if necessary, so devoted to their work that they will sacrifice personal well-being. This standard can only be maintained if one abandons family life entirely or has a partner or employee willing to manage childcare and household duties. At the turn of the century much energy was expended to create an asymmetrical family ideal in which women attended to family matters so that men were free to climb the professional ladder. This arrangement no longer prevails – most married women in the 1990s work in the paid labour force – but old attitudes linger and continue to justify discriminatory behaviour.

Women in Nova Scotia have made important inroads in chartered accountancy since Janet Dawe received her certification in 1956,[24] but this study suggests that they still face obstacles in advancing to the highest rungs of the profession. Although many respondents were aware of the barriers to women achieving equality in chartered accountancy, they seemed to accept the norms prevailing in the profession and remained sceptical about the possibility of radical workplace restructuring that would accommodate the family responsibilities of both women and men. With half of its new students women, the accounting profession clearly needs to address the gender issue, and accountants need to assess their 'family values' in other than family contexts. In her ground-breaking study *If Women Counted,* Marilyn Waring transcended the narrowly focused issue of women's status in any given sector by looking at what passes for economic analysis in modern society.[25] The problem of who is accounting, she argues, may well be more usefully approached by asking what are they accounting for. As the historically constructed divide between public and private and the market values assigned to them are increasingly called into question, both the scope of accounting and the structures that characterize the profession will almost certainly be profoundly transformed.

NOTES

We would like to thank Alan J. Richardson, of the School of Business, Queen's University, for taking the time to read our essay and sharing his knowledge of accounting history with us. In particular, we benefited from the information contained in the unpublished paper C.A. McKeen and A.J. Richardson, 'Education, Employment and Certification: An Oral History of the Entry of Women into the Canadian Accounting Profession,' presented at the Business and Economic History Conference, University of Maryland, March 1988.

1 Shari H. Westcott and Robert E. Seiler, *Women in the Accounting Profession* (New York: Marcus Winer Publishing, 1986), 42; Rebecca Sue Scruggs Legge, 'A History of Women Certified Public Accountants in the United States' (PhD thesis, University of Mississippi, 1988), 2–3.

2 Although Florence Herkins is recorded as having passed the final examination required by the Institute of Chartered Accountants of Nova Scotia (ICANS) in 1922, she seems not to have been formally registered in the province. See Alan J. Richardson, 'Development of Accounting Associations in Canada, 1879–1979,' in *A History of Canadian Accounting Thought and Practice,* ed. George Murphy (New York: Garland Publishing Inc., 1993), 580. Richardson notes (594) that Emma Morrison, the first woman to be registered by the Institute of Chartered Accountants of New Brunswick in 1949, had previously been a member of the ICANS. There is no record of Morrison having been registered to practise in the province, and where she took her exams has not been determined. Part of the reason for the confusion surrounding female 'firsts' in Nova Scotia is that accountants in public practice were not required by law to register with the ICANS until 1952.

3 Margaret Conrad, '"Not a Feminist but ...": The Political Career of Ellen Louks Fairclough, Canada's First Female Federal Cabinet Minister,' *Journal of Canadian Studies* 31, 2 (summer 1996): 5–28.

4 Cyndy Kathleen Allen, 'Current Perceptions of Gender and Chartered Accountancy in Nova Scotia' (MA thesis, Acadia University, 1996). Cyndy would like to thank her thesis supervisor, Paula Chegwidden, as well as Dianne Looker, both members of the Sociology Department, Acadia University, for their advice on this project.

5 This overview relies primarily on the work of Alan J. Richardson who has conducted extensive research on the accounting profession. See, in particular, 'Professionalization and Intraprofessional Competition in the Canadian Accounting Profession,' *Work and Occupations* 14, 4 (1987): 591–615; 'Canada's Accounting Elite, 1880–1930,' *Accounting Historians' Journal,* 16, 1 (1989): 1–21; and 'Educational Policy and Professional Status: A Case History of the Ontario Accounting Profession,' *Journal of Canadian Studies* 27, 1 (1992): 44–57; as well as his highly valuable chronology, cited in note 2, which includes an extensive bibliography. See also Horace Mann, *The Evolution of Accounting in Canada* (Montreal: Touche Ross, 1975).

6 Now the Canadian Institute of Chartered Accountants (CICA).

7 Richardson, 'Educational Policy and Professional Status,' 46.

8 H.P. Edwards, 'After Three Score Years and Ten,' *Canadian Chartered Accountant* 64 (1954): 358.

9 Richardson, 'Development of Accounting Associations in Canada, 1879–1979,' 570.

10 The 1941 census, for example, lists 31,384 male and 2,992 female accountants and auditors and 14,384 male and 20,924 female bookkeepers and cashiers. See Canada, Dominion Bureau of Statistics, *Census of Canada,* 1941 (Ottawa: King's Printer, 1946), 7: table 12, 330–7.

11 Richardson, 'Development of Accounting Associations in Canada, 1879–1979,' 578–80. Other accountant associations proved no more welcoming to female membership. For example, in 1921 the Certified General Accountants' Association decided by a vote of 44 to 3 that 'it was not in the interest of the Association to admit women.' See Reginald C. Stuart, *The First Seventy-Five Years: A History of the Certified General Accountants' Association of Canada* (Vancouver: CGA-Canada, 1988), 30.

12 Richardson, 'Development of Accounting Associations in Canada, 1879–1979,' 578, 585.

13 There is very little research published on women in the accounting profession in Canada. For Great Britian and the United States important sources include Ceil Moran Pillsbury, Liza Capozzoli, and Amy Ciampa, 'A Synthesis of Research Studies Regarding the Upward Mobility of Women in Public Accounting,' *Accounting Horizons,* March 1989, 63–70; Michael Trapp, Roger H. Hermanson, and Deborah H. Turner, 'Current Perceptions of Issues

Related to Women Employed in Public Accounting,' *Accounting Horizons*, March 1989, 71–85; Cheryl Lehman, '"Herstory" in Accounting: The First Eighty Years,' *Accounting, Organizations and Society* 17, 3/4 (1992): 261–85; Karen L. Hooks, 'Gender Effects and Labour Supply in Public Accounting: An Agenda of Research Issues,' *Accounting, Organization and Society* 17, 3/4 (1992): 343–66; Charles W. Wootton and Wanda Spruill, 'The Role of Women in Major Public Accounting Firms in the United States during World War II,' *Business and Economic History* 23, 1 (fall 1994): 241–52.

14 Carol McKeen and Meridee Bujaki, 'Taking Women into Account,' *CA Magazine*, March 1994, 30.

15 In 1993 women represented 18.5 per cent of the CAs in Ontario compared to 19.3 in Nova Scotia. Quebec and the Yukon have the highest female participation rates at 23 per cent. See McKeen and Bujaki, 'Taking Women into Account,' 30.

16 The tendency to explain developments in the Maritimes in terms of some underlying 'conservative mentality' has been called into question by Ernest R. Forbes in a series of well-argued articles published as *Challenging the Regional Stereotype: Essays on the 20th Century Maritimes* (Fredericton: Acadiensis Press, 1989).

17 We are grateful to Ross Towlor and the staff at the Institute of Chartered Accountants of Nova Scotia for taking the time to assist us with this project.

18 Numbers and letters were assigned to respondents to protect their identity. A bracketed number refers to the individual survey from which a particular quotation was taken. Letters (A through J) refer to interviews conducted for this study.

19 Twenty-seven per cent of female juniors and 19 per cent of female managers believed that men were encouraged into more-prestigious specializations. Only 6 per cent of male CAs supported the assertion of inequality.

20 This reaction was consistent with the findings of the Canadian Institute of Chartered Accountants Diversity study in 1995, which underscored 'the significance of the changing expectations and values of Generation X ... who want to work to live, not live to work.' See Canadian Institute of Chartered Accountants, 'Diversity in the C.A. Profession: Results of Brainstorming Sessions,' December 1994–February 1995.

21 Peter V. Marsden, Arne L. Kalleberg, and Cynthia R. Cook, 'Gender Differences in Organizational Commitment,' *Work and Occupations* 20, 3(1993): 368–90.

22 The problem of remuneration is discussed in McKeen and Bujaki, 'Taking Women into Account,' 29. Research indicates that men's compensation, promotions, and job satisfaction begin to exceed women's after the first five years,

and that both men and women perceive that women's opportunities decline with increasing seniority.

23 See Mary Kinnear, *In Subordination: Professional Women, 1870–1970* (Montreal and Kingston: McGill-Queen's University Press, 1995), 153.

24 Janet Dawe's career offers insights into the strategies that even the most advantaged women must still pursue in order to triumph over obstacles placed in their paths. The daughter of a land developer in St John's, she attended Trafalgar Boarding School in Montreal and enrolled in commerce at McGill University before transferring to Dalhousie, where she received a bachelor of commerce degree in 1956. Dawe's interest in accounting was advanced by her friendship with Heather Martin, the only other women in her class, whose father was a partner in the accounting firm of Lee and Martin in Halifax. After graduation, she did her internship at Lee and Martin and then applied for a position with the Newfoundland taxation department. Despite the fact that there were no CAs in the department, she was turned down for the job. In the end, the first female CA in Newfoundland was employed by her father's firm, Chester Dawe Ltd. She married a fellow accountant, and while her three children were young, she worked part-time. Currently CEO of Chester Dawe Ltd, Janet Dawe Gardiner continues to chalk up female firsts with her appointment to a number of boards in her native province.

25 Marilyn Waring, *If Women Counted: A New Feminist Economics* (New York: HarperCollins, 1988)

Caring as Work for Women Educators

SANDRA ACKER

In the essay that follows I explore a certain kind of experience that I believe is common in the caring professions and in university teaching, particularly for women. The work required in these occupations often calls on a 'caring script,' a set of expectations that mimics women's traditional work in the home. These expectations are often unrealistic in the conditions of the work world, but they may form part of the worker's sense of self, as well as being reinforced in various ways from the outside, and thus be difficult to dislodge, even when not well rewarded in material or status terms. The nearest I have come to a name for this syndrome is Jean Baker Miller's phrase 'doing good and feeling bad.'[1] To develop and illustrate my argument, I draw on two sets of data, concerned respectively with teaching at the elementary and the post-secondary levels.

Gender and the Caring Professions

It is no secret that women's experiences of the professions have been disproportionately concentrated in a restricted range of occupations, notably teaching, nursing, and social work.[2] Sometimes 'professional' and 'women' have been regarded as virtually incompatible concepts. In commenting on the sociology of the professions, Judith Glazer remarks that 'the professional ideal is based on the male experience and on values generally associated with masculinity,' namely, 'status, exclusivity, individualism, and power.'[3] Scholars have tried to find ways of describing professions with women in them, coming up with labels such as the infamous 'semi-profession.'[4] Teaching, nursing, and social work have all struggled over time to gain professional status by various stratagems based on models of the established professions: for example, by raising the level of qualifications necessary to enter the field. A relatively recent phenomenon is quite different and involves reclaiming and celebrating the traditionally feminine aspects of these occupations. For instance, Nel Noddings argues that caring should be at the heart of teaching.[5] Nursing theorists and educators have worked to develop a mode of practice and curriculum that embraces caring as a central principle.[6]

These developments have drawn on a perspective sometimes called relational feminism. Influenced by scholars such as Carol Gilligan,[7] relational feminists believe that women's preferences have been submerged as men's predominance in public life has narrowed conventional ways of organizing occupations and workplaces; instead, a typically or even stereotypically feminine way of operating, one that emphasizes caring and connectedness, has much to commend it and should be adopted more widely.

Relational feminism has been criticized on a number of fronts. Detractors make the following points: (1) it institutionalizes an essentialist view of women, neglecting diversity among them; (2) it contributes to the tradition of low pay and exploitation associated with 'women's work'; (3) it obscures the hard work involved in occupations when they are thought merely to be expressions of natural tendencies in women; and (4) it reserves to women responsibility for caring and emotional aspects of life while men are free to pursue other avenues. Marjorie DeVault encapsulates the paradox of reclaiming caring as the crux of women's work: 'Caring as skilled and significant work can be a source of pride and identity; caring as personal service can draw women into self-sacrifice and resentment.'[8]

I turn now to empirical examples of cases where women are fulfilling the caring script, yet experiencing 'outlaw emotions.'[9] My first example comes from elementary school teaching, a clear case of a 'caring profession' with mainly women workers. The second example is from a more traditional profession, university teaching, which has a minority of women. The specific focus in the latter case is on academics in faculties of education, sites that might be expected to encompass some of the values from the teaching profession and be more hospitable to women than other sectors of the university have been. Both examples are situations where the protagonists are 'doing good' (living out the caring script, as extended to both nurturing and service roles) but 'feeling bad' (conscious that something is wrong).

A Study of Teachers' Workplace Culture

My interest in what might be called the emotions of teaching[10] stems originally from ethnographic research I conducted in the late 1980s and early 1990s on primary (elementary) school teachers in England. I became interested in the extent to which the small work group of mostly female teachers at 'Hillview School' (a pseudonym) could be seen as a 'women's culture,' a group that embodied the values which relational feminists argue are characteristic of 'women's ways': kindness, cooperation, sharing, connectedness, and so forth.[11] Hillview is an urban school with about two hundred children, mixed in social class and ethnicity. At the time of my study the staff included the head teacher (principal), a deputy head teacher (assistant principal), and five other full-time and three part-time teachers. There were indications of deep attachments between teachers and their classes as well as incidents where teachers put others' (especially colleagues') welfare ahead of their own.[12] Yet there were frequent frustrations. Material conditions were poor; space restricted, resources scarce, and discipline difficult.

When I was asked to write an article to be submitted to a special issue of a journal on the 'emotions of teaching,' my thoughts turned to the rather submerged, less-positive sentiments that bubbled up from time to time.[13] Hillview's teachers worked extremely hard, held themselves to high standards, and cared for the children and each other. Yet there was also a sense in which they frequently felt underappreciated. The school's ethos, which stressed tolerance for differences and encouragement of assertiveness, meant that teachers could not rely on pliable pupils. Children could be self-centred and resistant. At times it seemed to the teachers that neither the children nor their parents appreciated their hard work. At a greater distance was the barely disguised scorn coming from the government of the day, which was trying to make major changes in the curriculum and the pedagogy of primary-school teaching.[14]

Parents, although certainly appreciated by the teachers as helpers and partners in children's schooling, could be particularly problematic. The teachers believed that they were not always treated with the respect that other professionals such as doctors or dentists received, when parents felt free to interrupt them at any time.[15] Nor did parents always cooperate with the teachers' efforts to reach out to them: extensive preparations for a parents' meeting or educational evening might produce only a few participants. In contrast, a small number of parents took on activist roles and pushed the school to redouble its efforts to combat racism and sexism, ignoring the teachers' existing attempts to reform the curriculum.[16]

Here is a discussion among four teachers at Hillview – Debbie, Sheila, Kristen, and Rosalind – which shows some of these themes (all names are pseudonyms). A mother had complained to the head teacher about Sheila's testing of the children on multiplication tables. This extract from my field notes indicates that the teachers felt resentful and misunderstood, but found it hard to know where to put the blame for the situation:

Debbie says, 'You can't win, you've got to sit and take it from all directions.' Sheila: 'Apparently I test too quickly.' 'Do you know,' says Debbie, 'I do this and the class says they know their tables, then I say two threes and they say oh, no, miss. They don't really know them.' The talk turns to parent interviews, and particular children, including one named Jane. Kristen says, 'She was writing with biro [a pen not allowed]. She's so rude, looking right at me, saying I don't care if I have to leave this school.' Rosalind agrees: 'She's manipulative, tries to set you up. She got her mother early in the term to believe I was down on her. Ever since then I always talk to her with Debbie present.' [Other children and their rudeness are discussed.] Debbie says, 'I'm fed up with being treated like a door mat.' 'The pleasant humanities of person to person are missing,' Rosalind adds. 'I asked Harry to pick up something ...' Debbie interrupts, 'I can tell you what he said – it's not mine.' Rosalind is nodding. Sheila asks, 'Is it our fault?'[17]

As Sheila's last remark suggests, the teachers were uncertain whom to hold responsible when things went wrong. Often they blamed themselves. Teachers felt guilty when they experienced anger or resentment. For example, one of the teachers told me: 'I lost my temper with Jake, I was shouting and shouting ... then lay awake thinking it must be my handling of him, how can I do it differently?'[18] They coped by developing a strong, supportive culture that allowed them to express doubts to one another and reinforce their shared commitments.[19]

The teachers rarely spoke about feminism. Few, if any, would call themselves feminists. Yet it was apparent to all that men in primary schools had career advantages over women. At Hillview the head teacher was female. There was a tacit understanding that the deputy should therefore be male. During most of my research that understanding continued. Liz Clarke was the head teacher, Dennis Bryan the deputy head teacher. But then Dennis went overseas for a year, and Debbie Stevens became acting deputy in his place. Debbie began to notice how her experience of being deputy head differed from Dennis's. The year before, Debbie and Dennis had taught two adjoining classes and had conducted much of their teaching as a team. In British primary schools deputy heads often have full class timetables and struggle to perform both roles adequately. To help Dennis, Debbie would keep track of dates for him, act as a sounding board, and bring him a sandwich if he were unable to leave the office at lunchtime. Now no one was backing her up in the same way, although she believed that colleagues would do so if she asked. In an interview she reflected on whether she was at a disadvantage through being a woman in the role:

There are situations in which I find myself thinking – for example, with that difficult parent – if I'd have been *Dennis*, perhaps the situation wouldn't have arisen. The father wouldn't have dreamt of threatening Liz, because Dennis would have been around ... Just the simple fact that he's a very charismatic, prominent male figure and I will never be that [laughs] ... I don't know if I feel I've got to do everything twice as well, but I do know a lot of parents look around and assume that a man's got better discipline and assume that he's not as approachable as I am, that they haven't got the right to encroach on his time ... There are things that people come and perhaps talk to me about that I think Dennis wouldn't have got ... So, if, say, dinner ladies [lunchtime staff] would come up and mention to me a problem that they had ... or if a teacher has come up and said to me about something they've been concerned about, actually they will be more frank and honest with me because I am a woman than they would be with Dennis. There are a lot of things that go on that Dennis never knew, or will never know, because people don't unburden themselves to him ... [It's] not because they don't feel that he was approachable but because they wouldn't have thought of approaching him in that way.

She continued:

Liz has got the same with being a woman head. I do think that if a man was sat in the chair down in the office, that there would be fewer interruptions. I mean, I know it's awful and perhaps I'm just – no, I do think it's true – if Ronald Grant [head of a neighbouring school] was sat in that office downstairs, people wouldn't come and knock on the door and say 'So and so's just tied my shoelace together.' Even for the children, I think there's this sort of distance thing about it and it's a protection for a man, in a way, that they can get away with not having to be this sort of nurturing, helpful type of character in the school.

Debbie noted that the school has had a male deputy for at least twenty years. She wanted to make sure that Liz did not regret her decision to ask Debbie to do the job. Her highest priority was to make sure the staff felt 'happy': 'That was something that I was really aware of, keeping everybody feeling happy and stress-free in their job because I was actually sorting something out in the background or the sidelines.'

At the time Debbie held this position, she was pregnant with her third child, and she also had a full class responsibility for the most difficult class she had so far encountered at Hillview. From one perspective she could be seen as trapped into taking on too large a share of the nurturing and service work in the school; but at the same time she also derived pleasure from living out that image of herself.

A Study of Academics in Canadian Faculties of Education

At the end of 1990 I changed jobs and moved to Canada. Although I still kept in touch with the Hillview staff and continued to write papers based on my ethnographic work, I also began new research in Canada. This time it was a study of academics, both women and men, in the four professional fields of education, social work, pharmacy, and dentistry. This research is being conducted by a team of colleagues and is funded by the Social Sciences and Humanities Research Council of Canada. While the Hillview study relied on participant observation as well as interviews, the Canadian project is based on interviews collected from across the country. The four fields were chosen to represent a continuum of 'feminization,' a concept referring mainly to the increased presence of women and secondarily to the possibility of a culture arising that reflects values traditionally associated with women, such as caring. Judged by the proportions of women in the student body, the continuum runs from social work at the high end through education and pharmacy to dentistry at the low end. Given that proportions of women faculty rarely equal those of women students, we wondered what the effects of 'feminization' in these fields had on the centrality or marginalization of women faculty, on the workplace culture, and on the curriculum.

My own involvement has been primarily with the academics from faculties of education. I could see some parallels with my previous research on Hillview, in that once again I was interested in teachers' (or instructors') work and their workplace cultures. Many of the academics had previously been employed in elementary or secondary schools; so there was additional continuity in choosing this group for study after the Hillview teachers. There were obvious differences as well. In the field of education, university departments are usually administered by men, and women are in the minority, typically around a third of the faculty. Moreover, even the smallest faculties are generally larger than a school such as Hillview. Elementary school teachers have had to fight for designation as professionals (see note 15), while university teachers generally take professional status for granted. Yet despite the differences in the settings, the 'doing good and feeling bad' response seemed equally evident among the women academics as it had been among the women teachers.

In the interview transcripts[20] I looked for expressions of emotion about work and related statements about workload, type of work, and extra work. It was clear that although there were many positive sentiments expressed about research, teaching, and colleagues, both women and men showed a degree of alienation, not surprising in an era of retrenchment and intensification of workloads. Almost unique to the women, however, was resentment focused on caring and service roles taken and the lack of reward in the formal system for this kind of work. These sentiments were more likely to be expressed by women at the associate and full professor level, that is, those in mid-career and senior positions, than by the relatively junior assistant professors, although there were exceptions. Like the Hillview teachers, the women academics felt somehow disappointed and dispirited by their situation. More-detailed examples are given below.

Doing Good

The women talked about how hard they worked, how they supported others, especially students, and how they acted as 'good citizens' in their departments. Many of them said that they had high standards or were perfectionists or 'workaholics.' They talked about their strategies for getting work done, such as rising early, staying up late, and working through breaks. Statements about 'time' figured frequently in the interviews, especially but not exclusively for women with young children:

Once I was tenure-track, I have to tell you I would work through my noon hours. I never took a coffee break. I had no downtime for me, personally, because when I got home and picked up my children from child care, or from school, I had to attend to their needs and get organized for the next day. (Diana)

Well I write ... at 10:00 at night till 3:00 in the morning. Last night I came back at 8 and worked till midnight. Sometimes I have breakfast meetings with students at

8 in the morning. I don't have another life; my life when I get home is my children. (Moira)

I don't have to be somewhere from 9 to 5, but the other side of that is that you also don't have a 5:00. There is no turnoff time. There's no time when it's not work time. (Laurie)

I'd love to have a secretary, so I don't have to go home and do my admin work at night ... Sometimes I don't get to bed till 3:00 and then I get up at 7:00 if I have an 8:30 class, you know. There's no other way I can do that because as you can see, the students are usually out there all the time and the phones ringing in the afternoons. And I'm here all the time. I gave up taking lunch hours a long time ago ... So I'm basically here all day long and they just come in. They know where to find me. (Penny)

Like Penny, many of the women academics spoke about the help and nurturing that they provide to students. The following quotations are just a few examples.

I guess that grad students that I work with directly, as supervisor, I guess they feel that I mentor them too. Because I do take their work quite seriously. And I guess they end up talking to me about other problems, apart from their academic problems. And I try to be a good listener. (Grace)

Many students will show up at my door with a problem and I can't turn them away. This happens often before my teaching even though I tell them to make an appointment. But they're in a crisis; how can I say I'm not available? (Olivette)

One of the students that was waiting for me outside my office as I was talking to my doctoral student said to me afterwards, you know, just hearing you talk is so exhausting: so much support, so much nurturing. (Wendy)

I never realized I shouldn't have to speak to my students in the evening at home. Finally a male colleague said that he doesn't allow that unless it's an emergency. It wouldn't have occurred to me otherwise. I don't have the same understanding of boundaries as he does. (Estelle)

Caring could extend to helping junior colleagues:

[As an administrator] I spent more time getting to know the individuals. I think I was more honest with them about why things were being done as they were. I shared more information with them. I encouraged a lot of people to apply for scholarships for different kinds of things ... I would never say to an individual, you're teaching so and so ... I would negotiate with them ... I always tried to read papers that people had written ... and that was also very, very much appreciated. (Judith)

Women also talked about their responsibilities in the department or faculty. For example, Lucille thought that her original appointment years earlier was based on an assumption that she would 'be the housewife,' that is, take departmental committee and student supervision responsibilities. Even now, she is 'the person ... who can be called on to do whatever needs to be done.' After a description of her activities on committees and working parties, Terri concluded: 'I think we [women] are just great department citizens.'

Feeling Bad

As may be evident, these women took a certain pride in their capacity for hard work and in their caring and service activities. Yet negative emotions surfaced frequently during the interviews. Although, as we saw earlier, the women believed that they *should* be caring for others, the results could be disappointing or at least mixed. For example, they discovered that students would become upset when their caring teacher found it necessary to emphasize standards or take a critical stance: 'If you ask what I worry about, I worry when I give a response back to my graduate students that I'm too harsh, you know – that they're going to take it the wrong way' (Helen). Like the Hillview teachers, these academics thought that students often took their extra efforts for granted or failed to reciprocate with efforts of their own: 'Sometimes it's quite insulting. I remember one in particular, this one student who was sort of dry running a thesis proposal, and at one point I said "You really shouldn't be talking to me, I'm just a [thesis] committee member. You should really be talking to your supervisor about this." And she said point blank: "Well ... I wanted to make sure it was good before I went to him"' (Terri).

There was a widespread sense that the women worked 'too hard.' Sometimes it seemed that they blamed themselves: 'I've done more than the average person in the department but I've done it by choice' (Katherine); 'I find the workload heavy at the moment but it's a self-imposed stress' (Iris). But there were also *systemic* sources of overwork.

The preferences of women students (especially graduate students) to work with women faculty members was one source of extra work. These faculties of education all have a majority of women students, while women make up around a third of the faculty members:

I think another thing you'll notice about women's work here is that probably we have more graduate students than men ... we've got lots of women who are going to university now and they want to work with women. And we just keep taking them on because we don't know how to say no. (Kay)

There are fewer women in the graduate faculty, but the few women that are in the graduate faculty do something like 70 or 80% of the supervision and teach the courses. So even though we're a small group, we're working, I would think, much harder than the average man in this faculty. (Rosanne)

An ironic consequence of efforts to introduce gender-equity policies in these faculties was that women ended up doing more committee work. Zoe explained: 'We have to have a woman on every committee and if there are only x number of women around, that means we're serving on many more committees than the men are.' Senior professors felt the pressure most strongly: 'You're asked to be on twice or three times as many committees as a comparable male would just because they need that female balance. What I didn't discover until I got promoted to full professor was a lot of them need senior professors' (Katherine).

University policies for tenure, promotion, and merit pay came in for particular criticism, both because of the stress and anxiety caused by trying to meet ever-rising and ambiguous standards and because work such as nurturing students and service on committees was not greatly rewarded. The theme of 'women working harder' surfaced again: 'The women seem to work harder and they're more anguished than the men. I was so careful to cover all my bases for tenure: publications, research grants, supervising and teaching. I said to myself I can't do more. But I was full of anxiety. I rewrote my tenure dossier ten times; the men only do it once! We [women] have a sorority of anxiety' (Solange).

A number of women questioned the criteria for tenure, promotion, and merit pay, which they saw as shifting, ambiguous, too limited, or counter-productive:

I invest heavily in teaching and supervision and I'm not satisfied by it because that's not what's rewarded in the final analysis. The research is. (Olivette)

I collaborate on everything I do ... That has been a major issue. [They say] how do we know what you're doing? Why wouldn't you do this independently? How do we know you can be an independent scholar? ... and that's a woman's issue. I think women do collaborate more than men ... It's questioned, and it doesn't get rewarded. (Ruth)

Some women were also disturbed by the difficulty of deciding when they had done 'enough' or whether their work was 'good enough.' 'I remember going through at some point really agonizing about tenure – had I done enough ... and then at some point realizing if this isn't enough this is the most I can do' (Terri). 'If you're going to succeed in academe, you're very self driven, and you're never doing a good enough job. That's the way I feel, and it's stressful' (Beth). 'Am I good enough? I'm not good enough. Constantly, not good enough. I constantly feel not good enough ... This job makes one feel not good' (Barbara).

Men and Women

I do not mean to suggest that every woman responded in identical fashion, or that women and men held sentiments with no overlap. I am pointing to tendencies, not absolutes. Transcripts for the men were scrutinized to see whether themes appeared similar to those identified above. Men had their complaints too: there were stories of, for example, an abusive department head and unfair practices. Many men spoke about their families, and those with young children believed that their efforts to be 'good dads' were not always recognized and that balance between work and family was difficult to achieve for men as well as for women. Edward had recently been divorced and had his small children with him about 60 per cent of the time: 'I have a nanny who takes care of the kids till 5, so I have to leave here [the university] at 5 – it doesn't matter what's happening. I have to take my kids to school, so I can't be here until 9:30. It doesn't really matter who's having what meeting ... it's just not on.' Daniel pointed out that, while family responsibilities were taken into account when women with young children came up for tenure, for men this was not the case: 'I don't think that the family issue has ever been addressed. And I know that in terms of tenure and promotion that, frankly, there was absolutely, you know, no mention of my role outside this place ... and no mention whatsoever of the fact that, yeah, I'm raising three kids, and I have an 83–year-old mother who's ill, and a father who died, all of this kind of stuff.'

Certainly, some of the men noted that they had a heavy workload. Several thought that they were on too many committees. Arnold noted the lack of consideration of teaching and service in tenure and promotion decisions. He was also the only man to speak at any length about time spent with students, in this case graduate students: 'The demands that are made on us from the point of view of supervision are very great, or so it seems to me. And they are endless ... PhD students don't go away, ever.'

Tenure procedures were stressful for some of the men, as for some of the women. Solange, quoted above, may have underestimated the amount of work that certain men do in preparing a tenure case. Steve described his strategies for gaining tenure: 'I always do more than what I think they're going to expect. So, I had more journal articles than the previous people who got tenured the year before. I did a lot of writing and made sure I had refereed journal articles. My teaching was above average, so I didn't have any problems at all getting tenure or promotion ... I had more articles and more teaching.' One man, Elliot, with a very heavy workload and few publications, thought his prospects for tenure did not look very good: 'That's going to be an issue and I may appear calm at the moment, but I'm not feeling very calm about it.' On the other hand, Adam, who was just coming up for contract renewal prior to tenure, was indeed very calm: 'It's not a thing I'm worried about at all ... [my] publishing record is really strong and the teaching evaluations have been right up there ... and there's just no shortage of opportunities for service, so I'm not worried about that.'

Concerns about workload and evaluation did, then, appear in the interviews with men, but to a markedly lower degree than in the women's narratives. There was little evidence of extensive nurturing efforts for students and almost none of the angst apparent in women's accounts of being judged for tenure, promotion, or merit. Although men, especially those with families, stressed that balance was difficult because the job demanded so much, they did not give the extended accounts of going to bed late, getting up early, and working through breaks that the women provided.

Most striking were the differences in responses to questions about health and stress. Men were far less likely to admit to poor health or too much stress in their work, whereas these were common responses from the women. In interpreting these responses, we should keep in mind that men (broadly speaking) are socialized not to disclose their feelings, and the extent to which they do worry about being unable to control their work situation may not be readily revealed in an interview. Moreover, women may have felt more comfortable talking about their problems with a woman interviewer. But if we take the responses at face value, we do see quite a difference between the typical responses of men and women to this set of questions. For example, Victor, who did not yet have tenure and had a heavy teaching load, nevertheless could say in response to the interview question 'What kind of health do you enjoy': 'Wonderful ... there are some stresses sometimes but I don't consider that I've been sick and I think I'm, well I'm told by my wife, that I'm one of these incredible optimists.' He added that he had some worries about being overweight. In contrast, Helen, a female assistant professor of about the same age, responded to the question this way: 'I'm a pretty strong person and I'm quite athletic. But I would say that this level of stress and fatigue really wears on me. And my health is pretty good but I think emotionally it wears you down and ... it's aging me actually ... I think current, untenured academic life is quite stressful and draining. And demanding. And that it fills all of your waking hours. It would fill every minute of my week if I didn't walk from it.'

The more senior men did not show any increased tendency to find work stressful or to complain more about health problems. Patrick, an associate professor, simply said, 'I don't get stressed about things,' and his sentiment was echoed by others at his rank. Colin, a full professor, observed, 'I've been tremendously healthy thus far, touch wood.' In response to a question about stress, he added, 'I think it [academic life] can be terribly stressful but it can also be enormously rewarding and therefore can relieve the stress.'

In contrast, many of the women associate and full professors gave extended accounts of illnesses and stress. For example, to the question on health, Aline replied, 'Yes I could tell you about my health. The burnout was diagnosed as chronic fatigue syndrome.' She then described her symptoms, the early responses from doctors, the measures she then took, and her eventual partial recovery.

Both men and women had problems in the university. Although some men believed that their childcare responsibilities were not recognized and allowed for, it was primarily women who talked about stress and health concerns, anxiety over evaluation, extreme time pressures, and disproportionate responsibilities for nurturing students and departmental service.

Conclusion

This essay has investigated the parameters of an emotional response that I regard as fairly widespread in the caring professions, as well as among at least some women academics: a belief that one is 'doing good' but, as a result of factors outside one's control, ends up 'feeling bad.' The body of the essay has featured two examples of situations where women in teaching, at elementary-school or university level, tried to live out the caring discourse and be good professionals, with rather perplexing consequences. In both cases the women worked hard and made extra efforts to care for and support others and be 'good citizens,' not because they were forced to do so, but because they had internalized these ways of working as the right thing to do, the moral way to be. Yet reward systems and community responses did not seem to reflect those norms. Why was it that elementary school children and their parents could not see how hard the teachers worked to meet their needs? Why was Dennis spared the interruptions and concerns that staff and children brought to Debbie? Why was it that all that 'good citizen' effort and student support was not usually recognized in university tenure, promotion, and merit reviews, yet was a layer of extra work apparently reserved for women academics?[21] Why did so many women feel stressed and suffer health problems?

Thus far I have mainly emphasized the similarities between the responses of two groups of women from different workplaces: a small primary school in England and faculties of education in Canada. We could ask why the similar responses occur. The most obvious conclusion is that women at work are faced with similar expectations in different settings, and that they hold common orientations to their work that reflect stereotypical ideas about women being caring, conscientious, and good with people as well as, in the case of some of the academics, 'good department citizens.' Thus we are focusing on the *sameness* of women and by implication their difference from men. This route takes us into some difficult terrain, as many feminist writers have come to understand; for there is inevitably much diversity among women, and by emphasizing sameness we downplay diversity. Not every woman academic gave the same response to the questions, for example, but I have smoothed out their differences in an attempt to find broad trends. There are similarities related to being women in a workplace, but there are also differences related to various other facets of the women's subjectivities and to the particularity of the workplace. In the elementary school, women are the majority, and at Hillview they had a woman administrator as well. The teachers have inherited a legacy of work with children being regarded as an extension of mothering,[22] a natural occupation for women, and they can feel comfortable with their contribution to society. It is only when parents, children, and others fail to appreciate their efforts or when the material situations in which they work are shabby and crowded that they express some distress. If Mrs Clarke had been a less-successful manager, their resentment would likely have been much greater.

In contrast, the women academics cannot help but know that they are in a man's world. When they look around for an apt group with which to compare their situations, they see the men in their own faculties. When they see these men apparently contributing much less to the smooth running of the department and the nurturing of the students, yet more readily receiving rewards such as promotions and high salaries, they react unfavourably. By and large, the women academics are more aware than the elementary school teachers of the contradictions of caring. Debbie, at Hillview, is something of an exception, because she had the chance to compare her situation with Dennis's in the same role of deputy head teacher. Perhaps also the academics' wider reading and greater exposure to feminist thought exacerbates their sensitivity.

Similar findings come from studies conducted on women academics in other countries, including Kenya and New Zealand.[23] It is possible that women in fields such as education, where they are fairly well represented, will be less content than those in certain other areas where they are clearly extraordinary to be present at all (see, for example, the essays on physicists by Alison Prentice and on foresters by Peggy Tripp-Knowles in this volume). Women who can, on the one hand, make common cause and share perceptions with others in the same situation and, at the same time, observe the greater rewards that men attain in their fields may be more likely to take men as the reference group and thereby feel relatively deprived and unhappy in consequence.

Neither the women elementary teachers nor the academics displayed much overt anger, at least not in the presence of the researcher. Resentment, bitterness, and anger would be 'outlaw emotions,' inconsistent with the social scripts for women. They may even be dangerous. What kind of career would a woman elementary school teacher have if it appeared that she were openly angry at her students and their parents? Would a woman academic receive tenure if it were said about her that 'she resents caring for her students'? The literature on academics suggests that the university can be a very uncongenial setting for those who defy its norms.[24] Negative sentiments are safer when shared among colleagues in the staff room or in a one-to-one interview situation where anonymity has been promised and rapport established. When I used some of the data on the women academics for another article, the response of one reviewer to the initial submission included this observation: 'It comes across to me as a prolonged whinge [whine] on how women are treated in the world of work.'[25] The comment illustrates the point rather well that the complaints of women are not received as entirely legitimate. Women are expected to go on 'doing good' but to keep quiet about 'feeling bad.'

NOTES

I would like to acknowledge the support of the Social Sciences and Humanities Research Council of Canada for the research on academics described in this essay. Thanks also are owed to my faculty and student colleagues on the project, including Carol Baines, Marcia Boyd, Grace Feuerverger, Linda Muzzin, Lisa Richards, and Amy Sullivan; to Carmen Armenti, Margaret Njoki Kamau, and Alison Taylor for help with the project at various points; to Janet Ryding, Josephine Mazzuca, Nancy Roszell, and Gina Valle for transcribing; and to the academics who participated in the study. Further heartfelt thanks go to Liz Clarke and the staff of Hillview School.

1 Jean Baker Miller, *Toward a New Psychology of Women* (Harmondsworth: Penguin, 1976).
2 It should be noted, however, that in recent years women's representation has increased in many of the professions traditionally associated with men. For example, in 1995–6 women made up 65, 52, and 44 per cent of undergraduate enrolments in pharmacy, law, and dentistry respectively; Statistics Canada, *Education in Canada 1997*, Cat. no. 81–229–XPB (Ottawa: Minister of Industry, 1998), 63–5. See also Katherine Marshall, 'Women in Professional Occupations: Progress in the 1980s,' *Canadian Social Trends*, spring 1989, 13–16.
3 Judith S. Glazer, 'Feminism and Professionalism in Teaching and Educational Administration,' *Educational Administration Quarterly* 27, no. 3 (August 1991): 321–42.
4 Amitai Etzioni, ed., *The Semi-Professions and Their Organization: Teachers, Nurses, and Social Workers* (New York: Free Press, 1969).
5 Nel Noddings, *The Challenge to Care in Schools* (New York: Teachers College Press, 1992); Nel Noddings, 'An Ethic of Caring and Its Implications for Instructional Arrangements,' in Lynda Stone, ed., *The Education Feminism Reader* (New York: Routledge, 1994), 171–83.
6 Nel Noddings, 'Feminist Critiques in the Professions,' in Courtney B. Cazden, ed., *Review of Research in Education* 16 (Washington, DC: American Educational Research Association, 1990). For other discussions of caring in the professions, see Carol Baines, 'Women's Professions and an Ethic of Care,' in Carol Baines, Patricia Evans, and Sheila Neysmith, eds., *Women's Caring: Feminist Per-*

spectives on Social Welfare (2nd ed., Toronto: Oxford University Press, 1998); Mary Field Belenky, Blythe Clinchy, Nancy Goldberger, and Jill Tarule, *Women's Ways of Knowing* (New York: Basic Books, 1986); Deborah Eaker-Rich and Jane Van Galen, eds., *Caring in an Unjust World* (Albany: State University of New York Press, 1996).

7 Carol Gilligan, *In a Different Voice* (Cambridge: Harvard University Press, 1982).

8 Marjorie DeVault, *Feeding the Family: The Social Organization of Caring as Gendered Work* (Chicago: University of Chicago Press, 1991), 240.

9 Alison Jaggar, 'Love and Knowledge: Emotion in Feminist Epistemology,' in Alison Jaggar and Susan Bordo, eds., *Gender/Body/Knowledge* (New Brunswick, NJ: Rutgers University Press, 1989), 145–71.

10 See Andy Hargreaves, *Changing Teachers, Changing Times* (New York: Teachers College Press, 1994); Jennifer Nias, ed., *The Emotions of Teaching*, special issue, *Cambridge Journal of Education* 26, no. 3 (1996).

11 My fieldwork in the school took place between April 1987 and December 1990, totalling at least a thousand hours. I observed classrooms, participated in school activities, collected documents, conducted and taped interviews with staff (sometimes on several occasions), and attended staff meetings. I kept in touch with the teachers after I moved to Canada and saw them on a number of visits to England. The full report of my research appears in Sandra Acker, *The Realities of Teachers' Work: Never a Dull Moment* (London: Cassell, 1999).

12 Sandra Acker, 'Carry on Caring: The Work of Women Teachers,' *British Journal of Sociology of Education* 16 (1995): 21–36.

13 Sandra Acker and Grace Feuerverger, 'Doing Good and Feeling Bad: The Work of Women University Teachers,' *Cambridge Journal of Education* 26, no. 3 (1996): 401–22; Nias, *The Emotions of Teaching*.

14 Sandra Acker, 'Primary School Teachers' Work: The Response to Educational Reform,' in Gill Helsby and Gary McCulloch, eds., *Teachers and the National Curriculum* (London: Cassell, 1997), 34–51; Bob Jeffery and Peter Woods, 'Feeling Deprofessionalised: The Social Construction of Emotions during an OFSTED Inspection,' *Cambridge Journal of Education* 26, no. 3 (1996): 325–43.

15 There is an enormous literature, both historical and sociological, that considers questions of teachers as professionals: for example, whether teaching is a profession, whether teachers have been deprofessionalized, and how gender relates to professionalism. Some recent studies include Richard Altenbaugh, ed., *The Teacher's Voice* (London: Falmer Press, 1992); Michael Apple, *Teachers and Texts* (New York: Routledge & Kegan Paul, 1986); Sari Knopp Biklen, *School Work* (New York: Teachers College Press, 1995); R.W. Connell, *Teachers'*

Work (Sydney: Allen & Unwin, 1985); Ivor Goodson and Andy Hargreaves, eds., *Teachers' Professional Lives* (London: Falmer Press, 1996); Hargreaves, *Changing Teachers, Changing Times*; Martin Lawn, *Modern Times? Work, Professionalism and Citizenship in Teaching* (London: Falmer Press, 1996); Martin Lawn and Gerald Grace, eds., *Teachers: The Culture and Politics of Work* (London: Falmer Press, 1987); Jenny Ozga, ed., *Schoolwork* (Milton Keynes: Open University Press, 1988); Andrew Pollard, Patricia Broadfoot, Paul Croll, Marilyn Osborn, and Dorothy Abbott, *Changing English Primary Schools?* (London: Cassell, 1994); Geoff Troman, 'The Rise of the New Professionals? The Restructuring of Primary Teachers' Work and Professionalism,' *British Journal of Sociology of Education* 17, no. 4 (1996): 473–87.

16 Sandra Acker, 'Managing the Drama: The Head Teacher's Work in an Urban Primary School,' *Sociological Review* 38 (1990): 247–71.

17 Acker, 'Carry on Caring,' 29.

18 Ibid.

19 Ibid.

20 For this analysis I worked with transcripts of interviews with thirty-two women (twelve full professors, fourteen associate professors, and six assistant professors) and, for comparison, sixteen men (five full professors, eight associate professors, and three assistant professors). These transcripts were all in English; I also read relevant translated excerpts from seven interviews with women academics in education faculties conducted in French (four full professors, two associate professors, and one assistant professor). Interviews came from five universities in four Canadian provinces.

21 Shelley Park, 'Research, Teaching and Service: Why Shouldn't Women's Work Count?' *Journal of Higher Education* 67 (1996): 47–84.

22 Kate Rousmaniere, *City Teachers: Teaching and School Reform in Historical Perspective* (New York: Teachers College Press, 1997), 40.

23 For Kenya see Margaret Njoki Kamau, *The Experiences of Women Academics in Kenya* (Unpublished PhD dissertation, Graduate Department of Education, University of Toronto 1996); for New Zealand see Ann Brooks, *Academic Women* (Buckingham: Open University Press, 1997). There are also studies with different results. Brooks's questionnaire to women academics in the United Kingdom did not produce the same expressions of discontent as she found when conducting in-depth interviews in New Zealand. In Costa Rica Susan Twombly's interviews with women in positions of academic leadership revealed that these women did compare themselves with other women and saw themselves as leading privileged lives: Twombly, 'Paradoxes of Professional Life for Female Academic Leaders in a Latin American University,' *Higher Education* 35 (1998): 367–97.

24 Paula Caplan, *Lifting a Ton of Feathers: A Woman's Guide to Surviving in the Academic World* (Toronto: University of Toronto Press, 1993); Chilly Collective, ed., *Breaking Anonymity: The Chilly Climate for Women Faculty* (Waterloo: Wilfrid Laurier Press, 1995); Patricia Gumport, 'Fired Faculty,' in Daniel McLaughlin and William G. Tierney, eds., *Naming Silenced Lives* (New York: Routledge, 1993), 135–54; see also Linda Muzzin, 'Pawns between Patriarchies,' in this volume.

25 Acker and Feuerverger, 'Doing Good and Feeling Bad.'

Pawns between Patriarchies: Women in Canadian Pharmacy

LINDA MUZZIN WITH PATRICIA SINNOTT
AND CLAUDIA LAI

The Six Patriarchies and Their Ideologies

This history of women in pharmacy is organized around a picture of the profession of pharmacy in which women pharmacists, academics, and policy-makers can be described as 'pawns' in a series of power struggles among competing and interlocking patriarchies. Chess provides an appropriate metaphor for this history because the warring patriarchies involved may be visualized as plotting various long- and short-term strategies against each other, sacrificing their professional foot soldiers, and game-playing for profit. Two main struggles in the field can be identified in the past century in Canada: those between physicians and pharmacists and between independent pharmacists and corporate owners of drug stores. Women have played an important role in both sets of confrontations.

These oppositions can be placed within the context of a global struggle that has taken centre stage in contemporary times between global multinational pharmaceutical manufacturing firms and national states. In this confrontation, nation states such as Canada are unable to protect their domestic drug manufacturing industries or control drug prices. Multinational manufacturers regularly checkmate such government policies, as they did recently in Canada by reversing our patent legislation allegedly through a 'deal' made during the North American Free Trade Agreement negotiations.

The two sets of confrontations described here can also be contextualized within the universities, where health professionals are trained. These professional schools are composed of two *additional* patriarchies of phar-

maceutical scientist-professors and administrators. Here the confrontation is between scientists, who wish to maintain autonomy over the
content of their work, and their administrators, who are anxious to
ensure the survival and reputation of their schools. In Canada, as in the
United States, the administrators make contracts to turn over the labour
of their scientists to the pharmaceutical industry for money. Women scientists have been involved voluntarily and involuntarily. Students of the
health professions, now mostly women, are also caught in the middle of
this struggle.

Thus the six interlocking patriarchies with whom women in pharmacy
have had to deal are (1) independent pharmacy and its associations;
(2) hierarchical medicine, in which physicians who practise specialty
medicine dominate the division of labour and other health professions
are 'handmaidens' to them;[1] (3) corporate chain drugstores such as
Shoppers Drug Mart and Wal-Mart; (4) the multinational pharmaceutical
industry, represented by the voluntary association of brand-name drug
manufacturers, the Pharmaceutical Manufacturers' Association of Canada; (5) the scientists who 'manipulate molecules' to design contemporary drugs; and (6) university administrators. The story is very complex
because each patriarchy uses as its weapons *ideologies* or ways of thinking
about the world that are presented as inclusionary world-views but which
in reality represent *their* interests – that is, the interests of the powerful.
The dominant ideologies put forward by the six patriarchies discussed
here to justify their activities are held partly in common and partly in
opposition. They are (1) 'guild' or 'free market' capitalism, espoused by
independent pharmacists and academic scientists; (2) hierarchical medicine; (3) chain-store professionalism; (4) molecular science; and (5) global corporate monopoly capitalism, embraced by multinational corporations and members of national governments and university administra-
tions alike. I call the six hierarchies 'patriarchies' because over 80
per cent of each is composed of men *and* because the activities and rhetoric of the groups can be characterized as hegemonic and androcentric.[2]

A Relational-Critical Feminist Perspective on the Pharmaceutical World

The ideas put forward here are based primarily on my own work over the
past decade, which has involved interviewing and surveying thousands of
Canadian pharmacists from Newfoundland to British Columbia, teaching
graduate and undergraduate students, and participating in university life

and governance in the largest of the nine faculties of pharmacy in Canada, located at the University of Toronto. Together with two practising pharmacists who have been my graduate students, I examine critically what has been important to women in pharmacy over the century, their disadvantaged position in the health-care hierarchy, and how and why their ethical ideals have been so compromised. My student-colleagues have each done thesis research with twenty to thirty pharmacists which was intensely personal for them, as they struggled to understand the profession that they had chosen.

In our work all three of us have celebrated how pharmacists try to realize their ideals of caring in practice.[3] Specifically, we have noted how many women (and men) pharmacists place great importance on relationships which orient them towards others in responsible and caring ways. In their everyday work, rather than focusing on the marketing of drugs, they emphasize relationships with their clients and resist moral indignities that they feel are inappropriate for the practice of a profession. Their behaviour includes gentleness in dealing with angry customers, care in following up problems encountered with them, being responsive to unspoken health and social problems faced by these clients, and resisting an oppressive workplace pressure towards marketing. We are critical of the worlds in which the women pharmacists are oppressed; we are also in despair about what can be labelled their 'false consciousness,'[4] or a general inability to 'see' their oppression in its global context, of their 'silence' or ethical paralysis in protesting the corruption of their ideals, and of their 'co-optation' or recruitment by powerful patriarchies. The theme of co-optation is at the centre of our argument, since we see the ethical orientations of the women – their 'options' or 'choices' – overridden by a group consensus that pre-empts their opposition. While we may appear to set ourselves up as judges who override the women's voices, we would prefer to see ourselves as providing a context for understanding how their betrayal in pharmacy has been perpetrated with their complicity.

The 125–year history briefly reviewed here is divided into three eras: the 50–year period between the granting of the first monopoly to practise pharmacy in Ontario and the point at which the first direct influence of women on pharmacy is visible in the 1920s; the 50–year period from the first blush of women's resistance to androcentric commercial pharmacy to the beginning of the 1970s, when the 'women's movement' took hold in Canada; and the past 25 years, in which women have 'feminized' Canadian pharmacy by their numbers, changing its public face. At the same time, women have found themselves ghettoized within its six patriarchies and buffeted by the local, national, and international professional, inter-professional, corporate chain store, scientific, and multinational corporate and governmental crossfire that accompanies the selling of drugs for profit.

The women have been pawns in these struggles in two ways. First, they provided some of the 'man' power for the battles. But more important, in the struggles described here the women resisted one patriarchy by joining another that promised to provide them the freedom to realize their ideals. This pursuit of ennoblement, however, has been co-opted by the more powerful patriarchies, thus lending a 'caring face' to an otherwise sordid business that involves, at its heart, drug making and selling as exploitation of ill health for profit.

The First Fifty Years

Before 1871, when Ontario granted a monopoly to pharmacists to compound and dispense drugs, Canada looked very different from what it is today. Ontario and Quebec were the most populated provinces, but apart from British Columbia the country west of Manitoba was called the North-West Territories.[5] There were population centres along the American border in those 'two solitudes' of anglophone Ontario and francophone Quebec,[6] but Canada was agrarian, consisting of a patchwork of small, family-owned farms. The south-central part of the country was a network of towns built around churches and surrounded by these farms. There were doctors in the towns, but they were only consulted by the affluent; most farmers sought an over-the-counter drug solution to their health problems wherever druggists (sometimes called 'poor men's doctors') were established. Thus many drugstores later became the social centre of their towns. Atlases and family and town histories compiled at this time reveal that the largest farms were owned by prominent families from the British Isles who also dominated the politics of the small towns.[7] Quebec was similarly agrarian. Canada north of the Ottawa River was a wild, dangerous place.[8]

Who were the first Canadian pharmacists? According to an unpublished analysis of records,[9] there were hundreds of male graduates of the Ontario College of Pharmacy (established in 1882 in Toronto) in its first quarter-century of operation, virtually all of whom, as pioneering entrepreneurs, subsequently established the first drugstores in central Canada; but only four women appeared at the college. (There are now nine schools of pharmacy in Canada, two of which are in Quebec, and none in

New Brunswick or Prince Edward Island.) The numbers of women in the largest pharmacy school increased only very slightly from the turn of the century to the First World War, but we know little about these women beyond their names. As in many other areas of male-dominated professionalism, we can say nothing about their hopes and dreams, let alone their accomplishments. The story is slightly different for Quebec, where Johanne Collin has documented the efforts of pharmacy students to establish a francophone school.[10] Beyond this work we know virtually nothing about the social circumstances and ideals of practice of these early women in Canadian pharmacy. Similarly, although Ernst Stieb has laid the groundwork for understanding the motivations of the men who founded pharmacy,[11] little is known about the attitudes and practices of early independent male pharmacy owners. The *Canadian Pharmaceutical Journal*, the voice of the national association of pharmacists, was published from 1868 onwards, so that there is the possibility of reconstructing this history; but it has not yet been done.

The Second Fifty Years

In turn-of-the-twentieth-century Canada male pharmacists practised their trade as independent business people, finding honour in their successes as technical or 'guild' workers doing extemporaneous compounding of simple chemicals. They had small drug businesses in the 'free' market[12] of their communities, selling low-priced liquid tinctures, dried herbs, and patent medicines. Druggists served the poor, while doctors ministered to the rich. Since women tended not to inherit businesses and married women who worked shamed their breadwinning husbands, there was no opportunity for women to have a direct influence on this patriarchical organization of independent pharmacy and its provincially and federally based professional associations.

All of this began to change after the First World War when women started to slip into pharmacy unnoticed via their family ties.[13] They had never been barred from becoming pharmacy apprentices and attending pharmacy school, but there were only 3 to 6 women per class of 140 to 300 students in the inter-war years at the largest school of pharmacy, Toronto. A few found their way into commercial practice as employees or owners' wives or daughters. These women have reported to me that they did not see themselves as subservient to their husbands and fathers but as 'pioneers,' making unique contributions to the profession. As one doctor's daughter claimed, women's early involvement in pharmacy was the 'start of the feminist movement' because medicine and pharmacy were the first two professional faculties at the University of Toronto to accept women. Despite her enthusiasm about their acceptance into the *university*, however, it can be argued that women never really managed to enter the patriarchy of independent pharmacy in most parts of Canada; in the 1990s, based on my examination of anglophone licensing board records, I discovered that in some provinces such as Manitoba less than 10 per cent of owners are women. (Quebec has the highest proportion at 30 per cent.)[14] Nationally, although over half the approximately 22,000 Canadian pharmacists are women, the vast majority are employees.

The real resistance exhibited by women to a pharmacy patriarchy based on free-market capitalism, from which they were almost totally excluded, came with the establishment of a new *kind* of pharmacy practice without commercial overtones in the 1920s and 1930s. Partly because this new branch of pharmacy – in hospitals – was poorly paid and involved living an austere institutional life, women were the first pharmacists to take it up. Although contemporary male pharmacists claim that *they* were the founders of hospital pharmacy in Canada, the accounts of the women whom we have interviewed suggest another story.[15] Catholic sisters who were nurses running voluntary hospitals have told me that they decided to acquire pharmacy training after critically observing the practices of physicians working in their hospitals. Other women pharmacists who began to work in public hospitals in Montreal, Toronto, and other cities idolized the physicians with whom they worked. This was the 'golden era' of medicine in Canada,[16] when new antibiotic and sulfa drugs first became widely available and the physicians who administered the drugs were regarded as 'miracle workers.' The women pharmacists felt that they were able to fulfil their ethical goals of serving the sick without selling drugs for profit, which they saw as the preoccupation of their male colleagues. A few who had worked as employees within the independent pharmacy patriarchy before choosing what they judged to be the 'more ethical' route of hospital practice expressed disgust to me at the business orientation and attitudes towards clients and staff in some of the drugstores where they had been employed.

As part of a whole army of women who peopled the lower rungs of the medical hierarchy that formed in Canada during these decades, these women strengthened the medical patriarchy that was finally institutionalized within the government-subsidized medicare legislated in the 1970s. The subsidization of hierarchical medicine, by this time based virtually entirely on molecular science, by Canadian governments placed physicians at the top of a powerful patriarchy that has partly co-opted the pharmacists by making them dependent upon prescription business for the 'professional' aspect of their work. Specifically, although community pharmacists are empowered to dispense prescriptions, they do not have access to medical records and cannot give patients advice beyond warning of side effects and how the medication should be taken. All other medical decision-making, including diagnosis, treatment, and choice of medication and its dose and duration, are the professional territory of the physician. As part of government attempts at cost-cutting, pharmacists are allowed to substitute a cheaper generic drug when filling a prescription, but not if the physician has written 'no substitution' on the prescription. Pharmacists also sell non-prescription drugs and sundries for profit, but their work would not be characterized as 'professional' without the act of dispensing prescriptions written by physicians.

The Past Quarter-Century

In 1971 central Canada was no longer a patchwork of family farms controlled economically by a few elite families who originated in the British Isles, as it had been a hundred years earlier. By then the family farms had begun to disappear, and the majority of Canadians had moved to urban areas. The prairies were no longer part of the North-West Territories, but were now billed as the 'world's breadbasket' and produced a tenth of its wheat. Elite families, however, still 'owned' the country.[17] Although a pattern of alternating francophone and anglophone prime ministers had evolved, Canadians had just experienced a violent episode in which Quebec separatists had murdered a provincial cabinet minister.[18] Northern Canada was no longer dangerous, but it was still largely unpopulated. Physicians were everywhere, as were druggists, in virtually every small town and city in the country; Canada had just passed the medicare legislation that subsidized health care for everyone from Newfoundland, which had joined Confederation in 1949, to British Columbia and the north. The future of the Canadian medical patriarchy seemed assured, with pharmacists, nurses, and an army of other health-care workers as their minions in the medical hierarchy. Drugs were not covered by universal government insurance, but medicare promised to subsidize the elderly and the indigent.

But independent pharmacists were not safe or sheltered by physicians and medicare. By the late 1960s those who owned stores faced a new battle, with a corporate patriarchy. We are surrounded by the relentless corporatization of services in Canadian society formerly offered by independent business people, such as the sale of hardware, cinema, groceries, furniture, eyewear, gasoline, and virtually every other commodity-based service. Pharmacy is no exception. The one-pharmacist-owner one-store pattern so characteristic of independent pharmacy had involved an interesting dialectical tug-of-war between those who placed the emphasis on being 'professional,' as in the image of the elitist medical doctor, and those who placed the emphasis on 'discounting' or providing drugs as cheaply as they possibly could by *whatever* means. This split within commercial pharmacy had traditionally served to provide 'discount' drugs for the poor as well as functioning in a more-upscale, 'professional' way for middle-class patients. It provided an opening on the chessboard for a corporate takeover.

The battle was fought first between chains and independents, but the original struggle has been transformed in the past three decades into one of corporate professionalizers versus corporate discounters. The idea of elitist 'professionalism' (reflecting the elitist origins of medicine) was actually *marketed* by early chains such as Tamblyn's, where George Tamblyn would show up at his downtown stores and run his white glove along the display cases, threatening to fire any pharmacist-manager who let dust accumulate anywhere. This white-and-clean 'chain store professionalism' gained favour with the public and is best illustrated by the contemporary corporate franchise chain Shoppers Drug Mart (SDM), which grew from two stores owned by Murray Koffler in the 1950s to its currently estimated one thousand stores, making it the largest in the country, concentrated in the most profitable urban locations. SDM is a franchise corporation, but the pharmacist-franchisees no longer have their autonomy; they must follow accounting and other practices determined by head office and can be fired.[19] Other corporations such as Superstore, Zellers, K-Mart, Safeway, and Wal-Mart have reproduced the 'discounter' pharmacies of independent origins by incorporating pharmacies into department and grocery stores.

Women are again involved in the battles, this time in very great numbers. The massive influx of women into the labour force that corresponded to the coming of age of the 'baby boom' population in Canada has had a significant effect on the make-up of pharmacy, as it has on workplaces and families everywhere. In fact, pharmacy was one of the fastest patriarchies to feminize during this time, at least on its lower rungs.[20] American feminists have speculated that this may have been so because independent pharmacy no longer held the lure of windfall profits, since it was already struggling with corporate chains that undercut the autonomy of the independent pharmacist.[21] The key to understanding how women have contributed to this takeover can be found in where they work: predominantly employees rather than owners, they have been attracted to corporate chains.[22]

The women's 'choice' to work in chain stores has come about partly because the independent pharmacy hierarchy excluded them, but also because of their own ethical preferences. Like their predecessors of fifty years ago, they prefer an 'ethical practice' – one in which they clearly serve the patient rather than sell drugs for profit. And like those earlier women pharmacists who 'ran into the arms' of the powerful patriarchy of physicians, only too happy to serve the sick, contemporary women pharmacists find themselves opting for what many of them consider a more 'professional' practice in a corporately owned store, where they are not bothered with financial concerns. If they are going to be employees anyway, why not leave business concerns to the store manager and concentrate on the clinical aspects of the work? In interviews some expressed concern that, in working for SDM, they are employed by a company no longer owned by Murray Koffler but instead by Imasco, which is mostly owned by British-American (Imperial) Tobacco, the largest tobacco company in the world. It is widely known that smoking is the major cause of lung cancer and that lung cancer is now the major killer, among all the types of cancer, of both men and women in Canada.[23] Thus contextualized, their 'ethics' appear to have gone awry. Although legislation banning the sale of cigarettes in pharmacies has been passed in Ontario, such stores continue to be major vendors of cigarettes in other provinces. But the women, concerned with everyday/everynight issues of childcare and supplementary breadwinning, have little time to worry about this contradiction in their work, the consequences of the loss of their professional autonomy and the co-optation of their professional ideals by a multinational corporation.

As the independent pharmacy patriarchy struggles so ineptly with national corporations that can compete by securing the most favourable locations and leases in malls, buy out any competitors, and attract large contracts from government institutions wishing to save money through a discounted dispensing fee, a minority of women have purchased ailing independent stores, trying valiantly to run them according to their ethical consciences. While they reject the 'marketing professionalism' mode of their colleagues, these women are having great difficulties in a playing field that is not level. The majority of their female classmates, by way of contrast, have opted to work within the more powerful patriarchy of corporate pharmacy, which is only too happy to have *whoever* will make a profit, including women employees who want to 'make a difference' for their clients. Thus just as surely as women helped to people the lower rungs of the medical hierarchy, as we have described above, so they serve, just like pawns, to fill the lower rungs of a corporate pharmacy that either markets professionalism or exploits them to sell drugs along with any other commodity that can be discounted. In discount sweatshops these pharmacists, mostly young and mostly women, fill as many as two hundred prescriptions in an eight-hour shift, or about one prescription every two minutes, hour after hour, with no break or time to advise the patient properly on his or her medications.

It is in this way that the lower rungs of the corporate hierarchy are kept in place and given a caring face. Here ethical resistance leads to an even more fundamental co-optation than the one that preceded it: a patriarchal hierarchy uses 'feminist' ethical orientations to, paradoxically, build a stronger patriarchy. The partial vision of the women who willingly take part in this type of pharmacy, in the form of commitment to a corporate ideology, recruits them as foot soldiers for the positions they theoretically oppose. They are taken in by the commercials that SDM flashes past them on their television sets, showing them to be caring women attending to the needs of their communities. In the process, they buy into a patriarchy that subordinates caring and the maintenance of health to profit-making and further devalues their importance.

The World Context of Pharmacy Practice

It has been argued to this point that women in pharmacy have been unwitting pawns of warring patriarchies that subordinate their ideals of ethical and professional practice to what may be called the 'business of health.' However, besides being present 'in the trenches,' women may also be found (albeit in very small numbers) at the top of academic, political, corporate, and scientific hierarchies. These women are important to the Canadian feminist movement in raising the profile of women in Canada. In view of their positions, it is more difficult to see them as pawns in the confrontations described above; however, it will be argued here that they also, perhaps against their intentions, contribute to the subordination of concerns of health to those of profit-making. In order to understand the situation of these elite women, which will be discussed below, it is necessary to appreciate the context of Canadian pharmacy practice.

Most important is the role of the Pharmaceutical Manufacturers' Association of Canada (PMAC). There are approximately (since they are continuously merging, splitting, and renaming themselves) sixty-five members of the PMAC, which differ in size and include the giant multinationals such as Glaxo, Merck, Novartis (a merger of Sandoz and Ciba-Geigy), and Bristol-Myers-Squibb. As Joel Lexchin has pointed out,[24] these companies tend not to compete with one another but instead stake off territories or 'niches' in which they market drugs. Eli Lilly, for example, is known for antibiotics and drugs such as Prozac,[25] which it was instrumental in developing. Hoffman-LaRoche is infamous for its drug Valium, among the most prescribed in the world and known as the drug that doped a generation of housewives.[26] These brand-name companies are not owned by Canadians but have Canadian branches. They call themselves 'innovative' because, they argue, *they* do research and development, while their counterparts, the generic-drug companies, do not. This has been their justification for the twenty-year patent protection they recently achieved. In critical perspective though, the world average of research and development expenditures as a proportion of profit, according to three Swiss-based multinationals, is about 11 per cent.[27] And since these companies have been estimated to spend about 15 per cent of their profits in Canada on *advertising*,[28] it is difficult to 'buy' the argument that they need special governmental concessions.[29]

The PMAC espouses the ideology of global corporate monopoly capitalism, which is in the best interests of the huge corporations. It has successfully convinced Canada's political leaders that globalization is advantageous to Canadians, as compared with the government's own drug policy, which was legislated to keep drug prices down by encouraging the growth of domestic generic-drug manufacturing firms. The concept of generic drugs is now familiar to all Canadians through the operation of discount grocery stores. Their manufacture in Canada was supported by the ability of the pharmacist to substitute these cheaper versions of a drug, as well as by a policy, in operation from 1969 until 1993, that favoured these 'home-grown' generic companies by allowing them, within about four or five years of the marketing of a new (typically expensive) brand-name drug, to begin to 'copy' it and market it more cheaply to the public. Although only a small proportion of the Canadian market belonged to the Canadian generic by 1993, patent protection was raised from what had effectively been four years to twelve before generic companies could apply to begin this process. Representatives of the generic firms warned the public about higher prices in 1992 when Bill C-91 was being debated. They observed bitterly that national governments *usually* fight to protect their own industries.[30] News reports highlighted the haste with which the bill was passed through the House of Commons and the Senate, with closure invoked at each level, despite its major financial implications for Canada. As a consequence of high prices, the provincial drug-benefit plans have had to cut back on their coverage for medication for seniors and are hard-pressed to control expenditures.

Why did this change occur, since it seems to make no sense from a Canadian perspective? News reports have suggested that multinational corporations wrote to the U.S. trade negotiator during the NAFTA negotiations in 1992 demanding that the agreement end compulsory licensing in Canada. Thus it appears that Canada's federal drug policy became a trade-off in an international agreement such that it cannot be renegotiated by future governments. The leader of the PMAC, Judy Erola, was quoted as saying at the ratification of the agreement, 'This is an important day for medical science.' Ralph Nader, on the other hand, speculated that it was just the beginning of corporate ultimatums that would start to bring Canadian standards for health, safety, and wages down to the level of those in other countries. And Dalton Camp observed, 'Those who vote for C-91 are voting for greed and exploitation, and they know it.' In her later statements, Erola continues to emphasize the benefits that this multinational hegemonic patriarchy has planned for Canada.[31]

University-Based Molecular Science, Drug Research and Development, and Elite (Academic) Women in Pharmacy

The critical literature on medical education has pointed out that the science conducted at universities today is out of synchrony with the education of health professionals. Samuel Bloom, for example, characterizes medical education (of which pharmacy education is a close copy) as a contradictory mix of reductionist molecular science and what he calls the 'social ecology' challenge to reductionism (in which 'caring' is as important as 'curing').[32] This approach, he says, reflects the *competition* between scientific research and professional education, and it forces the medical school to depend upon and be influenced by those who fund scientific research. According to this argument, the presence of the pharmaceutical industry explains why the curriculum in pharmacy schools is almost all molecular science and why professors of pharmaceutical science spend so much time in the laboratory, rarely making the connections with practice and rarely teaching the broader context of health and the health-care system that their young, mostly women, students wish to learn about.

Where do those few women who gave up practising pharmacy to research and teach pharmaceutical science fit in this context? Having experienced this world first-hand, I would argue that they, like women employee pharmacists, can be characterized as pawns. This time the struggle is among a more-complex set of patriarchies to control what is researched and taught at universities. Like other women in male-domi-nated academia, they tend to be marginalized and are thus more vulnera-ble to pressures to conform than their male colleagues. And, I would argue, the pressures to conform to prevailing ideologies are considerable in the contemporary university. For example, university-based molecular scientists, like independent pharmacists, often consider themselves to be 'guild' or technical professionals. But the scientists, who may see them-selves working in a 'free market' of ideas, are increasingly at the mercy of multinational pharmaceutical corporations. Industry representatives show up in the laboratory, encouraging these scientists to write grant pro-posals which they would like to support. These 'scientific detail men' appear at an opportune time, because it is increasingly difficult to acquire funding of scientific research through the main government agency in Canada for this purpose, the Medical Research Council (MRC). For example, in the competition for funding announced in January 1997, $16 million was available to scientists in grant support to operate their labora-tories and carry out experiments, but only 253 of the 1,111 grant propos-als submitted were funded.[33] Professors in this country who lose their funding are not 'locked out' of their laboratories as they are at some pres-tigious American institutions, but the loss of funding represents a disaster in terms of the scientist's research staff, students, and equipment. In fair-ness, many scientists resist the temptation to take the 'easy money' offered by the pharmaceutical firms, but their ethical stance is no longer relevant because the PMAC has been finding ways to support MRC in what can be seen as a marriage of convenience. In 1988 the Canadian gov-ernment spent almost $100 million more on the funding of medical research than the PMAC, but the association became the largest funder of medical research in Canada in 1991.[34] The PMAC has also targeted young researchers since 1987 by providing, together with the MRC, $8 million worth of scholarships.

How does the PMAC–MRC collaboration work? The situation is ideal for the pharmaceutical multinationals: until recently, they might fund 80 per cent of particular projects that were of interest to them as potentially profit-making, as long as the proposal was favourably reviewed by MRC referees. This policy meant that there might be a 60 per cent chance of being funded if one *could interest a PMAC company* in funding one's research. It is money that university departments would not turn their noses up at, and unlike federal money, the funds could be used to meet overhead costs, an increasingly important consideration in the days of cutbacks in university funding by provincial governments, the non-existence of money for capital building projects, the decay of buildings constructed during the boom of the 1960s, and the growing costs of maintenance at universities. The preference for funding with the prestigious MRC stamp of approval (regardless of the PMAC engine that drove it) thus pleased the university, and the continuation of funding satisfied the need to maintain laboratory and research staff. But overall, the consequence was that research *relevant to drugs* was much more likely to be carried out; that is, there was a steering effect of the pharmaceutical industry on MRC – in the direction of molecular research and profit. Unfortunately, women are more vulnerable to these pressures than their well-established male peers.

The process that I am describing is much more advanced in the United States,[35] although Canada is catching up quickly. In 1997 the University of Toronto signed over the rights to any drugs or other therapies that emerged from research on Alzheimer's disease at the Hospital for Sick Children for up to $34.5 million from Schering Canada, a subsidiary of the pharmaceutical firm Schering-Plough.[36] A university spokeswoman rejoiced that this university–drug company collaboration would 'put Canada in the forefront of the competition for new treatments.' But Schering is only one of many companies competing for the attention of scientists to work on problems of particular interest to them. The molecular science that interests pharmaceutical firms takes many forms. The discipline of pharmacology has been revolutionized by the discovery of receptor systems in the body that mediate bodily functions and can be 'turned on' or 'off' by drugs designed to make a molecular 'fit' with the receptor sites. Thus pharmacologists study the nature of the receptor systems as well as design the drugs that interact with them. Work is also ongoing to design genetic material (as a kind of drug) to inhibit the production of proteins that contribute to disease. Beyond disease, claims have also been made for 'magic bullets' that could help cure, for example, cocaine addiction. But most recently pharmaceutical firms have declared their intention to 'divide up' and 'cure' world diseases.[37] University researchers will be part of their attempts to achieve these noble goals. And the women (and men) students whom they teach, many of them eager to fulfil their professional roles in caring for and serving the sick, will continue to be pawns in the worldwide drug trade.

Conclusions

It has been argued here that women in pharmacy have been largely silent pawns in patriarchal wars over power in a biotechnology and health-care chess game. Pursuing their professional ideals but excluded from independent pharmacy, they historically chose to work with physicians, joining an army of labourers supporting the medical patriarchy. Subsequently, within pharmacy they have chosen to work for a patriarchy of corporate professionalizers, ignoring the underpinnings of the corporate ideology into which they are buying. And currently, having entered the labour market in large numbers, a few elite women have found their way into the academic part of the drug world. At our universities they are participants in the education of young women (and men) for the professional roles that they will play in the next millennium, when drug companies promise to eradicate world disease.

NOTES

Research on women's and men's orientations towards business in pharmacy was supported by Social Sciences and Humanities Research Council of Canada grant no. 816–93–0076.

1 The concept of medical dominance is taken from the work of Eliot Freidson in *Professional Dominance* (Chicago: Aldine, 1970). For a discussion of the gendered nature of the medical hierarchy in Canada, see Juanne Clarke, 'The Medical Care System: Critical Issues,' in *Health, Illness and Medicine in Canada* (Toronto: McClelland and Stewart, 1990), 224–48.
2 The term 'androcentric,' widely used by feminist critics of science, refers to 'the virtual absence of a feminist voice in the natural sciences,' as summarized in Ruth Bleier, *Feminist Approaches to Science* (New York: Teachers College Press, 1991), 1.
3 Evidence of these ethical positions is presented in Linda Muzzin, Claudia Lai, and Pat Sinnott, 'Realizing Ideals of Caring in Pharmacy Practice,' presented at the 9th International Social Pharmacy Workshop, 11–14 August 1996, University of Madison-Wisconsin. The gender differences being discussed here are examples of what Weber called 'ideal types,' rather than referring to *all*

men and *all* women. This distinction is particularly important in pharmacy, where many young men appear to be indistinguishable from many young women in their professional orientations. It at first suggested to me that the dimension of interest may be power or a lack of it rather than gender; these explanations, of course, are difficult to separate, but when men's and women's accounts of their store-ownership experiences were compared, the gender differences were quite apparent. For example, in my interviews with them, women owners tended to speak of delegating business considerations to an employee or partner and subordinating business concerns to consideration for patients, staff, and their families, while men owners tended to talk about competition with other stores, business strategies, and coping with the political and economic climate for business in their particular province.

4 'False consciousness' is a Marxian term which tries to explain one of the most persistent of all sociological findings – that social action often produces results other than those intended by the actors, and quite often the *opposite* of what is intended (e.g., see Georg Lukacs, *History and Class Consciousness. Studies in Marxist Dialectic* [Cambridge, Mass.: MIT Press, 1982], 46ff). Specifically, neo-Marxists have been concerned with the question of why workers in Western society have been seemingly 'unaware' of their self-interest in organizing and overthrowing capitalism. Their answer is that for a revolution to occur, the workers must recognize that their best interests are not being served by their corporate bosses. However, workers who are 'falsely conscious' identify with the ideology of capitalism such that they are unable to act in their own best interests. A contemporary discussion is that by Raymond Boudon in *The Analysis of Ideology* (Chicago: University of Chicago Press, 1986). The idea of 'false consciousness' is relevant to the feminist concept of 'silence' popularized by Mary Belenky, Blythe Clinchy, Nancy Goldberger, and Jill Tarule in *Women's Ways of Knowing: The Development of Self, Voice and Mind* (New York: Basic Books, 1986).

5 See the map and history in Maggie Siggins, *Revenge of the Land* (Toronto: McClelland and Stewart, 1992).

6 See Richard Joy, *Languages in Conflict* (Toronto: McClelland and Stewart, 1972). The phrase was originally used by novelist Hugh MacLennan.

7 An example of this type of publication is the *Illustrated Historical Atlas of the Counties of Haldimand and Norfolk* (Toronto: H.R. Page and Co., 1877).

8 William Spaulding, 'Smallpox control in the Ontario wilderness, 1880–1910,' in Charles Roland, ed., *Health, Disease and Medicine: Essays in Canadian History* (Toronto: The Hannah Institute for the History of Medicine, 1984), 194–214.

9 Gail Coulas, 'The Initial Feminization of Pharmacy, 1867–1927' (unpublished paper, Department of Sociology, McMaster University, 1986).

10 Johanne Collin, *Changement d'ordonnance: Mutations professionnelles, identité sociale et féminisation de la profession pharmaceutique au Québec, 1940–1980* (Montréal: Boréal, 1995).

11 Ernst Stieb, 'A Century of Formal Pharmaceutical Education in Ontario: Part One,' *Canadian Pharmaceutical Journal* 116 (1983): 104–7.

12 The market in drugs is not 'free' now because they are regulated in various ways. For example, prescription drugs are chosen by the physician, there are legal restrictions on the dispensing of drugs such as narcotics, and there is legislation regarding the safety and the production of drugs. See Chester Mitchell, *The Drug Solution* (Ottawa: Carleton University Press, 1990).

13 See Linda Adam and Ernst Stieb, 'Women in Ontario Pharmacy, 1927–1952,' *On Continuing Practice* 17, 3 (1990): 23–6. I have been able to locate and interview fifty pharmacists who began to practise in the period between the two world wars, fifteen women and thirty-five men. See Linda Muzzin and Roy Hornosty, 'Formal and Informal Training in Pharmacy, Ontario, Canada, 1917–1927,' *Pharmacy in History* 36, 2 (1994): 71–84, and 'Competition and Cooperation among Pharmacists and Physicians in Ontario, 1920–1940,' in H.Z. Lopata and A.E. Figert, eds. *Getting Down to Business*, vol. 9 of *Current Research on Occupations and Professions* (Greenwich, Conn.: JAI Press, 1996).

14 In smaller provinces such as Prince Edward Island and Newfoundland these estimates were based on my hand count of women owners in 1992. In other provinces the licensing boards themselves counted the numbers of women owners for me. The figure for Quebec is more recent, reported by Jeanine Matte in 'The Role of Women in Pharmacy: Leadership of the Future,' at the Women in Pharmacy Lunch of the World Congress of Pharmacy, 3 September 1997, Vancouver. I reported the figures for anglophone Canada at a talk, 'Women in Pharmacy in Canada, 1920–1995,' at the same conference on 4 September.

15 Linda Muzzin and Roy Hornosty, 'The Effect of the Great Depression on Ontario Men and Women Pharmacists, *Pharmacy in History* 36, 4 (1994): 160–8.

16 S.E.D. Shortt, '"Before the Age of Miracles": The Rise, Fall and Rebirth of General Practice in Canada, 1890–1940,' in Roland, *Health, Disease and Medicine*, 123–52.

17 Diane Francis, *Controlling Interest: Who Owns Canada?* (Toronto: McClelland-Bantam 1986). See also the series of books written by Peter Newman, beginning with his *The Canadian Establishment*, vol. 1 (Toronto: McClelland and Stewart, 1975).

18 Pierre Trudeau, *Memoirs* (Toronto: McClelland & Stewart, 1993).

19 Frank Rasky, *Just a Simple Pharmacist: The Story of Murray Koffler, Builder of the Shoppers Drug Mart Empire* (Toronto: McClelland and Stewart, 1988). For a dis-

cussion about a recent case in which a pharmacist was fired, see Fiona Hendry, 'SDM Settles Out of Court,' *Pharmacy Post* 5, 4 (1997): 1.

20 Roy Hornosty and Gail Coulas, 'The Feminization of Pharmacy – Is the Analysis Right?' *Canadian Pharmaceutical Journal*, February 1988, 93–8.

21 Polly Phipps, 'Industrial and Occupational Change in Pharmacy: Prescription for Feminization,' in B. Reskin and P. Roos, eds., *Job Queues, Gender Queues* (Philadelphia: Temple University Press, 1990), 111–25.

22 Linda Muzzin, Greg Brown, and Roy Hornosty, 'Consequences of the Feminization of a Profession: The Case of Canadian Pharmacy,' *Women and Health* 21, 2/3 (1994): 39–56.

23 National Cancer Institute of Canada, Statistics Canada, Provincial Registries, and Health Canada, *Canadian Cancer Statistics*, 1994, 13.

24 Joel Lexchin, *The Real Pushers: A Critical Analysis of the Canadian Drug Industry* (Vancouver: New Star Books, 1984).

25 For a critical account of the process by which Eli Lilly obtained permission to market this drug, see Peter Breggin, *Talking Back to Prozac: What Doctors Aren't Telling You about Today's Most Controversial Drug* (New York: St. Martin's Press, 1994). The more conventional statement about the drug can be found in the best-seller by Peter Kramer, *Listening to Prozac* (New York: Penguin Books, 1993).

26 Ruth Cooperstock, 'A Review of Women's Psychotropic Drug Use,' *Canadian Journal of Psychiatry* 24 (1979): 29–34. See also Jim Harding, 'Social Basis of the Overprescribing of Mood-Modifying Pharmaceutics to Women,' in B.S. Bolaria and R. Bolaria, eds., *Women, Medicine and Health* (Halifax: Fernwood, 1994); Kathleen McDonnell, ed., *Adverse Effects: Women and the Pharmaceutical Industry* (Toronto: Women's Educational Press, 1986); and Rachel Weiss, *A Critical Re-examination of Tranquillizer Use by the Elderly: A Secondary Data Analysis of the 1990 Ontario Health Survey* (PhD thesis, Department of Behavioural Science, Faculty of Medicine, University of Toronto, 1996).

27 Interpharma (association of the Swiss-based pharmaceutical industry), *Working for Patients – Swiss Pharmaceutical Research* (Basel, Switzerland: Interpharma, 1992).

28 Joel Lexchin, 'Pharmaceutical Promotion in Canada: Convince Them or Confuse Them,' *International Journal of Health Services* 17, 1 (1987): 77–89.

29 Pharmaceutical Manufacturers' Association of Canada, 'Bill C-91 Review: Patent Legislation a Win-Win for Canada,' *PMAC News*, special issue January-February 1997.

30 A sample of newspaper coverage included this argument in 'Opponents in Debate Millions Apart,' *London Free Press*, 24 November 1992.

31 Judy Erola, 'Pharmaceutical Industry and Health Care in Canada,' Seminar presented at the Faculty of Pharmacy, University of Toronto, 21 April 1995.

32 Samuel Bloom, 'Structure and Ideology in Medical Education: An Analysis of Resistance to Change,' *Journal of Health and Social Behaviour* 29 (1988): 294–306.

33 Pennefather, Peter, 'Open Letter concerning Federal Funding of Fundamental Science' (unpublished, Toronto, 1997).

34 Pharmaceutical Manufacturers' Association of Canada, *A Five-Year Report on the Canadian Brand-Name Pharmaceutical Industry* (Ottawa: PMAC, 1993).

35 According to Tim Beardsley, in 'Trends in Biological Research: Big Time Biology,' *Scientific American* 271, 5 (1994): 90–7, in the United States, 1,300 biotechnology (including agricultural and pharmaceutical) corporations performed half the American health research in 1994, compared with the one-third funded by the National Institutes of Health (the counterpart to our MRC). The NIH had grown 150–fold between 1945 and 1965, but private funding took over, and the proportion of NIH funding slowed in the 1970s and 1980s. By the latter decade half of the eight hundred biotechnology professors at forty universities consulted for private research. Consulting is lucrative, making a noticeable gap between the incomes of those who do it and those who do not.

36 'U of T, Drug Firm Join Forces to Seek Alzheimer's Cure,' *Hamilton Spectator*, 28 January 1997, C9. In addition to individual arrangements between American scientists and the biotechnology industry, some American universities have made significant contractual agreements with multinational corporations. The most widely publicized was one between Scripps Research Institute of California (which received $70 million that year from NIH) and Sandoz, the Swiss pharmaceutical firm. Before a public outcry, led by NIH, charging that public money was being used for private gain, Scripps was said to have contemplated selling the right of 'first refusal' or the right to license most of their scientists' future inventions for $30 million a year for ten years. The outcry led to a renegotiation of the agreement to be more favourable to Scripps, and similar arrangements have been made by other American universities – for example, between the University of Washington and Monsanto and between Stanford and SmithKline Beecham, another pharmaceutical firm.

37 Like their predecessor, the Rockefeller Foundation, drug companies have declared that they will stamp out world 'epidemics' such as diabetes, which is the market interest of Eli Lilly. See that company's new magazine, *Outcomes: A Look at What's Ahead in Diabetes Management* 1, 1 (1997).

Contributors

Sandra Acker is Professor, Department of Sociology and Equity Studies in Education, Ontario Institute for Studies in Education of the University of Toronto. Her most recent book is *The Realities of Teachers' Work: Never a Dull Moment* (Cassell, 1999).

Cyndy Allen is Human Resources Consultant with the Bank of Montreal. Her master of arts thesis in sociology at Acadia University examined gender and the professionalization of chartered accountancy.

Carol Baines is Professor, School of Social Work, Ryerson Polytechnical University. She is a co-editor of *Women's Caring: Feminist Perspectives on Social Welfare* (Oxford University Press, 1998).

Paula Bourne is Coordinator, Centre for Women's Studies in Education, Ontario Institute for Studies in Education of the University of Toronto. Her current research deals with gender issues and schooling.

Ruth Compton Brouwer is Associate Professor of History, King's College, University of Western Ontario. Her current research deals with three Canadian professional women in Asian and African missions in the twentieth century.

William Bruneau teaches in the Department of Educational Studies at the University of British Columbia. He is finishing a full-length biography of Jean Coulthard, preparing a new edition of his history of the UBC Faculty

Association (1st ed., 1990), and continuing work on a history of post-secondary education in British Columbia.

Margaret Conrad is Professor of History, Acadia University. She is the co-editor of the *Canadian Historical Review.*

Janice Dickin is Professor, Faculty of General Studies, University of Calgary. She is currently finishing her biography of Aimee Semple McPherson for the University of Nebraska Press.

Robert D. Gidney is Professor Emeritus, Faculty of Education, University of Western Ontario. With W.P.J. Millar, he is the author of *Professional Gentlemen: The Professions in Nineteenth-Century Ontario* (UTP, 1994) and several articles on the professions in nineteenth- and twentieth-century Ontario.

Ruby Heap is Associate Professor of History and Director of the Women's Studies Program at the University of Ottawa. Her main areas of research are women and education and women and the professions. With Meryn Stuart, she is preparing a manuscript on nurses and physiotherapists during the First World War.

Claudia Lai and **Patricia Sinnott** are practising pharmacists and graduates of the Faculty of Pharmacy, University of Toronto.

Wyn P.J. Millar is an independent scholar based in London, Ontario.

Linda Muzzin is Associate Professor, Department of Theory and Policy Studies in Education, Ontario Institute for Studies in Education of the University of Toronto. Her research and teaching focuses on professional education, university-industry relationships, and critical autoethnography.

Alison Prentice is Professor Emeritus, Ontario Institute for Studies in Education of the University of Toronto, and Adjunct Professor, University of Victoria. Her most recent Canadian book, edited with Beverly Boutilier, is *Creating Historical Memory: English-Canadian Women and the Work of History* (UBC Press, 1997).

Elizabeth Smyth is Associate Professor, Northwestern Centre, Ontario

Institute for Studies in Education of the University of Toronto. As part of her work on the history of Canadian education, she is engaged in research on women religious as teachers in English Canada.

Meryn Stuart is Associate Professor, School of Nursing, University of Ottawa. She is a member of the International Nursing History Collective and author of *Nurses of All Nations: A History of the International Council of Nurses, 1899–1999* (Lippincott-Raven, 1999).

Peggy Tripp-Knowles (currently Peggy Tripp) is Professor, Department of Biology and Faculty of Forestry, Lakehead University, Thunder Bay. From a background in forest genetics research work, she has recently changed her scholarly pursuits and teaching to women and science, eco-feminism, and environmental ethics.

Illustration Credits

Andreas Poulsson, CSC: Jean Coulthard

Archives of the Sisters of St Joseph of Peterborough: Music Teachers Workshop. Reproduced by permission

The Gillespie family: Ada Gillespie and First World War nursing sisters (author's collection)

Lloyd Carr-Harris: Marguerite Carr-Harris (author's collection)

United Church Archives/Victoria University Archives, Toronto: Dr Florence Murray and Korean doctors

University of Saskatchewan Archives: University of Saskatchewan Physical Society

University of Toronto Archives: Clara Benson, A78-0041/002; Elizabeth Govan, B79–0027; Annie Laird, B79-1113; University of Toronto's Mathematical and Physical Society, 1898; University of Toronto's Mathematical and Physical Society, 1926

William Morrow and Co.: as printed in Lately Thomas, *Storming Heaven: The Lives and Turmoils of Minnie Kennedy and Aimee Semple McPherson* **(New York: William Morrow and Co., 1970):** L.I.F.E. students cheering Aimee Semple McPherson

Index

academic men: and career advancement, 286–7, 288, 291; caring responsibilities of, 287–9

academic women: caring work of,
284–7, 289–92; experiences of,
9–10; finding work in the U.S., 119,
120, 125; gender bias against, 45–6,
47–8, 51, 55, 60, 61, 101–4, 131–3,
134, 162–3; mentors and cultural
support, 47, 128; pay equity for,
54–5, 61; prohibitions against
advancement, 128; at University of
Toronto, 139n39

accountants, 8; associations of, 256–7;
history of, 256; in Nova Scotia: ability to generate new business, 267
(table), 267–8; —, career-and-chil-
dren conflict, 261–2, 265–6, 269–70,
272; —, client bias against women,
270–1; —, demographics, 260; —,
gender-based job assignments,
262–4; —, gender and commitment,
268, 269 (table), 270–2; —, gender
hierarchy and advantage, 263
(table), 271; —, obstacles for
women, 272–3; —, partnership and
career advancement, 264–5, 266–7,
270; —, specialization, 264; —, types
of work, 260, 261 (table); —, unequal salaries, 266–7; professionalization and status of women, 257–8,
274n11; struggle for gender equality
in, 259; women and men in, 258
(table)

Acker, Sandra, 6

Adaskin, Harry, 100–2, 103–4, 105,
113n28

African-American women, 11

Aisenberg, Nadya, 46, 47, 61

Allen, Cyndy, 256

Allin, Elizabeth, 9; academic
struggles of, 128, 131, 133; career
at University of Toronto, 119, 128,
134, 135, 136; doctoral student in
physics, 125, 126; involvement
in physics community, 127, 128;
relationship with Dorothy Forward,
128; studies at Cambridge,
126–8

American Dietetic Association, 146,
151–2, 160

Archer, Violet, 102

artists, 4; survival in BC, 97–8, 111n12.
See also Coulthard, Jean
Atrill, Alfreda, 175–6, 178
Australia: social work education in,
48–9, 60
autonomy, 15; of military nurses,
173–4, 178; of public-health nurses,
181–2

baptism by fire, 26–7
Bateson, Mary Catherine, 13
Benson, Clara C., 142, 143, 148, 150;
integration into male-dominated
profession, 155, 161–2; moves from
chemistry to biochemistry, 152–3;
and professional women's associations, 155; research at Faculty of
Household Science, 152, 153–4;
research in food chemistry, 154;
teacher and leader in food chemistry, 155–7
Bevier, Isabel, 147
bible college: and professional training, 37–41
biography: of women, 16, 120
Bloom, Samuel, 307
Boniface VII (pope), 236–7
Bonner, Thomas Neville, 69–70
bookkeepers, 255, 257, 274n10; and
career advancement, 259
Born, Max, 128
boundary: of gender in physics community, 133–4; in professional
development, 5; between voluntary
and state intervention, 14–15
Bourne, Paula, 6
British Columbia: artists in, 97–8,
111n12; women chartered accountants in, 258–9. See also University of
British Columbia

Brooks, Harriet, 125, 126, 138n16
Bruneau, William, 10
Bryn Mawr College, 122, 123, 124
Burke, Sara, 45
Burpee, Helen, 259
Burwash, Nathanael, 145

Cambridge University, 119; women in
physics at, 126, 128, 129–30, 133
Camp, Dalton, 307
Canadian Army Medical Corps, 184;
military nurses in, 173–7, 178
Canadian Association of Physicists,
120–1, 128, 134–5; gendered promotional material of, 133–4
Canadian Dietetic Association, 146,
151–2, 160, 161, 170n83
Canadian Federation of University
Women, 3
Canadian League of Composers, 98,
105, 106
Canadian Music Centre, 98, 112n17
Canadian Welfare Council, 52
career advancement: for academic
men, 286–7, 288, 291; for professional accountants: barriers against,
259, 264–8; —, bias against women,
270–1; —, and gendered job assignments, 262–4; —, job commitment
and, 268–70
care-giving, 46, 62
caring: in academic women's work,
182–7; 291–2; ethics of for women
pharmacists, 298, 301, 304–5; in
teacher's workplace culture,
279–82; 290–2; as women's work,
278–9
Carr, Emily, 4, 97
Carr-Harris, Marguerite, 171, 193n66;
childhood and education, 177–8; as

military nurse, 178; as public-health nurse, 179, 181–3

Cassidy, Harry, 61; and welfare bureaucracy, 51

children: and careers in accounting, 261–2, 265–6, 269–70; whether to have, 12. *See also* family

China, 34–5; medical missionaries in, 66. *See also* Peking Union Medical College

Chittister, Joan, 250–1

Coburn, David, 10

Cohen, Elizabeth, 125, 126, 127, 128

Collin, Johanne, 300

Conrad, Margaret, 255–6

corporate pharmacy: and chain-store professionalism, 303–4; women's participation in, 304–5. *See also* pharmacists; pharmacy

Cott, Nancy, 66, 76

Coulthard, Jean, 9, 15; compositions of, 96–7, 98–9, 107–9, 110, 115n43; marginality in artistic community, 106; marginalized career at UBC, 99, 101–2, 103–5, 106–7, 109–10; mother's influence on, 101; musical form and language, 105–6; musical training, 101; networks of, 99, 101, 104; reputation as composer, 96–7, 102–3; retirement, 109–10; strategies for artistic survival, 98, 107; teaching methods, 99, 109, 116n46

Crehan, Mary Ellen, 257–8

Crossley, Kathleen, 128

Curie, Marie, 120, 128, 134

Curie, Pierre, 120

Curzon, Edith, 153

Danylewycz, Marta, 242

Davis, Marjorie, 217, 218, 225

Davis, Natalie, 234

Dawe, Janet C., 255, 259, 272, 276n24

Deacon, Beatrice Reid, 125, 126, 128

Deegan, Mary Jo, 56

Depression, the: affects on careers of academic women, 128, 131, 133; role of accountants during, 257, 259; women's enrolment in medical school, 216, 222, 231n20

DeVault, Marjorie, 278

Dickson, E. MacPherson, 179

dietetics: emergence of, 144; in hospitals, 150–1, 157–8, 159; in hotels and restaurants, 160; in institutional food services, 158; in military hospitals, 158–9; as new profession for women, 141, 149; professionalization of, 142, 151–2, 161

Dominion Association of Chartered Accountants, 156, 157

Douglas, Allie Vibert, 9; academic career of, 119, 120; astrophysics studies at McGill, 130–1; childhood and life in England, 129; dean of women at Queen's, 131; and gender bias in academy, 133, 134, 135; studies in physics at Cambridge, 129–30

Durand, Laura Bradshaw: and *Maclean's* coverage of household science, 149–50, 155, 157, 158

Eaton, Margaret: community kitchen work, 157; launches commercial dietetics, 160

eco-feminism, 195, 206

Eddington, A.S., 130, 131

education: work of women religious in, 234, 240–2, 243, 245–8. *See also* higher education; teachers

Elgqvist-Saltzman, Inga, 12–13

enrolments: of medical students, 215–17; and quotas, 217–18, 227–8

Erola, Judy, 307

ethics of caring: of women pharmacists, 298, 301, 304–5

Etter-Lewis, Gwendolyn, 11

Faderman, Lillian, 44, 59–60

Fairclough, Ellen, 256

family, 12, 46; and balancing medical career, 224–5; commitments and ties to, 55–6, 62, 200–1; and male academics, 287–8; responsibilities as detrimental to accounting careers, 262, 265–6, 269–70, 272; and support for women medical students, 218–19, 230n12

feminism: 'modern,' 66, 76; and political analysis, 202, 204–5; relational, 278, 279

feminists: and equality in the academy, 133, 135; and equality in the labour force, 159; women religious challenge papal authority, 150–1

feminization, 282; of pharmacy, 298–9; of science, 142, 162, 164n9

First World War, 13, 68; and demand for professional accountants, 257; and dietetics in military hospitals, 158–9; and emergence of dietetics, 151; military nurses during, 171, 172–7, 187n2; services of women scientists during, 154; and women's enrolment in medical school, 215–16, 219, 228

Flexner, Abraham, 68–9

food chemistry and research: women's leadership in, 153–4, 155, 157

food services: dietetics and systematic improvements to, 158; launch of commercial dietetics, 160

forestry, 9; gender barriers in, 195–6, 199–202; educational programs in, 206 (table); masculine portrayal of, 194, 207; women in educational programs, 206–10; women in professional literature of, 205–6; women professors in, 197; women's career paths in, 194–5, 196–7; women's impact on, 196, 202–5; women students in, 197, 198–9

Forward, Dorothy, 128–9, 135

Franklin, Ursula, 208

funding: bias in scholarships, 121, 133; fellowships for women in physics, 122–3, 124; for pharmaceutical research, 308–9; women's access to, 6

Gauld, Flora, 223

gender: and advancement in chartered accountancy, 260–73; analysis of women in forestry, 206–10; barriers in forestry, 195–6, 199–202; and development of professions, 7; discrimination against academic women, 45–6, 47–8, 51, 55, 60, 61, 101–4, 131–3, 134, 162–3; hierarchy: in Pentecostal church, 39–41; —, in chartered accountancy, 257, 259; imbalance in Scripture, 29; and physics in the academy, 120, 122, 127, 128–9, 131–5; and political power, 14; relations, 8; shifts in traditional Korean culture, 66, 74–6, 81, 84. See also masculinization; maternalism; motherhood

gendering: of professions, 8–9, 10, 15;

of the social order, 177–9, 186; of war, 173

Gidney, R.D., 4, 8, 238

Gillespie, Ada, 174

Gilligan, Carol, 278

Gingras, Yves, 120, 128, 134–5

Gipson, Olive, 181

Glaistor, Deborah, 225

Glazer, Judith, 277

Glazer, Penina, 10–11

glossolalia (speaking in tongues), 26, 27–8; women as interpreters of, 33–4

Govan, Elizabeth, 9, 15; academic career at University of Toronto, 46, 50, 51–2, 54, 61; academic work at University of Sydney, 48–50; doctoral studies at University of Chicago, 52; educational discrimination against, 47; family life, 55–6, 62; personal relationships, 45, 47, 57–60, 62; —, with Norma Parker, 49, 56; professional discrimination against, 54–5, 61; professionalization of social work education and practice, 49–50, 51–2, 58–9, 60, 61; studies at Oxford, 44, 47–8; studies at University of Toronto, 47, 48; work with Canadian Welfare Council, 52–4

government: influence on health care, 14; influence on women's professions, 14–15. See also state, the; welfare state

Grenville, Ina, 181

Gunn, Jean, 184, 192n54

Guyart, Marie, 234

Halifax Medical College, 68–9

Hall, Radclyffe, 173

Hardman, Anna, 225

Harrington, Mona, 46, 47, 61

Harris, Anita, 11

health care: government influence on, 14; work of women religious in, 234, 242, 245, 247 (table), 248

Heeley, Marjorie, 178, 180

Hendry, Charles, 51, 54, 55, 61

Herkins, Florence, 258, 273n2

Hicks, Gideon, 97

hierarchy: in chartered accountancy, 257, 266, 271; in organized Pentecostal church, 40–1

higher education: for chartered accountants, 257, 259, 260; for Korean girls and women, 85, 94n112; for nurses, 171–2, 179, 183–7; for women in professional forestry, 206–10; for women religious, 240–1, 247–8

Hilliard, Marion, 218, 228

historians: obstacles against women as, 134; of women religious, 235–6, 244–5, 253n15

home economics: expansion of in the U.S., 144, 166n23; as feminized field of science, 142, 162, 164n9; opposition to, 145, 147; professionalization of, 147. See also household science

Hoodless, Adelaide, 142, 143, 144, 148, 149, 164n5

Hospital for Sick Children (Toronto): internships in, 222–3

hospitals: dietitians in, 150–1, 157–8, 159; medical internships in, 222–3, 225; women pharmacists in, 301; women physicians in, 225, 226. See also medical missionaries; military hospitals

household science, 163nn2 & 4; aca-

demic curriculum for, 145, 147–9;
emergence and growth of, 141–2;
opposition to, 147, 148; practical
training for, 149; professionalization of, 142–3, 161–2; women physicists in, 126. *See also* dietetics; home
economics; nutritionists
Howell, Charlotte N., 258–9

identity: of military nurses, 173–4; of
public-health nurses, 177, 178–9,
181, 183, 187
Innis, Mary Quayle, 3, 4, 8
Institute of Chartered Accountants of
Nova Scotia: first woman admitted
to, 255, 259; women members of,
260
inter-war years: career opportunities
in physics, 126, 131; women in medical school, 216–17, 222, 228

Jacobi, Mary Putnam; 69
Jamieson, Agnes, 225
Japan: colonial rule in Korea, 70–1, 78
Jewish professionals, 15; prejudice
against, 126; quotas against, 5, 222,
232n31
Jewish women, 5–6, 227
John Paul II (pope), 249–50
Johns, Ethel, 183

Kelly, Farley, 120
Kent, Susan, 186
Kessler, Winifred, 208; overcoming
gender barriers, 199; professor of
forestry, 197; pursues wildlife management, 198
Kinnear, Mary, 4, 8, 11, 13, 14, 46, 224,
226, 272
knowledge: for certain professions, 14

Korea: gender relations in, 66, 74–5,
75–6, 81, 84; under Japanese colonial rule, 70; medical missionaries
in, 71–85; women's higher education in, 85, 94n112

Laird, Annie Louisa, 123, 146, 154;
broadens nutritional sciences,
149–50; childhood and education,
143; develops professional educational curriculum, 145, 147–9; helps
to establish dietetic profession,
158–9, 160; honours and awards
received, 150; organizes the Canadian Dietetic Association, 151–2;
professor and head of Faculty of
Household Science, 121, 141, 142,
148, 150, 162, 163; promotes household science, 141, 161; as single
career woman, 143, 162; studies at
Drexel Institute, 144–5
Laird, Elizabeth Rebecca, 9; childhood
and early studies in physics, 121–2;
fellowship for European studies,
122–3; physics instructor at Mount
Holyoke, 119, 125; pursues career in
the U.S., 120, 125, 133; research at
University of Western Ontario, 119,
125; studies at Bryn Mawr, 122–3,
124; studies in Berlin, 123–4
Lawrence, Barbara, 15
Lawrence, John, 49
lawyers: restrictions against, 5
leadership: appropriate behaviour
for women, 52, 54–5; bias against
women in positions of, 45–6, 51,
60–1, 280–1; of public-health nurses,
183, 187; of women religious, 235,
239, 242, 247, 250–1; of women scientists, 152

Lee, Grant, 75
lesbians, 45, 60, 202. *See also* same-sex relationships
L.I.F.E. Bible College: and professionalization of evangelism, 37–41
Lillian Massey School of Household Science, 157: founding of and curriculum, 145; merges with University of Toronto, 148, 153; and pioneers in food chemistry and research, 153. *See also* household science
Lynch, John J. (archbishop), 241–2

Macallum, Archibald Byron, 153, 154, 155
McClure, Janet, 223
McCullough, John, 179–80
McGill University, 129; women teaching physics at, 119, 131
Mackenzie, Margaret Thomas, 100, 101
Mackinnon, Alison, 12
McPherson, Aimee Semple, 15; Angelus Temple: founding of, 36–7; —, successor to leadership of, 39–41; childhood, 31–2; daughter (Roberta), 29, 31, 35, 39; father (James Kennedy): religious influence of, 29–30, 31; interpreter of speaking in tongues, 33–4; marriage: leaves to pursue calling from God, 28; —, to David Hutton, 35; —, to Harold McPherson, 35; —, to Robert Semple, 29, 32–5; missionary work: in Chicago, 34; —, China mission, 34–5; —, establishes Los Angeles mission, 35–6; —, Hebden Mission (Toronto), 33–4, 38; mother (Minnie Clark Kennedy): religious influence of, 29–30; —, works in Aimee's mission, 35; and Pentecostal church, 25, 28; —, founds L.I.F.E. Bible College, 36, 37–41; reinterprets Scripture, 28–9; Salvation Army as training base, 29–30, 31, 35; siblings, 25; son (Rolf), 35, 39–40, 41; widowhood, 34
management: and gender division in accounting, 261 (table), 261–71
Manitoba: chartered accountants in, 256; study of professional women in, 11, 46, 272; women physicians in, 5, 13, 226
marginal positions: in male-dominated professions, 12, 13, 21n36, 61; and separation of public and private lives, 44–5; of women composers, 99, 101–5, 106, 109–10
Marillac, Louise de, 237
Marquis, Welton, 105, 107
marriage, 11–12; and interruptions in medical careers, 224–5; leaving profession for, 125; and professional careers, 33, 46, 76, 79, 126, 134, 161; sacrificing for professional calling, 18
married women: discrimination against, 272; in medical careers, 224–5; prejudice against, 46, 128
masculine imagery: in forestry, 194, 207
masculinization: of nutrition, 162–3; of physics, 133–4
Massey-Treble, Lillian, 143, 144, 157; pioneers teaching household science, 145, 148, 149
maternalism: and public-health nursing, 171–2, 177–9, 186
medical missionaries: in Korea, 71–85;

and separate-spheres approach, 65–6; training of, 69–70; women physicians as, 223. *See also* missionaries; Murray, Florence Jessie

Medical Research Council, 308–9

medical schools: quotas in, 18n8, 217–18, 227–8; reforms to, 68–9; women's access to, 5, 13, 215; women students in, 8. *See also* medical students; University of Toronto

medical students, female: academic records and achievements, 219–21, 227; —, enrolments, 215–16; —, experiences in male-dominated schools, 228–9, 233n52; —, graduates, 221–2; —, internships, 222–3; —, professional careers of, 223–4; —, quotas for, 217–18, 227–8; —, socio-economic backgrounds of, 218–19, 226–7; —, at women's medical colleges, 69–70; male: academic records and achievements, 220–1, 227; —, enrolments, 216–17; —, graduates, 221–2; —, internships, 222–3; —, socio-economic backgrounds of, 218–19, 226–7. *See also* medical missionaries; physicians

medicine: professionalization of, 66, 68–70, 74; reforms to medical education, 68–9; women practising, 223–6. *See also* medical students; medical missionaries; physicians

Meiklejohn, Harriet, 179

Meitner, Lise, 120, 134

Merici, Angela, 237

methodology: for study of professions, 8–15

midwives, 14

Millar, W.J.P., 4, 8, 238

Miller, Jean Baker, 277

Minden, Karen, 66

military hospitals: dietitians in, 158–9; female physicians in, 225; nurses' work in, 174–7. *See also* hospitals

missionaries: changes in practice and purpose, 67; Pentecostal evangelists, 33–4, 36–7; professionalization of, 37–41. *See also* McPherson, Aimee Semple; medical missionaries; Protestant missions

Morantz-Sanchez, Regina Markell, 69–70

Morrison, Emma, 273n2

motherhood: imagery of in First World War, 171, 172–3, 186. *See also* children; family

Mount Holyoke College, 119, 125

Mowat, Wilhemina, 173–4

Murray, Florence Jessie, 15: disapproval of Korean mission hospitals, 71–4; medical mission in Hamhung, 71–2; —, improves medical practices and infrastructure, 77–8, 84; —, leadership in hospital management and training, 81–3; —, training Korean men as physicians, 66, 79–82, 92n83; —, training Korean women as nurses, 78–9; as a 'modern feminist,' 66, 76; professional standards of, 66, 69, 70, 71, 73–4, 82, 85; rejects separate-spheres medicine, 75–6, 84–5; upbringing and training, 67–8, 69, 70; views on marriage, 79; work with tuberculosis patients, 77, 83, 84

musical theorists and composers: in American universities, 103 (table), 114n33; at UBC, 102–3. *See also* Coulthard, Jean

Nader, Ralph, 307
narrative: and telling of stories, 11
National Research Council of Canada, 120, 131–3, 154
networks, 47: as influence for musical careers, 99, 104; of male professionals, 6; among professional women and educators, 6–8, 9, 13; among social work educators, 56, 60
New Brunswick: chartered accountants in, 273n2
Newman, Jean, 225
Noddings, Nel, 278
North American Free Trade Agreement, 296, 307
Nova Scotia: chartered accountants in: professional association of, 255, 256; —, women as, 8, 258, 259, 260–73. *See also* Halifax Medical College
nuns: as different than sisters, 237; role in Catholic Church, 236–7
nurses, 13, 17n1; in First World War, 171, 172–7; higher education for, 171–2, 183–6; public-health, 171–2, 177–83; training programs in Korea, 78–9
nutritionists: academic curriculum for, 148, 153–4; masculinization of, 162–3; as new profession for women, 141, 144, 149, 152, 155, 157. *See also* household science

Ontario: chartered accountants in: banning women from profession, 257; —, professional associations, 256, 257; —, women certified as, 259; Jewish professionals in, 15; nurses' training in, 183–6; pharmaceutical profession in, 299, 300–1; public-health nurses in, 178–83;

women lawyers in, 5; women physicians in, 5, 13
O'Reilly, Gwen, 197; overcoming gender barriers, 201–2; and women's impact on forestry, 204–5
Ouditt, Sharon, 172, 173

Park, Edna Wilhelmine, 149, 155
Park, Ruth, 149
Parker, Norma, 49, 56, 60
patriarchy, 11; of Catholic Church, 235, 236; corporate, 303–5; medical, 301–2; in pharmacy, 298, 300–1; of welfare state, 60
Patterson, Irene, 258
pay equity: for academic women, 54–5, 61; for chartered accountants, 267. *See also* salaries
Payne-Krapotkin, Cecilia, 130
Peking Union Medical College, 74, 82
Pentecostal evangelism: doctrine of, 26–7, 41; Hebden Mission, 33–4, 38, 41; missions of, 33–4; professionalization of, 25, 28, 37–41; women-founded ministry (Angelus Temple), 36, 38–41; women's leadership role in, 39–40
Pentland, Barbara, 102–3, 105
Persons Case, 258–9
Perutz, M.F., 120
Pharmaceutical Manufacturers' Association of Canada, 297; funding medical research, 308–9; generic vs corporate drug manufacturing, 306–7; multinational membership of, 306
pharmacists: and the corporate patriarchy: women's work in, 303–5; corruption of ideals of caring, 298,

304–5; enter hospital pharmacy, 301–2; enter independent businesses, 300–1; independent vs corporate owners, 296, 297; and the medical patriarchy: involvement with, 301–2; in pharmaceutical science, 308; the pharmacy patriarchy: and corruption of women's caring ethics, 298; —, women's entrance into, 300–1; —, women's resistance to, 301; in schools of pharmacy, 300–1; working in corporate drugstore chains, 303–5

pharmacy: corporatization of, 203–5; funding for molecular science research, 307–10; globalization of, 296, 297; incorporated into hospital care, 301; as independent trade, 300; in Ontario, 299; multinationals: and funding of pharmaceutical research, 308–9; —, and globalization of drug manufacturing, 306–7; —, as members of PMAC, 306; schools of, 300; women enter business of, 300–1

physicians: balancing family and professional life, 224–5; in hospital and private practice, 225–6; Korean men as, 79–82, 83; Korean women as, 79, 83, 84; as medical missionaries, 223; restrictions against, 5; service during wartime, 225; in the UK, 15. *See also* Murray, Florence Jessie

physics: decline of women in, 131–5; identity of 'physicist,' 120–1, 134–5; scholarship bias, 121–2; shifts in gender relations, 120–1; women in societies of, 122, 127, 132. *See also* Allin, Elizabeth; Douglas, Allie Vibert; Laird, Elizabeth Rebecca

pioneers, 7, 11; in dietetics, 157–61; in household science, 143–52; in nutrition, 152–7

Podmore, David, 12

Pound, Vivian Ellsworth, 125

power: imbalance of in Pentecostal church, 41; of professional groups, 14; of women in professions, 15

Prentice, Alison, 6, 10

Presbyterian missions: in Korea, 67, 74

priesthood: women's ordination to, 235, 250

professional associations: for women, 155; women's membership in, 257–9

professionalism, 5; of corporate drugstore chains, 303–5; definition of, 8; mystique of, 6–7

professionalization, 10; of medical practice, 66, 68–70, 74; of missionary medicine, 77–85; of nursing, 171–2, 183–7; of nutritionists and dietitians, 142–3, 151–2, 153–4, 155, 158, 159, 160–1; of Pentecostal evangelism, 25, 28, 36–41; of social work education, 48–50, 50–1, 59, 60–1; and status of women accountants, 257–9; of women religious, 234–5, 236, 239–42, 244–5, 247–8, 249–50; women's motives and strategies, 10–11; of women's work, 13–14

professionals: definition of, 5, 272–3, 277; education of, 5; male networks, 6; women's integration as, 155

professional women: associations of, 155; definition of, 3, 4

professions: choosing knowledge for, 14; definition of, 4, 7–8, 278–9; entry of women into, 5–6, 13–14, 259, 272; government control and influence, 14–15; and male mem-

bership, 14; women's religious life
as, 236–9
proletarianization, 10
Protestant missions: inter-war changes
to, 67; in Korea, 70–1; women missionaries in, 65, 69
public and private spheres: influence
on household science, 141–2; influence on role of public-health
nurses, 177–9, 186; and nurses in
the military, 171, 172–3; separation
of, 44–5, 55–60, 62. See also separate-
spheres approach
public-health nurses, 171; autonomy
of, 178–9; education of, 184–6;
in Ontario, 179–83; as women's
work in private sphere, 177–9,
186

Quebec: chartered accountants in:
professional associations, 256; —,
women certified as, 258–9; —,
women denied status as, 258; pharmacy schools in, 299–300; —,
women students in, 301
Queen's University: barring women
medical students, 215; women
teaching astrophysics, 119, 131
Quinlan, Florence, 125, 126, 128
quotas, 5, 13; in medical school enrolments, 18n8, 217–18, 227–8, 233n51

Rauter, Marie: as a career forester,
196–7; overcoming gender barriers,
199–200; studies at University of
Toronto, 198; and women's contri-
butions to forestry, 203
Rayner-Canham, G.W., 125
Rayner-Canham, M.F., 125
Red Cross: funding nurses' training,

172, 185; recruitment of nurses, 171,
172, 179
Reed, Helen, 150
restaurant and hotel industry: com-
mercial dietetics in, 160
Richards, Ellen Swallow, 144, 147, 150
Roman Catholic Church: future of
religious life in, 249–50; and institu-
tionalization of virginity, 236–7;
vows for nuns and sisters, 237;
women's unequal roles in, 234, 235–
6, 250–1. See also Second Vatican
Council; women religious
Roman Catholic women. See sisters
(Catholic); women religious
Rosenberg, Rosalind, 76
Ross, Christine, 255
Rossiter, Margaret W., 126, 133, 135,
142–3, 161, 162
Rotenberg, Mattie Levi, 125, 126, 128
Russell, Kathleen, 185, 186
Rutherford, Ernest, 125, 128, 130
Ryley, Violet, 143, 150; dietitian for
military hospitals, 151, 158–9; education and community work, 157–8;
launches commercial dietetics, 160;
pioneer in dietetics, 142, 161, 163;
professionalizes hospital dietitians,
159–60; systematizes university food
services, 158

salaries: for chartered accountants,
255, 266–7, 275n22; for public-
health nurses, 180. See also pay
equity
Salvation Army: influence on evangelical women, 30–1, 35
same-sex relationships: among nurses,
177; among professional women,
44–5, 56–60, 128. See also lesbians

Saskatchewan: women accountants in, 258

scientists, 121; biographical studies of, 120; home economics and, 142, 162; and household science, 150, 152–3; and molecular research, 297, 307–9; as pioneers in food chemistry and research, 154; and professions in forestry, 198–9, 203; struggle for research autonomy, 297

Second Vatican Council (Vatican II), 236: reforms for women religious, 238, 244–5

Second World War, 83; effects on women historians, 134; effects on women in physics, 119, 128, 131, 134; post–Second World War: women's enrolment in medical school, 217, 219, 227–8; and professional work for women, 13; women in medical practice during, 225; and women's enrolment in medical schools, 215, 217, 218, 219, 226–8

separate-spheres approach: in medical training, 69–70; in missionary work and medicine, 65, 73–6. See also public and private spheres

Severance, L.H., 74

Shiva, Vandana, 206

Shoppers Drug Mart: women pharmacists in, 303–5

single women, 12, 46; in military nursing, 173–4; in public-health nursing, 179; in public sphere, 143; in science, 162

sisters (Catholic): as professionals in secular world, 239–42; religious preparation for, 238–9; as role for women in the church, 237–8; as

pharmacists in public hospitals, 301. See also women religious

Sisters of St Joseph: as professional educators, 240–2. See also women religious

Slater, Miriam, 10–11

Smith, May Annetts, 125

Smith, Sandy, 208; family commitments and career, 200–1; professor of forestry, 197; pursues agricultural studies, 198–9; and women's impact on forestry profession, 203–4

Smyth, Elizabeth, 6

social service: women religious in, 234, 242, 246 (table), 247 (table)

social work: and development of welfare state, 51, 60; gender divisions in, 45, 60; history of women in, 45–6; network of women educators in, 56, 60; social policy vs social reform, 49–51, 61. See also Govan, Elizabeth

Speisman, Stephen, 15

Spencer, Anne, 12

Squires, Edna, 181

state, the: and development of social welfare, 51; and rise of public-health nursing, 171–2, 179–83. See also government; welfare state

Stieb, Ernst, 300

Strong-Boag, Veronica, 216, 224, 228

Summers, Anne, 173

Sweden: women's research funding in, 6; workshop on women and higher education, 12

systems of employment, 10

teachers (elementary): caring work of, 279–82, 290–2; (general): of household science, 144–5, 148–9; —, women religious as, 140–2, 143

Technical Assistance Administration of the United Nations, 52

Toronto General Hospital: nurses' training in, 184, 186; women physicians in, 225, 226

Tripp-Knowles, Peggy: career path in forestry profession, 194–5; gender and social barriers to higher education, 195–6

Tucker, Sara W., 66

United Kingdom: caring work of elementary teachers in, 279–82, 290–2; military nurses in, 174, 176; women practitioners in, 15

United States: home economics movement in, 142, 144, 150, 161; hospital internships in, 222–3, 232n34; household science in, 147; musical theorists and composers in, 103; social work education and practice in, 50–1; social work educators in, 56

universities: degree for nurses in, 172; women in forestry programs of, 206–8, 209 (table); women's access to, 5; women teaching in, 13. *See also* academic women; Cambridge University; McGill University; Queen's University; University of British Columbia; University of Toronto; University of Western Ontario

University of British Columbia: marginalization of women composers in, 100–5, 110; professionalization of musical education, 106–7, 109; School of Nursing, 183

University of Saskatchewan Physical Society, 132

University of Toronto, 14; dietetic improvement to food services, 158;

Faculty of Household Science, 121, 141, 142, 148, 152, 153–4, 156, 161; Faculty of Medicine, 8; —, academic qualifications for, 219–20; —, background of women students in, 218–19; —, drop-outs from, 221–2, 226; —, hospital internships, 222–3; —, quotas for, 18n8, 217–18, 227–8, 233n51; —, students' academic achievements, 220–2, 227; —, women enrolled in, 215–17, 228–9; female academics in, 139n39; forestry: women students in, 197, 198, 203–4, 209 (table); gender bias against academic women, 51–2, 54, 134, 162–3; Mathematical and Physical Society, 122, 127; nursing programs in, 172, 184, 185; pharmacy, 298, 301; —, and multinational funding for research, 309; physics: decline of women in, 131–3, 134, 135–6, 140n43; —, doctoral students in, 125–6; — women teaching, 119, 128–9

University of Western Ontario: barring women medical students, 215; nursing programs in, 172, 185; women in physics research, 119, 125

upper class: and community kitchen work, 157

Ursulines, 234, 237. *See also* women religious

Urwick, E.J., 48, 50

Valverde, Mariana, 177

Wacker, Grant, 67

Waring, Marilyn, 273

Weir, George, 183

welfare state, 15; and evolution of

social welfare, 51, 60; and rise of
public-health nursing, 171–2,
179–83. *See also* government; state,
the
Weston, William, 97–8
Witz, Anne, 10
women religious, 9; academic qualifications of, 247–8; ages of, 247;
arrival in New France, 234; difference between sisters and nuns, 237–
8; dual professional lives of, 234,
236, 239–40, 250–1; effects of religious reform on, 244–5; exclusion
from priesthood, 235, 250; and feminist challenge to papal authority,
250–1; historians of, 235–6, 244–5,
253n15; leadership of, 250–1; numbers of, 246–7, 248–9; occupations
of, 242, 245–6, 248–9; religious
preparation for, 238–9; role within
Catholic Church, 234–5, 236; as
teaching sisters, 239–42, 243; and
vowed virginity, 236–7
Women's College Hospital (Toronto),
14; internships in, 222, 225; women
physicians in, 226
women's medical colleges, 69–70. *See
also* medical students
'women worthies,' 9, 20n26
workplace culture: bias against family
responsibilities, 265–6; and caring
in educational settings, 279–92